"My brothers have my back"

# "My brothers have my back"

## *Inside the November 1969 Battle on the Vietnamese DMZ*

LOU PEPI

FOREWORD BY Sterling Eugene Kelly, Jr.
AFTERWORD BY Clyde "Bud" Wagner

McFarland & Company, Inc., Publishers
*Jefferson, North Carolina*

Library of Congress Cataloguing-in-Publication Data

Names: Pepi, Lou, 1948– author.
Title: "My brothers have my back" : inside the November 1969 battle on the Vietnamese DMZ / Lou Pepi ; foreword by Sterling Eugene Kelly, Jr. ; Afterword by Clyde "Bud" Wagner.
Other titles: Inside the November 1969 battle on the Vietnamese DMZ
Description: Jefferson, North Carolina : McFarland & Company, Inc., Publishers, 2018 | Includes bibliographical references and index.
Identifiers: LCCN 2018047651 | ISBN 9781476675169 (softcover : acid free paper) ♾
Subjects: LCSH: Pepi, Lou, 1948– | United States. Army. Infantry, 61st. Battalion, 1st—History. | United States. Army. Infantry, 61st. Battalion, 1st—Biography. | United States. Army. Task Force 1-61—History. | Vietnam War, 1961–1975—Campaigns—Quảng Trị (Province) | Vietnam Demilitarized Zone (Vietnam)—History. | Vietnam Moratorium, 1969. | Vietnam War, 1961–1975—Peace. | Vietnam War, 1961–1975—Regimental histories, American. | Vietnam War, 1961–1975—Personal narratives, American.
Classification: LCC DS559.5 .P43437 2018 | DDC 959.704/34—dc23
LC record available at https://lccn.loc.gov/2018047651

British Library cataloguing data are available

**ISBN (print) 978-1-4766-7516-9**
**ISBN (ebook) 978-1-4766-3430-2**



Printed in the United States of America

*McFarland & Company, Inc., Publishers*
*Box 611, Jefferson, North Carolina 28640*
*www.mcfarlandpub.com*

For my wife Pat, who by finding and loving me
undoubtedly saved my life.

For my children Mike and Gretchen, with sorrow for being
preoccupied with all this and not being a better parent.

For my grandson Sam, so that he will have
a record of what his Papa did in the war.

For Captain Robert P. Gallagher
and the other 14 men who gave their lives.

And for all the men of Task Force 1-61, including all
5th Infantry Division support units that took part
in the 1969 November battle on the DMZ.

# Table of Contents

*Foreword by Sterling Eugene Kelly, Jr.* 1
*Preface* 3

1. Three Generations of Military Service 7
2. The Train to Fort Dix 9
3. Fort Dix, April to July 1968 11
4. 52nd Ordnance Company, July 1968 to June 1969 16
5. The Drawdown 21
6. The First 100 Days 27
7. The First 10 Days of November 44
8. Overview of the November Battle 66
9. Veterans' Day, 11 Nov 1969 (DAY 1) 70
10. 12 Nov 1969 (DAY 2) at the Jump CP 83
11. 12 Nov 1969, Mission "Bald Eagle" 119
12. 13 Nov 1969 (DAY 3) 128
13. Unfriendly Fire and Survivor's Guilt 158
14. Going Home 161
15. Utah Mesa and Bravo Company—18 Jun 1969 165
16. Chris Martin and the Americal Division 171

*Epilogue* 175
*Afterword by Clyde "Bud" Wagner* 177
*Appendix A: What They Are Doing Today* 179
*Appendix B: Awards Index* 183
*Appendix C: Valorous Unit Citation* 186

*Appendix D: Glossary* 189
*Appendix E: Communication Logs, 11–13 Nov 1969* 192
*Appendix F: The "Rules" of Engagement* 213
*Chapter Notes* 215
*Index* 217

# Foreword by Sterling Eugene Kelly, Jr.

*Alpha Company 1\61, Fifth Infantry Division (Red Devils) "WE WILL"*

Lou Pepi's book is unlike other military histories. It is from the "grunt's" perspective on the war. There will be maps, photographs, and some documents, to be sure, but my friend and brother-in-arms, Louis Pepi, tells the story of the lead up to—and the battle for—Hill 100, a.k.a. Gallagher Ridge, from the standpoint of an active participant.

The author has invested thousands of hours diligently researching and interviewing surviving participants of this engagement. Through personal testimony and after-action reports from the field, this book will give the reader a good idea of what was going on during this significant battle for Hills 100 and 162—plus the amazing level of cooperation demonstrated by infantry, artillery, armor, and air support.

There are many books about Vietnam, and Lou Pepi's narrative provides one more significant page in the story. Here we see the contribution of the First Brigade of the Fifth Infantry, which has seemed at times to be eclipsed by larger units. In fact, we took over a key area, formerly the domain of the Third Marine Division, in a very hot area of operation—the demilitarized zone (DMZ) of the northernmost portion of the Republic of Vietnam.

Lou has always been a stickler for accuracy, and he pulls no punches here. There is no gratuitous gore, although it was plenty bloody for sure. What is apparent are the sacrifices we made for each other when life was on the line. Lord knows we carry a huge rucksack full of graphic memories from that collision of fire, steel, and flesh. Maybe Lou's legacy to us will put some of those scenes to rest.

My pride and love are evident for my comrades, without whose valor I would not be here and I am privileged to write this foreword. Now, we will let Lou tell the story—he is the author.

Thanks, Louis.

*PFC Sterling Eugene Kelly, Jr., served with A Company, 1/61, 5th Infantry (Mechanized) from August until December of 1969.*

# Preface

The men I interviewed have all spoken and their words are on paper. The tears have passed too and are now a distant memory. My friends and family are frightened for my well-being. They think I have gone back to horrible times past. They see the writing of this book as a remanifestation of the malady in me—my PTSD. They are wrong, though—they have mistaken the sickness for the cure. I know it now. Actually, they do not know one way or the other. They cannot know. Most have never been in that place of sheer terror, the type they most likely will never see in their lives. Yes, we have all seen that moment of a tragic accident, or loss from an illness, but I am talking about the terror that seeps into your soul—day after day—week upon week—month after month until you think you cannot bear it another moment. You even ponder giving up and letting it end. Somehow, you bear it—you even laugh about it with dark humor when you are in the middle of it because it is all you can do. You resign yourself to death. You are walking dead. This terror probably is undescribed—but I am trying here. Some have simplified it: "You have seen the elephant." After that, you are marked as your brothers are—and we can see it in each other.

When I came back to the world, I was deathly sick inside. There was no goodness for me—I saw the evil in everything—for thirty years. Then I turned the corner. One day in 2008, while surfing the Internet, I discovered that all 58,220 of the fighting men who died in Vietnam had an individual memorial page, a guestbook for mourners—acquaintances and strangers—to write testimonials. From the search engine of the Vietnam Virtual Wall, I typed in "Robert Gallagher." Suddenly, my heart missed several beats, there was a flash in my brain and my face flushed with heat like standing in front of an opened door of a blast furnace. Everything went from fiery burning red to a blinding white light. Suddenly I was there—back in Vietnam—and of all places on Hill 100. I had the feeling of wanting to run—but where? Let us face it; I was in my home sitting in front of my laptop. This is classic PTSD.

As my vision returned, I saw the heading: "Capt. Robert Patrick Gallagher," and below it were some vital statistics: Age—32, Race—Caucasian, Sex—male, DOB—Jun 7, 1937, From—Wyoming, RI, Religion—Episcopal/Anglican, Status—married. The next page had more information, and still half-stunned, I read it. There was information about things like "Quang Tri Province," "multiple fragmentation wounds," and the "body was recovered."

Then I flipped to the next page and there were testimonials written by friends, relatives, strangers and other soldiers. A niece named Dawn wrote that she only knew him when she was three and asked if someone would email her and tell her about him. I eventually tried to contact her eight years later but without success. She must have changed her email address. His stepdaughter wrote that she also wanted to know what people had to say about him. Strangers left "thank yous" and "God blesses." One of them said, "He came to help us." The writer was Tim Hurley. I found out later that he was one of the trapped and surrounded mortar-men on Hill 100. I read what he wrote:

> One night, in November 1969, about 30 of us were on a hill just south of the DMZ. Things were happening all around us and our outlook was bleak. The word that we got was Captain Gallagher was back at a base camp "safe and sound" and he volunteered to come and help us because he knew if we were attacked we probably would not have made it. For the 30 of us, we all owe our lives to the Captain and his men. Attacked by hardcore NVA, the 30 of us would not last very long. Because of him, I am able to be typing this today. Sir, thank you. I am sorry that you never returned to your family. I have talked to your radio operator and he said that you were a soldier's soldier and I read what Col Swaren wrote about you and I have the utmost respect for him and he felt the same way about the Captain. Captain Robert Gallagher will always be in my thoughts. Sir, I salute you. Thank you.
>
> Tim Hurley, Nov 28, 2006

As I read his moving tribute to our fallen leader, I thought, "I was on that hill!" The memories came back in a landslide and I swam frantically through my thoughts in an emotional sea of frenzy. The memories tumbled by me in vivid freeze-frames. The helicopter air-assault—foxholes frantically dug—waking up to a thousand mortar blasts—actually seeing the mortar rounds lobbing in and out. I saw the advancing enemy pith helmets just appearing over the curve of the hill into the eerie illumination of the "Willie Pete." I saw—again—the unfriendly green tracers snapping in every possible direction—even from behind. Moreover, I saw the red friendly tracers shattering into all those pith helmets. Worst of all was that cruel chaotic growl of the sound of battle—the Dogs of War.

I stood up and walked away from my laptop—thinking that I had had too much too fast. Nevertheless, I was drawn back like a magnet—I had to read more.

Next, I read what one of his OCS classmates wrote about the plaque with his name on it at Fort Benning, Georgia:

> Fellow OCS Graduate
>
> On Wednesday, March 7, 2007, it will be 40 years to the day that we graduated from Infantry OCS at Ft. Benning, GA.—and your classmates will again gather at that very spot to re-dedicate the memorial we placed in 2002 honoring you and the others from Class 14–67 including two of our TAC Officers who gave all in support of your comrades. We will bring you flowers, share stories of those 6 months we spent together earning those gold bars and afterwards we will raise a glass to all who cannot be with us.
>
> Mar 3, 2007

As I read all this, my brain was still swirling. Again, I remembered the mortar emplacements. I remembered my foxhole. In addition, I remembered Capt. Gallagher making the rounds to each position—checking field of fire and foxhole depths. He had a word of encouragement for each of us and told us as he moved on to stay alert. I know that the main reason so many of us survived that night was his keen eye for detail, but more importantly, the aura of the professional soldier that he projected. Let us face it—we were all 18- to 20-year-old kids. He was the professional soldier.

Feeling a need, I wrote a paragraph and posted it on Captain Gallagher's page. I wrote about what I remembered of the night and how I could not understand why I survived—

and others did not. I called him one of our country's finest and that he was a soldier "that rode to the sound of the guns"—a quote that I now see as a little bit clichéd, but there it is. The funny thing was that the act of writing that paragraph made me feel better about Vietnam than I had for decades. For 38 years, I did not have much to share about my time in Vietnam—other than frequent bouts of rage toward friends and loved ones followed by deep depression. Of course, they did not see this as sharing anything. Maybe if I wrote some more I might feel even better.

The seed of a manuscript was planted that day in the compost of my scribblings over the last 40 years and it has finally sprouted into this book. If not a medicinal cure, this book has actually saved me. I firmly believe that. I no longer see myself as a casualty of Hill 100, for I now see myself as a messenger of the courage and the good in the men who lived and died with me.

I wrote Tim Hurley in 2006 and there was a string of a half dozen emails. I still have them. Eventually we met eight years later on Vietnam Veterans Appreciation Day on March 29, 2014, just around the corner from Alice's Restaurant in Stockbridge, Massachusetts. Bob Ziessler, another 1-61 vet, was at this reunion as well. We were all a little nervous about what to expect of our meeting, but within ten seconds, we knew that we would be lifelong friends. I found others by Internet search or email. The list grows every day and numbers close to a thousand now. To me, these men are the salt of the earth. They are the ones who lived while others died. The gift from the dead to us was a life to live and those who died now live through us and hopefully through this book.

Soon after this encounter, I began writing. After three years of writing, I realized that my memory was not that clear and I needed the memories of others. More importantly, I needed facts. I needed military records, and they were in several places—but mostly in the D.C. area. I needed to get to repositories in College Park, Maryland; Alexandria, Virginia; Fort Knox, Kentucky; and Montgomery, Alabama. Over a two-year period, I did just that. The fruits of this were 50,000 pages of Department of Defense documents. I now had more information in front of me about the November Battle than any man on earth did. I dove into it, hashed it, and rehashed it. With all these facts, I was ready to start interviewing others with the knowledge that I could now separate fact from fiction—the real from the surreal. This was important because—like me—all these men would also suffer from varying degrees of PTSD.

I started with email and telephone interviews. They were all fraught with emotion and I began to worry about injuring someone emotionally. To my relief, I began to receive replies of appreciation for helping them deal with decades of repressed memories. The word passed and I started to receive offers of interviews from men who wanted to take part in my project. In early 2016—coinciding with my retirement—I began to plan a ten-stop trip from Massachusetts to Florida to do face-to-face interviews along the way. The first few, including the battalion commander, an aerial observer pilot and a dustoff crew chief, went smoothly—so smoothly, in fact, that they produced instant friendships that I knew would be lifelong.

Then I arranged a meeting with a veteran in a grocery store parking lot in Florida. We approached each other, shook hands and exchanged pleasantries. Eventually, we agreed to sit in my truck and start the interview. I turned on my recorder, entered some cataloging data and nodded for him to start. Instead, he broke into tears and left the vehicle. I got out too and walked up to him and put my hand on his shoulder. After a while, we got back in the truck, but again, he broke out in tears. I indicated that we should stop, but he insisted he would do the interview. Finally, the interview proceeded, but it was very emotional throughout with several more stops. After the interview ended, he said goodbye and left abruptly. I was extremely concerned for him and tried to call him several times with no success. I was worried for his well-being. Maybe this book was a bad idea. I certainly did not want to cause anyone injury. I was in a depressed state all the way back to Orlando. However, that evening I received a call from him saying that he was fine and he was grateful to me that I had helped him remove this great weight from him he had been carrying for decades. He'd finally come to terms with a dark period of his life. In turn, I came to terms with my doubt and continued my interviews.

Thank you, Tim Hurley, for being the catalyst. You were the first contact I made and that has grown into hundreds more. It began with that first email and I will forever be indebted to you for your response.

Over the last five years, one of the great difficulties I encountered was coming up with a title. Over that time, I came up with at least a dozen. In every instance, I instantly disliked them. They were not altogether bad, but none of them rang true. Friends would ask if I had come up with a title yet and I would proclaim the latest. They were met with a forced smile or silence. Then, I was on the phone one night with John Ginty, a fellow Alpha Company trooper. John and I were both in the third platoon—first squad, but at different times. He also helped me immensely come to terms with my PTSD. We talk often. I had called him following the 2015 Fifth Infantry Reunion in Pittsburgh to tell him that several of his Alpha Company brothers had asked about him and wished him well. He told me that he had attended a mini-reunion with two fellow veterans and their wives. They were having dinner at a restaurant in New York City one night and an odd thing happened—at least John's wife Fran thought so. John and Fran were sitting facing Jerry Reising and Bruce Walmsley at the table. The oddity was that John had his back to the entrance of the restaurant—something that Fran had not seen him do—ever. He had always insisted on facing the door, the residual effect of hyper-vigilance. Fran questioned him on the occurrence and John immediately responded by saying, "I'm fine. My brothers have my back." There it was—the search for a title was over!

Therefore, in the spirit of brotherhood, I commit this book to all the men of the Fifth Infantry Division, and specifically:

- the 1st Battalion of the 61st Infantry Regiment,
- Delta Company of the 1st Battalion, 11th Light Infantry,
- the 1st Battalion of the 77th Armor,
- 5th of the 4th Artillery,
- Rotary Aviation—Ghost Riders, Lancers, Batman, & Dustoff
- Fixed Wing Aviation—220th RAC, 20th TASS,
- Jet Fighter/Interceptor—Gunfighters

I especially offer this book to Captain Robert Patrick Gallagher (posthumously) who saved my life twice—once in the flesh on November 13, 1969, through his keen professional eye for setting up defenses and fighting positions, and a second time in the abstract, on December 23, 2006.

Hurrah Red Devils—We Will!

# 1

# Three Generations of Military Service

My family's experience in America started at the dawn of the twentieth century, during the final wave of the Great European Migration. Both my maternal and paternal grandparents were of hardy peasant stock. To my knowledge, neither they nor their parents ever had any formal education. Bettering oneself and family, specifically through education, even if based on some vague promise of America, must have been one of the main reasons they decided to sever all ties from family, friends, and country, and embark on a dangerous and frightening, albeit exciting adventure. Five generations of my family live, or have lived, in America.

The patriarch of my family was my grandfather Giovanni—changed to John when he reached Ellis Island. His courage and quiet persistence were the chief qualities that got him across the Atlantic—that, and his dream of bettering himself. Giovanni preferred the solitude of toil to conversation, and he had the ability to complete colossal tasks of manual labor that most would not even attempt. Giovanni was born in the mountain village of Alto Piegiao, Italy, on September 16, 1891. A simple peasant man, he farmed the steep terraced hillsides and walked the narrow cart paths that switch-backed to the hilltop where the town stood. The village remains in the same state today.

He was a dreamer who had a grand scheme: to come to America and raise a family that had greater opportunity than he had. So, on May 22, 1914, the twenty-three-year-old, without his betrothed Ascenzina Bartolome, made his way from Italy across France to La Havre with his brother Allesandro, and boarded a ship bound for Ellis Island. Their final destination was Worcester, Massachusetts. His dream took nearly ten years to accomplish; but in that time, he got a job, bought a house, joined the army in World War I to fast-track his citizenship, contracted the Great Influenza—and then survived it. He never reached the front in Europe, but instead convalesced at Fort Devens in Ayer, Massachusetts. His recovery took 6 years.

Finally, his health returned and he applied for a six-month visa to return to Italy, where he married Ascenzina on December 19, 1923. She had been waiting patiently nine and a half years for his return. Then, on March 22, 1924, the thirty-three-year-old newlyweds boarded the *Dulio* and embarked to America. My father Louis Sr. was born on December 16, 1924. He was schooled in the Worcester public school system. He applied for admission to several colleges, but he settled on Syracuse University. He arrived at the Syracuse campus in September of 1941 and distinguished himself with excellent grades for three months, preceding the attack on Pearl Harbor. He remained in college after the attack, but prepared for war. In late December, he joined ROTC on campus, but eventually dropped out of the Officer Candidate Corps and joined the Army Air Corps. In 1944, he found himself in the Northern Marianas, the Pacific island chain that was the staging area for the bombing of Tokyo. When he was half a world away from his hometown of Worcester, Massachusetts, on the Island of Saipan, Syracuse University was the last thing on his mind.

My father distinguished himself in the Air Corps, flying 39 missions in B-29 Superfortresses with the 883 Bomb Squadron of the 500th Bomb Group as a left door gunner. Thirty-five of his missions were over Japan. He shot down two Japanese fighters and damaged three others. He participated in the firebombing of Kobe and Tokyo, as well as several missions to the Mitsubishi & Hitachi Engine Factories and the Musashino Ball-Bearing Factory. The other missions were in support of the invasions of Okinawa and the island of Truk. He was awarded two Distinguished Flying Crosses and the Air Medal with five bronze stars. Dad never talked about his war experience, nor did he ever show any interest in discussing mine with me.

I was born to Louis Pepi and Teresa (Palladino) Pepi on March 8, 1948, at St. Vincent's Hospital in Worcester, Massachusetts. I was the oldest of five siblings, and was followed by three sisters—Linda, Lisa and Nancy—and a brother, John. We lived in the middle floor of my maternal grandmother Josephine's three-decker on 3 Fay Street in Worcester until I was five, when the family—now with my two-year-old sister Linda—moved 10 miles to a brand-new three-bedroom ranch house on 21 Linden Street in the suburb of West Boylston.

As I grew up, I always planned to attend college; I breezed through public school. I managed to attain very good results—high honors, actually—with little or no study. When it came time to entertain college, I had second thoughts. My father thought that Syracuse would be a good choice. I did not. Then he began pushing Worcester Polytechnic Institute, which was also his dream rather than mine. It was only ten miles away, and he said it was "a very good engineering school." I was eventually accepted to WPI in November of 1965, a year before I actually graduated from high school. I started matriculation in September of 1966 as an electrical engineering student and was enrolled in the mandatory ROTC program. My heart was not in study, though. I figured I could make my way without college as Giovanni had. There was no shame in emulating him. Hence, I left WPI after three semesters, telling my father I needed a year off and promising him that I would go back. From his personal experience, he knew that I probably would not. It was the fall of 1967.

In January of 1968, I received a letter from the Selective Service Board. To this day, I remember the first word of the letter—*Greetings.* Two months later, I found myself on my way to the train station in the neighboring town of Clinton, Massachusetts. At the front entrance of the train depot, I said my goodbyes to my father and family. I have no memory of the words exchanged. My life was about to take a drastic turn.

# 2

# The Train to Fort Dix

My first recollection of being alone in the world to fend for myself was while sitting on a train at the depot in Clinton, waiting to depart for the United States Armed Services Induction Center in Boston. We had been organized and led to and onto the train by a Marine recruiting sergeant. From the moment I met him he had been very friendly, polite and cordial. As I boarded the train, I sensed that it would not be that way for long. Of course, I had had friends who had been—and were now in—the service, and they had forewarned me. The specter of the verbal abuse and grueling training that I would surely have to endure over the next eight weeks really didn't bother me, though. I viewed it more as a game, but something else bigger hit home as I looked at my parents through the window. They had waved several times from the platform as the train lingered and their fortitude began waning a little each time they hand-flapped at me, until I could finally see the worry in their eyes showing through. I was suddenly struck with an epiphany. I was no longer under the sphere of influence and protection of my parents—instead I was now entirely on my own. A twinge of fear rose up my spine as I contemplated this, but that was somewhat diluted by the romantic excitement of the unknown. Little did I know that by the end of the day, I would be struck by a new and more profound advancement of this same epiphany, increasing in profundity with each stop that the train made.

The track up ahead had a long curve in it and I actually saw the engine at idle, diesel smoke lightly rising from its stack. When the diesel finally revved, I was looking at it. It started moving, first by itself, then there was a loud iron clang and the second car joined in the movement. This sequence continued and a loud bang announced the initial movement of each car, increasing progressively in volume and tempo as this phenomenon moved closer and closer to the car where I was seated. When it finally reached my car, the engine had already moved a full ten feet, and the jerking motion whiplashed my head with a fair amount of forcefulness. Had I really known how the events of that day were to proceed, I would have seen the increasingly violent momentum of the train as a symbol of what was to come.

When the train pulled into the induction center in Boston, the Marine sergeant stood abruptly and barked some unintelligible words, yet we all stood immediately, fully understanding his intention. We moved in a ragtag formation as he marched this rabble into the building. Totally out of step, each of us at least once tripped over the heels of the inductee in front of us. Stopping in a large barren rotunda of a room inside the building, we stood for what seemed an eternity. Then another Marine walked through a door in front of us—a captain this time—and instructed that we count off. We did this, and in doing it, found that we were one hundred fifty-five strong. He then instructed that every fifth man reassemble in a separate group to our left. My number was ninety-four.

"Those of you in the new group will be Marines and the rest will be inducted into the Army," he barked with a malicious tone. I was in the larger stationary group. Then he said, "In a few moments I will ask you all to take an oath of allegiance. Then I will ask you to take a step forward. When you take that step forward, you will cease to be civilians. If you refuse to take a step forward, we will take you in to the Battalion Commander, and you will have one more chance to comply. If you refuse, you will be clapped in irons and sent to Leavenworth Prison—Portsmouth Prison for you Marines. It's entirely your choice, men—military service or prison." As we all took a step forward, he paused for a moment, and then said, "Raise your right hand and repeat after me."

As the officer spoke, I repeated:

"I, Louis Pepi, do solemnly swear that I will support and defend the Constitution of the United States against all enemies, foreign and domestic; that I will bear true faith and allegiance to the same; and that I will obey the orders of the President of the United States and the orders of the officers appointed over me, according to regulations and the Uniform Code of Military Justice. So help me God."

I boarded the train again with the rest of the Army recruits with our small carry-ons and the bag lunches we were given at the induction center. Shortly, the steel wheels were rattling monotonously toward Fort Dix, New Jersey. It was late March and one of the first warm days of the season. As the train rolled south, the advance of the spring season progressed with it. By the time we entered New Jersey, the trees were in partial bloom. The train moved through, as most train lines do, a rural wooded countryside, seeming somehow to avoid the frequent urban centers of the northeastern corridor, which were only occasionally visible in the smoggy distance. It was a special train, for it only stopped once in New York City to pick up more inductees, before it continued on to Newark, New Jersey. There, we were transferred onto a fleet of buses for the final push to the training camp at Fort Dix.[1] Little did we realize the firestorm that we were to walk into as we disembarked the buses at the barracks of our training unit, our new home for the next sixteen weeks.

# 3

# Fort Dix, April to July 1968

As we entered the army base—it was late in the evening—it was brightly lit in a very surreal way. We passed row after row of barracks, situated neatly on a maze of parallel and perpendicular streets, positioned in such a way as to create giant oblong drill fields that formed the back yard of each full block of buildings. Each barracks was lit front and back by floodlights, which gave it the look of a prison. Each window seemed to be dimly lit, suggesting that there was a lonely light burning in the recess of almost every room. Not a soul stirred and the movement of the bus seemed to cause the only disturbance in the silence everywhere. Then, as the bus slowed and turned a corner, one building stood out from the others. It was even more brightly lit. It seemed that every possible bulb in the building was turned on. As the bus pulled to the curb, it gradually slowed to a halt. Where it stopped, a row of smart-looking soldiers stood perfectly aligned at parade rest. They all wore sergeant stripes and donned the typical "Smokey-the-Bear hat" of a drill instructor. As the door opened, two large search beacons that were situated behind the row of "spit-shined" soldiers were switched on and blinded us all in the bus.

One of the soldiers jumped through the open door and began screaming at the top of his lungs, using some of the foulest language I had ever heard to that point in my life. The gist of his crude ranting was that we all get off the bus at the risk of our lives, and do it with all haste. We all jumped up like coiled springs and pushed through the narrow door like a herd of stampeded cattle, only to find the other drill instructors waiting just outside the door of the bus, arranged in a gauntlet and slinging every possible rank term of belittlement at us as we passed by. It seemed uproariously comedic that they could do all this—and with straight faces—and this caused a dim smile to form on my face. That was a big mistake.

"Something funny, shithead?" one screamed so loud that his voice cracked.

"Nooo…," I began, not smiling anymore.

"No what—scumbag?"

"No sir," I said.

"No sergeant, idiot."

"No sergeant."

"Shut up, puss nuts," he screeched in another broken scream.

"Gimme that sissy bag of yours, pea-brain!" I held it up to him. "Get at attention," he yelled. I stiffened. He grabbed it and flung it back at my head. I flinched slightly and jerked my arms up to catch it. "I said attention, piss-brain," as he yanked the bag back and threw it at me again. Again, I flinched and caught the bag. "This pissant is disobeying a direct order," he screeched louder than I imagined someone could yell. "Now attention!" he barked as two of the other spit-shined soldiers moved alongside me and held my wrists to my side. His third assault caught me square in the nose, causing a small trickle of blood that dripped on the ground between my feet.

"You're soiling my clean drill field, worm." The two soldiers released me, but I remained at attention thinking: *So this is the game. OK, I can play it.* The soldier's eyes softened almost imperceptibly and it grew silent for a moment. Finally, the sergeant reached into his back pocket, pulled out a clean and smartly folded green handkerchief, and tossed it to me. It hit me lightly in the face and fell to the ground but I remained motionless. A little smirk blossomed on the corner of his mouth as he walked away. "Clean yourself up, recruit."

Basic training consisted of all of the usual aspects of military training. We were taught to march in step and we practiced every day on the drill field. Conditioning was grueling—we ran one mile or more every day, and did push-ups, sit-ups and the rest of the daily dozen. We were issued M-14s and we learned to field-strip them and put them back together blindfolded. Then there was the obstacle course and the infiltration course at night with live-fire machine guns and exploding TNT in sandbagged craters. After a period of familiarity with our weapons, we double-timed to the range every day for live-fire shooting practice. I excelled at this, as I had been a hunter since I was a teen. At age 17, I had owned my own deer rifle, a 30-06 bolt action. While I was very familiar with the techniques of accurate shooting, I did learn a wealth of additional information on the subject.

Then they taught us bayonet training and fighting with pugil sticks. The terms are imprinted in my mind.

"Parry and thrust." I even still remember all of the required dialogue as well from the first day.

"What's the spirit of the bayonet?" Sergeant Luff yelled.

"I don't know, sir."

"Don't call me sir, shithead. I work for a living."

"Sergeant, I don't know, Sergeant."

"You don't know? Are you stupid?"

"Sergeant, no Sergeant."

"Then answer me."

"I don't know, Sergeant," I howled at the top of my voice.

"Turd, the spirit of the bayonet is, 'Kill—kill—kill!' Say it."

"Kill—kill—kill, Sergeant," I screamed.

"So help you…" another DI chimed in and hang-fired—waiting for me to add the final word.

"Sergeant, so help me God, Sergeant."

"No, puss nuts," he screamed. "SO HELP YOU BAYONET." He screeched the last word so loudly; his voice cracked and cut out again.

"SO HELP ME BAYONET," I bellowed even louder.

Then another sergeant jumped in: "And when you have some VC good and skewered, how do you get him off, dirt bag?"

"Sergeant, I kick out and yank back, Sergeant."

"No, pea brain. YOU SHOOT HIM OFF."

"Sergeant, I SHOOT HIM OFF, SERGEANT."

On and on it went. I'm sure it ended up with 50 push-ups. Oh, excuse me—applying pressure to Fort Dix, New Jersey, 50 times.

The grenade range was for the most part uneventful. Only one trainee dropped a grenade and it was picked up and tossed away safely by Sergeant Luff. I believe that poor guy suffered a little that day with quite a few applications of pressure to Fort Dix and maybe a mile run, but that was it. There were a few screw-ups on the obstacle course that resulted in repetition for the whole group each time. That was just a little teamwork practice thrown into the mix. Finally, one evening, we negotiated the live-fire infiltration course and it went smoothly. The indoor classes were tough because it was hard to stay awake, but the classroom training ran its course as well.

There was one poor soul and I still feel sorry for him today. His name was REDACTED—I'll call him Red—and the poor kid was tortured nearly to death. Red showed up on the second day of AIT. He hobbled into the barracks on crutches sporting casts on both feet up to and over his ankles. He had some sort of a defect and his ankles had been broken and reset by an army surgeon. He told us that he had been in AIT two months earlier and failed to pass due to the ankle problem. When they operated, they found a congenital issue and they performed additional surgery on both ankles. For those months, he had been trying to get a discharge due to obvious health issues while he was on medical profile and was placed on continual KP detail and company area cleanup. It sounded like he had a good case, but the army didn't think so. Instead, they viewed him as a slacker, stating continually that he was lazy and was just faking.

While he was telling us all this for the first time, a couple of drill sergeants burst through the door and we all snapped to attention. Red reacted as quickly as he could and hobbled into line while balancing on his crutches. One sergeant moved rapidly across the barracks, channeling straight to Red. "I said attention, Red," he barked as he bumped him. Red fell to the floor with a deflating groan. Not expecting this, Red cracked his head loudly on the linoleum-covered concrete floor. There were several seconds of silence—at least until the DI began a loud tirade.

"Get up and stand at attention," he shouted as he kicked the two crutches out of reach. Red struggled painfully to his feet, shifting his weight from one leg to the other several times to alternatingly relieve the pain before falling back to his knees. He rose again and continued to bob back and forth, as the DI kicked the crutches toward him, shook his head and walked away. That was the last we saw of Red during the day except at chow time at the mess hall. He could be seen scrubbing pots and pans or leaning heavily on a mop as he swabbed the floors of the dining hall. In the evening, he would return to the barracks just before lights out and would talk to whoever would listen. He was asking for a hearing and expected to be discharged in a few weeks. This separation from the company went on for a time. Red was eventually hobbling around on the heels of his casts in a very unbalanced gait since he had now given up his crutches. He had also started participating in the classroom part of our training, but returned to the mess hall when we had PT or we jogged to the range.

Then one day when we had returned from a two-mile run from the range, Red was sitting dejectedly on his bunk and cleaning his rifle. He was in a very depressed state as he explained that his appeal to be discharged had been denied and that he was told that he would be expected to run to the range with the company the next day. He was always assigned to our platoon, but now, he was specifically assigned to my squad, and I was the squad leader. Tearfully he began to claim that he might be able to walk but there was no way that he could run. I told him that he would at least have to try. He didn't think he could because he had attempted to double-time around the barracks earlier while he was waiting for us to return from the range and could not make more than two laps. Again, we encouraged him to at least try and that we would help him if allowed.

The next morning Red fell out with the platoon and participated in physical training. The drill sergeants were very tough on him, taking turns taunting him about his technique as well as doubting the effort he was putting into the exercises. At one point, all three drill instructors were on him together and made him demonstrate squat thrusts and jumping jacks—the two exercises that gave him the most trouble. The whole company was stopped to watch this solo performance. Red continued to stumble disjointedly through a round of squat thrusts. At one point one of the DIs looked at me and shouted, "Pepi, you're his squad leader. Aren't you working with him?"

"Sergeant, yes I am, Sergeant," I regurgitated instinctively.

"Not good enough, Pepi. Drop and give me twenty-five."

Instinctively, I fell to the ground and rattled off twenty-five in the normal rhythm—snapping smartly through the first fifteen, then slowing progressively through the last ten. Then the DI turned back to Red and asked for twenty-five jumping jacks. Again, he was clumsy and lost his balance several times.

"I suppose you worked on those with him too," the DI spat at me. I replied as before. He dropped me to the ground again for twenty-five more, but this time the rest of the squad was punished in like manner as well. The second twenty-five were a little more of a challenge for me, and when I finally finished, the rest of the squad had been on their feet and at parade rest for nearly ten seconds. Then drill instructor Sergeant Milazzo announced that the whole company would be punished along with Red for his short-comings. The company was dismissed for chow—but not until one of the drill instructors announced that my squad would have to run three laps around the parade ground before we could eat.

After chow and a thorough "police-call," we were instructed to get our rifles, steel pots and webbed gear—including full canteens—for the two-mile jog to the range. Back out on the parade ground with Sergeant Luff in the lead, the company was progressively marched into columns of two. Our platoon fell in last with my squad bringing up the drag. We marched out of the parade ground as two other drill instructors fell in on either side of Red. They immediately began to deride his instability and his inability to keep an even cadence. As we turned up the road to the range, things went very badly. As soon as "double-time-march" was called for, Red started to fall behind. He fell once, and one of the drill instructors had two of us drag him back to his feet, but he fell again. We then hauled him in shifts, but eventually Red was completely winded and in tears. He finally stopped trying to run and was now just dead weight on our shoulders with the toes of his boots dragging through the dusty gravel. In twos, the guys in the squad traded off all the way to the range. We finally arrived at the range twenty-five minutes behind the rest of the company who were already firing their weapons. Red was completely exhausted and claimed that one of his ankles was re-broken. Somehow, his canteen cap had loosened and he had no water. We did manage to sneak him a few mouthfuls.

Sergeant Luff spotted someone giving him water at one point and just turned away shaking his head. He now wanted no part of what was being heaped on Red and it was obvious. Luff was a draftee who enlisted for the third year in return for a ticket to Drill Instructor School. Here he was—a short-timer with only 60 days left in this man's army—

having been a combat infantry instructor for almost two years without ever spending a minute in a combat situation. He was a good man, though. He had taken a shine to Dan Perkins and me and made us both squad leaders. Perkins eventually became the platoon leader. Luff encouraged us both to sign up for OCS. Perkins finally did, but I had misgivings. I finally realized that I had no will to be an officer because as a good Marine friend of mine had told me before I was inducted, "Shave-tail lieutenants in Vietnam get their asses shot off on a regular basis." Besides, I had no desire to send men to their death. Luff finally talked me into applying for DI School.

Red, as the day wore on, became racked with more pain and he complained that his feet were swelling in his casts. He was in bad shape. As we formed up for the "double-time" back to the barracks, it was announced that Red would no longer be in my squad and was assigned to another because of our failure to rehabilitate him. As our punishment we had to do an about-face and double-time three laps around the range staging area and then catch up with the company. It was also stated that Red's new squad would be first in line and would lead the way back to the barracks, and if need be, Red would be dragged all the way. If they failed to rehabilitate Red, they would have to run back to the range and then catch back up to the company. Then the next squad would have a shot at Red. This handoff would continue back through each successive squad until we neared the company area.

As we set out in columns of twos, my squad again was positioned at the back of the column because of our additional run. Now, a full training company of two hundred twenty men stretches out for a pretty long distance. As we took up our position in the rear, my squad had no indication of how Red was progressing, but eventually at about the halfway point we all began to notice some type of a disturbance up ahead. After a time, a squad appeared as it passed the column and headed back toward the range. Before long, a second squad ran by, also on a reverse course. Eventually, squad-size groups were passing the column at regular intervals. It was obvious that each successive squad that passed us was displaying more and more anger, most likely because their round-trip distance was growing in length. Then the reversing squads stopped passing by us. Meanwhile, Sergeant Luff kept up his double-time cadence as we passed two other anxious DIs. Red lay on the ground between them—eyes glazed over and staring skyward. The last squad had been ordered to drag him face down. That is the last time we saw Red. Sergeant Luff told us that he finally got his medical discharge.

The rest of basic and AIT was uneventful. Two hundred twenty trainees graduated. I was promoted to Private E-2 out of basic and PFC soon after leaving AIT. Following the advice of Sergeant Luff, I signed up for DI School, as did Jerry Heinemann, and we were issued orders for drill instructor training at Fort Campbell, Kentucky. Prior to that, though, I received two weeks leave and returned to Massachusetts for a short vacation in my hometown of West Boylston.

# 4

# 52nd Ordnance Company, July 1968 to June 1969

Fort Campbell was a bust. When Jerry Heinemann and I arrived at the replacement company, we were told that DI School was filled up. Instead, we would be assigned to the 52nd Ordnance Company to be part of a guard detail for a special weapons stockpile. The 52nd Ordnance was actually at Clarksville Naval Base, which was an annex of Fort Campbell. At the replacement company, we were told that we'd be lucky to be at the 52nd for a month before we were levied to Vietnam. All I could think was, "Fucked by Uncle Sam again."

Without any choice in the matter, I took my orders and checked into the naval base. The barracks and other accommodations were better than any I had seen in any Army facility anywhere so far. If this lasted for a while, it might not be too bad, but I was told it wouldn't. The 52nd Ordnance was a holding pen for the Vietnam levy.

The first order of business at the company headquarters was to be cleared for a secret security clearance because of the nature of the ordnance I would be guarding. While I was waiting for my clearance, I was assigned to barracks cleaning duty as well as all-purpose spit-shine detail. This wasn't too bad either, because there were about a dozen other new guys also awaiting clearances and assigned the same duty. It was obvious that this was going to be a "spit and polish"-type unit—totally strac. The first two guys I met were Chris Martin and Dennis Shine—both from Worcester, Massachusetts, which was a moderately-sized city adjacent to my hometown. *What a coincidence,* I thought. There was also John Crutchfield, Don Rich and Tony Steerman—Southern boys who turned out to be great guys. Along with Joe Lehner and John Miles, we formed an inseparable group, augmented by the fact that we were assigned to the same guard team. We were also all promoted to PFC.

Chris Martin was the social director and orchestrated the comings and goings of the group. He had enlisted under the buddy system with his hometown best friend, Dennis Shine. Dennis was a soft-spoken gentleman who was also a little naïve. Chris was his protector.

Depending on our guard schedule, one evening each weekend was spent at the Marine EM Club, and although there was common respect, there was the occasional tussle. Whenever the Marines messed with Chris, it was a mistake. In addition, if they messed with Dennis, it was an even bigger mistake because Chris would jump in. Once a pair of Marines decided they were going to push Dennis around a little just because he always displayed that vulnerable look. Chris knocked one Marine to the ground and the other was pinned across the bar before they knew what hit them. You didn't mess with Den-Den when Chris was around. Shine was married and the father of two infant children. He enlisted in the Army on principle to fight for his country. He was really a fish out of water in an infantry company—he was just a gentle soul. Chris enlisted—I believe—to take care of Dennis. Chris was eventually shipped to Nam and served with the Americal Division. During his tour, he was awarded a Silver Star, two Bronze Stars, and an ARCOM for heroism, along with three Purple Hearts. He came home and went to work for the Post Office in Worcester, Massachusetts. His route was on Main Street and you could always find him walking his beat in the busy business district stopping from time to time to hold court for his endless flood of friends.

Dennis was assigned to the 101st Airborne Division and lasted barely two weeks in the Thua Thien area of the Southern I Corp. He was killed setting out a mechanical ambush—he simply blew himself up. Chris always regretted that he wasn't with Dennis in Vietnam and carried that weight with him his whole life. The Babe Ruth League team in Dennis's neighborhood named their ball field after him. Today, the scoreboard displays in large block letters: Dennis Shine Babe Ruth League. His gravestone sits in St. John's Cemetery. He died on August 19, 1969. His unit was C Co, 2nd Bn, 506th Infantry, 101st ABN Div. He was awarded the Purple Heart.

Chris ultimately died of cancer. Vietnam got him in the end. He was one hell of a guy. I attended Chris's funeral in 2010 and met his son. Tony Steerman had these words to say about Chris in his obituary guest book:

> I served with Chris at Ft. Campbell Ky. and in different battalions in Viet Nam (same division); I have wondered for years where he was. My first son was named after Chris. I have pictures in my album of us together near Chu Lai. I have always told my kids that he could walk into a room with 100 strangers and every one of them would assume that he was in charge.[1]

Don Rich and John Crutchfield were best of friends in the same way as Chris and Dennis were, and Tony Steerman, Joe Lehner and John Miles rounded out the rest of the group. Eventually all of us were shipped to Vietnam. I have never reunited with Rich and Crutchfield, but I have not given up trying. I reunited with Tony Steerman about four years ago and we converse regularly by email. He still suffers from a service-connected back injury. I plan to meet him face to face at some time.

As it turned out, my time at the 52nd was much longer than a month. As spring of 1969 rolled around, I had less than a year to serve to complete my debt to Uncle Sam, but he eventually got me again by levying me to Vietnam with a scant nine months left before I was due to be discharged. The odd thing was that this levy coincided with President Nixon's planned troop reduction that he had promised to the American people. On the levy with me were all the close friends I had made during my one year with the 52nd.

We did have a slew of good times at Clarksville Base. Guard duty consisted of twenty-four hours on and forty-eight off with every other weekend off. It was a spit-and-shine outfit. There were two entrances leading to the lab at this special weapons depot that disassembled nuclear warheads for disposal. The Marines guarded one entry point and the 52nd Ordnance guard detail secured the other. There was a continual flow of high-ranking coming and going. The generals always tried to walk on by the guard detail claiming their rank precluded them from showing an ID. We always detained the generals because we were warned that letting them walk by unchecked would be a court-martial offense.

In my eleven months at this duty post, I never ventured into the depot or the lab. To my knowledge, neither did any other men of the guard detail. I could only accept the rumors as to the nature of the weapons I was guarding. Years later, I found that the rumors were true.

On our off days, we spent a great deal of time applying Kiwi shoe polish and Brasso. We also spent a great deal of time at the range. We fired for score with the M-16 twice. I scored a 26 and a 28—good for second and first place in the company. I qualified with the BAR—expert again. Finally, I qualified with the 1911A 45-caliber pistol. There was a turkey shoot before Thanksgiving with the 45 ACP. I believe the first sergeant won.

There was an inspection every day. Demerits were easy to accrue if you were slack. I received demerits once and it cost me a promotion to corporal. One particular morning, prior to a company inspection, I was "getting my shit in order" at the last minute when I realized that I didn't have a pair of polished boots. Neither did anyone else have an extra polished pair. I had no choice but to put on a scuffed pair. Lieutenant Terry gave me a demerit and I was sent to the company commander. The old man asked me if I had an explanation and I offered no excuse. The result was an Article Fifteen. The next week everyone in my detail was up for promotion to corporal. I remained a PFC and was not promoted to Spec 4 until I got to Vietnam in September 1969.

There was one notable series of occurrences at the 52nd Ordnance. As I said, we were always at the range, and we all were looking for ways to smuggle live ammo off the range to use in a long-running game we were playing with the Marine guard detail. The live ammo that was passed out for guard detail by Lieutenant Terry every day was counted and recounted at the start and finish of each shift. The 5.56mm was emptied out of the magazines, counted and then reloaded. The same process was carried out with the .45 ACP magazines. Then the gun safe was checked. The cartridge count always had to be exact. It took about six weeks but Chris and I managed to squirrel ten rounds of .556mm from the range. It involved lying to the range officer: "No brass—no ammo, sir." That could have been another court-martial offense.

Several weeks later, the time was right, and Chris and I were on the graveyard shift—midnight until 0600. Steerman, Crutchfield, Shine and Joe Lehner were sound asleep. Miles and Rich—the alternate guard detail—were playing pool in the day room. Our euchre game with Lehner and Steerman had broken up at midnight when we replaced Shine and Crutchfield on guard. It was now 0300 and Chris said it was time. We had already loaded five rounds each of our ammo stash into empty magazines. We took the twenty-round clips out of our weapons and "locked and loaded" the fives. Chris nodded and we walked outside and got into the jeep to make the hourly rounds. Out at one of the angles of the security fence there was a clear view of the Marine detail that was making their hourly rounds too. We slipped out of our jeep as planned and eased the muzzles of our M-16s through the chain link fence.

"Aim about five feet over that jarhead jeep," Chris whispered. "That way the rounds will fall harmlessly into the rifle range."

"OK," I responded, "One—two—three. Fire!"

The night silence was broken by our hail of fire. In less than five seconds, we were back in the jeep. I drove the jeep while Chris was already field-stripping his weapon. As we pulled up to the guard shack, the others were awake at the door in their skivvies. They knew exactly what had just happened and they all had wide grins. Chris jumped out of the jeep cradling the pieces of his field-dressed weapon and I threw mine to one of the others. Within three minutes, both rifles were patched, oiled, reassembled and reloaded as Lt. Terry was beeping at the gate. We walked out and let him in and told him that we heard the shots, too, outside the security fence, but he didn't believe a word we said—or rather what *Chris* said. He did all of the talking, because he was the Corporal of the Guard. Terry went back to the guard shack and recounted the ammunition for two hours to no avail while the other six guys shot billiards. He eventually called the Marine lieutenant who said that his Marine detail had backed up our story about the shots coming from outside the security fence. Chris smiled about that after Terry left. The Marine detail knew what really happened, and we knew that they knew. We also knew they were planning something as well—payback. It would most likely involve squirreling ammo from the range. That was Chris—always in charge—always with a plan. Nothing would ever rattle him no matter how desperate. Those traits would shine through in Vietnam. That Silver Star was a downgrade from a DSC and a Medal of Honor nomination because he refused to extend his tour in Nam as part of the deal.

The Marines eventually did fire back, but it was only one round. With a single round, it is over so quickly that anyone hearing it cannot come up with any accurate identification, let alone direction and distance calculations. It really wasn't much of a payback.

Another good friend at the 52nd Ordnance was Joe Focceri. Joe had DEROS-ed from Vietnam to the 52nd to bide his time for his last eight months until he was discharged back to his home in New York City. When he wasn't on guard, Joe was at the billiards table. He beat all comers at the EM Club, but I was the only one who knew how good he was. He was a pool hustler—the real thing. He would always just barely beat his opponents and would even let them win a few to keep them coming back.

One day Joe and I were driving through downtown Clarksville, Tennessee, and we passed a pool hall. He told me to find a place to park so we could play some pool. We walked in, rented a table, and started playing eight ball. There was a guy sitting against the wall watching Joe. He was very interested in Joe's play and studied him for a good while. Joe was aware of this and went into his rope-a-dope mode. After a few mediocre games, Joe ran the lows and sunk the eight ball on me. The guy walked over and asked Joe if he was interested in playing for money. Joe suggested nine ball—$20 a game. Joe won three games in a row—sinking the nine on the break twice. This wasn't exactly rope-a-dope; it looked more like luck. He was still hustling the guy, though. The stranger then suggested a game of straight pool to 125 for $500—winner takes all. Joe agreed and gathered the balls in the rack—all but two. With the $1000 stacked on the rail, they lagged for break and the stranger won. Joe set the rack and they were off. The stranger then broke and ran nearly fifty balls before missing. The whole room stopped what they were doing and watched intently. Joe started in and never looked up for nearly eight full racks until he dropped the 125th ball. With no fanfare, Joe nodded to me, then to the stranger—picked up the stack of cash—and we beat for the door. We jumped into my car and I looked back through the rearview mirror as the pool hall emptied out and watched us leave. It was the greatest display of pool skill I ever saw firsthand. Back at the day room of the barracks, he returned to his stumblebum way of "just barely winning."

In late May of 1969, we all got orders for Vietnam. Chris and Tony were headed for the Americal Division. Don Rich and Dennis Shine were bound for the 101st. Crutchfield and I were headed for the Fifth Infantry Division on the DMZ. On June 6, I shipped home for a 30-day leave. That was the fastest thirty days that I had ever experienced. It went by in the blink of an eye. I met Chris and Dennis somewhere—at one of the Worcester

VFW Posts, I believe, for a few drinks and farewells. We traded home addresses, but I don't believe we ever contacted one another while in Southeast Asia.

July 6 finally arrived and I vividly remember saying my goodbyes to my family. My dad was quiet and told me to be careful. "How do you do that?" I thought. My siblings Nancy, Lisa, John and Linda were 9, 12, 13 and 18 respectively. The younger ones were a little confused with emotion and really didn't comprehend what was happening. My father knew, though.

The commercial airline took me to SEATAC Air Base and I was bused into Fort Lewis. Several days later I was on another commercial airline—Pan American—bound for Southeast Asia. We landed in Honolulu for a two-hour holdover and a change of crew. Back in the air, we settled into the long hop to Guam. As entertainment, we played poker. The steward and one of the stewardesses sat in and we took them for several hundred dollars. After a time, cards got boring and we just sat uncomfortably and watched the endless Pacific below pass by. We touched down in Guam to refuel again and they let us out for an hour to stretch our legs. When the door was opened, the humidity hit us like a ton of bricks. It was a harbinger of what was to come.

Back in the air, we got underway again on the hop to Ton Son Nhut Airbase. We landed under darkness and were bused to a filthy barracks to spend the night. The humidity was so intense that I lay in a puddle of sweat and never slept a wink. The next morning we were fed a breakfast of slop and were soon bussed back to the tarmac to catch a C-130 to Da Nang. The humidity was again unbearable. The C-130 landed and eventually we boarded another fixed-wing plane to Camp Red Devil, home of the Fifth Infantry Division. I was trucked to Alpha Company, 75th Support Battalion for a day and a half of supposedly *grueling* jungle training. It was nothing more than an over-staged presentation. We went out on a patrol, walked into a mock L-shaped ambush and learned how to set up a trip-flare and a claymore mine. That was it—we were now "ready for combat," they said. Most of the *newbies* took a scornful view of the jungle training. My new unit—Alpha Company, 1st Battalion, 61st Infantry Regiment, Fifth Infantry Division (Mech)—was in a place called Qua Viet—about a mile from the DMZ. Oh, boy—and I thought it couldn't get any worse.

# 5

# The Drawdown

On July 8, 1969, coincidentally about the same time that I landed at Tan Son Nhut Air Force base outside of Saigon, President Nixon announced the first troop withdrawal. That very first U.S. troop withdrawal occurred when 800 men from the Ninth Infantry Division were sent home. The phased troop withdrawal then proceeded in fourteen stages from that time through November of 1972.[1] The U.S. Army and the government in general could have saved a lot of money and jet fuel if they just cancelled our flight to Vietnam—it seemed to me that that was the sensible thing to do. FUBAR.

When Richard Nixon had taken office that January, 25,000 American soldiers had died in Vietnam over the previous four years. The war was starting to become unpopular and it was time he had a new plan to present to the American people. So he declared, on behalf of the United States, what he called the Nixon Doctrine, and was "quite emphatic on two points" in dealing with our Asian allies. First, he assured America's friends in Asia, "We will keep our treaty commitments." However, "as far as the problems of military defense, except for the threat of a major power involving nuclear weapons," the United States would be adopting a different stance. In relation to military defense, America would now "encourage and has a right to expect that this problem will be increasingly handled by, and the responsibility for it taken by, the Asian nations themselves." He concluded that his recent talks with several Asian leaders indicated, "They are going to be willing to undertake this responsibility."[2] The Nixon Doctrine also marked the formal announcement of the president's "Vietnamization" plan, whereby American troops would be slowly withdrawn from service in the country and would be replaced by American-trained ARVN forces. Nixon, Secretary of State Henry Kissinger, and the rest of the executive branch portrayed a very hopeful attitude about this idea in speeches and news media releases, but behind the scenes, confidence of success on this issue flip-flopped one hundred eighty degrees.

Still they groped publicly for a way to provide a legitimate reason for our forces to be fighting there—when in fact there already was a good reason. Previous administrations had supported the "Domino Theory" that simply expounded that America halt the growth of Communism in Vietnam to ensure that adjacent countries would not follow suit one by one. In fact, the passage of time has proven the Domino Theory was a complete success, as no other countries have succumbed to Chinese or Russian influence since. However, the Nixon staff thought that they had to put a different slant on this policy to re-convince the American public. This is reflected in a letter from Secretary of Defense Eliot Richardson to Henry Kissinger in November of 1969. They seem to be trying to re-convince themselves more than to persuade the American people. It was clear in the correspondence that the plan was never to win the war but simply not to lose it. Among the politicians this was political hair-splitting at its most absurd, while any military man from the Joint Chiefs on down to the lowliest private knows that not winning a war and losing it are one and the same. Richardson to Kissinger:

> In thinking about the opportunity—and the need—for a Presidential restatement of our purposes and plans for Viet-Nam, I keep coming back to the pivotal question: why are we justified in calling for additional sacrifices of American lives and the continuing diversion of American resources for something less than victory but short of defeat? It is not enough, I believe, to point to the goal of self-determination for the people of South Viet-Nam. Only a few of the world's peoples enjoy that privilege, if by it we mean the exercise of free choice through fair and honest elections. Nor is this goal made sufficient by the circumstance that in South Viet-Nam the major danger to its fulfillment is externally supported insurgency: the President himself, in his Southeast Asian tour, made clear that assistance against insurgency, even though externally supported, will not hereafter justify the involvement of U.S. combat forces. There is, however, an element in the South Vietnamese situation that significantly distinguishes it from other situations in which the exercise of self-determination is threatened by external force. This is that we have made a commitment—a promise—to the people of South Viet-Nam to help them preserve the opportunity to determine their own destiny. Whether or not it was wise in the first instance for us to have undertaken such a commitment is not now in issue: the important fact is that we have undertaken it.[3]

The American public and the peace coalition did not buy in to any of this, yet it was decided that slow troop withdrawal and Vietnamization were now the path to follow.

Trying to finish what they had started, Henry Kissinger, in the name of the U.S. government started secret meetings in Paris with Le Duc To on August 4, 1969, to form a peace agreement. Representatives from Hanoi arrived as well. To add fuel to the fire, on August 15, the first organized "Moratorium" demonstrations were staged in many of America's major cities. Coupling these events with the huge American losses suffered in mid-June, including the 46 Americans killed on Hamburger Hill, the end was evident—although it took better than four years and 25,000 more American lives to achieve it.

Still, the government tried to downplay the demonstrators as misguided youth who would come around or would be brought to ground by their parents. The parents of that generation were the "Silent Majority," and Nixon wanted to revive it. Nixon downplayed the power of these demonstrators no matter what advice his advisors gave to him. It was unheeded, as was the advice below from Under-Secretary of Urban Affairs, Daniel Patrick Moynihan—whom Nixon once described as "One of those Harvard bastards."

> Last night Teddy White related to me your hopes for reviving the Eisenhower-Nixon majority. This seems to me altogether a worthy goal, and a perfectly feasible one. But I fear we may be jeopardizing that outcome by certain present postures that are now in no way central to any of your other goals or policies. The Eisenhower-Nixon majority was broad-based. (Ike got 20% of the black vote in 1952 and twice that in 1956.) But its bedrock consisted of the business and professional class of the nation. These provided the brains, the money, [and] the élan. Clearly your overall policies are ideal for mobilizing that group once again. Your fixed intention to get us out of that war in Asia; to put the economy back in balance; to restore the authority of public institutions; to achieve social progress with social stability—all these are precisely the goals of that group. I think, however, you could lose much of it—needlessly—if their children begin to take personally your necessary, proper and essentially impersonal opposition to their own effort to make foreign policy in the streets. It must be remembered that to an extraordinary degree the demonstrators are an elite group.—I would hazard that half their parents are Republicans.—I

> would not be surprised if those parents contributed half the funds spent by either major party in the 1968 election.—Note, for example, that much of the money behind this weekend's demonstration comes from General Motors and Singer Sewing Machine fortunes. (The *Ole Mole*, the radical journal in Cambridge, is financed by the granddaughter of Merrill, Lynch, Pierce, Fenner and Smith. There is no end to such examples.) As with most such groups, they really are kind of arrogant. Teddy White told a (private) story. His son will be down from Harvard this weekend, demonstrating with his girlfriend. She is an Auchincloss. As she put it, "Uncle Mac [Bundy] and Uncle Bill [Bundy] made a terrible mistake about Vietnam, and I feel I must help rectify it." They can also be wonderful. Maureen Finch who took part in the Moratorium worked for me this summer, and was superb. I gather that Mel Laird's son who also took part is equally an attractive young man. And in the mass they are powerful. One of the least understood phenomenon [*sic*] of the time is the way in which the radical children of the upper middle classes have influenced their parents. That is why *Time* magazine, *Life, Newsweek*, NBC, CBS, the *New York Times* and the media in general will take their side against anybody whatsoever: the Democratic Party, the Pentagon, Mayor Daley. Or, if it should ever come to it ... you. In the course of the rioting at the Chicago convention Tom Wicker of the *New York Times* uttered the famous remark "But those are our children down there on the street." It remained for Pete Hamill to comment that "You'd think no cop ever had a mother." No matter; the kids finished Humphrey. Their parents are in a curious way proud of them. Last Saturday at half time at the Harvard-Princeton game the Harvard Band lined up and began its march with the announcement "Ladies and Gentlemen, the Effete Harvard Corps of Intellectual Snobs." There cannot have been less than $10 billion bucks of Republican money in the Stadium at the time, and as one man it roared approval, i.e., unity with the undergraduates in the face of an outsider who dared affront them. After all, they are Harvard men, etc. (Try to remember that I went to the City College of New York on the subway. So I am not writing about anybody I know!) I sometimes like these kids. More often I detest their ignorant, chiliastic, almost insolent self-confidence. But I think it extremely important for the administration not to allow itself to become an object of their incredible powers of derision, destruction, and disdain.[4]

Nixon paid no heed to Moynihan, but Nixon needed a Democrat and Moynihan needed a president. The fact that Nixon was not cast in the mold of his beloved John F. Kennedy didn't seem to bother him.

The duo of Richard Nixon and Daniel Patrick Moynihan was a most odd pair, but—again—Nixon needed a Democrat, and Moynihan needed a president.

> Indeed, in his new book, "The Professor and the President," Stephen Hess, a Republican journalist who worked with Moynihan for Nixon in the White House before a long career at the Brookings Institution, asks whether "Of all the odd couples in American public life, were they not the oddest?" Nixon, scowling and paranoid, the most combative (though not the most conservative) of Republican politicians, had survived eight often humiliating years as Ike Eisenhower's vice-president. When he ran for the White House in 1960 he was beaten by John Kennedy by a handful of votes. He became a laughing-stock for the press when he failed to become governor of California two years later. Moynihan was six foot five inches (nearly two meters) of Irish brawn and charm, one of the "Harvard bastards" Nixon disdained but sometimes employed. He liked to say he was "baptized a Catholic but born a Democrat." He had idolized Kennedy and helped to inspire Lyndon Johnson's 1965 Howard University speech, the high water mark of liberal commitment. Then, to his bitter disappointment he found himself ostracized by his fellow liberals for "blaming the victim" in his report, "The Negro Family," written when he was assistant labor secretary.[5]

Little did we know the large role that the Fifth Infantry would play that fall in the struggle between the Hawks and the Doves and between Nixon's Silent Majority and the Vietnam War Moratorium protesters. With the secret talks now taking place between Henry Kissinger and Le Duc To and the Paris Peace Talks about to resume, the Nixon administration was looking for any way to withdraw from Southeast Asia. The troop reduction had already begun, and it was evident that victory was no longer the goal, but instead it was to turn tail and run—albeit in a dignified and honorably perceived way. The North Vietnamese government saw this and were just waiting for the perfect opportunity to engage a large American military unit and defeat them in a totally crushing way. They would find their patsy several months later in the Fifth Infantry that was preparing to take over the Northern I Corps from the Third Marine Division who were withdrawing from Vietnam to Okinawa in November. They would bide their time—and watch and wait.[6]

On September 2, 1969, in the wake of the brutality of Typhoon Doris on North Vietnam with over 50 inches of rain and one hundred plus mile per hour winds, Ho Chi Minh died of a heart attack at age 79. He was succeeded by Le Duan, who publicly read the last will and testament of Ho Chi Minh, urging the North Vietnamese to fight on "until the last Yankee has gone."

On October 16, demonstration organizers finally received praises from North Vietnam's Prime Minister Pham Van Dong, who stated in a letter to them, "[M]ay your fall offensive succeed splendidly," marking the first time Hanoi publicly acknowledged the American antiwar movement. Dong's comments infuriated American conservatives, including Vice-President Spiro Agnew, who lambasted the protesters as Communist "dupes" comprised of "an effete corps of impudent snobs who characterize themselves as intellectuals."[7]

North Vietnam finally knew that they had an ally in the peace demonstrators. What Dong didn't say was that the beginning stages of their fall offensive against the Fifth Infantry on the DMZ were in motion as well. Task Force 1-61 looked to be a good candidate to use as an ace in the hole in Paris. A few days later, an unofficial cease-fire was agreed to and the secret talks began. It would turn out to be an opportunity to build NVA forces near the DMZ and would eventually be one-sided. Still, Nixon appeared on TV with his "Silent Majority" speech in a last futile attempt to offset the effects of the demonstrations on public opinion. He would find out that that "Vocal Minority" and "Silent Majority" would be a total juxtaposition.

Here is the conclusion of President Richard Nixon's Silent Majority speech:

> In San Francisco a few weeks ago, I saw demonstrators carrying signs reading: "Lose in Vietnam, bring the boys home."
>
> Well, one of the strengths of our free society is that any American has a right to reach that conclusion and to advocate that point of view. But as President of the United States, I would be untrue to my oath of office if I allowed the policy of this Nation to be dictated by the minority who hold that point of view and who try to impose it on the Nation by mounting demonstrations in the street.
>
> For almost 200 years, the policy of this Nation has been made under our Constitution by those leaders in the Congress and the White House elected by all of the people. If a vocal minority, however fervent its cause, prevails over reason and the will of the majority, this Nation has no future as a free society.
>
> And now I would like to address a word, if I may, to the young people of this Nation who are particularly concerned, and I understand why they are concerned, about this war.
>
> I respect your idealism.
>
> I share your concern for peace.
>
> I want peace as much as you do. There are powerful personal reasons I want to end this war. This week I will have to sign 83 letters to mothers, fathers, wives, and loved ones of men who have given their lives for America in Vietnam. It is very little satisfaction to me that this is only

one-third as many letters as I signed the first week in office. There is nothing I want more than to see the day come when I do not have to write any of those letters.

I want to end the war to save the lives of those brave young men in Vietnam.

But I want to end it in a way that will increase the chance that their younger brothers and their sons will not have to fight in some future Vietnam someplace in the world. And I want to end the war for another reason. I want to end it so that the energy and dedication of you, our young people, now too often directed into bitter hatred against those responsible for the war, can be turned to the great challenges of peace, a better life for all Americans, a better life for all people on this earth.

I have chosen a plan for peace. I believe it will succeed.

If it does succeed, what the critics say now won't matter. If it does not succeed, anything I say then won't matter.

I know it may not be fashionable to speak of patriotism or national destiny these days. But I feel it is appropriate to do so on this occasion.

Two hundred years ago this Nation was weak and poor. But even then, America was the hope of millions in the world. Today we have become the strongest and richest nation in the world. And the wheel of destiny has turned so that any hope the world has for the survival of peace and freedom will be determined by whether the American people have the moral stamina and the courage to meet the challenge of free world leadership.

Let historians not record that when America was the most powerful nation in the world we passed on the other side of the road and allowed the last hopes for peace and freedom of millions of people to be suffocated by the forces of totalitarianism.

And so tonight—to you, the great silent majority of my fellow Americans—I ask for your support.

I pledged in my campaign for the Presidency to end the war in a way that we could win the peace. I have initiated a plan of action that will enable me to keep that pledge.

The more support I can have from the American people, the sooner that pledge can be redeemed; for the more divided we are at home, the less likely the enemy is to negotiate at Paris.

Let us be united for peace. Let us also be united against defeat. Because let us understand: North Vietnam cannot defeat or humiliate the United States. Only Americans can do that.

Fifty years ago, in this room and at this very desk, President Woodrow Wilson spoke words that caught the imagination of a war-weary world. He said: "This is the war to end war." His dream for peace after World War I was shattered on the hard realities of great power politics and Woodrow Wilson died a broken man.

Tonight I do not tell you that the war in Vietnam is the war to end wars. But I do say this: I have initiated a plan which will end this war in a way that will bring us closer to that great goal to which Woodrow Wilson and every American President in our history has been dedicated—the goal of a just and lasting peace.

As President I hold the responsibility for choosing the best path to that goal and then leading the Nation along it.

I pledge to you tonight that I shall meet this responsibility with all of the strength and wisdom I can command in accordance with your hopes, mindful of your concerns, sustained by your prayers.

Thank you and goodnight.[8]

As it turned out, the Silent Majority was a shadow of its former self, and the vocal minority was growing every day. The organizers of the Moratorium, bolstered by the success of the August demonstrations, were organizing more aggressively for the next round of protests planned in mid–November. Considered the largest political rally in U.S. history, the November 15, 1969, march of over 500,000 protesters on Washington, D.C., in the frigid autumn cold, was billed the most influential protest ever. The protesters didn't know, however, that the specifics of troop withdrawal and Vietnamization were already written in stone in the White House. They didn't know that North Vietnam would break the cease-fire when they saw the opportunity to trap Task Force 1-61, and that they would play for that ace in the hole on Hill 162 and Hill 100. We didn't know it then, but in October of 1969, the stage was set for what was an inevitable showdown that would involve three battalions of the 27th NVA Regiment against Task Force 1-61 of the Fifth Infantry Division—primarily four companies of infantry with support units—just south of the Demilitarized Zone on November 11, 1969.

# 6

# The First 100 Days

On July 13, 1969, I started my tour with A/1-61. When I reached Qua Viet in the back of a deuce-and-a-half with a half dozen other troopers, the company was on a mid-day stand-down squaring up their gear. We had made a side trip to LZ Sharon, which is where the battalion headquarters were, to get our issue of personnel gear. The gear comprised an M-16, fourteen magazines of .556-millimeter ammunition in a pair of green cloth bandoleers, a steel pot and camo cover, a poncho and liner, 2 quart-sized canteens, a rucksack, web gear, bayonet, a pair of jungle boots, a first aid pack, and a B bag for personal gear. We turned in our duffel—called our A bag—with some personal stuff, dress uniform and khakis to be stored away in a Conex. I asked for a Kabar and a PFC found one for me. Then we were trucked up to Qua Viet Naval Base—the second northernmost base in Vietnam—to link up with Alpha Company, which was providing security in that area.

We were called troopers—that was new lingo for me—because we were a mechanized unit. Eventually, I was assigned to third platoon, first squad. The company's sixteen Armored Personnel Carriers were impressively parallel-parked inside Qua Viet Naval Base. Each PC had a 50-caliber Browning machine gun mounted in the center turret on top. There was another smaller turret angling rearward where the M-60 machine gunner sat. A coil of chain link fence and two metal posts were rolled up on the top deck to be used as an RPG fence, and five coils of concertina wire were fastened to the back to be ringed around a segment of a company night defensive position. I was told everyone sat on top of the tracks and not inside, where an NVA shape-charged Rocket Propelled Grenade could wipe out a whole crew. The interior was loaded with about a ton of supplies—assorted ammo, several cases of grenades, spare cans of diesel fuel, smoke, Willie Pete, extra Ma-Deuce barrels, our B-bags, and God knows what else.

The first squad comprised six other men—Allen Jones (AJ), Don Sarsfield, Stretch Cragholm, Skip Hager, Gary Kent (Coolbreeze) and Tut, our Kit Carson Scout. Rounding out the squad was Cri Cri, our track driver. Stretch and AJ were short-timers and were rarely in the field with us, but they were our mentors—especially AJ. He was willing to work with us, helping us with the little things that would help us stay alive even if we were FNGs. With the inclusion of a few others who came in August, these were my closest friends. None of the group had a cause to fight for—we simply fought for each other. We saw death all around us and we didn't want to see it in the squad, but realized that some of us would die.

Cri Cri—who also went by the nickname of Jo Jo—was the shortest, and I knew

**Third platoon of Alpha Company, First Battalion, 61st Infantry Regiment, 5th Mechanized, circa August 1969. Top: Sgt. Kevin Priest, PFC Gary Kent, PFC Sterling Eugene "Bo" Kelly, SSgt Charles Krabel, unknown replacement, "Jo Jo" Crieder, Tut (Kit Carson Scout). Bottom: PFC Donald "Mark" Marksberry, PFC Alton "Skip" Hager, Sp4 Steven "Smitty" Smith, Sgt. Carl "Stretch" Cragholm, Sp4 Allen "AJ" Jones.**

little about him except that he and AJ were the two best and most experienced troopers in the squad. They were both Spec 4s and the brass would not promote them to sergeant and make them squad leaders. They were upset, rightly so, about not getting promoted.

Sp4 Don Sarsfield:

> AJ was a black man—a real gentleman. When I first arrived AJ and another guy ["Jo Jo" Creider] had been there a while and there was definitely a lot of prejudice in our unit. They probably were the best soldiers in the third platoon and they refused to give them sergeant stripes and make them squad leaders. AJ was the most experienced veteran and justifiably so should have been promoted.

Carl "Stretch" Cragholm was from California. The three of them had been in two Khe Sanh engagements—one on April 28 and the other on June 18. Cool-Breeze was a big farm boy from Georgia and one of the strongest guys I ever met.

Sp4 Don Sarsfield:

I remember the first time Coolbreeze came into the squad. We were in our bunker on a stand down and we were probably all drunk and high I'm sure. Anyway, I told him to do something and he actually came over and picked me up by the shirt and held me off the ground and said, "What are you going to do about this?" So I said to him, "Are you married?" And he said, "No!" And I said, "Do you plan on having kids?" He said, "Yah why?" And I said, "If you don't put me down, I'll guarantee you'll never have kids." That was the last problem I ever had with Coolbreeze.

Donny Sarsfield became one of my best friends over there. He was from Rochester, New York, and turned out to be very cool under fire. At one point he was our track driver, replacing me from a short stint at that position. Eventually he was promoted to squad leader.

My first mission was going to be a dismounted one, so we were leaving our tracks at Qua Viet. We were given an SP Pack and we divided up the goodies and cigarettes. The cigarettes went fast, but nobody wanted the Lucky Strikes or Camels, so I took both cartons. I put three packs in my ruck and the rest I stashed in my B bag in the 3-1 Track. "That should last me until morning," I thought. I also thought it was a shame leaving all that ammo behind, but I did add six M-26 grenades, a claymore mine and 2 belts of M-60 to my already substantial load. AJ waved me over, beckoning with a roll of electrical tape in his hand. He took the grenades one at a time from my shoulder straps and wrapped two coils of tape across the spoon and around the body of each one. "We've had a lot of accidents lately. That would be a bad way to start." I nodded dumbly. Hell, I was scared.

***Top:* Sp4 Louis A. Pepi Jr. (author) on the 3-1 squad track at LZ Sharon. *Middle:* Sp4 Steven "Smitty" Smith, member of the third platoon, A/1-61. *Bottom:* Tut, the third platoon, A/1-61 Kit Carson Scout.**

Shortly after 1200 hours, we exited Qua Viet—dismounted—to make cloverleaf sweeps south of the Qua Viet River. We moved out in platoon strength groups at about 1500- to 2000-meter intervals. We all had full canteens and C-rations as we would not return until morning. "Oh boy," I thought, "no grace period for me. Right into the fire." I was scared. The short-timers picked right up on it.

AJ said something like, "Relax, it's not going to be bad. Nothing happening around here lately." It didn't do much to alleviate the fear. I decided to just shut up and watch the others. The others didn't seem to be too worried, but that didn't help. It was the unknown.

Brigade Op Order sent to all units:

> During the months of May and June, the Brigade has suffered an appalling number of accidental injuries due to shooting and detonation of various types of explosive devices. At the present rate of non-hostile injuries, during a normal year tour, two full rifle companies would be senselessly killed or maimed. The accidental losses that have occurred in the first brigade during the past two months will not be further tolerated. Commanders and leaders at all echelons will take vigorous action to insure [*sic*] that proper care and respect is afforded to the safe handling of weapons and explosive devices in use in the brigade. Small arms, hand grenades, claymores, demolitions and pyrotechnics can be used safely and effectively if soldiers use common sense and are adequately supervised by their commissioned and non-commissioned officers.

Outside the Qua Viet gate, the first platoon and the CP took the lead. Second platoon followed and third platoon brought up the rear. Following the river, the platoons peeled off at 1500-meter intervals and patrolled south—then west—before turning north back to the river. Eventually a few hours before dark, the LT found a brushy knoll and we set up a perimeter about 300 meters from the Qua Viet River. I do not remember the LT's name. He wasn't with the platoon much more than another few weeks and would be replaced by Lieutenant William Miller in early August. As we dug foxholes, the LT "bracketed" our perimeter, walking artillery in to four registered spots in case there was a need in the night. "Now they know exactly where we are," I thought. My foxhole buddy that night was Alton Hager, our 60 gunner. Each of the other squad guys—except Tut—dropped the M-60 belts they were carrying, giving us a total of 1400 rounds. All the firepower that we had handy made me feel quite a bit safer until Hager mentioned offhand that if we were attacked, the NVA would concentrate on our tracers first off. As we were finishing up our foxhole—the digging was a breeze in the fine white sand—Stretch Cragholm came by and directed Hager to show me how to set the claymores.

Skip Hager was from Missouri and was truly a happy-go-lucky guy. He always had a smile on his face, but more importantly, he was one hell of an M-60 gunner. Pulling out his claymore, he motioned me to get mine. There are five parts to a claymore—the clicker, the wire, the blasting cap, the circuit tester and the mine itself. As he put his clicker in one of his side pockets, he motioned me to mimic the process. He put the blasting cap in his shirt pocket, clutched the claymore under his side with his arm and tied the end of the wire to his machine gun barrel. He then walked out in front of our position, uncoiling the wire as he went. About 30 meters out, he set the spool down and looped a knot about two feet back from the blasting cap. He then crouched to set the claymore down and adjusted his aim with the peep sight. He removed one of the priming adapters, inserted the wires through its slot, and screwed the blasting cap into the hole. Then he fastened a peg into the ground to secure the knotted wire, so pulling on the wire wouldn't topple the claymore. We then moved ten meters or so laterally and I placed my claymore.

Back at the foxhole, we tested the circuits, then connected the firing devices. We disconnected the clickers temporarily to let a two-man LP slip out of the perimeter just before dark.

Then it got dark. I wondered how I could be more scared than I was during the day. That was nothing—a cake walk. Hager took first guard at 2000 hours and said he would wake me up at midnight. I never slept. I lay on my back as the mosquitos devoured my flesh. I was on fire everywhere. I wrapped myself tightly in my poncho liner but they found their way in and were voracious. After an eternity, my wristwatch struck midnight and Hager finally reached over and tapped me. I sighed and sat up. He showed me where the claymores' clickers were and fell onto my sleeping spot. He was snoring lightly in less than a minute.

Clouds had moved in and it was the blackest of possible nights. I waved my hand in front of my face and couldn't see any movement. I must have looked like a carnival cat, my eyes were so bugged out. I went long periods without blinking and that began to dry my eyes out painfully. It was so quiet my ears were ringing. The funny thing is that they still ring like that today—the result of tinnitus from a thousand explosions. The terror of it was that some sapper could sneak up to me and slit my throat and I would never have seen it coming. I thought I imagined movement and rustling in front of my position, but it was only partially audible through my ringing ears. I swore to myself that the noise was real. I wanted to fire the machine gun—just a 10-shot burst of recon by fire. I was tempted because I could hear—something. I stared for so long that the black blindness began to undulate like heat waves on a desert floor. That made it worse because now I really thought I could see something. I wanted to wake up Hager and whispered out to him. Hager sighed in his slumber and rolled to his side, resuming his light snoring.

Then it started to rain—not a couple of indiscernible drops that escalated into a steadier freshet, but rather an instant deluge like a violent waterfall. I jabbed out in the darkness, feeling for my poncho, but it was already too late when I slipped it over my head. All sound and sight, imagined or otherwise, were drowned out in an instant by this—this monsoon. Within five minutes, my foxhole had a foot of water in it and I was shivering uncontrollably—so badly that the fear was gone—there was no room for it. As the foxhole filled, the water felt warm in comparison to the cold night air. It had been 95 degrees in the heat of the day, but now it must have been in the fifties. By 0200, I was waist-deep in water. I reached over and tapped Hager a few times—who woke with an angry sigh this time. I climbed out of the pond that was my foxhole in a seizure of chilling cold shakes. I spent the rest of the night and early morning trembling in the fetal position.

The weather cleared at dawn and I dried out rapidly as the temperature rose through the eighties not long after sunrise. The first order of business at daylight was to break down the claymores in reverse order of the way they were set up. While we were cooking breakfast, the LPs returned to the perimeter. The beans and franks breakfast—heated with a chunk of C4—warmed me from the inside out, and the cold night became a distant memory with the onrush of the heavy humidity into the saturated wet jungle.

At about 0730, after drying all our gear, we were saddled up and regrouped in company strength at a point on the river south of Qua Viet. While the three platoons loitered in separated groups, two Navy river patrol boats appeared, making their way towards us from a bend in the river. We were told that in the night one of the PBRs fired on approximately fifteen individuals—small people, they were called—and Alpha Company was given the task to "search and destroy" anyone in this "free fire zone." The PBRs eased up to the shore and extended a gangplank to dry land. It was about 0745. The first platoon loaded in two groups for the short ferry ride to the north side of the Qua Viet. As the diesel engines revved in reverse, they churned up red swirls of silty mud in a slow turn to the far shore. The third platoon watched from the south shore as they waited their turn.

That awaited return was interrupted by a loud explosion and a rooster-tail of water rising about thirty feet at the bow of the first boat. Simultaneously, the boat lifted out of the water. Five bodies were seen arcing out of the boat into the water—two Naval personnel and three 1-61 troopers. What ensued next was an instant panic of the shoreline bystanders. They all hit the ground and dispersed, awaiting a further eruption of chaos. It did not come. Four of the human missiles were soon seen bobbing in the muddy water. They quickly made their way back to the capsized boat that was sinking fast. They were noticeably shaken and wounded in varying but slight degrees. The second boat picked up the wounded before ferrying the first platoon to the north shore.

The fifth individual thrown by the blast was Spec 4 Terry Hawkins of Waterville, Ohio. He did not surface and the boats and troopers searched downstream on both shorelines for several hours before pronouncing that Hawkins was MIA. Eventually Hawkins's body washed up on the south shore of the large island downstream two days later and his status was changed to KIA. PFC Darrell Alexander, who was in the boat that hit the mine, stated that Hawkins was sitting just below the quad fifties and was slammed headfirst into the barrels and then ejected overboard. He was probably dead before he hit the water.

From the 1-61 Daily Journals July 14:

> 0755 Juno CP Qua Viet—14075H—303673—Clearwater Navy Patrol boat hit a mine and sunk. Four WIA and one MIA. Two WIA and one MIA from A/1-61. Two WIA from Navy. Medevac complete at 0805 Hours. Searching area for MIA

From the 1-61 Daily Journals July 16:

> In reference to mining incident in Qua Viet River, the MIA was found at approximately 0600 and pronounced KIA vicinity of YD309673

The ferrying resumed and soon it was third platoon's turn to board the lone remaining PBR. I strained my eyes to stare into the murky water to see any object that might resemble a mine, not even knowing what they actually looked like. This was a new level of fear as I expected to be blown out of the boat at any moment. It did not happen, and we waited on the far shore for the final groups to cross.

By 0900 all of Alpha Company was across the Qua Viet and heading northwest toward the DMZ—some three miles distant. The third platoon got the middle quadrangle near the destroyed city of Bac Vong starting out in grid square YD2664. The area was flat paddy country dotted with destroyed and abandoned villages of small thatched huts. I did not know what I would face. The blackness of the night before was bad enough, the mine incident was even worse, and the ferry ride while expecting another blast was yet a higher degree of terror. What level of fright could be next?

I soon found out: it was walking point. As we were about to start out, I made eye contact with the LT and he motioned me to join AJ on the point, stating that it was as good a time as any to learn. I made a mental note never to make eye contact with a lieutenant again. AJ waved me along and instructed me to do exactly as he did. You could tell by his expression that he did not agree with the lieutenant putting a green trooper on point. We started out hugging the brush about ten meters apart and heading west to another brush line, then north to a more barren wilder country with vegetated red bluffs and another brush line about 600 meters away. The ground was low undulating red heights with concealed areas at every turn. AJ moved out from the tree line and the next level of fear hit me head on. I lingered at the edge until AJ looked back and waved me out and beyond him to the point.

It dawned on me that calling this maneuver a "search and destroy" was totally deceptive for the grunts performing it. A better term would have been "bait and switch." We were the "bait" and air support or artillery was the "switch." Actually, military tacticians had a better term for it. They called it "hammer and anvil." It was a very simple slant on the ancient tactic in Vietnam. Put a small vulnerable-looking force of infantry out in the open to draw out a more superior enemy force and then use an air support and artillery combination to hammer them against the human grunt anvil. It was a very successful tactic that usually produced 10 to 1 casualty ratios—but not so good for a small infantry unit that was used as bait. In Vietnam it was always about body count and never about territory. Tacticians had another phrase—they called it a "war of attrition."

Those 600 yards took an eternity to negotiate, and I expected a bullet in the chest at every turn. It had taken barely two days, but I had already resigned myself to the fact that there was no scenario that would allow me to survive this place. I was simply a dead man walking and I was already reconciled to it. Somehow this caused a lessening of my anxiety and I was relieved to come to terms with my certain fate. The only question now was—when? As I turned to look back at the rest of the platoon, AJ looked back at me and instantly picked up the new resignation in my demeanor and nodded with approval. I guess I had met the test.

When we got to the tree line, we stopped for a breather in the 100-degree heat. I was exhausted more from fear than from the heat, thirst and the load I was carrying. AJ gave me some words of encouragement and then walked over and spoke to the lieutenant, who announced that AJ and I could fall back to the middle of the platoon when we resumed. Donald Sarsfield, another FNG, was called up to take my place and Kevin Priest replaced AJ.

The rest of the day was uneventful except for the complete feeling of exhaustion when we returned to the ferrying point at the river. The boats returned us to the south side and we dispersed in platoon strength again to set up platoon-size killer-team ambushes. The third platoon's area was the furthest west and we had humped maybe two miles by 1600. The lieutenant found us a little hill and he again registered the area with artillery. A chopper dropped in with water and hot chow, which lifted my spirits for the first time in my 36-hour baptism of fear. That was short-lived, though, when it became apparent that artillery registration and chopper landings were just broadcasting exactly where we were spending the night. We set up our claymores again and set shooting stakes for Hager's M-60. Then we sat in our wide foxhole as dusk fell. Our position faced northwest and we stared out toward the western mountains and watched them dim into the clear starlit night. The dominant landform was a steadily rising peak that was taller than the other three or four peaks slightly to the south of it. I didn't realize it then, but the large peak was Hill 162 and the smaller ones were called the Three Hundreds. They would play a dominant role in the collective lives of Alpha Company in about four months. The lieutenant gave us one of the starlight scopes and I was mesmerized by the way it transformed the distant vegetation into shimmering emerald images. The problem was the darker it got, the more everything looked like it was moving.

I was given first guard, which lasted until midnight, and I settled into the foxhole to smoke a cigarette out of sight under a poncho liner. This night was brightly starlit and the starlight scope really was not necessary. It was quiet except for the distant call of jungle birds, singing their evening chorus. Then the idea occurred to me that the birdcall might be sappers signaling each other as they crawled toward our perimeter to throw in satchel charges or slit our throats. Consciously, I unbuckled the clasp on my Kabar sheath and curled my hand around the steel-gray handle. I had been sharpening it for a week—starting during the truck ride from LZ Sharon and continuing every chance that offered itself. It was sharp enough to shave with—attested by the fact that I had removed nearly all the hair off my right forearm testing its keen edge. Lately, I was working on the top edge—two inches back from the tip—to shape it like a Bowie knife.

I was startled out of all this idle thought with the appearance of three human forms crossing the trail to the river about 200 meters to my front. My heart leapt and I slapped Hager awake and pointed emphatically to our front. He jumped into the hole and peered out, but they were already in the brush to the right of the trail. Meanwhile, the lieutenant saw the activity at our position and crawled to us. He told us to fire if we caught sight again. Hager saw movement at that moment and opened with several short bursts on the M-60—maybe 10 or 15 rounds. The lieutenant stopped him with a hand on the shoulder as his RTO, Doug Free, crawled up. Before calling in some coordinates, the lieutenant signaled someone in the next position to lob a few M-79 HEs to the point of interest. That done, the first artillery round came in from 155s somewhere and hit right on the mark. The lieutenant nodded back to the RTO and the call was to fire for effect. Nothing could have lived through that barrage, but still there was no evidence of success when one of the squads searched the area in the morning.

The company continued those search and clears—sometimes mounted and sometimes dismounted—for about another week. We alternated between ambushes out in the white sand area and security inside the Qua Viet Base itself in platoon-sized forces. Then, on the 22nd of July, the company moved about 17 miles south to LZ Sharon, where battalion command was. Alpha Company acted as a security force for the neighboring LZ Angel for the next 21 days. Captain Robert Patrick Gallagher joined Alpha Company as our commanding officer on July 26. Officers rotated in and out of units every six months. He was a no-nonsense, by-the-book commander, airborne qualified. He was clean-shaven with a short crew cut and always had a starched clean uniform. He expected us to shave every day—even out in the field—but there was not much he could do about our filthy uniforms, since we were never issued a new set of jungle fatigues until the old pair rotted off.

Sergeant Ken Leach, first platoon squad leader:

> And as for Gallagher—he ran a tight ship. I remember I had not shaved for two or three days one time and Gallagher came up to me and said, "Leach, you didn't shave this morning." He was a real stickler—even out in the field. I remember there on Hill 100 in the morning—I shaved with cold water in my steel pot. He went by the book and I think everyone respected him—I know I did. He had leadership qualities.

Gallagher was not popular with the battalion brass, I believe because he refused to lose a few men to justify a big enemy body count. He looked out for us and we truly appreciated that. An anonymous higher battalion source told me that for this reason, brigade was considering relieving him of command. He also admitted that that was a grossly incorrect review of his soldiering qualities. As a result, Alpha Company did not roll up enemy body count numbers like the other companies, but after Terry Hawkins died on July 14, we did not have another friendly KIA until November 13, in the big firefight. During the same period, the other rifle companies in Task Force 1-61 collectively suffered 56 friendly KIAs. If nothing else, the company respected Captain Gallagher for that. He was hard on drugs—administering swift punishment when he found troopers with them. This seldom happened, though, since we were nearly always in the field, where the problem was not as widespread and accessible as it was in the rear.

Lieutenant Colonel John Swaren, Battalion Commander:

> When you are down there in Quang Tri and [LZ] Sharon you've got race problems, you've got drug problems, and you've got serious problems. But up there in the AO, those things were reduced. You still have them but not nearly so bad.

As stated, in late July, Alpha Company was still based inside LZ Sharon but was occupied most of the time providing security inside and outside of nearby LZ Angel. During the day, though, the rifle companies ran platoon-sized cloverleaf "search and clears" outside LZ Sharon, both north and south, but rarely ranged beyond Jones Creek to the north. On the off chance that third platoon ranged further north than this, the battalion had a portable tank bridge along to aid in crossing the Thach Han and its tributaries, including Jones Creek. Jones Creek is significant because several tracks became stuck approaching the water, including the motorized tank bridge.

Dismounted and mounted patrols would find a variety of NVA equipment on a daily basis. There were Ho Chi Minh sandal tracks everywhere in the loose dirt and red mud. One day they would find NVA web gear and pith helmets and the next they would find Chicom grenades, RPGs and AK-47 ammo. From time to time, they would find various sizes of pots, pans and assorted mess gear. When NVA bodies were found, they were always stripped naked and wrapped in U.S. tarps or ponchos. The odd thing was that with all the signs that were found, there was surprisingly little contact. It was almost like the NVA were watching but avoiding contact.

About this same time, the rumor mill was indicating that the Third Marine Division would be pulling back to Thua Thien soon, and eventually would leave Vietnam completely for redeployment on the island of Okinawa. This rumor would turn out to be true. This meant that the Fifth Division would now take over operational control of the Northern I Corp. The official transfer date would be November 1.

During early and mid–August, the company received a fresh batch of new troopers. Among the group were Gene (Bo) Kelly, Joe Vetrano, Don (Mark) Marksberry, Bobby Vandergriff, David Nicholson, Steve (Smitty) Smith and Lieutenant William Miller. Kelly was assigned to third platoon first squad with Hager, Priest, Kent, Sarsfield and me. Kelly was from Shasta, California, and his hometown gave him one more nickname. He would eventually replace Sarsfield as our track driver sometime after Sarsfield launched Sergeant Priest off the 3-1 PC while making a high-speed "milk run." He was medevacked to the hospital ship with a broken coccyx vertebra. He would spend the rest of his time in the rear with a medical profile. Vandergriff was a Sp4, but was promoted to sergeant and took over one of the other squads of third platoon. Marksberry was assigned to first squad, as was Smith. Joe Vetrano was also assigned to Vandergriff's squad, but being a good friend of Kelly's, he spent a lot of his down time with us.

**Members of the first squad, third platoon, Alpha/1-61: PFC Donald Marksberry, PFC Gene Kelly, PFC Alto "Skip" Hager, unknown new replacement, Sp4 Allen "AJ" Jones, Sp4 Donald Sarsfield.**

On August 13, Alpha Company left the area around LZ Sharon and Angel to travel north again to the AO in and around Qua Viet. Alpha Company was placed under the operational control of Delta Company, 1–11 Infantry until August 22. This area was familiar to most of us as we had been there in mid–July. The benefit of being assigned to base security at Qua Viet was the good Navy chow and the outdoor movie theater. One particular instance comes to mind when the company had been out on mounted patrols south of the base all day and got back to Qua Viet at dusk to stand down until 1200 hours the next day.

Captain Gallagher was anxious to get the company through the chow line in quick order so that the whole company could watch a Clint Eastwood movie that night called *The Good, the Bad, and the Ugly*. It was almost show time as the last of the company finished chow. Gallagher, not wanting to miss the start of the movie, ordered everyone to mount up on our PCs and drive them over to the movie site. We pulled into the seating area and since there was nowhere to park, Gallagher divided the tracks into three columns and sent them down the center and two side isles. The other army and navy personnel that were already seated watched in amazement as a mechanized infantry captain, flailing his arms like a traffic cop, directed each driver, until all fifteen tracks were parked in three neat rows. We had the best seats in the house and everyone enjoyed the movie.

**PFC Joseph Vetrano standing next to a third platoon track.**

On August 22, Alpha Company was placed under the operational control of A/1-77 Armor and was charged with security of LZ Nancy and the surrounding area out onto Wunder Beach. Following this short stint, on August 26 A/1-61 was charged with the security of Fire Base C-2. This was an uneventful time, but the company did get their first taste of the western foothills in and around Hill 162. Several times they ranged out to this area and set up company perimeters with ambushes and LPs. The weather got hot and there were heat exhaustion medevacs on the 26th and 27th of August. On the 29th, five NVA were pushed out in the open briefly at about 0900 hours by a squad-sized search and clear patrol from the fourth platoon. Alpha company trained two 50-caliber machine guns on them and fired about 200 rounds. Barky was on site later in the day at 1800 hours and two fast movers were brought in to drop napalm. A bunker was found set up as a makeshift hospital and stocked with medical supplies. It was destroyed with C-4. On August 30, Alpha Company set up a night perimeter on Hill 100. They would return to this hill on November 12 in a night "Bald Eagle" insertion. This was the same day that

Sarsfield would launch Sergeant Kevin Priest and the rest of the squad on his high-speed run back to C-2. Priest was medevacked by Batman 17. On September 1, a trooper had two fingers blown off by a blasting cap while disarming a claymore mine. The company picked up camp and moved to C-2 to stand down the rest of the day for maintenance.

**Sergeant Kevin Priest, third platoon, A/1-61.**

On September 2, Typhoon Doris struck Vietnam. On the morning of the second, gale winds were blowing a deluge sideways and Alpha Company was assigned the task of maneuvering around C-2 on a mounted search and clear mission. The mission began at 0700 hours, and the first four checkpoints were reached in platoon-sized mounted patrols by 1100 hours. The company then dismounted in 70-mile-per-hour winds—with gusts to 100—and walked to the next 2 checkpoints. The rain was coming down now at a rate of more than 3 inches per hour. Everything was flooded as the company moved along in foot-deep standing water.

In this set of weather conditions, bomb craters were hidden by the standing water and there were numerous instances of the point elements plunging to the bottom of these hidden craters. In several instances, they dropped and discarded web gear and rifles to prevent drownings. Several M-16 rifles and quite a bit of web gear were lost. Sgt. Bob Ziessler recounts that he was walking along in ankle-deep water when he stepped into what would turn out to be a bomb crater. As he struggled to keep from falling forward into an abyss, a huge gust of wind hit him head-on—and coupled with the weight of his M-60 machine gun that was slung over his shoulder, he was hurled backwards into shallow water. He lay on his back like a turtle until several members of his squad lifted him back to his feet. Huge lizards—possibly Komodo dragons flooded out of their underground dens by the deluge—were flushed out into the open by the approaching column. At about 0200 hours, we finally made it back to the APCs and headed into C-2 for shelter.

At C-2 there was chaos in the now 90-mile-per-hour sustained winds. The roofs had blown off the four hooches we were to be billeted in, so we were put in tents. There were rivers of water running through the tents. Smitty (Steve Smith) found a leech on his leg that must have been sucking his blood all day. It was so gorged with blood that it measured four inches long and two inches in diameter. There was corrugated metal flying through the air everywhere. Some of that flying metal killed two rear echelon soldiers. Then the tents started to blow away, so the company packed into the tracks and rode out the typhoon in relative safety. The aftermath of the typhoon was wind damage and significant flooding from the 52 inches of rainfall. There were several instances of tanks, APCs and other vehicles that were abandoned on the muddy service roads until the weather subsided.

On September 4, Alpha Company was again placed under the operational control of the 77th Armor—and was attached to their Alpha Company tankers. This attachment extended out to September 26. The area of operation for the first week was west of Con

**Sgt. Robert "Bob Z" Zeissler, machine-gunner for first platoon A/1-61.**

Thien along the DMZ. During that time, various pieces of enemy equipment were found including several cached AK-47s, plus a decomposed NVA body that had been there for about a month.

On September 11 there was a noteworthy occurrence near the DMZ in AO Orange. A new NCO, a master sergeant, was assigned to first platoon as their platoon sergeant. A mounted mechanized mission was assigned to Alpha Company 5 clicks east of Con Thien and less than two clicks south of the demilitarized zone. As the company closed within 2 clicks of the DMZ, a temporary company perimeter was formed, and three patrols of ten troopers each from the three rifle companies were dismounted and formed to make cloverleaf search and clears across the DMZ, then sweep north and then east—keeping just south of the international demarcation line. With the temperature above 100 degrees, the new platoon sergeant—overweight and out of shape—succumbed to heat exhaustion just north of the DMZ. His patrol had been moving through a long stretch of stifling elephant grass and he fell in complete exhaustion.

Because of the precarious location, a medevac was a decision of last resort. We were in no man's land, and technically, we were not supposed to be there. In lieu of a medevac, Captain Gallagher decided to have an APC pick up the sergeant and take him back to the company defensive perimeter, where he could be medevacked south of the "no fly" zone. Don Sarsfield and I were atop the 3-1 track manning the fifty-caliber machine gun and Gallagher waved us over. Giving us a dead reckoning direction by sighting down the length of his arm, he pointed out for us where the sergeant was down. He ordered us to traverse the relatively open country and bring the sergeant back to the company perimeter where he could then be medevacked. Knowing that Sarsfield was our regular driver, he ordered him to drive and me to man the fifty—to which we both nodded to the affirmative. I had done a stint as a driver previously and Sarsfield had made the recent switch.

As we were walking back to the track, Sarsfield asked me if I wanted to drive to which I quickly said no. As I jumped into the fifty turret, we expected the mission to take only a few minutes as the patrol was on the return leg just over a knoll that could be seen about 300 meters north of the perimeter. The problem was that a small tributary of the Ben Hai River was situated just south of that knoll and we had to cross it. We made the 250 meters to the bank of the stream where we stopped to reconnoiter a crossing.

Right away, we were reluctant. Although the stream was only about twenty feet wide, there was a steep bank rising up out of the water on the other side, and we had no reason to believe that that steepness did not continue under the water to a depth too great to negotiate. We sat on the track staring at the stream, convinced that crossing at this point was a mistake. At the same time we were pondering the crossing, the company commander's RTO radioed us asking what the holdup was. The reply was that we doubted we could cross successfully. Meanwhile, one of the platoon patrols appeared upstream on their return route. They had crossed the stream several hundred meters upstream to the southwest. The officer in charge of the patrol, having heard our doubts about crossing on the company net, stated that he had just crossed upstream and the streambed was very firm and the water was moderately shallow and static as it appeared to him in front of us. He then gestured us to start moving. In the spirit of the old military adage that enlisted men are not paid to think, we immediately obeyed the order and motored down the bank—only to smash headlong into the steeper opposite bank. The water was about seven feet deep—considerably deeper than the crossing upstream. We tried to back out, but only succeeded in digging in deeper. Captain Gallagher was notified and the command track appeared at the scene a few minutes later with two other PCs. It was soon discovered that there was no tow cable. It was now late in the afternoon—almost 1700 hours—and this was a bad place to be stranded.

The rest of the company was contacted and instructed to break camp at the temporary perimeter and move about 2 clicks southwest to a new NDP. An hour later at 1800 hours, a Batman from the brigade aviation detachment showed up and threw out four tow cables before he medevacked several troopers with heat exhaustion, including the staff sergeant. One of the tracks was backed into place and was cabled to the 3-1 track. It immediately was sucked into the mud. A second track was backed in and hooked up in tandem only to become stuck as well. A call was made to A-4 for an M-88 Tank Recovery Vehicle. In the meantime an M-48 tank, part of the group we were attached to, was backed into place with negative results. It became bogged down in the mire too. At 1945 hours, with the aid of a recovery vehicle, the tank and the three PCs were pulled out of the hole and clear of the mud. Gene Kelly was summoned to the 3-1 track, and Jack Collins, one of the other company track drivers, towed him and his derelict PC back to LZ Sharon, where the diesel engine was replaced. Gene would officially become our new track driver at that moment.

It was now 2100 hours and the remaining contingent of five tracked vehicles started the trek across the western foothills under darkness. Their destination was the new company NDP. At 2145 a request was made for an airburst "Willie-Pete" round to illuminate

**Sp4 Don Sarsfield, first squad, third platoon, A/1-61 sitting in the 3-1 squad track submerged in a tributary of the Ben Hai River.**

the way back to the NDP, but the request was denied. At 2345 the command track, with the three other PCs and an M-48 tank, finally closed with the rest of Alpha Company at the NDP, 2½ miles to the southwest of the scene of the day's event. We were now in the shadow of Hill 162. Somehow there was no enemy contact.

On September 26, Alpha Company was released from the 77th Armor and returned to LZ Sharon. The company remained in that vicinity until October 5, spending most of that time running mounted and dismounted search and clears around LZ Sharon. Each line platoon would spend two nights out of three out on ambush and the third inside with base security. It remained a quiet time. Again, there was plenty of enemy sign and equipment found with little or no contact. We had the feeling, though, that we were still being watched.

**Two Alpha Company tracks stuck in mud attempting to pull the 3-1 track from a tributary of the Ben Hai River.**

During this time, we lost one of the scout dogs attached to our squad. The dog and handler had been with us nearly a month and we all became attached to the dog. The dog was friendly to everyone in the squad except for the unlucky person who pulled the guard shift just before the handler's slot. It was a very delicate undertaking waking up the handler without being chewed up by the dog. To put it mildly, the dog did not like anyone shaking or touching the handler at night while he was asleep. The dog had been out of sorts during the day and was bleeding internally through its nostrils that night. A strategic practice of the NVA was to place poison-laced meat when they saw that we had a scout dog. The dog was in obvious physical distress but a medevac was refused because another company in Leatherneck Square was engaged and had wounded. A medevac did not arrive until 0600—unfortunately, the dog was nearly gone by then. We never saw this dog or his handler again.

On October 5, Alpha Company was put under the operational control of the 3rd/5th Cav to replace the Marine detachment that was guarding the Cam Lo Bridge. On October 8, the 3rd/5th Cav was relieved from bridge security and the 77th Armor replaced them. Alpha Company remained at the Cam Lo Bridge, billeted at Cam Lo Fire Base until October 22. Bridge security turned out to be good duty, protecting it from harm at night. The quiet times continued for Alpha Company. On October 23, the company returned to LZ Sharon and remained in the area until October 31, when an advance party of all the 1-61 units was sent to Firebase C-2 to move the entire battalion operation there. The balance of the line companies remained at LZ Sharon, packing for the move. There was a definite change in the air as the entire 3rd Marine Division was preparing to leave Vietnam for the island of Okinawa and pass the Northern I Corp over to the 5th Infantry Division. Task Force 1-61 would be on center stage now.

On November 1, Alpha Company/1-61, Delta Company/1-61 and A/1-77 were ordered to set up their billets at Con Thien. Bravo/1-61, Charlie/1-61 and Delta/1-11 were ordered to Firebase C-2 along with Headquarters and Headquarters Company. This new push was called Operation Fulton Square, and the battalion commander had ordered his OH-1 for observation of AO Orange for each of the next six days. A distinct change was about to occur.

# 7

# The First 10 Days of November

November 1 started with 74-degree temperatures, unrestricted visibility and 15-mile-per-hour winds. The outlook for the day was partly cloudy skies and highs of 85 degrees. Sunrise was 0648 and sunset was 1822. The beginning of morning nautical twilight was 0626 and the end of evening nautical twilight was 1845.

The systematic movement of Task Force 1-61—numbering about 700 men—started with the Scout Platoon exiting LZ Sharon at 0930 hours with the mission of linking with a platoon of tanks—the 1/6 element of A/1–77. Their mission was then to proceed to Fire Base C-2 as a Ready Reaction Force for the firebase. This was followed by Alpha Company at 0935, the battalion Command Post at 1000, Charlie Company at 1015, and Bravo Company at 1030. D/1-11—already at C-2—was put under the operational control of Task Force 1-61. Alpha Company proceeded toward C-2 to their jumping off point, and then maneuvered west to the general vicinity of Hill 162. Just before dark, Charlie Company took five rounds of incoming with no casualties.

On November 2, Alpha Company brought in its ambushes at dawn, and by 0745 hours had moved east six clicks past C-2 to an area on the edge of a large plain of rice paddies near the destroyed village of Dao Xuyen. They then divided into mounted patrols and searched four to five clicks east-northeast. The patrols fanned to the south, on a line toward Con Thien. The third platoon patrols found three heavily used trails—one heading north and two northwest—with multiple footprints in the loose dirt. At midday a report was received by the TOC that A/1-61 was receiving incoming, but this communication was later proven false, when it was confirmed that the ARVN 7th Mech in the next sector had received that incoming. At 1500 hours, the fourth platoon command track—directed by Lieutenant Chelsea Korte—split off the column and drove to Con Thien to pick up hot chow. They met up with the rest of the company at the evening NDP four clicks southeast of Con Thien. After the evening chow was complete, night acts of ambushes and LPs were put out.

Bravo Company patrolled further west of C-2 and had an uneventful day other than calling for a medevac when two men were severely stung by bees and were having allergic reactions. They were medevacked in the late afternoon. The company was committed to a search and destroy mission several clicks to the west when a sniffer sensor detected approximately 20 little people in the vicinity and moving west. An artillery mission was fired on the spot before they resumed the mission several hundred meters to the west to block any retreating action. Bravo Company later reported negative findings after searching the area.

Charlie Company patrolled west of Bravo Company in the area of the Three 100s and had an uneventful day reporting only that a trooper had been bitten by the scout dog and medevacked. At 2200 hours, another sensor detected movement of twenty or more individuals, and several dashes of TAC Air were sent to drop ordnance on the area.

Delta Company of the 1st of the 11th Infantry—now under the operational control of TF 1-61—and having set up an NDP three clicks west of Firebase C-2, reported one of their mechanical ambushes exploding and indicated that they would have more information in the morning. Delta Company, 1st Battalion, 11th Light Infantry was commanded By Captain Stanley Blunt. As stated, on November 1, D/1-11 was placed under the operational control of Task Force 1-61. In late 1969, Captain Stanley Blunt was already halfway through his third tour in Quang Tri Province—this time with the 5th Division. He had earlier in 1966 and 1967 served as an advisor to a battalion of the Army of the Republic of Vietnam. He went on to serve another tour as an advisor to units of the ARVNs in a program that was known as Vietnamization. He was renowned as a courageous—but very unconventional—commander by the Army staff. His men revered him and followed him anywhere he asked. He knew his profession as a combat infantry officer. More importantly, he knew every crook and cranny of the country along the DMZ. But most importantly, he knew the enemy he was fighting—maybe better than they knew themselves—certainly better than the high command. He knew their tactics and strong points. In so doing, he knew their weaknesses and always capitalized on them. In a war where soldiers were limited to twelve-month tours, he had been in Northern I Corps for better than two years. He knew his area of operation second to none. On the other hand, most arrivals, no matter whether they were officers, noncommissioned officers or enlisted men, would show up at Camp Red Devil ignorant of the tactics of jungle warfare. To help prepare them, they were attached to the 75th Support Battalion for the previously mentioned. In other words, it was a crash course, and as Blunt put it, "Mickey Mouse"

Task Force 1-61 had another issue. Earlier in July, the First Brigade of the Fifth Division had gone through a 100 percent rotation of personnel. Since the division had arrived exactly one year earlier, en masse in an amphibious landing, this complete rotation of personnel had ensued. In route to Vietnam, the brigade had traveled overland from their home base at Fort Carson, Colorado, to San Diego where they had boarded transport and cargo ships for Vietnam. The Kansas National Guard's 69th Division had filled the gap at Fort Carson for the corresponding period and remained a part of the Fifth Division until it returned to the control of the state of Kansas in December of 1969 when the 1-5 returned. The jungle training offered by the 75th Support Battalion, however scant, was now more important, since the entire brigade was now comprised of very green replacements and the inexperience was evident in all support of the units, but most importantly, in the two premier infantry battalions—the 1-11th Light Infantry, a.k.a. the Wandering Eleventh, and the 1-61 Mechanized Infantry, a.k.a. Roadrunners. To compound matters, July through October had been comparatively quiet months and many of the men were not yet battle tested.

In the face of all this rawness, Blunt was the consummate teaching soldier who always led from the front. His men were more at home in the western hills because of Blunt's steady teaching hand. They had spent more time in those foothills as "defensive aggressors" rather than "passive decoys" waiting to be found by the enemy, only to employ "hammer and anvil" tactics.

Stanley Blunt became notorious with his mechanical ambushes. Actually, he learned the technique from a soldier nicknamed Wahoo and Sgt. "Big Daddy" Hammond. The way it worked was that Blunt established several "killer teams." One particular incident that Joe Prince recalls was during a day of platoon patrols. As late afternoon approached, Blunt assigned Sergeant Phil Phillips's killer team to lag behind and set a booby trap. Included in the team was Sergeant Joe Prince, along with EMs Dan Switzer, Bobby Strack, and Bobby Preece. While the main force of the company stealthily meandered their way to the top of the hill in small groups to set up a night defensive position on top, the killer team searched the valley for a well-used trail to set the booby trap. Typically they would look for a portion of the trail that was a natural funnel. On this particular day, they found a good spot and set up the device. Once the trap was armed, they moved off the trail and meandered their way to the perimeter.

Less than fifteen minutes after they arrived at the company site, there was a large explosion and a huge cloud of smoke and dust billowing up out of the valley. Blunt—believing that the device detonated spontaneously—sent the team back to check the site. This was out of character for him because he liked to call artillery in and wait until the next morning to reconnoiter. Still believing the blast was spontaneous, the men were instructed to view the spot from a distance and not actually go to the bottom of the hill.

As the team worked their way down the hill, they spotted a lot of red in the grass—presumably blood. Acting on their own and moving cautiously, they made their way down the hill and found three dead NVA. It appeared that one of them may have spotted the trap and bent over to look at the wire across the trail and the next PAVN soldier behind tripped the secondary wire, killing all three. The lead man had the whole top of his skull blown off from the eye sockets up, suggesting he had bent over to take a closer look when the setup exploded. From the documents they had on their persons, it appeared one was a paymaster. They found three weapons and hid them in the bushes so they could find them in front of the lieutenant the next day and claim them as booty of war.

Blunt's killer teams became so adept at this practice that the NVA gave them the nickname of Bushwhackers. Eventually the 27B Regiment put a price on Blunt's head. A few weeks after this episode, D/1-11 was setting up another night perimeter. By mid-1969, there was no suitable hilltop that was not used many times over for a night position. This spot was no different. As the company split into twos, they touched up the ready-made positions with their entrenching tools. Blunt was no different, finding a hole in the center of the "military crest" that appeared to be previously used as a command position. As he thrust his shovel into the center of the hole, it struck a metallic object. Digging around it he found a mine—which he assumed, probably correctly, was meant for him. "Damn Gooks—those fuckers are trying to kill me," he barked. This hill would be named Gallagher Ridge in the not-to-distant future.

Sgt. Joseph Prince, 2nd Squad, 2nd Platoon:

> We had four man teams that would set up the unmanned Claymore ambushes. The group I was with consisted of Phil Phillips, Tom Strack, Bob Preece, and myself. We would pick out a trail that looked like it had been used on a regular basis. We would try to read the direction of travel that was used the most and direct our ambush accordingly. The booby-trap team would then stay behind with a couple of guys for security while we were setting up the ambush and the rest of the platoon would move on down the trail. The platoon would find a good site for an NDP and carefully make their way into some thick cover so as not to leave a path revealing where they were. They would then proceed to set up the NDP. The ambush team would join them when the ambush was set. The platoon would leave the NDP each day at dawn and move to a remote location to do the cooking, reading, letter writing, resting, etc., away from the NDP, then return about dark to spend the night. This way the NDP was not compromised and could be used for several days. We

used a plastic spoon from the C-ration pack. We would cut the handle off and bore a hole in it, then attach it to some tripwire and covered it with electrical tape. We would attach that to a bush and stretch it across the trail to use as a trigger. At the other end, we attached a wooden clothespin to a bush on the other side of the trail with another short piece of tripwire. The clothespin had a thumbtack on the inside of each ear that would make contact when the spoon was sprung by walking into the trip wire. We ran a wire to each tack and ran that to a battery hidden somewhere off the trail. The clothespin was then covered with friction tape to hide it in the brush. The spoon handle was placed between the tacks to keep it from completing the circuit. The electrical connection at the battery was made with one wire run from the clothespin ear and connected to the negative terminal on the battery. The other wire from the other clothespin ear was connected to the claymores via a blasting cap.

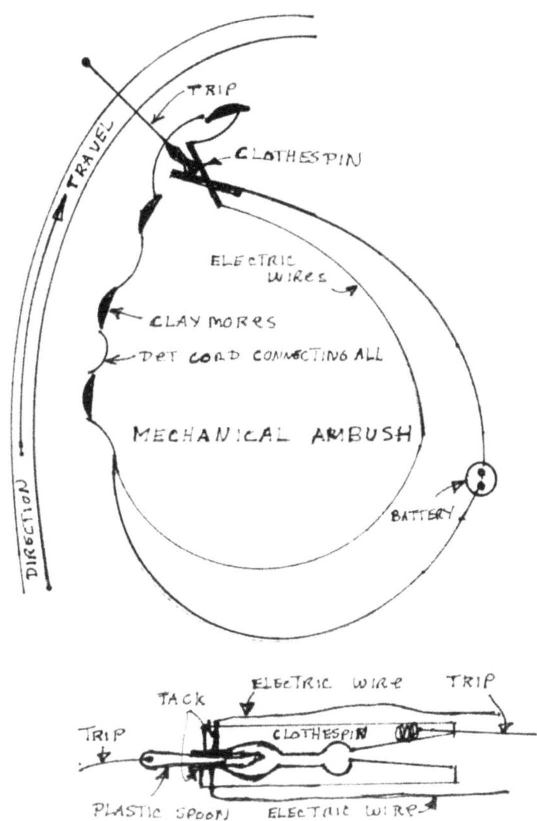


***Right:*** **Diagram of mechanical ambush set-up.** ***Below:*** **Sgt. Kenneth Leach, first platoon, A/1-61 with Kit Carson Scout Boitang. They are questioning civilians found in a "free fire zone."**

> Then the other wire from the blasting cap was connected to the positive terminal of the battery. This made a complete circuit if the plastic spoon was removed. We would then place 4 claymores on the trail connected in parallel to the circuit and together by det-cord. Number one Claymore was aimed directly at the tripwire. Number two was aimed just in front of the tripwire in case someone walked into the ambush from the wrong direction. The third Claymore was aimed so as to overlap the number one Claymore to cover the targets behind the person that tripped the ambush. The number four Claymore was aimed down the trail to catch anyone following on the trail from the anticipated direction of travel. That meant that you had one Claymore at the tripwire, one in front of the tripwire and two behind the tripwire pointing back down the trail.

I asked Phil Phillips who taught Blunt about the mechanical claymores. Phil says it was probably was Ron Gibson:

> I don't know where he would have gotten the idea for that, he wasn't in-country very long before me at all and I don't remember anything about it. Maybe he got it from hanging around Wahoo, who had been there quite a while and I believe had been in recon or something before that. Rumor was he was to be married in Hawaii and was stood up so he went AWOL and ended up in D/1-11. I cannot remember his real name, only that he was about half nuts. He would unscrew a grenade, disarm it, pull the pin, let it discharge and put it back together. Then [he would] open the door of the hooch and roll the grenade down the floor, letting the spoon flip off like it was the real thing. He would then roll on the ground in a fit of laughter when everyone dove through the screens. Or else he would prop a dead gook up against a tree after a firefight and sit back tossing M&Ms into his mouth—that is, if he wasn't prying a gold tooth out with his bayonet. NUTS! But he was fearless in a firefight.

Captain Blunt was one of only a few officers who actually understood Vietnam and how to fight that war. Unfortunately, the brass never listened to those few. Others like Paul Vann were similarly discounted for finding fault with the American strategy. Blunt was a classically trained infantryman. From Denver, Colorado, Blunt enlisted in the Army early in the war because he feared the war would be over before he could get a chance to get there. In his own words, he describes his early education, training, and tours:

**Captain Stanley Blunt, company commander of Delta/1-11 (courtesy Stanley Blunt).**

> Captain Stan Blunt: Thank goodness for sports in high school. That was a good time for us all. We had a good football team and basketball team, and it was part of life in Colorado—having after school time on the football field, the basketball court … darn near won a state championship. We got third place in football, third place in basketball too in the State Class A. We had a good team. [They were] good men. They went on to college, and I tried college for two years and said, "The hell with this, to heck with this shit…." Too much time in college. I was drafted and I don't know if my dad called the local draft board and got me drafted or [not]. The draft [notice] came and the next thing I knew I was on a train for Fort Leonard

**Sgt. Harold "Phil" Phillips, Sgt. Joseph Prince, PFC Ron Gibson of second squad, second platoon, D/1-11. Known as "Blunt's Grunts."**

Wood—and then for Ranger training in Georgia—Airborne training. I enjoyed that very much. It was challenging. And OCS was good too, because I had a physical nature and I enjoyed that, and we were pretty good. We had a good platoon with a good platoon sergeant. Viet Nam was starting. We had one platoon leader that had just got back from Viet Nam, who [was] wounded and I know he wasn't too happy about it. It dawned on me the importance of that, the conflict, and I thought it was going to be a short duration. I just had to get over there, what the hell. But it turned out to be long-range, and we were there ten years. I saw over four of it I guess. At Ranger School, we were down there with "Charging Charlie" Beckwith, they called him, and he was the boss. He tried to turn it into Special Forces. Eglin Air Force Base was where I was at for the third stage of Ranger training. We had patrols down there in swamps with big rattlesnakes! Big damn snakes we kept running into during the course of it. But it was good training. I just felt you [must] be hard-core to make it ... but you can only teach so much about Vietnam; put your Vietnam village up and all that crap. We didn't need those things. We needed to stay strictly Ranger. It was a good school. And "Charging Charlie" and I disagreed on the whole damn thing. But he was a good man. He had a point—village searches and crap like that, but I felt we could learn that in Vietnam. It was OK to push guys to make them proud and they come out of there as good leaders, but let them work on Vietnam when they get there. I don't know whether I was right or wrong ... I think probably right ... I think he was looking for training here in the States to have us ready to go over there and that's impossible. Every village was different. So, we learned again over there though. You learned fast what was right and what was wrong.... I stayed there a year [starting] in early '66 with the 173d Airborne, and everybody was trying to get a platoon, so, I [became] the company XO just waiting for a platoon to open up in the 1st of the 503rd. Finally, I got one it [but] it still looked like the war was going to be over any second. I had to make it quick. Search and destroys, we went on 'em. It was thick forest—thick jungle. You tried to keep it quiet. Thank goodness, we stayed off the trails. We had straight lines to go through, but when you look at what you actually saw, you saw a hundred meters of a thousand-meter area and you wouldn't see the other 900 meters. You saw a hundred meters of the area that you worked through, and they could be right there on the left or right and you'd miss 'em. It was War Zone "D" and "C," Bien Hoa, and around Saigon. On Saigon River we had contact with the NVA.

Well, first I was a lieutenant, a little lieutenant—then first lieutenant and finally to captain. I made rank pretty quick. Eventually I got wounded and was sent in to Fitzsimons Army Hospital. I was thinking about the whole god dang thing, and I thought, "I can't be finished," even though the doctor said, "Take your disability and get out of the military." Bull-crap! So I went to Washington and altered my records a little bit. Where it said I shouldn't go anywhere without a jeep and I should be protected at all times, and wear a steel pot anytime I was out of the orderly room, I reworded the damn thing and resubmitted my file. Then I requested to go back to Vietnam to use some of my thoughts about what we should be doing in that conflict.

So, I got to go back, initially, with the 1st ARVN Division as an advisor and that was '67–'68, so I was in a portion of almost every year. But I learned a lot with the 1st ARVN Division. They were good guys in the 1st Battalion, 2d ARV up in Quang Tri and around Da Nang and the Rock Pile, and Vandergrift Combat Base, and Khe Sanh, and A-Shau Valley. We were on Hamburger Hill [a year before the famous battle]. We were on the west side of it. The hill we tried to take [Ap Bia Mountain] was on the west side of the A-Shau. We watched it, and then we ran into contact too. It was on the main road into Da Nang from Laos. They had guards on it, and we ran into them. We took friendly artillery from a fire support base on ... I think it was on Fire Base Sarge. They fired short rounds, and we were on top of a hill where we could hear them whistling by, then those rounds hit the trees. It was nighttime and we had some men hit that were in ponchos that were in bed. We did the medevacs the next day and cleared out, and ah, WHAM!

After that, I ran into this little major, whom I never forgot, Major Ferguson. [laughing] Shouldn't use any names. And he was the battalion senior advisor, real mouse, that brought me in as staff advisor after this operation, and the first thing he did was, want me to go down to Da Nang and see about his Bronze Star, and I said "No, instead I'll go out and talk to the S-1. He wants me to find out how many ARVN soldiers were killed and are still drawing pay," because it was all going into the pockets of the Battalion Commander and Regimental Commander. I said, "I don't need to go to Da Nang. You go to Da Nang and get your damn Bronze Star." He was a major in a lieutenant colonel's position, and all he could think about was getting his records straight so he could get his medal. The last thing on my mind was having a record. I mean, it was about being out in the bush accomplishing the mission—knowing what you're doing and thinking about it. They had a lot of frags in that unit.

Eventually, I went in to the 5th Mech. It was '69–'70, and the 5th Mech was up in Quang Tri. It must have been July but I forget [chuckling] ... but I had a pretty good time with everybody there. I kind of knew my stuff there, thanks to the ARVNs that taught me an awful lot. I knew about I-Corps and northern I-Corps, and along the DMZ and A-Shau Valley and Khe Sanh. I knew the areas because we'd worked them before ... Vandergrift Combat Base, and I knew about Con Thien. I'd been there a couple of times and had some action with the ARVNs at each place. I learned a lot, because I insisted on staying in the bush. Oh yeah, good memories of the 5th. The 5th was a good unit. They were out of Fort Carson. I'd already been up there for a year or two before they came over to Viet Nam. They had a combination of a leg battalion, a mechanized battalion and a tank battalion, all of them under a brigade. It was pretty good unit, especially the legs, cause we didn't have to hit the roads and hit the mines. We knew what we were doing. I knew the area already as far south as the Ba Long Valley, to the Khe Sanh area and the A-Shau Valley.

We were starting to use booby traps—to hell with convention. We would use Claymore booby traps with pre-planned artillery, and then get the hell out of there. And go back into it very carefully. You'd unhook that battery and get your Claymores and move out—or put them back in and stay. We had them coming and going. We didn't hit the base camps but we got the places in between. And the army finally found that's what caused the big push in '72. It was the ambushes—the Claymore ambushes. I think that they simply couldn't resupply their units. They couldn't go out of their base camps and into the residential areas anymore, because everybody was using them—the Regional Force, the Popular Force and, and the ARVNs were using them too. The commanding officer of the 1st ARVN Division was a good friend and we taught them how to use them. I don't know what happened to him. His name was Di-Uy Ta. He became the regimental commander and he was my old battalion commander—good friend. We showed him how, and showed everybody how to make the Claymore booby traps—and they got good at it.

Captain Blunt—with his one-of-a-kind personality—definitely knew his stuff as a straight-leg company commander and definitely knew the area. His strategy was to keep his position hidden—to set up mechanical ambushes and booby traps that were preregistered with artillery. If a booby trap detonated, artillery was immediately called in to all the approaches while the company perimeter remained quiet and held fire. It was hinted that the NVA actually changed their strategy as the war wore on because the mechanical ambushes were so effective. Also, choppers were never allowed to fly into his defensive perimeters and give away his position—unless it was absolutely necessary. Because of this, there were never hot meals and purified water. His men ate C-rations and got their water—which they treated with purification tablets—from the streams they traversed. They stayed out in the field fifty to seventy days at a time. There was many an irate letter from the parents of his men echoing the entreaties of the soldiers for hot chow. Several that he did respond to immediately saw the justification of his orders and thanked him. He verbalizes this in his own words:

I said, "Let's just be quiet." "Well, what about a hot meal?" "No, we don't have hot meals. We hide out in the bush and you can listen to your radio, but keep it down." And don't go moving around much or they'll see you and then we got trouble. If you hear a 'boom' we want to put artillery on it immediately. I don't give a damn if it's pigs, or a water-buffalo or whatever's walked in there and detonated that thing. We got to put fire power on it and then H & I's and then we'll go in very carefully the next day and locate the battery, disconnect the damn thing and then go see if we got anything with it. And you pick up those Claymores and get out of there. "But we're going in careful. We're not gonna walk into an ambush they've set up. No, no." Supposedly that was violating the Geneva Convention, but who cares? Who cares? We are walking into booby traps all the time—let them walk into a few. And they would come down the trails lickety-split. They weren't messing around; they were always going where they're going on a trail. They never cut their way through the jungle. And so you mine the trails. And you cleared pre-planned, and were ready to fire. Have the tubes aimed there. We got pretty good at it along with the artillery. They knew we weren't messing around out there. At least you make them think about it. It got to be a dry spell in '71 and '72. They couldn't get their commanders to come down the trails anymore because this was going all over I-Corps and II-Corps. It was against the Geneva Convention, but who cares? Who cares? You're walking into booby-traps all the time, let them walk into them, of course....

Blunt's disdain for convention did not make him popular among the brass and they just couldn't see that his ideas were sound. The buzzwords of the day were "Search & Clear," or "Search & Destroy"—or in other words, move to contact. This notion continually got American men killed because the idea of body count was so critical to the politics of the war. Granted, the tradeoff was two, three, four, or even ten to one—but still, American soldiers were needlessly being lost, in his opinion. Back home the American people agreed and were more concerned with the one dead American in those ten-to-one tradeoffs.

Blunt's tactics received low appreciation from the brigade brass, but Blunt himself shared some reciprocal disdain of his own:

> Burke was bullshitter. He was a frustrated general. He made me frustrated. He'd walk around with his silver pearl-handled pistol, acting tough, but he was lost. He didn't last that long—Ol' Burke. I remember him coming in to one LZ and we had the company there, and were getting ready to go up a hill where we were supposed to go up to the thicket up there and set up quietly. He comes in and there's not a goddamned Viet Cong in that area that can't see us, right there in this LZ where the generals are walking around and giving us away. But they don't care because they are getting ready to go back in for the hot meal at night back at the base. And uh, I just avoided him like a plague because we had to go up that damn hill and I knew I was gonna either take casualties or they'd get the hell out of there. They'd know we're coming. It was a base camp on hill [162] with a bunker system coming out of the thickets there, big thickets on the south side of the hill. They had a base camp [bunker system] there and infiltrated all the time down this trail. We found the base camp and we were very lucky. But we were very careful too because I thought, "This is just so stupid, because they got to see us. We're in the elephant grass, and they're in the thicket up there. They got a choice to wait for us or get the hell out of there—one or the other. And it's going to take us a long time to get up this hill ... the west side of it, and to get to the top of that mountain. We should have been put on the top of the mountain first of all if we're gonna risk helicopters." I just thought, "Gee whiz, you guys still don't know what you're doing." And this was '69.... I had plenty of experience in that area, and Khe Sanh....

Captain Blunt disagreed with the U.S. strategy in almost all areas of the war. What is interesting is that all of his ideas have the ring of complete soundness today and most veterans and military historians agree that the war—once committed to—should have been fought to win instead of simply "not to lose." Here are his final thoughts on the subject:

> Well, there was a lot of embarrassment [laughing]. Like with the ranger units and some of the LRRP units—long range patrol and stuff. What a farce. I mean you get off the helicopter and go hide, and wait for something to come down the trail. You don't make any noise, because they can find out where you're at and eventually they come in on you or wait for you at the helicopter pick-up. And it's all so dang dangerous—very dangerous. And there were a few times when they go to insert and they'd take ground fire while they're inserting -no, no.
>
> Then there was Rocket Ridge, where they shot rockets off from all the time with time-delay fuses—water triggers. They'd set them up and figure out where they wanted them to go—Con Thien, or Alpha Three, Alpha Two and Charlie Two. And then they'd get out of there because there would be a delay fuse that would fire. Sometimes it would be six hours later before the thing goes up. That's the way they hit Charlie Two where they hit that bunker that had all the men in it. [He's talking about the rocket attack on Charlie Two on May 21, 1971, that killed 33 American soldiers—the majority of them A/1-61 troopers.] Yeah, it was like an R&R center—that bunker. It's the same one like in the movie *Platoon* where they had a bunker, they were dancing, and talking, that's the kind of bunker they were in—with a mess hall and music. It was a place where you went when you were coming in from the field. They had a delayed fuse on a 130 and WHOOM—it hit right in the middle of them. It killed 33 good men. God almighty—they were good men. Darn good men. We had the AO out to the west with all these trails coming into Quang Tri that we booby-trapped [to] hell.

On November 3, Alpha Company consolidated their ambushes in the morning and moved north along with a tank platoon from A/1-77. A little after 1300 hours, Recon Team 12 reported being surrounded just across the DMZ. Alpha Company was alerted along with the tank platoon to move north to a rendezvous point and be prepared to move to the aid of Team 12 and to extract them if contact developed. It was one of those situations alluded to by Captain Stanley Blunt. Recon Team 12 had been inserted by air and the NVA were simply waiting for their return. At 1400 hours A/1-61 and the tank platoon were ordered to continue their movement north to a grid point to assist in an extraction of Team 12 by air. At 1440 hours, while en route to that grid point, an APC from the tank platoon hit a mine. The mine was of unknown size, but four bogie wheels were blown off and there were 2 medevac casualties and one other slightly injured trooper. The crater created by the mine measured five feet by six feet by four feet deep.

Alpha Company, while heading to the grid point, found a bunker complex consisting of five bunkers and a ten-foot tunnel leading to a four-foot-by-four-foot room. The complex was destroyed and they moved on to their allotted grid point on the DMZ. As the afternoon wore on, Team 12 seemed to be out of danger and the extraction was canceled. A/1-61 was diverted east and set up in platoon NDPs with squad-sized ambushes and LPs just outside the northern boundary wire of Con Thien.

Charlie Company worked their platoons east to a final point where they set up their NDP several clicks west of Hill 162. In the course of the day, they found an area where approximately twenty men had slept the night before. They also reported the heavy use of the nearby trails, indicating the presence of many more than twenty individuals. Various pieces of discarded enemy contraband were found and kept as souvenirs. They had one medevac during the day for a toothache.

Bravo Company worked the area southwest of C-2, moving in the course of the day to a point about four clicks south of Firebase C-2. After setting up their new NDP, six fire-teams were situated outside the radius of the perimeter.

Delta Company (1–11) remained in the same general area it had been in the past three days, patrolling the adjoining areas as before, and picking thick covered areas for their meals and down time.

On November 4, Alpha Company again moved east of Con Thien and performed search and clears all day. At 1000 hours, the second platoon found three sets of footprints and patrolled in the direction of travel. At a turn in the trail, individuals were sighted and a short time later radar sensors spotted movement in the same grid. Artillery was called in and Alpha Company moved forward after the fire mission to assess the damage. The results of the artillery mission were negative at first. Eventually, the third platoon found a shattered rifle stock, and a little further on, found an AK-47 rifle barrel stuck in the ground. They also found one RPG booster and a 105 mm fuse.

Bravo Company worked the area 3 clicks northeast of Hill 162 and patrolled all day long. They found one RPG in the bushes and destroyed it. At 1745 they set up on Gallagher Ridge at YD 085645—the same hill where Captain Blunt had found a mine while cleaning up the CP foxhole with his entrenching tool. Bravo Company put out two ambushes and two LPs.

Charlie Company started the day west of Hill 162 and searched in an easterly direction. Several clicks south of Gallagher Ridge, they found an observation area consisting of two spider holes with observation ports. Behind the holes was a skinned tree that appeared to be for affixing an antenna and camouflaging it. There were also rocks with scratch marks on them seeming to indicate direction of travel put out by an advance group of an enemy unit. They also found a badly mutilated NVA body—probably a casualty of an artillery attack. It was estimated to be about two days old. It was also assessed that a platoon-sized force had occupied the area for a while and had abandoned it about two days earlier. They also found three TM41 mines, an NVA entrenching tool, a Chicom grenade, a shirt with bloodstains, a canister round, and one 57 mm recoilless rifle round in very new condition. All the items were evacuated, and this was all reported to Col. Swaren. Charlie Company set up their NDP 2 clicks south of Gallagher Ridge and put out their night acts—two ambushes and two LPs.

D/1-11 consolidated to their NDP of the night before and prepared for a significant movement west to the area of Hill 162. After moving west all day and passing in the vicinity of Bravo Company, they moved west-southwest of Gallagher Ridge at about twelve hundred meters' distance and set their NDP at YD 077637. They put out six LPs at a distance of one hundred meters from the perimeter.

On November 5, Alpha Company, after bringing in their night acts at dawn, was on the move early, and by 0735 hours was about four clicks east-northeast of the northern perimeter of Con Thien. Search and clears were initiated, and at 0840 hours, the third platoon found a northwest-traveling trail that had sustained heavy use in the past few days. There were maybe ten fresh sets of prints from the previous evening. At midday, the lead element of A/1-61 spotted fourteen individuals in their sector and evacuated them to Cam Lo for questioning and resettlement. Later in the day, in the early afternoon, the first platoon found ten bunkers measuring forty feet long, eight feet wide and five feet high. They also found eleven one-man foxholes, all with overhead protection. There was a tunnel complex to all the bunkers lined with pieces of bamboo—some of them with various writings on them. Also found was a GI poncho, a C-ration can, and an empty mortar charge. The bunkers and contraband were destroyed, but the bamboo writings were evacuated to S1.

Bravo Company conducted a search and clear of their area north of Gallagher Ridge and swept in cloverleafs, returning to their defensive position of the night before.

Charlie Company worked their sector two thousand meters south of Hill 162 on the south-facing ridge of Hill 124. They found a bunker system consisting of eighty spider holes with head cover. Russian 60mm ordnance was found, along with one poncho and one rifle grenade. The system seemed not to have been used in several weeks. Moving up Hill 124 dismounted, the third platoon found four Chicom grenades, one U.S.-made M-26 grenade, and an NVA hand grenade pouch. Twenty minutes later, the third platoon found another cache consisting of an RPG round and seventeen assorted hand grenades that were destroyed in place.

Delta Company (1–11) ranged northwest four clicks in the course of the day with large cloverleaf patrols, only to return to their NDP of the previous evening—on the southwest facing ridge of Hill 162.

November 6 was a bluebird day—clear skies, temperature 84 degrees and relatively low humidity. By 0720, Alpha Company was back from its night acts and in the company defensive perimeter, five clicks northwest of Con Thien and two clicks south of the DMZ. Charlie Company was four clicks south of Hill 162, fifteen clicks southwest of Con Thien and their ambushes were moving toward their NDP. Bravo Company was 4 clicks northwest of Charlie on Gallagher Ridge. D/1-11 was between the two 1-61 companies. The area of operation was known as AO Orange.

While sweeping around their NDP, Charlie Company found a foot trail going in a westerly direction. A mounted platoon patrol followed this trail for 900 meters. By 0920, the rest of Charlie Company's PCs had caught up with the lead platoon patrol and traversed together, another 1000 meters. While patrolling, they found fourteen bunkers—3 feet by 4 feet by 3 feet deep. They had recently been hit by airstrikes. While sweeping the area, the first platoon found an assortment of enemy equipment including five NVA shovels, a sixty-millimeter mortar base plate, two picks, four woven baskets, 3 RPG boosters, 186 AK-47 rounds, one RPD machine-gun clip, one Chicom grenade, one NVA soft cap, two NVA canteens, two NVA officer belts, four AK-47 magazine pouches, four RPG-2 fuses, one rucksack, five pairs of socks, two pairs of pants, two officer field hats, one 9-millimeter pistol magazine, three pounds of salt, ten pounds of polished rice, one pair of underwear, numerous graves and a copious amount of various propaganda materiel. Charlie Company's second platoon found an unexploded U.S. five-hundred-pound bomb that they blew in place. They also came up on ten more bunkers with various unserviceable materials and sundries, as well as one NVA flashlight, one pair of socks, one pair of pants, rice in cooking pots 24 hours old, one NVA handkerchief with "XVAN 1969" written on it, and three B-40 rockets that they blew in place. Sweeping its way back in the afternoon, Charlie Company set up its night defensive perimeter 800 meters south of Gallagher Ridge. Ambushes and LPs were strategically put out.

Bravo Company made its daily sweeps several thousand meters to the east of Charlie Company. Their day was uneventful except for one incident. While they were performing a recon by fire mission at approximately 1700 hours, a trooper had a 50-caliber machine gun blow up in his face. The man was in critical condition and a medevac was immediately called in. At 1735 hours, the dust-off was complete and the man did survive. They set up their NDP again about 1000 meters northwest of Gallagher Ridge and put out ambushes and LPs.

Delta/1-11 also made its daily sweeps and set up their NDP several hundred meters

**One of the three tracks damaged in the November 6 mine incident.**

north of their previous night's position, situated between Charlie and Bravo Companies on Gallagher Ridge. Blunt was again back at the scene of that booby-trapped foxhole on the "military crest." Their one event of the day was finding an antitank mine, an NVA blasting cap and det-cord, all which they blew in place. Because of the proximity to the other two companies, those patented Blunt mechanical ambushes were not set out that night.

Alpha Company had the unlucky draw twelve clicks to the northeast on this day. From their night defensive perimeter, they started a mounted sweep east in platoon patrols. About 2000 meters east of the NDP, half the company had split off and the remaining half was still on the main track trail. In a grassy area, and with the first platoon leader's PC in the lead, they hit a large tank mine at 0840 hours—probably command detonated. Lieutenant Maiorca remembers the blast and being thrown from the track, but is hazy on the details after that. Sergeant Kenny Leach, one of the first platoon squad, leaders remembers the incident as well.

> I was on the lead track—I didn't know it was November 6th exactly but it was around that time—so that was it. We hit a mine and I was thrown off the track about 10 feet in the air and got a Purple Heart. I remember the track tipped over on its side and I was thrown 20 or 30 feet laterally. I landed pretty far away and was banged up. There were about ten of us on that track and we were going up a hill. I believe it was detonated by someone. I didn't know there were two more tracks hit because I got medevacked. They shipped me out in a chopper but I was just banged up and bruised. They treated me and sent me back into the field. I remember all of us got Purple Hearts and citations for that, and someone in the rear said they would keep them safe for us, but that's the last that we saw of them. Somebody stole them, I guess, so I don't have that citation anymore, and that's why I didn't remember the date exactly.

PFC Sterling Eugene "Bo" Kelly—once in third platoon/ first squad but now driving for the medics—remembers with remarkable detail.

> So we were working out there in AO Orange. I was driving for the medics and we had some medics onboard the track. Right behind me was the maintenance track. I was the next to the last track in the column. As I recall, we went around a bend. I think we had half the Company with us. And the lead track went around the bend and I lost sight of the lead track and then I heard this WHOOMP! A big WHOOMP and then word came back to stop column. Soon more word came back for the medics to move forward. So, I think three medics went forward or all of them might have gone forward except for the gunner. And we were kind of sitting there in the dark, so to speak. We didn't have access to a radio or anything. So, I get word from the track in front of me and it appears that the lead track hit a mine and some guys got hurt and a dust-off had been called. The dust-off came and picked up our casualties.

Immediately, the order was given to dismount on both sides and form a defensive line in the grass. We were down in place well before the utterance was complete. Everyone expected small arms and machine-gun fire but it did not materialize. An LZ was set up and eventually a bird came in and eight men were evacuated. Two others were shaken up a bit but the second dust-off was canceled. The rest—half the company—lay in the grass facing out, as the journals read, "waiting for further information." The first platoon's command track had its hull split in two. It was field-stripped of all weaponry and all supplies. The hulk was to be left behind—as it was smartly flipped on its side, well off the

***Opposite, top:* Another of the three tracks damaged in the November 6 mine incident. *Bottom:* PFC Sterling Eugene "Bo" Kelly, track driver for first squad, third platoon and later driver for the company medic's track. He was an acting medic on Gallagher Ridge (Hill 100).**

track trail. The crater was about four feet wide and four feet deep—caused by an antitank mine estimated to be about thirty to forty pounds.

By the time the medevac was finished and the field-stripping of the PC complete, about two hours had passed. At 1045 hours, the order was given to mount the tracks and reverse direction. The other two columns were still sweeping west, while we were ordered back to our NDP of the previous night. At 1055 hours, now facing east, the column was given the order to move out while keeping widely spaced and following in our same tracks. It can only be imagined how the drivers and other troopers strained to see any telltale sign ahead for metal or det-cord. Not a minute passed and a second track hit a mine. Again everyone was dismounted and was in the grass even before the order was given. Bo Kelly recalled the second incident with equal detail.

PFC Sterling Eugene Kelly:

> The word came back to offload everybody on the tracks and to send out flank security, which us guys were part of that and they said, "OK, turn the column around." So that's what we did. I was solo in the medic track and the maintenance track had the driver and was behind me. We turned around, we headed back down the road the way we came and he was now in front of me. And the maintenance track was going back over this little rise, this little hump, and I noticed he started losing purchase with his tracks and he starts sliding backwards. I was trying to give him plenty of room in front of me, to maintain a distance from him. But my forward motion was still carrying me forward and he was sliding backwards and then KABOOM! On his right, it looked to me like his right rear idler (maybe just a little forward) hit a good-size mine. It really lifted that thing out and I didn't get hit with any of the shrapnel. Our track got some on the trim plane and on the left side, below the cockpit, but the concussion was just horrendous. And the PC came back down and landed and I [hesitated] there for a moment taking inventory of myself and I couldn't hear anything. I checked out my vision and I could still see. OK—so figured I was ok. And the medics came back. They got the driver out of the maintenance track. I don't remember his name. He had a broken jaw. He was pretty roughed up and they medevacked him. So, the word came back to continue on and Captain Gallagher came up on foot next to me and I couldn't hear a word he was saying but he made motions like—let me see your shotgun. I had the twelve-gauge pump shotgun and he pantomimed that. And that was the only weapon I had, so I didn't want to give it up, but he was a captain and I was a PFC, so I gave him my shotgun and I gave him about a quarter of a sandbag of double-aught buckshot. So, I was essentially unarmed and I was now the point track. So, he said go around the maintenance track and go back and rejoin the Company. So, that's what I did. I made my way around the maintenance track, got back on the trail, and I just kind of started skedaddling and I didn't know if those mines were command-detonated. I almost had a feeling they were. I was kinda putting on a little speed and I'm looking in front of me trying to see if there was anything I could see that was potentially lethal and I saw a little aluminum disk and I thought "Oh, crap, here it comes!" That was on my side, coming under the left-side of the track, then it dawned on me, it was a pop-up cap. So, I made my way back to the rest of the Company and pulled into the center of the perimeter. Here comes the rest of the company following in my trail pretty much. And I was rattled pretty good, but I was really kind of pissed that I didn't have my weapon with me while I was out there by myself. I met up with Captain Gallagher, put my hand out and kind of mumbled, "I'd like my shotgun back sir." So, he gave me my shotgun back. After that, for a couple of days, I was in a daze and didn't really remember much. I guess I had gotten a concussion then but didn't know it. You know, we were always so tired and pooped out; it really didn't make much of a difference.

The second track was a total loss as well—two road wheels and a track blown off. It was also field-stripped of all weaponry and supplies. It was left and towed back to A-4 a few days later by a recovery vehicle from A/1-77. The second mine also seemed to be command-detonated, but again the expected ambush never came.

PFC Sterling Eugene Kelly:

> You know what it looked like to me? From a tactical situation, being a PFC and not knowing a whole lot about tactics, but if I was going to ambush somebody, I would look at it like a snake. I would hit them in the head. When they turned around, I'd hit them in the tail. And I'd hit them from both sides.

PFC Ed Martin was seated on the weapons track that was always positioned in the rear of the column. Lieutenant Chelsea Korte, the mortar platoon leader, was on the mortar track as well and in radio contact through his RTO, Sp4 Tony Robinson, with the other elements on the company net. Martin remembers the day:

PFC Edwin Martin:

> I got into Nam on October the 15th of 1969. I landed in Cam Rahn Bay and flew up to the DMZ. I was with [1-61] for only a few weeks when all this started. I remember [the mine incident] very well and I remember that field very well. I was in the mortar track that was actually an M-113. We didn't have a proper mortar track—the ones that have the mortar built in. They must have lost it before I came into the outfit. We were in just a regular APC and we had all the mortar ammunition there—the mortar squad on the mortar track always traveled last in the convoy. We were out in a field in the middle of nowhere and the whole company had just dropped down a three-foot slope as we entered this large open field. All the rest of the APCs were in front of us and they were stretched out in a straight line in this field. We had just passed through that little entrance point and dropped down that slope. We were about 20 feet into the field when we heard this explosion up front. The first APC hit a tank mine and everybody froze. Eventually, Captain Gallagher ordered the second APC to peel off—reverse course and drive back to that little slope where we had entered. Then that number two track hit another mine about halfway back to the entrance point from where the first explosion was. The rest of the column [eventually] followed and cast around the number two track back to the entrance point. At this point, the new lead track was right beside our mortar track when they started up that little incline and there was a mine on it. They hit [that third mine] right [behind] us. The whole company rode over that mine, but that track was the first that returned to that [slope] and must have run over it at just the right angle and tripped it. I remember walking up to that track afterwards and there was a hole under it that must have been three feet deep. I felt so comfortable standing there because it had already blown and there was no danger then. After they medevacked the wounded out, the rest of us left that field, went off, and set up a perimeter.

Sgt. Don Sarsfield also remembers the mine incident: "The track I was on that day was one of the ones that hit the mines. It happened so quickly and I was fortunately thrown clear so that I wasn't hurt. The first thing that popped into my mind was, 'Shit, all my stuff is in the track.'" An additional dust-off was called for when one of the shaken troopers began bleeding from his ears. The others that were shaken, as Kelly was, remained with the company. Ambushes and LPs were put out, but it would be a quiet night.

The casualties of the day were all WIAs, and the dust-offs were listed in the Morning Report: PFC Jeffrey Brooks, 1LT Michael Maiorca, PFC Tommie Evans, Sp4 Robert Gawron, Sp4 Wayne Hall, PFC Gregory Lang, Sgt. Anatoli Puschkin, Sgt. Kenneth Leach, PFC Lewis Femiano, PFC David Nicholson. The other four incurred minor wounds and were not medevacked.

At 0100 hours on November 7, the observation tower at Con Thien spotted fifteen to twenty individuals four hundred meters west of the western perimeter at YD10707102 and heading toward the perimeter at an azimuth of 0800. An illumination and artillery fire mission was immediately called. During the fire mission these personnel were seen retreating at an azimuth of 0850 mils. At the same time, on the opposite side of the perimeter three individuals were seen blinking flashlights. These individuals were about one hundred seventy-five meters outside the western perimeter at YD13307028. Illumination and artillery were fired as well. Taking part on the western sighting were tanks, dusters, crew-served weapons and various small-arms fire. It was an extended mad minute. At first light, two platoons of tanks were sent out to search the area of earlier contacts. At 0830 hours the two platoons of tanks reached the grids of the previous evening's sightings with negative findings. Moving further northeast, one of the tank platoons found and destroyed a six-foot-by-four-foot-by-four-foot deep bunker made of dirt and logs. Later in the day the tankers found a total of fourteen bunkers, several ten to fifteen feet long and all of them roofed with logs and dirt. The last of them were destroyed at 1655 hours. Various other pieces of contraband were found, including an unexploded 1000-pound bomb that was also blown in place.

At 0900 hours, the scout platoon, moving from LZ Nancy to C-2, was ordered to check out individuals seven hundred meters east of C-2. Searching until 1300 hours, they found only recently used foot trails and returned to C-2 for base security.

At 1600 hours Lieutenant General Melvin Zais, commanding general of XXIV Corp, along with Major General Troung, the ARVN sector commander, were briefed by Lieutenant Colonel John Swaren, Task Force 1-61 commander, and Colonel John L. Osteen, 1st Brigade, Fifth Infantry Division Commander. It was now obvious—along with the ramp-up of sightings and engagements of the past week, and all this brass so close to the DMZ—that something pretty big was coming. Following this meeting, Ranger Teams 11, 15 and 17 were extracted. Team 12 and long-range recon were ordered to watch crossing points on the Ben Hai River and were en route to their grids. A message was sent out to all units to be on high alert the next four nights from November 7–11, taking special care to ensure that all defensive perimeters were extremely well prepared and mutually supported with preplanning artillery, mortar and TAC Air support. Additionally Alpha Company, whose NDPs were closest to the ranger teams north of Con Thien, was warned to be especially vigilant that evening and ready to assist in reinforcement, relief or extraction of either team by mounted ground or air-mobile assault. All units were also vigorously warned to be very vigilant when handling enemy bodies, due to the NVA practice of purposely leaving booby-trapped bodies specifically to be easily seen and handled by U.S. or friendly forces.

Alpha Company, shorthanded from the previous day's medevacs, recalled their ambushes and LPs and moved west-southwest in the direction of Con Thien as a northern blocking force for the fire base, while a tank platoon from Con Thien patrolled towards them. At 0830 Alpha had three platoons and a star team fanned out along the 71-northing line at easting grids 12, 13, 14, and 15 with negative sightings. At 1000 hours, the second platoon found five bunkers two thousand meters northeast of Con Thien and destroyed them with C4. Alpha Company set their NDP one click east of Con Thien and put out two platoon ambushes, two squad ambushes, and the Star Team for night acts.

Bravo Company, having been east of Hill 162, moved north to a point one thousand meters east of Gallagher Ridge. Moving to the north, the second platoon discovered a TM-41 mine on the tank trail that was exposed by the rain but had been run over many times. It was blown in place with det-cord. At 1830 hours, a squad patrol found an eight-pound tank mine lying on its side on a tank trail, and it too was blown in place. A half hour later, they found an RPG-2 round with a booster in very good condition and evacuated it back to C-2. Bravo Company set their NDP one click west of Gallagher Ridge and set up normal night acts.

Charlie Company moved around Hill 124 and circled Hill 162 as well, reaching a point on the northern slope of that peak. In the course of the day, C Company found signs of an enemy platoon in the area and various weapons and contraband—including twenty-six 82mm mortars and fuses, a large tin of NVA stew still warm, a wicker basket, and two stakes with paper wrapped around them pointing in the easterly direction. They then swept the area in a thousand-yard diameter around the spot. C Company set up their NDP two clicks east of Gallagher Ridge and established their normal night acts.

Delta Company (1–11), starting out south of 162, then moved northwest to a point four hundred meters north of Gallagher Ridge. They patrolled and swept this area all day and returned to their NDP of the past three days, where ambushes and LPs were put out.

Weather report for November 8: visibility unrestricted and wind out of the northeast at ten to twelve knots. The twenty-four hour outlook was for partly cloudy skies—high of 82 degrees and low of seventy-eight with 80 percent humidity—EMNT is 0627 and EENT is 1839—sunrise is 0649 and sunset is 1817—moonrise is 0501 and moonset is 1656 with lunar illumination of 5 percent. The darkest night of the month would be November 10–11.

Ranger Team 12 remained on the southern shore of the Ben Hai River northwest of Con Thien. At 0930 hours, the Tactical Operations Center announced that Killer Team 16 would be inserted into the DMZ in the afternoon and would move to the lower left corner of grid 1176 near the south shore of the Ben Hai River. These two reconnaissance teams were positioned about seven thousand meters apart. The plan also directed that they would stay in place for the next four days until November 12. At 1050 hours the TOC reported that C-2 had taken two to three rockets. Reverse radar measures were employed and it was determined that the rockets were fired from the western hills some ten clicks due west of the firebase. At the same time, Bravo and Charlie Companies reported seeing the rockets emanating several clicks southwest of Hill 162. There were no casualties. An hour later Charlie and Bravo reported seven to eight more rockets being fired from the same location. An artillery mission was ordered and adjusted by Bravo Company's forward observer, 1Lt Mike Cowart. As the fire mission continued, Bravo Company reported four secondary explosions. The result was that no more rockets were fired from that grid location.

Alpha Company began November 8 1300 meters northwest of Con Thien. All ambushes, listening posts and star teams returned to the night defensive perimeter just after dawn. After breakfast the company split into two groups. By 0940 hours, the CP and the fourth platoon moved fifteen hundred meters south to a point thirteen hundred meters east of Con Thien, while the first, second and third platoons moved northwest away from Con Thien to a point within two clicks of the DMZ. The command posts and mortar platoon continued their sweeps and found an exposed mine weighing twenty-five pounds and measuring seven inches in diameter, which they blew in place. It had been run over multiple times in the last few days. At dusk, Alpha moved into Con Thien for stand-down until late the following morning for maintenance. The rest was welcome, and so was a night's sleep in the relative security of a bunker, albeit rat-infested, filthy and laced with diesel fuel to hold down the vermin. Whoever came up with the idea that diesel would keep the rats down was mistaken. There was a standing contest for killing the biggest rat or centipede and the squads were very competitive in this sport. As it got dark and quiet and the troopers fell asleep, there was always someone awake to set out bait and wait for a rat or centipede to show its shadowy form. Critter-killing ammo was 45-caliber rounds altered by taking out the lead projectile and some powder and replacing them with a wad of candle wax—enough to safely kill a rat at close range. A shot fired with these light rounds would sound like a low thud outside, but the report was loud inside the bunker. The trophy would be hung on the game pole at the entrance of the bunker in the morning.

Bravo Company began the day on an elevated knoll halfway down the north-facing slope of Hill 162. At daybreak all night acts returned to the NDP. During the morning, as Charlie Company rotated clockwise to the north, then east, to Bravo's previous night position, Bravo made the same clockwise maneuver south, then west, to Charlie's previous night's position—reaching their destination by midday. In the afternoon, Bravo arrived at a hill one hundred meters in height. It was two clicks north northwest of Hill 162. This hill bore the same height as two other knobs, all oriented in a triangular shape, with about four hundred meters between each pair of hilltops. The land form was known as the Three 100s. On this evening, Bravo set up their night defensive perimeter on the southernmost hilltop that had a promontory that looked out at the northern slope of Hill 162. An hour before dusk, Bravo reported to TOC that while the company was firing DEFCONs, there was a secondary explosion. At dusk, three listening posts were set out north, from east to west—one hundred meters from the NDP. The fourth LP was set to the south—two hundred meters out and facing Hill 162.

Charlie Company initiated their day acts on a small bench one third of the way down the southwestern slope of Hill 162. Ambushes and LPs returned for breakfast chow after dawn in preparation for their daily sweeps. With the first platoon moving northeast toward Bravo Company's position of the previous night, they found various pieces of NVA equipment, including one Chicom grenade, an NVA pouch and a roll of communication wire. They continued to sweep the area. Meanwhile the second platoon, moving northwest fifteen hundred meters to a point twelve hundred meters west of the first platoon, found ten 4 × 4 × 4 bunkers with logs and dirt for overhead cover that had been hit a few days earlier by artillery. In the bunker were several unserviceable weapons and pieces of equipment. The troopers moved back carefully and then tossed a grenade in the bunker. From the several secondary explosions it was obvious that the bunkers were booby-trapped.

Sweeping further north, Charlie Company spotted eight to ten individuals out in the open in a southwesterly direction. Immediately, the weapons platoon plotted a fire mission from their track and lobbed a dozen 81mm at the fleeing PAVNs. Simultaneously the forward observer, attached to the company from the 5th/4th Artillery, called another fire mission, and the 175mm guns from Camp J.J. Carroll responded as well. After the mission, a platoon was sent down to sweep the area, finding no enemy casualties. They did find several pieces of unserviceable equipment along with a 51-caliber machine-gun tripod in very good condition. At 1450 hours, a Charlie Company sweep found two 82mm firing bunkers—two hundred meters apart—on an elevated bench one thousand meters north-northwest of Hill 162. They were reported to have appeared to be used for the last two or three weeks. Sweeping east for the rest of the afternoon, Charlie Company arrived at the westernmost hilltop of the Three 100s—500 meters northwest of Bravo Company's NDP. Setting up on that hill, they were following the directive given by the TOC earlier in the day for all units in the field to be mutually supportive. Six listening posts were set out—all one hundred meters or less from the NDP.

Delta 1–11 spent their evening four hundred meters north of Gallagher Ridge. They moved off to a secure location for chow before starting their daily sweeps to the south. During the morning, Delta worked south in platoon groups across Gallagher Ridge and continued to a point seven hundred meters to the south. When the directive from TOC earlier in the day was broadcast for all units in the field to be mutually supportive, Delta Company began a twenty-five-hundred meter trek to the northwest, coming to the easterly bench of the Three 100s. This completed the last act of all units in the field that day. LPs were put out at one hundred meters, and three-quarters of Task Force waited for what would turn out to be a quiet night.

At 0015 hours on November 9, Con Thien was probed. Perimeter guards on the eastern perimeter spotted individuals with flashlights at two hundred meters and engaged them with tank fire. The lights went out. At 0130, radar spotted five individuals to the east again at three hundred fifty meters and they were engaged with tank fire and artillery. At 0230, radar again spotted five individuals on the southeastern perimeter at about one thousand meters and engaged them with automatic weapons and tank fire. At 0300, radar again spotted five individuals on the southwestern perimeter at a distance of one thousand meters and engaged them with artillery and 40mm Dusters. At 0315 hours, radar spotted five individuals in the same area as fifteen minutes earlier, and artillery and duster fire resumed. From 0330 to 0415, five lights were sighted on the northwest perimeter intermittently for forty-five minutes and were fired upon at will with small arms and artillery.

All the probes came to naught, but hindsight would be telling. It would soon become obvious that these were feints to hold Alpha Company at Con Thien for base security and so prevent them from being inserted to reinforce any one of the three companies near Hill 162 in the western hills. Nobody knew it at the time, but the NVA were on the offensive, and the executive branch of the North Vietnamese government was hoping to be dealt that ace in the hole of wiping out an American fighting unit. In the next 24 hours they would break the cease-fire while still in secret meetings with American officials in Paris in an attempt to bring the war to an end.

The forecast for the day again was mid-eighties temperatures and high humidity with ten- to twelve-knot winds. The next two nights would be the darkest of this lunar cycle, with no moon and cloudy skies. Lunar illumination would be less than 1 percent. This would seem to be a perfect time for the NVA to attack if they so wished.

A/1–77 tankers sent three platoons out to sweep the previous evening's sighting and engagement locations. The third platoon found footprints along the southern perimeter in two locations. The three tanker platoons continued to sweep around Con Thien through late morning and found several twenty-foot-long tunnels with large vented underground rooms that they destroyed. At 1955 hours, battalion requested a bird for the next day from 0930 to 1000 to distribute Frag Order 2 of Op Order 11 to be distributed to all units in the field.

P Company of the 75th Rangers requested a four-square-kilometer grid location northwest of Con Thien along the DMZ, just south of the Ben Hai River, and it was granted. They would remain in that grid until November 13. At 1715 hours, the ranger team reported four NVA following them near the DMZ and several elements of A/1–77 Tankers were committed as a ready reaction force to chase them down. The small PAVN Recon team dispersed and the ranger team continued on its recon mission.

Alpha Company, still on stand-down, remained in Con Thien repairing equipment as well as refitting and loading three new APCs to replace the losses of the previous week. The company would remain in Con Thien and the bunker-wide rat hunt would be extended one more day.

Bravo Company began its day by moving off the Three 100s and moving south toward Hill 162. At midday they moved to just south of Gallagher Ridge. In the afternoon, they moved back north to Gallagher Ridge.

Charlie Company also started its day moving south from the Three 100s toward the eastern slope of Hill 162 and stopped for a breather between 162 and Gallagher Ridge. At midday they moved to just southwest of Hill 162. In the afternoon, they moved several hundred meters north and set up their night defensive perimeter.

Delta Company brought in its LPs at dawn and remained on the easternmost hilltop of the Three 100s. At midday they moved to just east of Gallagher Ridge. They remained there and dug in in the evening, and again the three companies were aligned in a triangle in mutual support of each other. Listening posts and fire teams were strategically set out to further support their sister companies. They were now in the epicenter of a ten-square-kilometer grid that they had swept and reswept over the past nine days. They had destroyed dozens of bunkers and tunnels, confiscated many pieces of equipment and the information that they passed on to intelligence, had hatched a major Frag Order and a change of OPORDER-11 coming the next day. The commanders now sensed that a major engagement was at hand and that they had done all that they humanly could to prepare Task Force 1-61 for what was to come.

On November 10, the weather report again was good, with clear skies, temperatures in the 80s, and ten-knot winds. Conversely, the night illumination forecast for the following night was 0 percent with the moon beginning its new phase—the portion of the lunar cycle perfect for enemy movement.

At 0055 hours, Con Thien radar picked up a motorized object or vehicle at nine hundred meters on the northern perimeter. The 8-inch guns fired 13 rounds as it kept moving toward the firebase. Illumination was fired by 4.2 mortars but visual detection was lost. A few minutes later the vehicle was detected again by radar and moving north at a high rate of speed. At 0900, Alpha Company tankers sent three platoon patrols to investigate. At 1230 hours, one of the patrols found, in the area of the previous night's radar sightings, four square holes that were one foot deep. They also found a Vietnamese newspaper. Intelligence was flown to the area. Another tank platoon discovered various pieces of enemy equipment including 51-caliber belted rounds and two RPG-2s. They were all blown in place. These would prove to be more diversionary tactics. Alpha Company spent still another night at Con Thien and was now assigned to close security of the firebase. The next few days would consist of night listening posts and ambushes along with daytime search & clears and sweeps close in to the firebase.

Bravo Company called in at 0800 and reported being in position on the western edge of Gallagher Ridge. They would patrol the area northeast to northwest for the day and set up on Gallagher Ridge for the night. Bravo Company's third platoon discovered a one-hundred-fifty-pound bomb that they blew in place. They also found several spider holes and a tunnel that was too deep to see if it opened into a room. All of the bunkers were destroyed. At 1505 hours an aerial observer in an O-1 aircraft from the 220th RAC spotted concentrated enemy activity on all of the trails west and northwest of Hill 162.

Charlie Company reported at 0230 hours taking one 60mm mortar with no casualties taken. The round hit harmlessly outside the perimeter to the west. Charlie Company moved back to Hill 124 southwest of Delta/1-11 and Bravo/1-61. They patrolled in platoons all day to the northwest. In the late afternoon, Charlie Company moved northwest to the top of Hill 162 and put out three listening posts one hundred meters from their NDP.

Delta Company reported at 0800 that they were positioned across a ravine from Hill 162. The three companies now were in platoon-sized units, spaced out in a straight line running northeasterly over a twenty-five-hundred-meter defensive line. Having been out in the field for nearly forty days, Delta Company was due to be airlifted back to Firebase C-2 the next morning for a well-deserved rest and stand-down.

# 8

# Overview of the November Battle

On November 10, 1969, three days of firefights involving Task Force 1-61 in an operation known as Fulton Square, that took place in the Northern I Corps, Republic of Vietnam, erupted 2 miles south of the DMZ in "AO Orange"—a.k.a. Leatherneck Square. The following account is accurate to the best recollections of nearly fifty of the participants who have contributed to this chronicle.

This narrative is not only a description of a battle fought by Americans against a determined adversary; it is also more importantly a story of brotherhood, teamwork and supreme sacrifice. Task Force 1-61 was matched up on the ground in the vicinity of Hill 162 with three reinforced battalions of the 27th NVA Regiment—outnumbering friendly forces most of the time by more than ten to one—and on November 13 by as many as 15 to 1. TF 1-61's great advantage was that they had superior firepower, unparalleled air and artillery support, precise intelligence, a seasoned core of officers, and NCOs to help lead the mostly green replacements. On the other hand, the indoctrinated PAVN forces were dogged and determined, and their leaders were amorally willing to sacrifice them to the last man to achieve victory by callous and cold-hearted attrition.

The names of the combatants, their recollections and some mention of the nearly 180 citations awarded, provide a broad-based summary of this combat action. What is true here, as is always true in war and battle, is that the memories of fifty men out of the nearly eight hundred combat infantry and support personnel who participated, tell only part of the story. Every man has his own story of what he experienced in his small corner of the field of battle. The fifteen brave men who were killed have taken theirs with them to the grave. Remembrance of and honor to them is the main driving force that has moved these many men to churn up and offer painful memories that have remained unspoken for decades.

Also involved were multiple rotary-wing flight crews with unit call-signs like Lancer, Batman, Dustoff, and Ghost Rider. The Ghost Riders also had personnel call signs like Spiderman and Chuckles. There were artillery batteries like the 5th/4th Arty from A-4 and the 4th/8th Arty from Camp J.J. Carroll that offered support. Above the battlefield was the constant and uninterrupted support of the 220th Reconnaissance Airplane Company (Catkiller) in their O-1 Cessna L-19s and the 20th Tactical Air Support Squadron (Barky and Basketball) in their OV-10 Broncos. On the ground with us were the 7th Engineers, 43rd Scout Dog Platoon, communication units and other support groups that took part in the action. Again, for this action, United States Army issued to combat infantrymen in the field approximately 180 citations for valor and heroism over those three days, but hundreds of other acts of bravery occurred that were regarded as just the normal actions of a well-trained combat infantry force simply doing its job.

Lt. Col. John Swaren, Bn CO:

> I changed my mind now but back in those days my theory was that with the infantry guys, it was their job to fight and to kill. So, if you did that, you were just doing your job. What the hell? You're going to get a medal for doing your job? And some people did more than their job.... Starr, Blunt. I believe they ought to get some kind of award, but GI Joe over there who shot sixteen magazines out of his foxhole because he was being attacked, that is what he is paid to do. Jesus, don't tell me he needs an award for doing that.

**Lt. Col. John Swaren, battalion commander, First Battalion of the 61st Infantry. West Point Graduate class of 1954. Two tours in Vietnam (courtesy John Swaren).**

At least 58 casualties rose to the level of being serious enough to warrant medevac, but nearly every man on the ground shed some amount of blood. Hundreds of Purple Hearts were awarded. Again, fifteen men made the ultimate sacrifice, while the rest of us have asked for more than 45 years, "Why them and not us?" This question has no answer, but we will continue to ask it, and this is why we will never forget them, nor will we let others forget.

Although all the units of the Fifth Division had been in and out of that area before November 1, they had now officially taken over operational control of the Northern I Corps from the Third Marine Division that had moved south to Thua Thien and Da Nang. Quang Tri Province was divided into Areas of Operation named after colors of the spectrum. There were AO Blue, Red, Gold, White and more, but AO Orange would prove to be the hot spot since it was in the foothills west of Con Thien and Charlie 2, adjacent to the DMZ. It came to be known to the troopers as the "Wild Wild West." The brigade plan was to rotate in and out—line companies of four battalions—two mechanized, one armored and one straight-legged light infantry. They were 1st Battalion, 61st Infantry Regiment; 4th Battalion, 12th Armored Cavalry; 1st Battalion, 77th Armored Tank Corp; and 1st Battalion, 11th Infantry. The 11th Infantry has had a long and noble history dating back to the American Civil War, and it was this unit that first adopted the motto "Semper Fidelis." The U.S. Marines also have a right through payment in blood to also take it as their own.

These four battalions were all part of the 5th Infantry Division (Mech), which also has an illustrious history, dating back to World War I under General Pershing, World War II under General George S. Patton, and in Panama in the 1980s.

The brigade strategy again was to rotate companies from these units in and out of AO Orange for 20-day stints. The idea was to give each of the unit commanders time to learn the lay of the land there. However, none knew it as well as Captain Blunt, and the learning curve was steep. That was how General Zais from XXIV Corps and General Burke from I Corps wanted to do business. On November 6, when the 5th Division took over from the 3rd Marines, the battalion "six" were summoned to brigade for a high brass powwow:

Lt. Col. Jack Swaren:

> We got a new Brigade Commander—he was a one-star general, named Burke. An armor guy but underneath all this armor shit he wasn't too bad. In fact, he was very good. I got in a corner with him and told him that this is ridiculous. "You've got people rotating in and out just when they start to get the hang of it and people were getting killed unnecessarily because they would lose their touch." He said, "That's true, and you're going to stay up there forever now, so have a nice day." And I smiled because it never hurt my feelings a bit.

As preparation for this takeover, the 1st Battalion of the 61st Infantry Regiment, based out of LZ Sharon, rotated their three rifle companies in an out of AOs in and around LZs Sharon, Angel and Pedro. They were practicing the cloverleaf search and clears that they would essentially use up in AO Orange, while Captain Blunt and D/1-11 and the rest of the 11th Infantry Battalion bushwhacked enemy forces in and around the DMZ whenever the opportunity arose. The journals show that August through late October were very quiet months although there was constant evidence of an enemy presence. Realizing through their intelligence that the Fifth I.D. would be taking over completely, the NVA occupied themselves with observation only of the regiment's mechanized tactics during the 60 days preceding the takeover and refrained, for the most part, from major offensive contacts. They then used this intelligence to stymie unit patrols on the 11th and 12th, at least for a time, before TF 1-61 could regroup and eventually crush the North Vietnamese force on the 13th.

During the last week of October and early November all of Vietnam was under a country-wide cease-fire as the Paris Peace Talks resumed. At one point during this period, Captain Starr and Charlie Company on patrol northeast of Con Thien sighted large columns of NVA marching south and waving at the hamstrung commanding officer, who was under orders not to fire unless fired upon. In Starr's own words:

> One night (I think in late October) we NDP'ed inside the DMZ on a bald hilltop.... [N]ext day we observed many NVA walking past at the bottom of the hill (west side) smiling and waving at us.... [R]equests to fire were denied due to Paris Cease Fire. Approximately two weeks later they broke the cease-fire, pinned down 1C/1/61. The rest is history.

The ramp-up of physical signs of enemy presence grew exponentially during the first 10 days of November, but contact was limited to antitank mine incidents, harassment and incoming. All mechanized units had events, but Alpha had the largest occurrence on November 6 when an M113 hit a mine moving northeast, away from Con Thien, and a second and third APC hit mines after the column reversed direction. There were 14 medevacs and several other dinged-up troopers. It could have been much worse. Several days earlier, an exposed 40-pound tank mine was spotted after a torrential rain. Luckily it was a dud, because it had been run over by literally every APC in the company. It was blown in place.

According to a *Time* magazine article, the capture of some NVA documents showed that the NVA believed a surprise attack on a significant U.S. unit could produce a timely victory and provide the bargaining chip for the peace accords. They could bring that

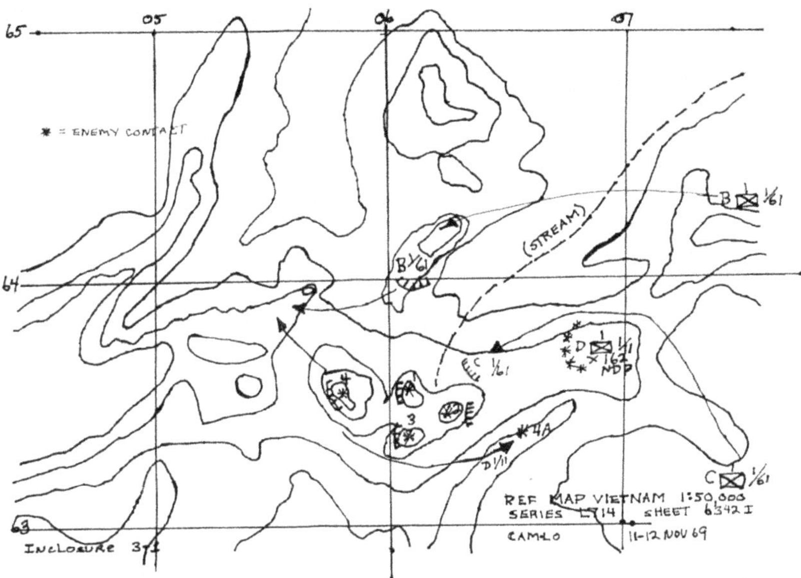


**Map #1 showing the location, movement and enemy contact of B/1-61, C/1-61, and D/1-11 in the early morning hours of November 11, 1969, and from which various patrols emanated during the daylight hours.**

chip to the table in Paris, and at the same time, sway U.S. public opinion and bring the Nixon administration to their will—an administration that was already looking for a way out. North Vietnam hoped these victories would coincide with the nationwide peace marches in the United States, organized by the antiwar movement, which were planned for the weekend of November 14–16.

*Time* magazine, Nov. 21, 1969, p. 42:

> On the military front, Saigon faced a more immediate challenge. The recent battlefield lull was shattered by Communist attacks all over the country. The renewed fighting apparently marked the start of the Communists' so-called "winter-spring campaign." They intended to stage sporadic coordinated attacks throughout the country [until] American public opinion forced a U.S. withdrawal. Though the campaign's start was scheduled long before last week's anti-war Moratorium demonstrations in the U.S., there was nevertheless an effort to get the fighting in step with the peace marchers. An enemy document captured southeast of Saigon recently urged intense action before November 14th and 15th "in support of the upcoming struggle of the American people for peace." The most vicious fighting of the week—and perhaps of the year—occurred just south of the Demilitarized Zone around Con Thien where troopers of the 5th Mechanized Infantry held off a North Vietnamese Regiment in three days of firefights. Although American forces were outnumbered ... superior firepower forced the enemy to retreat....

Hanoi broke the cease-fire on the 10th and the following chain of events ensued on Hill 162 that would culminate on Hill 100—a.k.a. Gallagher Ridge. The NVA did manage to surprise the Red Devils at first, but underestimating them, they proved inferior as the mechanized troopers, who were mostly on foot for this fight, ramped up to speed and spoiled Hanoi's plans. The three days of engagements would prove to be the fiercest fighting of the year in Vietnam.

# 9

# Veterans' Day, 11 Nov 1969 (DAY 1)

"Daily Journals: 0200—D/1-11 detected movement around their perimeter and fired organic weapons."

As evidenced from the excerpt from the daily journals above, on November 11, 1969—on the side-slopes and ravines of Hill 162—at 0200 hours, the first contact was made near the foxhole of Sp4 Raymond Arra and Sgt. Joseph "Sonny" Prince—2nd squad, 2nd Platoon, D/1-11. While on guard, Arra spotted movement through his starlight scope and informed Sgt. Harold "Iron-man" Phillips, his squad leader, who in turn had news of the sighting passed on to Captain Blunt. Blunt moved up and put the whole company on 100 percent alert. He instructed every man to be prepared and vigilant. Eventually an NVA prober set off a trip flare. Delta Company responded with return fire by throwing hand grenades and firing M-79s. Sgt. Prince recorded the first enemy casualty with his M-79. The NVA soldier was found several hours later in the morning, still alive but mortally wounded. Sonny Prince recalls it this way:

> We were on Hill 162 numerous times before November. This time was no different from any other until Sgt. (Phil) Phillips woke Ray Arra up for guard. Phil was crouched down in the foxhole getting ready to light a smoke when Arra told him that he sees gooks. Phil said, "Don't f**k with me Arra," and Ray said he did see gooks. Phil looked through the starlight scope that Ray was using and saw an NVA soldier pointing out our positions to others. He notified Capt. Blunt, who checked it out and told him to wake up all his men along his position. We all got into our foxholes and just as I got in a gook tripped a flare right in front of my position. I always kept a shotgun round in my 79 at night because I figured if I might have to use it much too quickly for an HE. It would also be too close for an HE (high-explosive) and a shotgun round would be the round of choice. I shut the 79 and fired at the gook in front of me and it didn't go off, so I re-cocked it and fired again: nothing. I checked and the 79 was empty. Someone—maybe me jumping into the hole—had knocked the round out into the bottom of the hole. Anyway, all hell broke loose in front of us as they were attempting to get close when the trip flare went off. We started getting arty flares after a bit and I had a gook running across in front of me about 50 meters away. When a flare went off he would get down and I would lob a round where he was, this went on for five or six times before he quit popping up. Then things got quiet for the rest of the night.

From his perspective, Sgt. "Phil" Phillips also described that first action in this manner:

> I probably can't give you any more than Joe could, his recollection is much better than mine. I do remember that as a result of Blunt calling for double guards in each foxhole that we were ready for them. My squad had 3 positions and Ray Arra and I [were] in the middle foxhole. Ray said,

**Joe Prince, Phil Phillips, Switzer and Strack with captured AK-47s found after an NVA patrol tripped their mechanical ambush.**

> "We have Gooks in front." With the starlight scope I could see them trying to skyline our positions. I told him to keep watch while I crawled up the hill and got Blunt to slide back down to our foxhole. After that things started popping fast and the old memory gets blurry about all the activity of each individual. When they popped a trip flare we let the claymores and grenades fly. I remember little people running for cover and scattering as it was obvious they weren't gonna get up Hill 162 on that night. We were raking them pretty good with small arms fire and Blunt called in the 155s and walked them up the ravine they had used to get close to us.

As Phillips explained, Blunt called for a mad minute and for pre-registered artillery fire along the various foot trails that meandered along the ravines around Hill 162. Unlike the American forces, who preferred the high ridgelines to move along, the NVA preferred the jungle valleys and elephant grass thickets to move through the trails undetected. Blunt disagreed with the American strategy and chose to keep his men hidden as they traveled, similar to the NVA strategy. But in this case he was tied to a noisy mechanized company on a spread-out battalion perimeter. Because of all the friendly activity, it was too risky to set up mechanicals, and he now was completely exposed to the enemy. Sp4 Ron Gibson was in an adjacent position:

> It was November 10, 1969, and I was in Second Platoon, Second Squad. We moved towards 162 and we'd been there before. I never could understand why we kept going back. Why we always got blown up from the same foxholes. I put out my Claymores and dug my hole a little deeper and then put up my grenades in the foxhole ready to go. Sgt. Phillips was our platoon sergeant at the time. He gave us our night watch I don't know when. I went to sleep and someone else took guard. Directly north of 162 a trip wire went off and I think three gooks ran across our position.

Captain Blunt, Sonny Prince and Phil Phillips saw half a dozen gooks below. Arra spotted them through the starlight scope. They threw grenades down at them all at the same time. The three ran across. We stayed at one hundred percent all night long.

One thousand meters to the southwest of Delta Company's night defensive perimeter, Charlie Company of 1-61 under Captain William Starr was set up in their NDP with fifteen M-113A1 armored personnel carriers and two M-125A1 mortar tracks. It was a relatively quiet night with some possible probing that was never positively confirmed. The response to the possible threat was to lob several rounds of HEs from the M-79 grenadiers. Starting out on fifty percent guard, Starr altered to full alert because the situation was being monitored on the battalion net over at Delta Company's NDP.

Meanwhile, that night, B/1-61 set up 1700 meters northeast with the same mechanized firepower as Charlie Company. They too heard the buzz about the movement outside the wire of the other two companies and remained on alert through the night. On the net too was Lt. Colonel Swaren, the battalion commander, and his S2/S3, 1Lt Fredrick Jelinek in the Tactical Operations Center at C-2 Fire Base. All units listened intently as Captain Stanley Blunt prepared to search the area from which contact had come the previous night.

Soon after first light, Blunt organized a company patrol with 3rd platoon in the lead followed by 1st platoon to sweep and clear and to assess enemy strength. They followed a well-used track trail down into the valley.

With the third platoon in the lead, made up of second and third squad men, the patrol ran into an ambush. Sgt. Ruben Carbajal and Sp4 Michael McQueer became the first U.S. soldiers killed in the battle, with 3 others wounded. Walking point in the sweep and clear, PFC Ken Kowalski was followed by McQueer, Carbajal, Lt. Bruce Horn, RTO Gary Ragle and Platoon Sergeant Clerf Adkins.

Immediately, Swaren and Jelinek leapt into motion. Several critical orders were given. Bravo Company was ordered to move west dismounted as a blocking force north of Delta/ 1–11s contact. Bravo Company was led by Captain William Spencer. He had been in with the company for nearly six months and was due to rotate in several weeks. Swaren also ordered Captain Starr and Charlie Company to sweep north and then west around D/1-11's night position and act as a blocking force to the west of the Blunt Company patrol. Finally, Swaren called for his Loach pilot and left Lt. Jelinek in charge of the Tactical Operations Center at C-2. Jelinek would play a key logistical role all day and into the night. Swaren then strapped on his combat gear and headed for the helipad. He was heading out to his battalion to lead from the front of his force.

Before those battalion wheels were put into motion, Ken Kowalski was the point man on Lt. Horne's third platoon patrol. Following are the words of the men in this patrol.

PFC Ken Kowalski, 3rd platoon:

I wasn't the normal point man but the guy who normally was on point was on R&R. So I kind of took his place. And it probably saved my life. We were doing a Search and Destroy in platoon patrols and we were walking along the base of a particular hill—maybe 162. And at the base of the hill, was a group of stones and they were pointed in the shape of an arrow pointing up the hill. So, I stopped the platoon. I called Lt. Horne. He was about the fourth man back in the patrol and he took a long look at it, and he was fairly new, but we knew something was going on. So, we worked our way up this hill and we spread out—walking. We took our time. We probably got two-thirds to three-quarters of the way up the hill and we walked into an ambush. The NVA were perched right near the top of the hill near a bomb crater and they were just waiting for us to come up. I heard the rounds go right past my head and they hit McQueer, who was right behind me,

> and Carjabal was somewhere behind too. McQueer died instantly. We stopped all forward movement and me and Lt. Horn and McQueer and Carbajal were pretty much pinned down. We were the closest to the top of the hill. You know, they were shooting down, throwing grenades back and forth and I don't know—I don't remember how much time it took, but after quite a while, the shooting and throwing of grenades eventually stopped. I remember that I had my rifle down by my knees, I pulled the pin on a grenade and I have this live grenade in my hand and one of the NVA grenades came down the hill and landed right up against my rifle which was at my knees.

Unconsciously, Kowalski rid himself of his grenade and jumped backwards down the hill. The Chicom grenade, stopped by his rifle, exploded and miraculously he was unharmed, cheating death for the second time in less than a minute. His M-16, however, was a complete loss.

2LT Bruce Horn, 3rd Platoon Leader:

> What I recall was there was a probe that night before, and we were going in that direction and I think it would have been to the northwest. There was ridgeline. My platoon was in the lead. I don't know whether the other two platoons were behind us but Blunt was. We'd been up that ridgeline before and we saw those old bunkers back then, but they had been pretty much destroyed from previous operations. We got to a point where there was this bomb crater and then it got a little steeper. We usually walked single file, but for whatever reason, I decided that we would have three of us abreast go up that little steeper part. We really weren't that far from the previous night's defensive position where we were hit. We ran into one of those old bunkers that had been refortified and rebuilt. I don't know how many North Vietnamese were in that bunker—probably 3 or 4. They opened fire on us. Everybody hit the deck as we began to take Chicoms and small arms fire and we fired back and threw grenades. We found out later we were throwing our grenades too far, and they too were throwing Chicoms over our heads. I think the guy that was hit first was Mike McQueer on the right. He was a young fellow that was in the platoon a few days. Kowalski was probably in the middle, and then I would have been on the left-hand side. Rubin was further back in the formation. He might have been the fourth or fifth guy. There was a lot of automatic fire and Chicoms being thrown and we were firing back. I laid there on the ground and kept throwing grenades and shooting my rifle. I do remember Rubin. He yelled, "LT, LT!" When he ran towards me, he was shot and he fell down. He had a wound in his chest. He was bubbling blood and he died very quickly.
>
> A little later Blunt came running up there and says to me, "Let's get out of here!" We just rolled down the hill towards the NDP and out of the line of sight. Blunt must have known where that bunker was. We came upon the end of this bomb crater where the rest of the platoon was and Blunt's CP. We proceeded to put down a lot of fire on that position. The platoon sergeant was Sgt. Atkins. He was a Korean War vet. He stood up to look out and he got hit in the arm. The platoon returned fire, shot up the bunker. Later, we called in artillery and fighter jets. They came in and took out the position.
>
> We pulled back temporarily and Blunt made the decision that it wasn't appropriate for the third platoon to go up there and retrieve their dead or wounded. I knew Rubin was dead, I didn't know McQueer was dead at that time, but I think Blunt had the first or second platoon go forward and consider an assault up against that position and they retrieved Rubin and McQueer. Then we just moved back down Hill 162 and medevacked out the platoon sergeant and Rubin and McQueer. They sent us back to the rear to C-2 later that day. Adkins went home.
>
> Then Blunt took Lt. Jordan, which was the second platoon, and they went back up. Blunt said to me, "You aren't going to have radio contact." I had two choices—stay on 162 or walk down to where the mechanized infantry people were. We stayed on 162.

As the ambush was popped on Lt. Horn and his patrol came under intense fire, the third squad was just below them, and machine-gunner PFC Vern Sondgeroth and point man PFC Jerry Shepard peeled off and crawled to that bomb crater where they had excellent enfilade fire on what turned out to be two NVA bunker positions. As they fired their

M-60, Captain Stanley Blunt directed the rest of their squad members to heave their belts of M-60 up to them—keeping them resupplied. As explained by Lieutenant Horn, the third platoon with the aid of gunships eventually managed to neutralize the reinforced positions and force a retreat of the rest of the enemy ambush force. Among the wounded was SFC Adkins. During the ambush, and seeing wounded at the front of the column, aid-man SSGT Richard Myers ran to the fallen men and was himself wounded.

PFC Vern Songderoth, 3rd Platoon, 3rd Squad:

> We headed down a small knob and there was kind of a flat point on the ridge that turned back up again and we stopped because the ridge went on and made almost a 90-degree turn. Something was a little different so Captain Blunt put the third platoon up front and put Second Squad on line and they started around that bend. They no more than got started around that bend and the two bunkers opened up on them. That's when Carbajal and McQueer were killed; Sargent Adkins and a medic got wounded also—Myers. The lieutenant, the platoon sergeant, the medic and the radio operator—Ragle—were up there in the front. They [NVA] opened up on them and from where I was at, back behind them a ways, I couldn't shoot because I would have been shooting over the right flank of the line. So I low-crawled off to the right of the hill and there was a bomb crater on the side of the hill. I crawled down into that bomb crater and then pushed my machine gun over the berm. Jerry Shepard, who was the point man for our squad, followed me to the bomb crater. When I pulled my machine gun up from behind me, I got hit in the arm. It just hurt like hell. I didn't want to look at it. It hurt so bad. Finally I took my other hand, touched it and I didn't see any blood on my hand so I thought, "OK, I can look at it." Evidently, it was the bottom plug of a Chicom grenade that hit me. It hit flat and cut a two-inch circle out of my shirt right where you flex your muscle—the bicep area. It hit right on that and cut a two-inch circle right out of my shirt. That ticked me off, and that's when I started firing.
>
> I opened up with my M-60 and Jerry was feeding ammo for me so that kept me going. Somehow, Captain Blunt got behind me—somewhere I could hear him hollering behind me. I never turned around to see where he was. He kept saying, "Don't just pull the trigger—shoot five-round bursts"—which is what I was doing anyway. Three- to five-round bursts. Blunt was also calling for other people to throw ammo into the bomb crater. So, one-hundred-round boxes of ammo were just flying into the bomb crater behind me and Jerry was rescuing them and hooking them up for me. I was able to keep the fire on the two bunkers because from my angle, I didn't hardly have to move my machine gun at all to cover both bunkers. I was actually firing at the bunkers from the side. With that, we had plenty of ammo and Captain Blunt told me and Shepard, "You keep going until I tell you to stop," and so I did, and he coordinated with Lt. Horn to pull them back away from the two bunkers. Then they brought in some gunships and F-4s that took care of the bunkers.

Below are portions of citation from the men of D/1-11:

**Citation—ARCOM/V**

PFC Ken Kowalski distinguished himself on 11 November 1969 while serving as a rifleman with Company D, 1st Battalion, 11th Infantry while on a combat operation near Con Thien. Company D was moving along a ridgeline searching unfamiliar terrain for suspected NVA positions when they were pinned down by intense enemy fire. Exposing himself to the hostile fire, PFC Kowalski employed hand grenades and his M-16 rifle to place effective counter fire on the enemy. Disregarding his own safety he braved the enemy fire to supply the machine-gunner with ammunition. On numerous occasions he exposed himself to the hostile fire to supply his comrades with critically needed ammunition.

**Citation ARCOM/V**

Lieutenant Bruce Horn distinguished himself by valorous actions while his platoon was the point element for Company D, 1st Battalion, 11th Infantry on 11 November 1969 on a search and clear operation near Con Thien. When his platoon was ambushed by an unknown size force of NVA soldiers, two friendly soldiers were mortally wounded and the remainder of the platoon was in a state of confusion. Lieutenant Horn exposed himself to the hostile fire and moved among his men shouting instructions and reorganizing them into defensive positions. After his platoon had established effective retaliatory fire on the enemy, Lieutenant Horn led several of his men to the exposed area where the two mortally wounded soldiers lay. He and his men secured the mortally wounded soldiers and moved back through the hostile fire to a secure position. The highly effective firepower that the rejuvenated platoon placed on the enemy positions forced the enemy to withdraw, and made the recovery of his two men possible.

**Citation—ACM-V**

Sergeant Clerf Adkins distinguished himself on 11 November 1969 while serving with Company D, 1st Battalion, 11th Infantry on a combat operation near Con Thien. Company D was moving along a ridgeline searching unfamiliar terrain for suspected NVA positions. Sergeant Adkins was in the point element when they were pinned down by intense enemy fire. Disregarding his own safety, Sergeant Adkins exposed himself to the enemy as he directed the retaliatory fire of his men. While he was moving through the hostile fire, Sergeant Adkins was severely wounded. Refusing medical treatment, he continued to rally and lead his men. He remained in the battle area until the enemy fire was silenced. Sergeant Adkins' outstanding leadership and exemplary actions in close combat were instrumental in the defeat of the enemy force.

**Citation—Bronze Star/V**

Staff Richard Sergeant Myers (then Specialist Five) distinguished himself by valorous actions on 11 November 1969 as a medic with Company D, 1st Bn, 11th Infantry. Company D was on a search and clear mission near Con Thien when they were engaged by an enemy force of unknown size. Hearing cries for help from a seriously wounded comrade, Sergeant Myers exposed himself to the enemy fire and ran toward the wounded man. While braving the small arms fire, Sergeant Myers was wounded and unable to walk. Disregarding his own safety, he crawled to the wounded man and administered medical aid. Despite the incoming fire and his own wounds, he stayed with the wounded man until the enemy withdrew. As a result of his courageous actions, the life of the wounded man was saved.

**Citation—ARCOM/V**

PFC Vernon Sondgeroth distinguished himself on 11 November 1969 while serving as a machinegunner on a combat mission near Con Thien with Company D, 1st Battalion, 11th Infantry. Company D was moving along a ridgeline searching unfamiliar terrain for suspected North Vietnamese positions when the point squad was pinned down by intense enemy fire. Disregarding his own safety, PFC Sondgeroth crawled directly toward the enemy fire to a position where he could place a sustained volume of machine gun fire on the enemy. Although the enemy concentrated their firepower on PFC Sondgeroth, he refused to abandon his hazardous position. He continued to place effective fire on the enemy until other members of his platoon came to his assistance. Because of PFC Sondgeroth's swift reactions and military discipline, the enemy force was defeated and friendly casualties were held to a minimum.

Captain Stanley Blunt, as told "in his customary short and sweet language": Yah, the memory I have is about the third platoon—we were with the Mech—and we walked towards their position and the Mech didn't have their guns ready. The 50 machine guns were supposed to be fired over us at automatic impulse as we headed up the hill towards 162. Then I went up the ridge to the third platoon, which was in the tree line on a ridge off Hill 162. I told the lieutenant—Lieutenant Horn—to go up and that the NVA would either come through the draw or be up on that tree line because we heard them digging in in the night. They opened up and I ran up and I threw hand grenades at the bunker and we came up with five bodies [laughs]. They had two machine guns and they were no more now—got them with hand grenades. Lt. Horn did it. I brought him up there because we had seen tracks up there the day before.

The battalion net was now ablaze and 1-61 "Actual" was orchestrating from the speeding inbound OH-6. The journals follow the words of the combatants and the reaction to the orders of the battalion CO.

*Daily journals* 0720 Commanding Officer of 1-61 directs B/1-61 elements to move dismounted to ridge vicinity of YD 066643 and to sweep southeast along the ridge.

0725 Commanding Officer of 1-61 directs C1/1-61 elements to move dismounted to position of D/1-11 to reinforce the element.

0725 Medevac on station, instructed to orbit east of C-2.

0730 Commanding Officer of 1-61 is now on ground and joins D/1-11.

0810 C/1-61 completes link-up to D/1-11 moves to north side of ridge and establishes fire. B/1-61 in vicinity of 062641 and establishes enfilade fire on NVA positions. Cobras on station NVA on 3 high spots with automatic weapons at vicinity of YD064635.

0835 Team Tank reaction force is on station at bridge between A-4 and C-2.

## At Con Thien: 0800

As the action ramped up out on Hill 162, Alpha Company was twelve miles northeast, under the command of Captain Robert P. Gallagher. They exited Con Thien and ran platoon sweeps around the firebase.

Con Thien, Vietnamese for "Hill of Angels," had definitely lived up to its name over the years, and especially in the earlier days when the U.S. Marines built the firebase as part of a crackpot idea known as the McNamara Line. This line was the harebrained idea proposed and fostered by so-called intellectuals, and it cost thousands of Marine lives in its building. Secretary of Defense Robert McNamara signed on and requested a plan for its construction. A plan was devised by Harvard Law School professor Roger Fisher to install a barrier of state-of-the-art electronic devices along the DMZ and the Ho Chi Minh Trail. The idea was turned over to the Jasons, an elite group of about 45 of the nation's leading academic scientists. They reached the same conclusion on the bombing issue and expanded the infiltration barrier concept to include two components:

1. An antipersonnel barrier, manned by military personnel, spanning south of the DMZ from Laos to the South China Sea, a distance of about 160 miles. The antipersonnel barrier was to be comprised of minefields, ditches, barbed wire, and defoliated strips with military strongholds at specified, geographically advantageous positions. Con Thien was one of the strongholds.
2. An anti-vehicular barrier to interdict traffic on the Ho Chi Minh Trail. The barrier was to consist of numerous sensing devices of various styles and applications, and monitored in Nakhon Phanom, Thailand.

The McNamara Line was first given the code name "Project Nine." MACV—U.S. Military Assistance Command Vietnam—then changed the name of the plan to "Dye Marker," following a compromise of the classified Project Nine sobriquet. At that time, September 1967, the North Vietnamese began Phase I of their "General Offensive, General Uprising" campaign by attacking Marine positions along the DMZ. That made it especially difficult to advance the McNamara Line's construction. As January 1968 came and went, NVA troops were massed for an all-out attack on the Marine base at Khe Sanh as part of the Tet Offensive. Sensors and hardware had to be diverted from other parts of the DMZ to Khe Sanh. After that siege ended in April, construction on the McNamara Line was abandoned.[1]

***Opposite, top:* SSgt Charles Krabel, third platoon sergeant, A/1-61. *Bottom:* Lieutenant William Miller, third platoon leader.**

Con Thien was the scene of several battles and long artillery sieges fought valiantly by US Marines of the 2/4 "Magnificent Bastards" and the 1/9 "Walking Dead." It was a nasty rat-infested place that was a red quagmire during the monsoon season and a filthy red-dust bowl in the dry season. The rats fought the American fighting men for ownership of the bunkers and many a GI lay awake on board slab bunks with loaded forty-fives waiting to dust off the vicious vermin for supremacy of their quarters.

Lieutenant William Miller was the third platoon leader. He was a recent college graduate with three years of ROTC and newly commissioned as a second lieutenant. Nonetheless, at the beginning of his tour, he watched and listened as Staff Sergeant Chuck Krabel ran the platoon. First platoon was run by Lieutenant Michael Maiorca, a Mid-westerner. The XO, Lt. Buford Bagby, oversaw the sector occupied by second platoon. The fourth platoon was commanded by Lieutenant Chelsea Korte. Alpha Company ran their cloverleaf searches as they kept one eye and one ear to the west where the battle was raging on 162. The staccato of small arms fire could be discerned above the thumping din of artillery and air strikes. Periodically, the buzz-saw sound of the Spooky gunships dominated the clamor.

The rumor was that Alpha Company would no longer have the plum assignment of firebase security with all the fringe benefits of hot meals and a roof over your head—rats or not. The skinny was that another company, possibly B/1-11, would be airlifted to Con Thien to free up A/1-61 if and when an insertion was ordered somewhere out in the Wild West where a shit storm was going on. It would turn out to be a long day of waiting and at the end of the day, Alpha would stay put for the time being.

## *D/1-11 on Hill 162*

Later that morning, Captain Blunt had sent third platoon back to the perimeter, and now working with the second platoon, he took a group, including Lieutenant Michael Jordan, Sgt. Harold Phillips, Sp4 Ronald Gibson, PFC Bobby Preese and Sgt. David Roberts and led them toward another bunker complex fortified with machine guns. They were immediately pinned down by the hail of enemy fire, but Captain Blunt began shouting orders and rallying his troops to respond to the dire situation. In this way, his encouragement and skilled soldiering got his men up and moving. In the course of defeating the fortified enemy position, they charged the emplacements—hurling grenades, firing small arms and securing their wounded to safe areas. Again the leadership of the company commander and the professional skill and teamwork of Delta Company turned another dire situation with a superior-sized force into success with only several wounded and no loss of life. Captain Blunt's DSC citation and several Bronze Star citations of the above volunteers read in part as follows:

**Citation—DSC**

Captain Stanley Blunt distinguished himself while leading his company during a search and clear operation through enemy controlled territory several kilometers south of the Demilitarized Zone in the northern area of I Corps Tactical Zone. On 11 November, his company was participating in a coordinated battalion attack on elements of the 27th North Vietnamese Army Regiment defending heavily fortified bunker positions. When his company's advance was halted by intense suppressive fire, Captain Blunt single handedly charged a heavily fortified machine gun emplacement and completely destroyed the position. In this same assault, he killed four other enemy soldiers at close range by hurling hand grenades into their positions.

Again, Blunt's words were short and sweet: "They had two machine guns and they were no more—got them with hand grenades." In response to the order by the battalion commander to the Delta company commander to refrain from leading assaults, the salty battalion CO had this to say about Captain Blunt's courage and valor.

> I'm just thinking, Delta Company had a contact with a machine gun and I was out there, physically trotting up that hill and I called Starr to bring up Charlie Company and I figured I'd run about two companies down that ridge line. We're all set to do that and that young company commander of Delta 1–11, the one that was a hero, trots down there and he says no, no, I'll walk down there by myself—sneak and peek and throw a hand grenade and get that machine gun. And he did! And I said, OK, that's a brave thing you did. And I tell him I'm going to court-martial your young ass for not doing what I told you to do! Now—one—I knew a damn court-martial would never go anywhere and—two—I'm going to put you in for a DSC for being brave running down that ridge line. And that's exactly what happened; he got his DSC, loaded him up with 1–11 and sent him home. Not home, but back down to the Fire Base at C-2. After walking around in that AO for four weeks, they were tired.

Now Captain Blunt didn't do all the fighting on that assault. He had help from his volunteers—or "Blunt's Grunts," as they called themselves. Portions of the citations speak for themselves:

**Citation—Bronze Star/V**

Lieutenant Michael Jordan distinguished himself by valorous actions on 11 November 1969 as a Platoon Leader with Company D, 1st Battalion, 11th Infantry. Company D was on a combat operation near Con Thien when they engaged a numerically superior force of NVA regulars. Lieutenant Jordan was leading the point platoon forward until it was halted by intense enemy fire. Disregarding his own safety, Lieutenant Jordan led his men through enemy small arms and automatic weapons fire in an assault on the fortified positions, and was directly responsible for knocking out an enemy machine gun position.

**Citation—Bronze Star/V**

Sergeant Harold Phillips distinguished himself by valorous actions on 11 November 1969 as a Squad Leader with Company D, 1st Battalion, 11th Infantry. Company D was on a combat operation near Con Thien, when they encountered a large force of NVA soldiers entrenched in bunkers and trenches. The commanding officer of Company D requested volunteers to form an assault team. Despite the difficult task of the assault team, Sergeant Phillips volunteered. As the assault team moved toward the enemy positions, they came under intense enemy fire. Sergeant Phillips spotted an enemy position, crawled toward the position and threw a hand grenade, killing two enemy soldiers. When one of his men was wounded, he again disregarded his own safety and went to his comrade's aid, pulling him out of the line of enemy fire. He then placed suppressive fire on the enemy until other members of his team could move forward. As a result of his courageous actions, a strong enemy force was eventually defeated and friendly casualties were held to a minimum.

**Citation—Bronze Star/V**

Sp4 Ron Gibson distinguished himself by valorous actions on 11 November 1969 as a rifleman from Company D, 1st Battalion, 11th Infantry. Company D was on a combat operation near Con Thien when they encountered a large force of NVA Regulars. When the commanding officer asked for volunteers to form an assault team, Sp4 Gibson volunteered. The assault team was given the mission of making the initial assault on the bunkers and trenches. As the assault team moved forward they were pinned down by heavy machine gun fire. Sp4 Gibson, noticing a wounded companion to his left, completely disregarded his own safety, crawled through the intense fire to the wounded man, and carried him back to a secure position. Sp4 Gibson administered aid until his wounded comrade could be evacuated. As a result of Sp4 Gibson's action, the wounded man's life was saved.

**Citation—Bronze Star/V**

Private First Class Bobby Preese distinguished himself by valorous actions on 11 November 1969 as a rifleman with Company D, 1st Battalion, 11th Infantry. Company D was on a combat operation when they came in contact with a large force of NVA soldiers. The enemy was well-equipped and solidly entrenched. Even though the company commander indicated that the mission of the assault team would be difficult and dangerous, Private Preese volunteered. He moved forward through enemy fire and threw a grenade that destroyed an enemy bunker and killed two enemy soldiers. As a result of the action, a strong enemy force was defeated and friendly casualties were held to a minimum.

**Citation—Bronze Star/V**

Sergeant David Roberts distinguished himself by valorous actions on 11 November 1969 as a squad leader with Company D, 1st Battalion, 11th Infantry near Con Thien. When a large force of well-entrenched NVA Regulars was encountered, the commanding officer of Company D requested volunteers to form an assault team. Even though the mission of the team would be difficult and dangerous, Sergeant Roberts volunteered. As Sergeant Roberts advanced through the hostile fire, he spotted an enemy solider and killed him with a burst of M-16 rifle fire. He then placed a sustained volume of fire on enemy positions, enabling the remainder of his element to advance. When one of his comrades was wounded, Sergeant Roberts disregarded his own safety and went to his aid, pulling him out of the line of enemy fire. As a result of the action, a strong enemy force was eventually defeated and friendly casualties were held to a minimum.

As enemy fire ceased originating from the bunker, Blunt ordered Lt. Jordan and his second platoon to gather their more seriously wounded and make their way down the ridgeline and back up to the company's defensive position. The several wounded were medevacked and the company packed their gear. They were miserably tired from the thirty-plus days they had been in the field and were emotionally wasted from the adrenaline drain of nearly twenty-four hours of constant vigilance and fighting. As Delta Company trudged back to their defensive position, the men of second squad, second platoon had gone on a little search and clear of their own and found two NVA—one alive and one dead. The prisoner was wounded critically and in sad shape. The angry Delta soldiers were primed for revenge—but all parties to a man thought better and no revenge was taken. Joe Prince and Ron Gibson describe it.

**PFC James Landry of D/1-11. His first day in the field was 12 Nov 1969 when he was choppered into Hill 162 and Delta Company (courtesy James Landry).**

Joe Prince:

At dawn Blunt took the other platoons and swept the ridgeline in front of us, he left us behind since we bore the brunt of the night before. That's when we went into a little draw and found the gook half bandaged up in the rocks. He was peppered with shrapnel and part of his skull was gone. We took him up the hill to wait for a chopper and that's when they hit some gooks and a Sgt. Ruben Carbajal was killed. Everyone liked him and that made us all mad. We grumbled about shooting

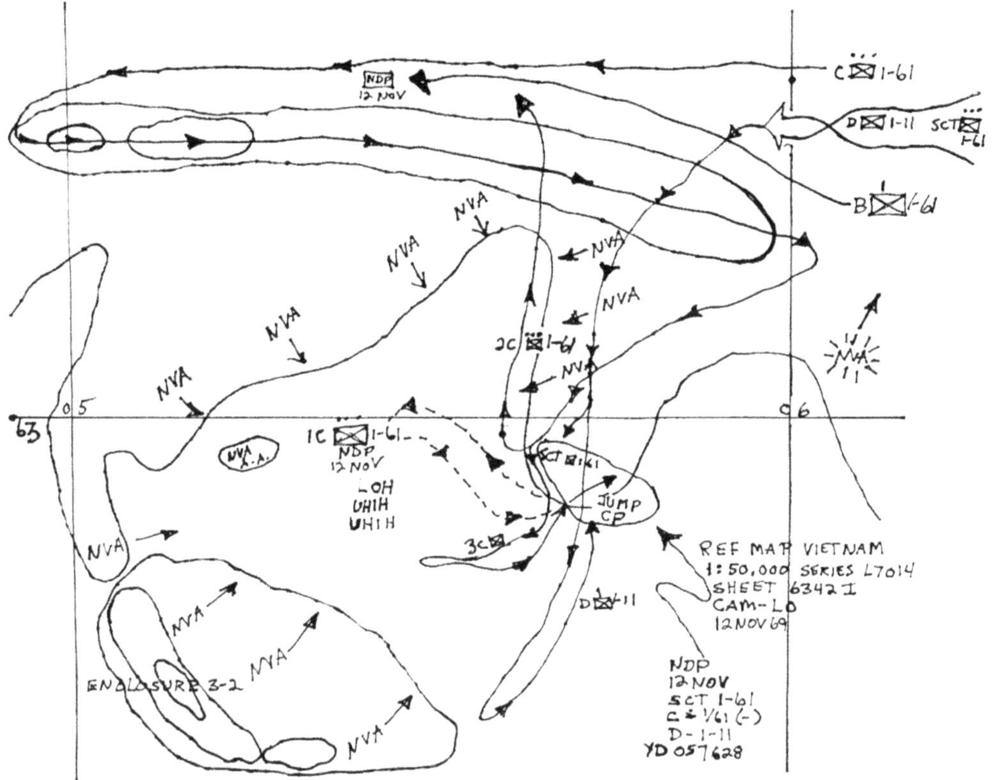


**Map #2 showing the location of the battalion command post "Jump CP," day patrols and the NDP of C/1-61, D/1-11, scout platoon near Hill 162, B/1-61 on Hill 1162 on 12 Nov 1969.**

the gook we had, but a sergeant, I believe his name was Reed, stopped us—the right thing to do. A resupply chopper came in with 3 new guys on it and airlifted the gook out.

Ron Gibson:

Morning came along and nothing much more had happened on the perimeter. Then I believe the intelligence guys came out and interrogated some prisoners. The one they were interrogating had seven bullet holes in him and the lid on the top of his head was smashed out so all you could see was spaghetti inside. Also, an M-79 blew up on his ankle and the nose cone from the 79 HE was embedded in it. He had tourniquets on all four limbs wired and twisted with pieces of wood. I remember helicopters picking up the two. A Montagnard interrogator and intelligence officer with an aluminum briefcase took them.

Two of the three new guys on the chopper were Jim Landry and PFC Dan Bostek. They must have been pretty awestruck to have been brought into such a dire situation on their first day in the field.

Sp4 James Landry:

I got into Vietnam on November 10 at Cam Ranh Bay and I was originally going to the 101st but they told me, "No you're not. You're going to the 5th Infantry because they're getting their ass kicked up north right now." I looked at the map and it was way up there on the DMZ and I said oh shit. So they sent me up there and when I got to C-2 the first sergeant got me and another guy named Bostek, and said you guys follow me. We followed him to supply and they gave us M-16s

> and some empty magazines but no ammo. Then we followed him down to the chopper pad and we helped load the chopper with chow and ammunition. They told us to get on and ride out to the field with the meal but they wouldn't give us ammo and we couldn't load our mags until we landed. We flew out and we unloaded the chopper and Joe Prince threw a wounded NVA into the chopper. They took us up to the CP and eventually assigned us a position. I was the RTO for Lt. Glazier.

At about 1700 hours, D/1-11 regrouped at the LZ and was flown back to C-2 to stand down for a well-deserved rest. "Higher" was under the opinion that the NVA would lick their wounds, pack up and make a run for the DMZ, as was there usual MO to hit and run. This did not happen, though, as sporadic small arms fire, RPGs and mortar fire began emanating from more and more places, and it was clear that the enemy was being reinforced, or that the force was much larger than previously expected.

Fifteen hundred meters to the north, Bravo Company ran several patrols down the ridge they were on, moving to the south and southwest after providing blocking fire for D/1-11 earlier in the day. They encountered RPGs and small arms fire, sustaining several wounded and inflicting 3 KIAs and capturing enemy equipment. Charlie Company as well got into several skirmishes, scoring many enemy KIAs without sustaining injury of their own. The total body count and captured enemy equipment for the day, according to the journals, is as follows:

Daily Journal:

> 1831 Total body count for today's contact was 12 NVA KIA, 2 NVA POW, 1 from C/1-61 and one from D/1-11. 2 NVA KIA from B/1-61 and 3 NVA KIA from C/1-61, 3 NVA KIA from D/1-11, 2 NVA KIA by gunships and 2 NVA KIA from artillery. Captured enemy equipment including 2 RPGs with 5 rounds, 1 RPD, 8 AK-47s, 1 SKS and 27 Chicom grenades.

Back at C-2 D/1-11, a well-deserved stand-down started with hot meals, hot showers and new changes of fatigues. That night, as chance was to have it, a group of Doughnut Dollies arrived at C-2. A surprise of coffee and doughnuts was planned for the battalion staff the next day, and D/1-11 would be told in the morning that they would be invited. As plans changed, that was not to be, and Delta/1-11 would be enjoying only a single night's rest, and be airlifted back into the field the next day at the order of the Battalion Commander, LTC John Swaren.

Meanwhile, after being resupplied by chopper, Charlie and Bravo Companies had reformed in new NDPs. Bravo moved east several clicks to an open rolling ridge known as Hill 100 and set up their NDP. Charlie had done the same but moved southwest 1000 meters, uniting with the Battalion Jump CP. Guards were established at every position, but the night consisted of minor probing and sporadic small arms fire. Back at C-2, Blunt's Hillbillies were enjoying hot meals and showers and their short-lived rest.

At nightfall, A/1-61 moved back inside A-4 and collectively breathed a sigh of relief, but tomorrow would bring an entirely different day.

# 10

# 12 Nov 1969 (DAY 2) at the Jump CP

At dawn of November 12, The battalion Jump CP was up and making plans for the day. Lt. Colonel Swaren was meeting with Captain Starr, commander of Charlie Company, and on the battalion net with Captain Spencer, the Bravo Company CO on his NDP, three clicks northeast at YD085645, and with First Lieutenant Frederick Jelinek back at the TOC at C-2. There had been a radio failure during the night—thought to be a breakdown of some relay equipment that was located in a camouflaged spot atop a nearby hill that offered a clear signal to both C-2 and Con Thien. Communication between the battalion CP on the back of Hill 162 and the TOC at C-2 had been cut off. This was a critical communication loss because it completely hampered resupply, medevac and air troop movement between the field and S3. A communication plan was devised where the Jump CP in the field would communicate their needs to a radio man at Con Thien, who would then relay the communication to C-2. This way, all units maintained a makeshift—but vital—communication link. Coincidentally, PFC Richard Coen of Charlie Company was sent back to base camp with an illness and would be that radio operator who would patch communications for the next twenty-four hours. Lt. Colonel Swaren described the communication patch in this way:

> Now, this is so [expletive] ridiculous. I'm down on that far side of that ridge line with the Jump CP. I've got an S-2 and an assistant S-3, and an artillery LNO and it turns out we cannot get FM contact back to Charlie Two. I can't talk to the TOC. Nobody can talk to the goddam TOC. I can talk to A-4—and there's some guy that could hear me and he would relay to TOC for me. So, it was kind of awkward but we had a little bit of radio contact.

Dawn (or in nautical terms, BMNT) arrived at 0628, which was late because of the start of the first phase of the new moon. The previous night was the darkest of the lunar cycle. The weather report called for cloudy skies in the 70s with a chance of showers. It was evident from the probes of the previous night that the enemy had not retreated, but rather may have reinforced and refortified their positions.

Daily Journals:

> 0635 Weather report from 120600–130600. Visibility 6 miles and winds are out of the Northeast at 8 knots. 24 hour outlook is for scattered showers. High of 78 and low of 70 is expected with humidity at 81%. BMNT is at 0628 and EENT is at 1838. Sunrise is at 0651 and sunset is at 1816. Moonrise is at 0908 and moonset is at 2038. Illumination is 6% in a new phase.

Plans for the day were made by 0730 and relayed to all parties by radio. Bravo would leave its mortar platoon and its APCs at their NDP and move toward but north of the Jump CP. They would divide into platoon searches five hundred meters apart and work the terrain of Hill162 and the surrounding hills. The plan was to have Bravo Company move two clicks east to the summit of Hill 162 and set up a perimeter on the military crest.

Charlie Company would move south and west of the Jump CP and hopefully trap any possible enemy forces in a pincer. C-2 was alerted through Con Thien to rally Delta/1-11 and airlift them back out to the field. Similarly, Lieutenant Hosfield's Recon Platoon was ordered to be airlifted out as well sometime during the day.

Daily Journals:

> 0743 From Battalion Commander to B/1-61 and C/1-61 Cos. B/1-61 to make thorough search of fingers and valleys of Hill 162. Check area for bunkers, bodies and equipment. C/1-61 to move west to south to east retracing the route they followed yesterday. Search all valleys, hills, draws, etc. using two days' time if necessary, making sure to check for bodies, bunkers, weapons and equipment. Making sure to try to make unit identification for S2. Also made C/1-61 and B/1-61 aware of enemy mortar attacks.

Now Lt. Jelinek would be able to demonstrate his skills at troop movement, resupply and medevac. Besides resupply of all units in the field, two groups had to be airlifted out to the Jump CP in the western hills, and there was still the possibility of Alpha Company entering the fray if they could be freed from security of Con Thien.

Joe Prince:

> The next thing I remember was being in C-2 as a reactionary force when the orders came to mount up. We were going back to Hill 162. A jeep drove beside us as we were walking to the helipad and we loaded up with ammo.

D/1-11 was airlifted to C/1-61's defensive perimeter near Hill 162. According to Lt. Colonel John Swaren, the scouts were to be deployed as a blocking force to the east of the Jump CP.

Lt. Colonel Jack Swaren:

> I called the scout platoon in and they came. Now, back in those days, the scout platoon was a pretty good size unit to put it in the field. They had rifles, as our company did. They were pretty strong. And I told them, I told Lieutenant Hosfield, the platoon leader—"Young man, you're going to get to the far end of those bad guys. You've just to get down there and circle all around all of them." And he did. He went down there.

Charlie and Delta spread their platoons at 500-meter intervals to search and clear the fingers and ravines of Hill 162 at the scene of the previous day's contact. Immediately contact was made. Bravo set up over the top of 162 as a blocking force. Individual units of Delta/1-11 and Bravo/1-61 became engaged in intense fire fights.

Sgt. Joe Prince:

> When we were dropped off at the base of Hill 162 another company started getting mortared so we were told to get up the hill as fast as possible. I had about 50 rounds of 79 ammo and couldn't run at all. The lieutenant shouted to get a move on and I gave him the finger, he just turned around and went up the hill. They moved us to where the action was and where a bunker line was stopping them from reaching the trapped element. The order came to get all the M60s and M79s (79, 60, 79, 60, etc.), on line and assault the bunker line. As we were moving and firing into the brush an RPG came out at us. I dove to my left and was turned in a somersault by the blast. That's when

> they ordered us back. The guy next to me was hit inside his thigh so I helped him back to the holes. We tried all day to get to the guys across a little draw from us but there were bunkers between us and them and we couldn't get through. We couldn't see the trapped element but we could see the smoke grenades going off in the burning choppers.

**1Lt Charles Matteffs, platoon leader first platoon C/1-61. He was instrumental in keeping alive the 22 survivors of his trapped platoon and several helicopter crews on 12 Nov 1969 until they were rescued in the wee hours of 13 Nov 1969 by Captain Blunt and a volunteer patrol in Starr Valley. Also later in his tour, he became Scout Platoon Leader of 1-61 (courtesy Charles Matteffs).**

**PFC Samuel Cornwell was a member of first platoon C/1-61 that was trapped and surrounded by NVA on 12 Nov 69. He was instrumental in rescuing several downed helicopter crews (courtesy Samuel Cornwell).**

The trapped platoon Joe Prince was talking about was Charlie Company's 1st platoon—and they were the first to get engaged. As lead element of the first platoon under Lt. Matteffs, squad leader Sergeant Larry Mosher moved down the steep hill towards a narrow ravine, PFC Stanley Samulak was the point man along with their Kit Carson Scout, who was nicknamed Elmer. As they reached the base of the ravine, Samulak and Elmer came upon an apparent outdoor NVA field kitchen area. Large 20-gallon pots simmered over small recently abandoned campfires. Instantly, Samulak, the scout and the other more experienced soldiers realized that they were up against a company element or larger. Elmer immediately pointed in the direction they were traveling and was positive the enemy was there—probably from his experiences as an ex-NVA soldier before he "Cho Hoy[ed]." A discussion ensued as to whether to continue or not. As PFC Sam Cornwell remembers, Lieutenant Matteffs instructed the platoon element to move on. They moved out in silence with Sgt. Mosher in the lead. Within a few paces, the point element was hit by machine-gun fire. Sgt. Larry Mosher was fatally wounded and two others were severely wounded.

Immediately, and with disregard for their safety, Lt. Matteffs and four PFCs (Stan

Samulak, Jerry Cobb, James Oetzel and medic Zeke Campbell) ran to their platoon sergeant's aid. He was dead but the other two needed to be dragged out of the intense volume of fire and attended to. Mosher was to the left. The citations for Matteffs's Silver Star and his four men tell the story:

**Citation—Army Commendation Medal/V**

Private Samulak distinguished himself while serving with the 1st Platoon of Company C, 1st Battalion, 61st Infantry while on a sweep and clear operations in the northernmost portion of South Vietnam on 12 November 1969. While maneuvering through enemy occupied terrain near Cam Lo, an unknown element from the 27th NVA Regiment opened fire on the point element of the 1st Platoon wounding the point man and the aid man. Disregarding their personal safety, Private Samulak and two comrades maneuvered through the intense fire and retrieved the two injured men and removed them to the safety of a covered position. Private Samulak's selfless courage undoubtedly saved the lives of the two men. His gallantry was in keeping with the highest traditions of the military service and reflects great credit upon himself, his unit, and the United States Army.

**Citation—Army Commendation Medal/V**

Private First Class Cobb distinguished himself by valorous actions on 12 November 1969 while serving with Company C, 1st Battalion (Mechanized), 61st Infantry on a sweep and clear operation near Cam Lo. While maneuvering through enemy occupied terrain, an unknown size element of NVA soldiers opened fire on the point element of the first platoon, pinning the small force down and wounding the point man. The aid man ran to his side and began treating the injured man when he too suffered a small arms wound. Disregarding their own safety, Private First Class Cobb and two comrades maneuvered through the intense fire and retrieved the two injured men and removed them back to the safety of a covered position. Private First Class Cobb's selfless courage undoubtedly saved the lives of the two men. His gallantry was in keeping with the highest traditions of the military service and reflects great credit upon himself, his unit, and the United States Army.

**Citation—Army Commendation Medal/V**

Private First Class Oetzel distinguished himself by valorous actions on 12 November 1969 as a member of Company C, 1st Battalion (Mechanized), 61st Infantry on a sweep and clear operation near Cam Lo. While maneuvering through enemy occupied terrain, an unknown size enemy element of NVA soldiers opened fire on the point element of the 1st Platoon, pinning the small force down and wounding the point man. The aid man ran to his side and began treating the injured man when he too suffered a serious small arms wound. Disregarding their personal safety, Private First Class Oetzel and two comrades maneuvered through the intense fire and retrieved the two injured men and removed them to the safety of a covered position where they were treated. Private First Class Oetzel's selfless courage undoubtedly saved the lives of the two men. His gallantry was in keeping with the highest traditions of the military service and reflects great credit upon himself, his unit and the United States Army.

**Citation—Bronze Star/V**

For heroism in connection with ground operations against a hostile force in the Republic of Vietnam: Specialist Ezekiel Campbell distinguished himself by valorous actions on 12 November 1969 while serving as a medical aid-man for the 1st Platoon of Company C, 1st Battalion (Mechanized), 61st Infantry during a sweep and clear operation in the northernmost portion of South Vietnam. That day a well-equipped and deeply entrenched company-size force of NVA Regulars initiated a fierce attack on Company C with grenades, small arms, and automatic weapons fire. During the initial contact the point man was seriously wounded. Disregarding his personal safety, Specialist Campbell rushed forward to the wounded soldier and began administering medical aid as the area was being saturated with enemy fire. Ignoring the intense fire around him, he continued to perform his duties even after he suffered wounds from an enemy grenade. His gallant actions were undoubtedly instrumental in saving his comrade's life. Specialist Campbell's courage and devotion to his fellow men was in keeping with the highest traditions of the military service and reflects great credit upon himself, his unit, and the United States Army.

**Citation—Silver Star**

For gallantry in action while engaged in military operations involving conflict with an armed hostile force in the Republic of Vietnam: Lieutenant Charles Matteffs distinguished himself by exceptionally valorous actions on 12 November 1969 while serving as platoon leader for the first platoon of C Company, 1st Battalion (Mechanized), 61st Infantry, during a sweep and clear operation in the northernmost portion of South Vietnam. A reinforced company of North Vietnam Regulars staged an attack against the 1st Platoon of C Company, effectively pinning them down. During the initial contact, Lieutenant Matteffs received a fragment wound from an enemy grenade that impacted near him. With total disregard for his pain and continuous loss of blood he constantly exposed himself to hostile fire for a medic who was attempting to extract a wounded soldier. While doing so, Lieutenant Matteffs was again wounded.

The platoon was now trapped in a three-sided ambush and could do nothing but take cover in a thicket of elephant grass which shielded them from the view of the bunkers where the intense enemy small arms and automatic weapons fire was emanating from. Sam Cornwell remembers bits and pieces of that day:

I don't remember a lot, but what I do remember is that morning we dismounted and we were on patrol. And I think Samulak was near the point and we came up on some cooking pots—they were cooking food in big kettles or something and it seemed like the group we were trying to flush out was too big for us. Well anyway, the platoon leader had us move on. So they took a few more steps. Mosher was then on point and he was the sergeant and they shot him up, they machine gunned him in half. Samulak was helping him. The lieutenant ordered smoke to be thrown for a medevac. They threw it and they shot the chopper down and then we had them with us. And of course Mosher died and I don't know exactly where we went to get cover. I had the M-79 and then it's all a blur to me. Anyway, in came another chopper and they blew that one up. And then we tried to get out of there and that's when they killed the ARVN that Stan had named Elmer. We called him Elmer. He got killed right in front of me. I was right in back of him. I didn't know which way to go and I really didn't know at the time that we were surrounded. So I guess I was supposed to be in charge of the squad at that point because everyone else was wounded or whatever. So I told Elmer you've got to tell us which way to go and he took a few steps and they filled him up with lead like I said.

The scene was chaotic. Eventually the enemy machine gun that had good enfilade fire on them was silenced, and Cornwell was given credit for that. Every man was wounded—including the two chopper crews. When the first bird was shot down in an attempt to medevac the wounded, Cornwell also helped in their evacuation to a safer position with the rest of the platoon. The Huey was from the Lancers. The crew chief, door gunner and pilot who were exposed out in the open to enemy fire were rescued and brought back to relative safety. Three men selflessly teamed to get all three wounded crew members to the platoon position. Again, the citations tell the story best:

**Citation—Bronze Star/V**

Specialist Samuel Cornwell distinguished himself by valorous actions on 12 November 1969 while serving as a team leader with Company C, 1st Battalion (Mechanized), 61st Infantry during a sweep and clear operation near Cam Lo. That day a well-equipped and deeply entrenched force of NVA Regulars initiated a fierce attack on Company C's dismounted maneuver elements. The intense fire caused the platoon elements to become separated and pinned down. In one gallant attempt to find an escape route for the entrapped platoon, Specialist Cornwell silenced an enemy machine-gun position with a grenade, but enemy fire from another position prevented his further movement in that direction. As the intense enemy fire inflicted several casualties, a request for an emergency medical evacuation helicopter was made. During one evacuation attempt, the craft burst into flames when it was hit by enemy rocket-propelled grenade fire. Disregarding his own safety, Specialist Cornwell ran through the hostile fire to the flaming helicopter, pulled the door gunner out and carried him back to a secure area. Although he was wounded himself, his selfless actions undoubtedly saved the gunner's life. Specialist Cornwell's gallantry was in keeping with the highest traditions of the military service and reflects great credit upon himself, his unit, and the United States Army.

**Citation—Bronze Star/V**

Specialist Ray Melarczik distinguished himself by valorous actions on 12 November 1969 while serving as a squad leader with Company C, 1st Battalion (Mechanized), 61st Infantry during a sweep and clear operation in the northernmost portion of South Vietnam. That day a well-equipped and highly motivated force of NVA Regulars initiated a fierce attack on the dismounted maneuver elements of Company C, effectively pinning them down with grenades, small arms and automatic weapons fire. Although initially wounded by grenade fragments, Specialist Melarczik refused medical evacuation and exposed himself to the intense hostile fire in order to carry his wounded comrades to a landing zone. When a helicopter crashed near his position, he unflinchingly ran to the burning helicopter and helped remove the passengers. He then directed intense suppressive cover fire with his M-60 machine gun in order to secure the landing zone while his comrades removed the injured men to safety. Refusing evacuation until the balance of the company was extracted that night, he remained with his men to lend them encouragement and leadership throughout the night. Specialist Melarczik's gallantry was in keeping with the highest traditions of the military service and reflects great credit upon himself, his unit, and the United States Army.

**Citation—Bronze Star/V**

Specialist Kenneth Hann distinguished himself by valorous actions on 12 November 1969 while serving as a team leader in the 1st Platoon of Company C, 1st Battalion (Mechanized), 61st Infantry during a sweep and clear operation near Cam Lo. That day a well-equipped and deeply entrenched company-size force of NVA Regulars initiated a fierce attack on Company C as they passed below a thickly wooded ridge. The ensuing action resulted in several personnel wounded, and immediately a request for a medical evacuation helicopter was sent out. In the midst of the intense fire, a helicopter managed to land and evacuate one of the more seriously wounded soldiers. During the second evacuation, the helicopter burst into flames when hit with a rocket-propelled grenade and small arms fire. Realizing the gravity of the situation, Specialist Hann braved the intense fire and ran toward the flaming helicopter. Although he sustained severe burns himself, he pulled the door gunner out and carried him back to a secure area. His selfless action undoubtedly saved the door gunner's life. Specialist Hann's gallantry was in keeping with the highest traditions of the military service and reflects great credit upon himself, his unit, and the United States Army.

**Lt Michael Cowart of B Battery 5th/4th Arty and attached to B/1-61 as forward observer. He directed fire of six artillery batteries on 12–13 Nov 1969 supporting friendly positions on Hills 100 and 162 (courtesy Michael Cowart).**

Lt. Charles Matteffs remembers that day philosophically:

I'm originally from Houston, Texas, and relocated to Akron, Ohio, in the summer of 1993 with my family. I realize now how fortunate we were that most of us that were down in that draw recovered from our wounds and led productive lives once we returned Stateside. I was stunned that so many of the guys that were with us in that ambush were wounded. Although my wounds were all superficial I still was hit on three separate occasions ... all very minor compared to others. One was a chi-com hand grenade when fragments got me in the back, while another was from an RPG that downed one of the medevac choppers that heroically came to our aid during the fighting. That fragment hit me in the right shoulder, but again, I could function with no problems. The 3rd injury was from fragments that took place when I was calling in Cobra gunships, trying to hit any NVA positions near us when we were pinned down and surrounded, and that made a real nice divot in my knee, almost like an axe (V-shaped) only real small/minor. I'm being very selfish in wanting to talk about it after all these years, as it's somewhat therapeutic to say out loud what I recall taking place at that time when I was only 25 years old. That's old, as most guys in my platoon were much younger than I! I was a 2nd lieutenant when this November contact took place. I was promoted later to 1st lieutenant. Regarding the medal associated with that contact, I'm a little uncomfortable ... almost as if I'm looking for a "pat on the back," and that's not it at all. I just need to get the guilt I associate with these awards out in the open before it's too late. I'm no spring chicken, since I'm now 73 years old! Honestly, I do not know why our lives were spared or how we were not assaulted that evening! When those choppers were shot down, we were very, very quiet, ... but, ... we could hear the NVA talking only a short distance away while we laid in that tall elephant grass! I'm going to share one thing with you that has always been bothersome to me up front. This may have happened after I got back from the hospital ship as I was approached by a clerk back at HQ who said, "Lieutenant, you need to write up something for the men in the platoon that were with you so they can be awarded for their bravery and commitment under these difficult circumstances..." and so I did. Then, he said, "You should also make a statement about yourself," and I refused, saying I could never do that! Bottom line, I was awarded a medal, the Silver Star, that to this day I do not feel I deserved as I felt I was only doing whatever it took to get my guys out of there, alive! Captain Starr, Captain Blunt, along with those seven young men that came to our rescue all are true heroes in my mind and always will be. Anyway, I've never told anyone about my feelings on that medal until now. Mentally, my main thoughts, no matter what mission was involved, was to make sure my guys were safe and returned to their families in good shape. I always felt I'd never ask them to do something that I was not willing to do myself. We're all very fortunate to be where we are today, especially with these memories so close to the surface whenever we meet, or correspond with someone that was there. The reception Stateside was so cold and indifferent from anyone other than our closest friends and our immediate family, that as American soldiers we were never able to put to rest that which we were involved in and did not have the solid support of our country. It has left a bitterness that will never ever go away for many of us. For me, that's a wound that has never healed, and whenever I meet someone that served in Vietnam, whether it was in my area or another, it's unspoken but understood that we have a unique connection in life that can never be forgotten and we're all family because of it. Perhaps, down the road I'll try to reach out to some of these guys.

### Lieutenant Charles Matteffs—citation, final portion—Silver Star:

[S]till disregarding his wounds he began encouraging his men to gain fire superiority so a rescue party could retrieve the occupants of a downed helicopter that had been hit with a rocket propelled grenade. After the successful rescue of the helicopter crew, Lieutenant Matteffs was wounded a third time while attempting to lead a flank assault on the enemy force. After an unsuccessful attempt, Lieutenant Matteffs called artillery strikes on the enemy positions. Although painfully wounded, he refused to be medevacked until his men were extracted that night. Lieutenant Matteffs' contagious courage and devotion to duty were instrumental in the repulsion of the enemy force. His conspicuous gallantry was in keeping with the highest traditions of the military service and reflects great credit on himself, his unit and the United States Army.

J.J. Jackson was a member of the Scout Platoon and was there when Lieutenant Matteffs replaced Hosfield as commanding officer when he (Hosfield) rotated to another duty. He had this to say about Matteffs:

Matteffs came to the Recon Platoon as platoon leader after he recovered from his wounds [from Helicopter Valley]. I remember we had set up an ambush and his RTO and FO both got hit and he had to call in artillery himself and I thought it was coming in about 50 meters from us. You know sometimes it seems real close but it was definitely closer than 100 meters. They stopped it when a tanker came out to support us. We had several wounded. He had to do all that. He was a short-timer by then. It was sometime in May. The average platoon leader had to spend only about 6 months in the field and I don't know whether they had offered him an XO position but they offered him the Recon Platoon and he took that. They liked to use an experienced platoon leader from a rifle com-

***Above:*** **LOH-6 helicopter flown by 1Lt Phillip Miller on 12 Nov 1969.** ***Right:*** **LOH-6 "Loach" pilot, 1Lt Phillip Miller, who voluntarily flew into a hot LZ and made a medevac under intense fire. He was shot down on his second extraction attempt. He retired from the Army a lieutenant colonel. He was awarded the DSC for his heroism on 12 Nov 1969 (courtesy Phillip Miller).**

pany. We were about 30 strong about then and sometimes they liked to think of us as another company and denoted us so often as a company symbol on a map. They definitely wanted an experienced platoon leader for us. Matteffs was not only very brave but also a good platoon leader for Charlie Company—I know he was for us. He was a quiet and soft-spoken guy.

As Charlie Company's first platoon relayed their distress on the communication net, Captain Spencer (Bravo Company) had divided the riflemen in his company into three platoon groups that were barely at fifty percent strength. As the depleted mortar platoon (which was about fifteen strong) watched, the three patrols moved across the open plain and to the southwest. Simultaneously, Charlie Company's mortar platoon approached the perimeter to consolidate their mortars with B Company.

In single file, Spencer and his divided force headed for the visible summit. The middle and right reconnaissance elements traversed a slightly sagging saddleback and moved on relatively high ground. Conversely, the left or most southerly element dropped somewhat into a wide ravine before climbing back to the approximate elevation of the other platoons. The last thousand meters rose to the summit. Now five hundred meters apart and in intermittent elephant grass and thicket, they slowed their approach. With one of the elements in the center was Lieutenant Michael Cowart. Cowart was the forward observer assigned to Bravo Company from battery D of the 5th/4th Artillery. His tech NCO, Sgt. Jon DeBoer, and his radio operator, PFC Frederick Dannefelture, moved along with him. As they moved near the front of the column, machine-gun fire halted their advance and they all hit the ground. The NVA ambush was only forty feet to their front. Two men were immediately wounded, but the impatience of the enemy ambushers was pivotal in avoiding more major injuries and fatalities. The entire patrol—who now lay prostrate on the ground—was protected from direct fire by a slight rise of the contour of the hill to their front. Too close for artillery shells, Cowart called for helicopter support, and two Cobras came in and eliminated the squad-sized ambush.

Lt. Mike Cowart, FO for Bravo Company:

I graduated from Ranger school August 27, 1969, and I was in Vietnam September 7. I went through that Mickey Mouse orientation program there at the base. Then I was sent out to the unit—actually I was assigned to D Battery, 5th/4th Artillery. I was then assigned to Bravo Company, 1st/61st as a forward observer for them. I remember I was choppered out to the unit after dark. The next day we got ambushed and a guy got killed about 50 meters from me—he had been shot in the chest. That was my first day. After that, it was relatively quiet leading up to the November Battle. We had that guy killed when we went in for inspection—friendly fire. I don't remember when exactly that was. Someone called us back into C-2 for an IG inspection and we went back after dark through a couple villages. Someone got nervous and unleashed an M-60 and a man was killed. That was kind of a sad and frustrating experience.

But on November 12 we were [on Hill 100 and were] moving east because a couple choppers had been shot down and some men were trapped from C Company—Captain Starr's company—which was engaged. We were heading to that engagement to help with that extraction and as a blocking force. As we moved in that direction, we were ambushed, and actually Colonel Swaren corrected me, saying we were actually moving to contact. We were on foot and we were going up this little berm. And maybe 40 meters away, we were opened up on. They were in bunkers—maybe 8 or 10 guys—NVA soldiers in that location. They opened up on us and the only reason no one was killed was that they got scared and fired wildly and too fast. We had one guy shot in the foot and another guy shot in the shoulder. There was just enough of a berm that we were able to hit the dirt and they couldn't hit us. Obviously we were too close to adjust artillery or bring in mortars. We tried to move around them but we finally called in Cobras. There were two or three of them and they engaged them and killed them. They got them with rockets and mini-guns and those grenades mounted on the front. We were close enough the blast threw dirt and body parts on us.

From 30 miles away—and listening on his radio—1Lt Phillip Miller, flying a small OH6A, volunteered to attempt a medevac of 1/C/1-61. After he dropped off a full-bird colonel and a major at the Jump CP, he then successfully extracted three of the more seriously First Platoon wounded. A fourth casualty had to wait because the small Loach would have been grossly overloaded. When he returned, he was asked by radio to check a friendly casualty and determine if he was KIA. Miller, hovering in place and under intense fire, hooked the man's shoulder with the skid of his Loach with the intent of dragging him closer to the platoon position, but the man did not respond. Presumed dead, this casualty would turn out to be Charlie Company's squad leader, Sgt. Larry Mosher.

On his second trip, the chopper heavily damaged from small arms fire, Miller took an RPG backing out of the PZ with three more wounded. The Loach crashed-landed upside down. Miller was knocked unconscious for a few moments and injured his back and knee. Now another chopper crew was cut off with the 1st Platoon—everyone wounded, and most of them nearly out of ammunition. 1Lt Miller would receive a DSC for his actions. Here are some of Miller's thoughts of his offer to help:

I was assigned to the 163rd Aviation Company and on 12 Nov 1969 I was flying a combat support mission for the CO of 326 Engineer BN. The SOP for all aircraft in Vietnam was to monitor the emergency frequency net and that's how I became aware of the fire-fight involving 1/61 infantry. Emergency medevac was being called for a downed air crew from B Company 158th Avn BN "Lancers." Because I had a very good friend with the Lancers I was greatly concerned when I heard that the dustoff aircraft would not attempt another extraction due to enemy fire. I contacted Catkiller 18 and told him that I was 10 minutes from the contact site and that I was in an OH-6 aircraft and that I would make the attempt. He told me to stand by and stay away from the contact site as there was a Huey down and he was working fast movers. I asked my passengers if they wanted to stay with me or be dropped off. They both agreed to stay and I landed at a nearby firebase to obtain M-16 rifles for them as they only had side-arms. Airborne again I contacted the FAC and told him I was available to extract wounded. The FAC requested that I keep my distance because of enemy fire. He told me that one aircraft had already been lost and that the ground unit was reluctant to bring in another aircraft due to heavy enemy fire. Listening to the radio communications between the parent company of the pinned-down platoon and their higher headquarters revealed that an American unit was in serious trouble and needed urgent help. I departed my holding position and proceeded north to the contact area. I again radioed the FAC and insisted that I be allowed to attempt the extraction of wounded personnel.

This time the FAC acknowledged my request and vectored me onto a hilltop east of the burning Huey. During my landing approach to this position I began to receive small arms fire from the west. Once below the ridgeline I was partially protected from the small arms fire and landed in the center of a company-size unit. LTC McClelland exited the aircraft and spoke with an officer, call sign "PIG-36" [Lt. Williamson White], to find out where the WIAs were located. He was told that they were approximately 100 meters west in a small valley, they had been trying to get to them but were not able to advance due to enemy fire coming from bunkers between the two units. After LTC McClelland returned, I departed the hilltop to the south. As I was climbing out, the FAC Catkiller 18 (Captain Arrington) advised me that the body of an American soldier was lying in the open near the burning Huey and asked me if I could check to see if he was alive. I turned right and made an immediate approach to the crash site. On short final I saw the body lying about 50 feet south of the Huey. The slope of the ground made it impossible to land so I began to nudge the body with the toe of the left skid of my aircraft. While trying to hook my skid under the arm of this soldier, I began to receive small arms fire, this time from the west. This meant the enemy occupied positions on both sides of the small valley entrance leading to the pinned-down platoon.

I asked my passengers and the on-site AH-1G gunships to return fire while I attempted to pick up the body with my skid. When my efforts turned the body over it was clear that the soldier was dead [Sgt. Larry Mosher]. This soldier was from 1/61 infantry and I never found out his name, I believe he was a staff sergeant. During my initial approach to the hilltop and while at the burning Huey my aircraft had sustained a number of small arms hits to the rotors and I could feel some vibration in the controls.

I now fully appreciated the very real danger of being shot down should I attempt to fly into the location where the pinned-down platoon was located. As I climbed for altitude I made radio contact with the pinned-down unit. I told them I was going to attempt an approach to their location to extract wounded, that I would be coming in hot and could not stay long. I asked if they could provide suppressive fire. They told me they could not offer much fire support but that they had five seriously wounded personnel needing immediate extraction. I was also advised of heavy ground fire from the east. I replied that I was dropping off my passengers at a friendly location to the south and that I would be back in five minutes. I told them to assemble their wounded and be ready. After dropping off my passengers, I made two low-level high-speed passes over the area to identify the best possible approach and landing site. Once satisfied, I initiated an approach and successfully landed next to the pinned-down unit. Upon touchdown, five severely wounded men were loaded onto the floor in back. I could not pick up the load and one was removed. I was on the ground no more than half a minute. I backed up away from the slope, turned left and departed down the valley as fast as I could. I received heavy small arms fire during this departure. Tracers were passing me on both sides and I remember thinking about the men in back and their lack of armor protection. Because of my overloaded condition and the damage I had sustained, I was not getting full performance from the aircraft and was unable to gain much altitude. Most of my instruments were indicating in the red and I asked one of the attack aircraft to stay with me in case of a forced landing. Despite my damage and overloaded condition I flew these WIAs to a combat aid station about 10 kilometers to the east.

As soon as the wounded were removed from the aircraft, I applied power and returned directly to the combat site to get the soldier I had left behind. The aircraft engine was now smoking and I had a pronounced lateral vibration, but I was still flying and power looked good. As I set up for my second approach into the PZ, the FAC advised me that the gunships were gone due to low fuel. I contacted the ground unit and told them I would again be coming in hot and to get ready. On this approach, it was clear that enemy gunners had repositioned to place effective fire on the landing site as well as the approach path into the site. As soon as I landed, three WIAs were loaded, I applied power, backed off the slope and this time I turned right instead of left. Had I turned left an RPG would have struck me in the cockpit and I would not be writing this. I was alone in the aircraft with three wounded soldiers lying on the floor in back. I had to back out of the PZ, as the hill was very steep, the main rotor was striking grass and brush directly in front of me and my rear skids were off the ground about a foot. I had completed my backout and was making a hovering turn to the right when the rocket hit. The RPG struck the aircraft behind and above the right rear door. The explosion severed the tail boom and blew out the [controls]. The aircraft pitched forward, violently striking the ground. During the crash sequence, I impacted the crushed windscreen, which knocked the wind out of me. The aircraft rolled over, causing the rotor blade to deform and cut the cockpit to pieces. I remember putting my hands above my head to brace myself as the aircraft starting rolling, but, as soon as I touched the roof of the cabin I pulled my hands back as I did not want the rotor to cut off my arms. My chest armor plate and seat no doubt saved my life. Once the aircraft stopped, I shut off the main fuel and turned off the battery. I then released my harness and fell up out of my seat and into the crushed canopy. At the time I didn't realize that I was upside down or that I had been hit by the RPG. I did not hear the explosion and could not hear anything for about 5 minutes. The plastic windscreen in front of the pedals was beginning to melt, and it was at that point I knew I was on fire. I exited out of the copilot door opening. I crawled about 20 feet away from the fire and waited until I could breathe better. Next, I loaded my .38 (I never flew with my sidearm loaded, as I didn't want it discharging during a crash) and crawled over to the platoon leader's location. He asked me if I wanted to assume command (I was a 1st LT and he was a 2nd LT) and I told him no, that he was doing just fine, but that I would help as best I could (at that point I could not walk due to knee and back injuries).

The level of fire from American forces to the east kept pressure on the entrenched enemy down the ridge from their location and west of our position. Night suppressive fires from aircraft and artillery kept the enemy in their bunkers and there was no attack launched on our position although we continued to receive small arms fire into our position. The heavy grass concealed our exact locations, preventing effective fire onto our positions. In the early morning hours of 13 Nov 1969, a small relief patrol made up of volunteers and led by a Captain Blunt ... he also received the DSC ... made their way into our position and we gathered the dead and wounded that couldn't walk and dragged/carried them north up the mountain and then east around the left flank of the known enemy positions and made our way to the parent unit. I was airlifted out later that day and flown to the USHS Repose. Three weeks later I returned to my unit and completed my tour.

Beleaguered as they were, the first platoon had to recover the downed Loach pilot along with the wounded who had been loaded a few seconds before. Samulak, Cornwell, Sweeney, radioman Hann and the rest sprang to action again. The citations best tell the story.

**Citation—Bronze Star/V**
**For heroism in connection with ground operations against a hostile force:**

In the Republic Of Vietnam: Sergeant (then Private First Class) Leon Sweeney distinguished himself by valorous actions on 12 November 1969 while serving as a team leader in the First Platoon of Company C, 1st Battalion (Mechanized), 61st Infantry during a sweep and clear operation in the northernmost portion of South Vietnam. That day a deeply entrenched, company-size force of NVA Regulars initiated a fierce attack on Company C as they passed below a ridgeline. As friendly casualties mounted, medical evacuation helicopters were called in to remove the wounded. When one helicopter crashed and burned from the enemy rocket-propelled grenade fire, Sergeant Sweeney disregarded the hostile fire and ran toward the burning craft and removed the crew members. Upon leaving the contact area, the helicopter he was riding in was shot down by enemy fire. Sergeant Sweeney was thrown out of the craft, but he returned to remove the pilot and the gunner from the burning wreckage. His selfless actions were instrumental in saving the lives of his fellow soldiers. Sergeant Sweeney's gallantry was in keeping with the highest traditions of the military service and reflects great credit upon himself, his unit, and the United States Army.

There was one other fatality in the first platoon and that was Sp4 Ken Barkley. After the battle, PFC Dan Webber, the company clerk, was told by one of the troopers who was in the field that Ken, while running for cover, ran directly over a spider hole and was shot by the NVA soldier who occupied it. Lt. Phil Miller also remembers:

The 12 Nov morning report entry for Barkley indicates, "missile wounds to entire body." The causalities placed on the rear deck of my aircraft were stacked like cordwood and the person on the top of the pile would have been exposed to the brunt of the exploding RPG. I remember crawling over destroyed sections of the upper rear fuselage as I moved up the hill to Lt. Matteffs' position. The panel I crawled over had hundreds of holes in it and I remember thinking that it looked like it had been shot with bird-shot from a shotgun. The panel came from a section of the fuselage over the rear seats and below the rotor hub. The number of holes in it would be consistent with the morning report entry for Sp4 Barkley. I do know that the body I [helped carry] was an American.

Now there were twenty-two U.S. servicemen trapped in this precarious position in a stand of elephant grass—and surrounded. They had retreated into a thicker and taller clump of elephant grass, and though the enemy fire was heavy, they could not pinpoint the first platoon with any accuracy. Everyone was wounded in some form and many were in great pain for lack of morphine. Ammunition supplies were very low—down two a few clips of M-16 and a few grenades. They could do nothing but wait for the battalion commander to come up with a plan. But he was also under attack from a line of reinforced enemy bunkers. They would have to sit tight for now and simply survive until another type of rescue could be attempted.

Back at the Jump CP, Lt. Col. Swaren greeted the full-bird colonel that pilot Lt. Miller had off-loaded. He got word to him that his Loach now had been shot down, but he did take solace in the fact that his pilot had survived the crash near the LZ—and was still alive. Swaren remembers the meeting with the full colonel as follows:

> So, anyway, this "06" Colonel comes over and I said well, look sir, you're the senior man in this crowd. Do you want to take command? Just tell me. I understand the rules of the game. He says, "Oh, no, I'm out here to help you. You tell me what you want me to do." Eventually it's getting dark and there's a little ravine coming up about where I wanted to spend the night. I said, "If you'd be so kind…." This guy carries a thump gun [M-79] and he's got this elephant gun loaded with Flechette rather than HEs. I said, "If you really mean that you can go down to the head of that ravine and get yourself a little cover and if anybody comes up, you can shoot them, you can just kill them." And it turns out, he was a good guy and he said, "Yeah, I can do that." And he did. We spent the night there.

By mid-afternoon, the Recon platoon had been inserted by helicopters. Lieutenant Hosfield was the platoon leader. There was some difficulty finding transportation for them because of all the downed choppers and the fact that every field grade officer in the I Corps had wanted to get in the air to see what was going on. Eventually, all that could be commandeered were three Hueys. In order to get 10 men in each helicopter they allowed only personal weapons and a single bandoleer for each trooper. Machine guns, rucksacks, claymores and even entrenching tools were left behind. PFC James "J.J." Jackson remembers:

> I was a PFC at the time. On November 12 they choppered us out and during that time we had 40 men. We operated with 10 armored personnel carriers. So there were about 40 of us then but we left our platoon sergeant and our 10 drivers at C-2, leaving about 30 of us. Danny Hosfield was our platoon leader. They landed us close to the battalion CP in three helicopters. They told us that we were going to guard a helicopter that had been shot down. Because they were putting 10 men into each helicopter plus the crew, the pilot told us no rucksacks, no entrenching tools, no M-60s, no claymores, but just carry a really light amount of ammo—one bandoleer, basically. I had an M-16 and one bandoleer but there were a couple of guys with M-79s. I also had one frag. I was with 2 guys at my position—one guy was Doug Humphrey from southern New Jersey, who had 8 days left in country that day, and the other was Robert Herrick—he had about 30 days. The only people I saw on the ground were the lieutenant colonel [McClellan] and a major that had been let off by the helicopter that had done some medevacs. When we landed, we were taking some live AK fire. Well, there was no helicopter to guard—Matteffs and 1st platoon had taken care of that, I guess. They didn't really know what to do with us so, they gave Lieutenant Hosfield some orders and we moved to a little hill to the east of Hill 162. We climbed it and it was very steep. When we got up there was a lot of blue commo-wire. I ran into a sniper once who had a Kit Carson Scout with him that had told him that when you ran into blue commo-wire there was at least an NVA battalion CP around that area. It was strung in the trees and one abandoned bunker there was full of empty 51-caliber machine gun cans and a lot of fresh bloody bandages. So the hill was probably occupied that day. It was about 4 in the afternoon and probably most of us only had about 140 rounds of ammunition and they left us there as a blocking force—as they said. We're on that hill and there was stuff going on all around us. I think we were all pretty exposed, but we weren't being shot at. I guess the NVA communication was as bad as ours was sometimes, and they weren't aware of us and how exposed we really were. That night we had

some movement in the valley on the side I was on. At our position there was only a single spider hole and we gave it to Humphrey because he had only 8 days left. It was so steep that if you fell asleep you would slide down the hill. So Herrick and I were virtually standing up with our necks stuck out. I can't testify that Doug wasn't shaking as much as I was, but I wasn't the only one shaking. We could hear something coming up that hill and we thought it was a pretty serious thing, and I told Herrick, "I've got a grenade." I was the only one that had a grenade. He said, "Get it out and get it ready. Straighten out the pin but don't pull it—just get it ready." We could hear something but it stopped. I believed that these were the ones that had 1st platoon of Charley Company pinned and were moving north to join up with the other ones that were coming in to hit [Gallagher Ridge]. And our FOs must have known about it because they were trying to fire artillery in there. But it was only 100–150 meters across to the next hill and trying to get artillery in there was difficult and it seemed they moved closer to the base of our hill to the extent that we really thought we were going to get hit. But then it got quiet again. By then my adrenaline was up so high I just told Humphreys, "I can't explain it, but I have to close my eyes. I have to go out for a minute," and it was almost like passing out drunk or something. So I was able to get my foot on a bush so I didn't slide down the hill and I just slept for about 2 minutes. We were very quiet the rest of the night and we only whispered.

Meanwhile, during the day, Charlie Company's second and third platoons set out on patrols in an attempt to rescue Lieutenant Matteffs and his men. They were also engaged in ferocious fire fights. The second platoon, in another one of those attempts to free the trapped first platoon, dropped down into the ravine and was immediately overwhelmed by small arms, grenade and RPG fire. They were caught in another L-shaped ambush by an enemy force that was entrenched on the higher ground. With the help of gunships, the second platoon fought their way out, finally silencing the enemy force, but Lt. William Pierpont was killed. Lt. Pierpont had only been with the unit a few days. Several Bronze Star Citations cite the heroism of the patrol members and tell the story:

**Citation—Bronze Star/V**

Sergeant Richard Dell distinguished himself by valorous actions on 12 November 1969 while serving as a squad leader with Company C, 1st Battalion (Mechanized), 61st Infantry during a sweep and clear operation in the northernmost portion of South Vietnam. When a well-equipped and deeply entrenched company-size force of NVA Regulars initiated a fierce attack on Company C's dismounted elements, effectively pinning down the friendly force, Sergeant Dell's platoon was called upon to serve as a reactionary force. While moving toward the besieged elements, his platoon came under heavy enemy fire, and Sergeant Dell reacted by organizing a tactical assault on the hostile positions. Upon reaching the high ground where the hostile fire originated from, the friendly force encountered a live enemy mortar position. Using fire and maneuver, the squad charged forward, neutralizing the enemy position, but losing the platoon leader to enemy automatic weapons fire. Instinctively, Sergeant Dell grasped complete command of the situation and directed the return of his men while simultaneously ensuring their safety by placing them into well-covered positions. Then, ignoring the intense hostile fire, he made his way back to the stricken platoon leader and carried him back to their covered position. Sergeant Dell's gallantry was in keeping with the highest traditions of the military service and reflects great credit upon himself, his unit, and the United States Army.

**Citation—Bronze Star/V**

Private First Class Richard Myllymaki distinguished himself by valorous actions on 12 November 1969 while serving as a rifleman with Company C, 1st Battalion (Mechanized), 61st Infantry during a sweep and clear operation in the northernmost portion of South Vietnam. That day, a well-equipped and deeply entrenched force of North Vietnamese Army Regulars initiated a fierce attack on Company C's dismounted maneuver elements as they passed below a thickly wooded ridge. The intense fire caused the platoon elements to become pinned down and separated. PFC Myllymaki's platoon, acting as a reactionary force, maneuvered by fire and movement in an effort to reach and free their entrapped sister platoon but were thwarted by the enemy's intense fire. Along with several other volunteers, PFC Myllymaki proceeded forward in a tactical manner in an effort to search out and silence the enemy resistance. While directing their assault on an enemy mortar position supported by enemy automatic and small arms, the platoon leader was stricken by a burst of heavy enemy automatic weapons fire. Disregarding his personal safety, PFC Myllymaki exposed himself to the intense enemy fire to provide intense suppressive fire to cover his comrades, permitting them to extract their fallen platoon leader. PFC Myllymaki's gallantry was in keeping with the highest traditions of the military service and reflects great credit upon himself, his unit, and the United States Army.

**Captain David Tousignant, pilot of Dustoff 708. He and his crew medevaced many 1-61 wounded on 12–13 Nov 1969, including Captain Starr and Lt. Korte (courtesy David Tousignant).**

### Citation—Arcom/V

Specialist Four Melquiades Villicana distinguished himself by valorous actions on 12 November 1969 while serving as a medical aid-man with Company C, 1st Battalion (Mechanized), 61st Infantry during a sweep and clear operation in the northernmost portion of South Vietnam. That day, a well-equipped and deeply entrenched force of North Vietnamese Army Regulars initiated a fierce attack on Company C's dismounted maneuver elements as they passed below a thickly wooded ridge, which caused the platoon elements to become separated and pinned down. The Second Platoon was organized as a reactionary force to free the entrapped First Platoon. While maneuvering to the First Platoon element they encountered a mortar position at the bottom of the ridge, supported by enemy snipers and machine-gunners. When the platoon leader took a seven-man volunteer squad down to silence the position, he became seriously wounded by the automatic weapons fire. Although the enemy maintained constant and intense fire on the area, Specialist Villicana, with utmost selflessness and devotion to duty, ran to the platoon leader and quickly threw two smoke grenades so members of the squad could safely evacuate their fallen comrade under concealment. Specialist Villicana's gallantry was in keeping with the highest traditions of the military service and reflects great credit upon himself, his unit, and the United States Army.

### Citation—Bronze Star

Private First Class Marvin Kelly distinguished himself by valorous actions on 12 November 1969 while serving as a grenadier with company C, 1st Battalion (Mechanized), 61st Infantry during a sweep and clear operation in the northernmost portion of South Vietnam. That day a well-equipped and deeply entrenched force of NVA Regulars initiated a fierce attack on Company C's dismounted maneuver elements as they passed below a thickly wooded ridge. The intense fire caused the platoon elements to be separated and pinned down. Disregarding his personal safety, PFC Kelly ran down the ridge, while constantly under intense hostile fire, in order to aid his fallen platoon leader. Running into the open, bullet-saturated area where his platoon leader lay, he dragged him to a covered area where some comrades joined him in the tedious evacuation. This completely voluntary and selfless act earned for him the respect and admiration of his comrades. PFC Kelly's gallantry was in keeping with the highest traditions of the military service and reflects great credit upon himself, his unit, and the United States Army.

Try as they did, the second platoon could get no closer than one hundred yards to the trapped First Platoon. Running low on ammunition, with several casualties and without their platoon leader, Captain Starr—C Company commander—radioed them and ordered they remain at their position and help would be on the way. As it would turn out, Captain Starr would soon have his own troubles to deal with. The job of extracting second platoon would be left to Bravo Company, who was now in position above and working their way down several steep draws from the top of Hill 162. Lt. Cowart and Captain Spencer also had been on the battalion net listening to the fight going on below them and were the closest element to the second platoon. It would be PFC Frederick Dannenfelture—the FO's RTO—who would get to Pierpont and carry him back to friendly forces. Cowart tells the story:

Lt. Mike Cowart, FO Bravo Co.:

> Our element was about 70 strong at the time, so we were two or three platoons. We left the mortar platoon behind. We were the center element and the rest were spread out on either side of us. As we continued forward, I was now towards the end of the column. We traveled through a series of ridgelines and ravines. There was elephant grass about chest high. As I moved forward, an NVA soldier stood up and looked me straight in the face. He then shot an RPG at me. I watched it come out of the tube—watched him and watched the RPG go right by me and hit behind us. When I popped up to take him, he was gone. After that, we moved on to the area we were supposed to occupy on Hill 162. We got to a position that we decided to occupy. It was a position that the NVA had formerly occupied earlier and we had to pull several bodies out of the holes before we could use the positions. There was a Chinese advisor there that was lying there who had been stripped naked of all his gear by the gooks. He was lying on that ridgetop. There was gunfire going on below as we occupied our positions. A young lieutenant was killed below not too far from our company—from Charley Company—I believe. My RTO was a guy named Frederick Dannenfelture—an Italian/Jewish guy—and we used to butt heads all the time but I loved the guy. He went down with three other guys and pulled the body back up and was awarded the Silver Star for that. They also brought back some of the fallen platoon leader's wounded men. The other guys who volunteered with him were awarded Bronze Stars, as I recollect. He was a good guy and I've tried to find him over the years with no luck. From that position we sent patrols down the hill to that area where the young lieutenant was killed. There was another guy, a first lieutenant from Charlie Company, that had a rifle shot out of his hand and was brought back to our position also.

It was now Captain William Starr and the third platoon who would take a shot at a rescue. The remainder of the second platoon returned up the hill, several of them wounded and without their young lieutenant. They were given positions on the battalion perimeter and ordered to dig into the edge of the hill. Starr quickly assembled another group to attempt to free his trapped first platoon. He contemplated leading his small force—comprised of third platoon members—in a rapid assault down the ravine in an attempt to traverse over those last hundred meters of heavily defended terrain. Instead, he had a chopper take him to a little knoll ahead and in the direction of assault beyond where they had stalled and where he could direct the reaction force from an elevated position. With his radioman refusing to go along in the chopper, Starr took the radio with him instead. There were concealed bunkers on every knoll. As the pilot came in under fire, he refused to land, but instead dumped Starr out the cargo door. He hit the ground and lost most of his equipment. Several pull-string grenades were tossed from bunkers, and Starr reacted. The fuses were smoking as he tossed them back, killing several NVA sappers. Finally, one blew up just as it left his hand and took off his arm below the elbow. His body took the brunt of the blast. Even wounded as he was, he killed several more NVA with his pistol—having to cycle the action using his exposed ulna and cradling it against his side. He then lapsed into semiconsciousness. Here is what he remembers of the ordeal today:

> The chopper pilot flew me to the knoll so I could direct my company's getting to 1st Platoon. The radio operator refused to go with me. Once in air near the knoll, the pilot said it was too hot to drop me off.... I did a very bad thing and pulled my .45. The pilot resented this and tipped the chopper and I slid out the door. Of course, the radio landed upside down and antenna broke off at base, rendering radio useless. The SKS I had been carrying went somewhere and I couldn't find it. So there I was on the knoll ... in the center of the HQ for 27th NVA Regt. They stood in a circle and began shooting at me. I'd like to apologize to the chopper pilot.
>
> As soon as I hit the ground ... from a height, I don't remember ... I looked around and made a very rapid assessment. No rifle ... radio useless ... three frag grenades ... a .45 with two mags. NVA were in a circle around knoll ... weapons pointed at me ... glassy-eyed from dope.... They fired.... I hugged the ground. They killed each other. At one point I looked behind me and saw that one of them had thrown a metallic grenade ... it was smoking from a pinhole.... I knew instantly that it was about to explode. Grabbed it with my left hand ... pitched it to right hand ... then threw it as hard as I could. It didn't go far before it went off. It hurt! Bad! I looked and saw that the hand was gone ... the ulna and radius bones remained with nerves dangling. By now, I had one grenade left. I had shot two NVA with a pistol but never got to the SKS. The NVA kept shooting at me and they threw lots of the old wooden potato-masher grenades. But the strings had slipped out of their hands or broke. I held the string and threw them back. At one point, I had to jack rounds in the .45 using ulna and radius. It seemed like forever before Tucker and Speer parted the grass and looked at me. At some point I put my belt around my right arm for a tourniquet but realized I wasn't bleeding anymore. It was years later that I was told it was the HQ of 27th NVA Regt that I had ended up on. By the time Tucker and Speer got to me, no NVA remained. I have no grasp of time that day. It was an eternity where I was. I caught shrapnel in army books in my left trouser pocket, in my wrist watch, in my left palm. Prior to leaving the knoll, I saw at least one chopper hit with RPG. I was hit everywhere but the chest ... machine guns, small arms, RPG, grenades.... I recall being on the USHP *Sanctuary* triage deck waiting to go to the OR. They took everyone but me and the dead. I sat up and asked two men if they were going to operate or not. One man was ship chaplain; the other was ship captain.

Starr lay on the knoll and somehow Tucker and Speer got to him and carried him back to the company defensive position. He was in bad shape and toe-tagged, as no one thought he would survive. He was medevacked by Dustoff 708, whose air commander was Captain David Tousignant. Tousignant adds his slant on that day's events:

> We were the 237th Medical Detachment—a.k.a. DMZ Dustoff. We deployed as a unit from Fort Meade in 1968. So we had brand-new aircraft and their tail numbers were sequential until we started getting shot up and got replacements. We didn't lose any ships during this particular time.
>
> During that particular day our primary support mission in that area was to the 1st Brigade 5th Mech. We were their dedicated air medical evacuation. We would have had that responsibility and even though the 101st came in, we would still have been involved in support of the Mech. Their medical evacuation group was called Eagle Dustoff and we worked with them a lot. My flight school roommate flew for them. We did missions together a lot and I'm sure at that point we supported each other. Normally we would fly three or four hours a day. But on the 10th of November I flew almost 8 hours, on the 11th I didn't fly at all, and the 12th—that was the big day—I flew 12.2 hours. And on the 13th—5.5 hours. By that time, I was a captain and I was getting ready to DEROS. I was at that time the most experienced pilot we had and I knew about the Fulton Square mission because we had been warned about it because we were the primary evacuation support for them. As the operations commander, I probably put myself there. That day I believe we had two medevac ships on duty. We operated out of Camp Evans at that time with the 18th Surgical and when we got to country we were in Quang Tri, but in 1969 we were in Camp Evans

again when they relocated at the end of my tour back to Quang Tri. We had a ship on site there and we had two more on standby down at Evans. There wasn't a lot of area up there to park at the 5th and you were always waiting for a phone call. I was the primary that day up there at Quang Tri—the primary aircraft.

It was a struggle all day to get into what was not only an intense but a prolonged action. As background on medical evacuation—you get a call that someone is wounded and a ground person, either a platoon leader or a company commander—or even a medic—would prioritize whether it was an urgent, intermediate or routine wound. If it was urgent you would need to get them out within an hour. Intermediate was within six hours and routine would be sometime that day. Routine would be slight burns, fevers, small injuries, cuts, bruises and all those silly little things. If you got the urgent call like that day, you jumped off quickly. The thing that I remember was that you know someone is wounded and you know what the wound is—a gunshot wound or a grenade blast, say. You don't necessarily know how or exactly what happened. Once we got them on board, we don't know the patient, of course, and we treat them in-flight. You triage them—you know you have a burn or a head wound, say—and there are certain facilities that treat certain types of injuries and also certain treatments you administer en route. The three facilities we had to use during this operation were the Quang Tri Surgical Hospital, and the hospital ships—*Repose* and *Sanctuary*—that were offshore on the DMZ. Once you got to the medical facility, that was it—you handed them off and you never knew. With Starr—I just knew his call sign, which was Pig-6—because we had worked all day with him getting his guys out while he stayed to the bitter end. That was the kind of person he was—he took his men ahead of him. When I finally got him on board, that's the only connection I had with anyone that day. We just spent the whole day trying to get in and out of that hill trying to keep ourselves from being killed and trying to get as many out as we could. It was just one of those crazy days where it was just one thing after another—all bad.

We came in the back door. Once I got Starr on the hospital ship, I never knew what happened to him. There was no way of tracing that. That's how it was. You put your life on the line to save someone and you never know how it turns out. That was one of those missing parts of our mission.

Below is a transcript of an email Tousignant sent to Bill Starr:

Pig 6, this is Dustoff 708, over.

I just looked up my flight records for NOV 69. Yeah, I still have all that s—t. I flew 7.9 hrs. on 10NOV, none on 11NOV, 12.2 hrs. on 12NOV, and 5.5 on 13NOV. You guys were in hell, and I was doing what we did best, save warriors lives! You have been the subject of one of my best combat stories for 47 years. One, because you refused to leave the site until all of your men were safe, two because when we finally got you on board I reminded our medic that we do not have room now for a KIA, but most famously, for what you said to me when I had my crew chief mike you up, so I could ask you if there was anything you NEEDED. Do you remember your response? It was the best line ever delivered, by far, by a patient on my ship. [Rough translation, "I could use a woman and a shot of whiskey."] Bill, I am so glad you are alive, because we never knew the disposition of those we risked our lives to save. You are closure in a big way. I have led an interesting and blessed life, and I pray yours is as well. Let's talk when you feel it's right.

[signed] Dave Tousignant a.k.a. "Dustoff 708"

**Starr's response.**

THANK YOU for all you did in that helicopter of yours! Countless lives were saved thanks to you. I understand that I was toe-tagged before the flight ... but I never lost consciousness, even when [my] heart rate was undetectable.

[signed] Bill Starr

In the late summer of 2017, Starr and Tousignant would meet and spend a great day together talking about their lives going forward after Vietnam. Starr would eventually receive a DSC for his actions. For the record, the NVA had put a price on his head. In Starr's own words again, he spoke of it:

> I was flown to the rear, I think A-4, but maybe C-2, in October '69 because the Corps CG, LTG Melvin Zais, had come to tell me that the NVA [monitored] radio transmissions had revealed that NVA had a major price on my head and were sending thousands of NVA across DMZ to kill me and my men. Later broadcasts by Hanoi Hanna confirmed this.

A portion of Captain Starr's DSC Citation reads as follows:

> The President of the United States takes pleasure in presenting the Distinguished Service Cross to William J. Starr, Captain (Infantry), U.S. Army, for extraordinary heroism in connection with military operations involving conflict with an armed hostile force in the Republic of Vietnam, while serving with Company C, 1st Battalion, 62st Infantry, 1st Brigade, 5th Infantry (Mechanized). Captain Starr distinguished himself while commanding a mechanized infantry company during a battalion sized reconnaissance-in-force operation just south of the Demilitarized Zone in northern I Corps Tactical Zone. As the friendly force was sweeping through a valley near the village of Cam Lo, it became engaged in fighting with elements of the 27th North Vietnamese Army Regiment. In the initial movement to contact, the First Platoon of Captain Starr's company was surrounded by enemy troops and pinned down by a heavy concentration of rocket propelled grenades and automatic weapons fire. Captain Starr quickly assembled a reaction force and led it in a rapid counter assault over some hundred meters of terrain swept by grenade and small arms fire. As he attempted to maneuver his relief force on the flank of the enemy's fortified gun emplacements, Captain Starr and his men were suddenly caught in an ambush of enemy grenades. When one grenade landed in the foxhole in which he and several comrades took cover, Captain Starr immediately scooped up the explosive device and attempted to throw it away, but before he could get the grenade off, the device exploded, severing his hand and part of his arm. Captain Starr's body absorbed the entire force of the blast, preventing any injury to the men who were with him. Captain Starr's extraordinary heroism and devotion to duty were in keeping with the highest traditions of the military service and reflect great credit upon himself, his unit, and the United States Army.

Sp4 Ron Gibson:

> When we did come back out [to Hill 162], we helicoptered out. We came back similar to the previous position, maybe around this crest and a platoon from the 1-61 was already trapped down at the bottom. We were being sniped at along that ridge all morning and the afternoon. I remember there was five of us trying to get down in the foxhole below the bullets and I was all pins and needles, which I eventually got sorted out. It was a very shallow hole and dug into the hill near the top. Eventually, we got out and dug a better position. They were shooting with heavy calibers across at us and sniping too. I saw a blade of grass near my right temple go down. I think there were possibly three or more attempts to bring out the platoon that was trapped, but none was successful. Tucker, the machine gunner, got down to the bottom once, within a hundred feet, but ran out of ammo. At one point, a Chicom went off while I was squatting down and I got blown up and I flew through the air. When I landed, I came down hard. I had a large diameter circle on my back where the blood had popped through the pores and you could tell it was a concussion wound, but I didn't have any shrapnel. I still have a scar from that in the middle of my back.

Among the men who came to Captain Starr's rescue were Thomas Tucker, Robert Towery and Speer. Seeing the company commander down and alone on that nearby knoll, they jumped into action and proceeded to secure their captain for a possible medevac.

**Citation—Bronze Star/V**

> Specialist Thomas Tucker distinguished himself by valorous actions on 12 November 1969 while serving as a squad leader in the Third Platoon of Company C, 1st Battalion (Mechanized), 61st Infantry during a sweep and clear operation in the northernmost portion of South Vietnam. That

afternoon a reinforced company-sized force of NVA Regulars initiated a fierce attack on Company C's dismounted maneuver elements as they passed below a thickly wooded ridge. When the First Platoon became encircled by the hostile force, the Second Platoon and Third Platoons made two assaults on the hill separating them from their entrapped sister platoon. Specialist Tucker, in a third attempt to reach the entrapped platoon, charged forward carrying an M-60 machine-gun and with devastating fire secured the frontal area of assault singlehandedly, enabling one of his comrades to extract one wounded member of their force. He also neutralized several enemy bunkers, and enabled his platoon to withdraw to safety. Specialist Tucker's gallantry was in keeping with the highest traditions of the military service and reflects great credit upon himself, his unit, and the United States Army.

**Citation—Arcom/V**

Specialist Four Robert Towery distinguished himself by valorous actions on 12 November 1969 while serving as a rifleman with Company C, 1st Battalion (Mechanized), 61st Infantry during a sweep and clear operation near Cam Lo. Specialist Towery was attached to an element led by his company commander when they came under heavy small arms and automatic weapons fire from a concealed bunker. In the process of assaulting the bunker, the company commander was seriously wounded by grenades. Specialist Towery, with complete disregard for his own safety, exposed himself to the enemy fire in order to lay down a base of fire, which would allow for the evacuation of the wounded and the retreat of the remainder of the unit to a safer place. Continuous accurate fire and movement finally enabled Specialist Towery to destroy the bunker complex. Through his heroic actions the mission was carried to a successful conclusion. Specialist Towery's gallantry was in keeping with the highest traditions of the military service and reflects great credit upon himself, his unit, and the United States Army.

Meanwhile, after Starr was medevacked, Charlie Company made multiple assaults in attempts to free the first platoon. Again and again they tried—and repeatedly they were driven back by superior numbers. It was evident now they were up against possibly three reinforced battalions of seasoned hardcore NVA. Some of those attempted assaults are described in the individual citations.

**Citation—Bronze Star/V**

Sergeant Robert Smith distinguished himself by valorous actions on 12 November 1969 while serving as a squad leader with Company C, 1st Battalion, 61st Infantry, during a sweep and clear operation near Cam Lo. That day, a well-equipped and deeply entrenched company-size force of North Vietnamese Army Regulars initiated a fierce attack on Company C's dismounted maneuver elements. The intense fire caused the platoon elements to be separated and pinned down. In retaliation, Sergeant Smith's platoon organized an assault on the entrenched enemy force in order to free one of the entrapped platoons. Armed with his M-16 rifle, Sergeant Smith charged forward, spraying heavy suppressive fire as he led his squad on the assault. Disregarding his personal safety, he exposed himself repeatedly to the intense hostile fire in order to direct his squad's fire until the enemy positions had been neutralized. His professional acumen and adept leadership contributed immensely to the success of the mission. Sergeant Smith's gallantry was in keeping with the highest traditions of the military service and reflects great credit upon himself, his unit, and the United States Army.

**Citation—Bronze Star/V**

Staff Sargent Timothy Thornton distinguished himself by valorous actions on 12 November 1969 as a Platoon Sergeant with Company C, 1st Battalion (Mechanized), 61st Infantry during a sweep and clear operation in the northernmost portion of South Vietnam. While maneuvering through a thickly vegetated draw, elements of his platoon suddenly became pinned down by intense enemy small arms fire from an estimated company-size force of NVA Regulars who were effectively camouflaged by natural cover. Commanding the balance of the platoon, SSG Thornton valiantly led his men on two determined assaults of the enemy positions, attempting to extract the entrapped elements of his platoon. Disregarding his personal safety, he charged forward, hurling grenades in a gallant effort, which considerably neutralized the well-entrenched NVA bunker complex. Although the head-on daylight assault was abandoned, a night extraction proved successful. SSG Thornton's courageous actions and exemplary leadership, while in conflict with a highly motivated and numerically superior enemy force, were in keeping with the highest traditions of the military service and reflect great credit upon himself, his unit, and the United States Army.

**Citation—Bronze Star/V**

Sergeant (then Private First Class) James Morgan distinguished himself by valorous actions on 12 November 1969 while serving as a team leader with Company C, 1st Battalion (Mechanized), 61st Infantry during a sweep and clear mission in the northernmost portion of South Vietnam. That day a well-equipped and deeply entrenched force of NVA Regulars initiated a fierce attack on Company C's dismounted maneuver elements as they passed below a thickly wooded ridge, causing the platoon elements to be separated and pinned down. Acting as a reactionary force, Sergeant Morgan's platoon organized an assault on the entrenched enemy in order to free the entrapped platoons. Armed with his M-16 rifle, Sergeant Morgan charged forward, exposing himself to the enemy fire in order to direct accurate fire into the enemy positions. Deploying his team in the most advantageous manner, he accomplished his mission with a minimum number of friendly casualties. Sergeant Morgan's gallantry was in keeping with the highest traditions of the military service and reflects great credit upon himself, his unit, and the United States Army.

**Citation—Bronze Star/V**

Private First Class Terry Reiner distinguished himself by valorous actions on 12 November 1969, while serving as a team leader with Company C, 1st Battalion (Mechanized), 61st Infantry during a sweep and clear operation in the northernmost portion of South Vietnam. That day a well-equipped and deeply entrenched company-size force of NVA Regulars initiated a fierce attack on Company C, which caused one of the platoons to become separated and pinned down. In retaliation PFC Reiner's platoon organized an assault on the entrenched enemy force in order to free the entrapped platoon. Armed with his M-16 rifle, PFC Reiner led his comrades in an aggressive manner, neutralizing several enemy bunkers. His intense fire and professional leadership enabled the entrapped platoon to withdraw safely and proved instrumental in securing a landing zone for safe evacuation of all wounded personnel. PFC Reiner's gallantry was in keeping with the highest traditions of the military service and reflects great credit upon himself, his unit, and the United States Army.

**Citation—Bronze Star/V**

Sergeant Lester Lawson distinguished himself by valorous actions on 12 November 1969, while serving as a team leader with Company C, 1st Battalion, 61st Infantry during a sweep and clear operation in the northernmost portion of South Vietnam. That day, a well-equipped and deeply entrenched company-size force of NVA Regulars initiated a fierce attack on Company C as they passed below a thickly wooded ridge, which caused the platoon elements to be separated and effectively pinned down. Acting as a reactionary force, Sergeant Lawson's platoon organized an assault on the entrenched enemy in order to free the entrapped elements. Armed with his machine gun, he charged forward, spraying accurate fire as he led his team in the assault. Disregarding his personal safety, he exposed himself to the enemy fire in order to draw fire toward himself, so he could spot the enemy positions and silence them. His accurate fire neutralized several enemy positions. Sergeant Lawson's gallantry was in keeping with the highest traditions of the military service and reflects great credit upon himself, his unit, and the United States Army.

**Citation—Bronze Star/V**

Specialist James Cooper distinguished himself by valorous actions on 12 November 1969 while serving as a machine-gunner with Company C, 1st Battalion (Mechanized), 61st Infantry during a sweep and clear operation in the northernmost portion of South Vietnam. That day a well-equipped and deeply entrenched force of NVA Regulars initiated a fierce attack on Company C's dismounted maneuver elements as they passed below on a thickly wooded ridge. The Second and

Third Platoons made two determined assaults on the hill separating them from the encircled First Platoon, but both proved fruitless against the enemy's intense fire. On a third attempt to reach the entrapped platoon, Specialist Cooper charged forward carrying his M-60 machine gun. With devastating fire he secured the frontal area of the assault singlehandedly, exposing himself to the enemy fire. Although his aggressiveness and courage did not bring about the extraction of the besieged platoon at this time, he personally neutralized several enemy bunkers and enabled his platoon to withdraw to safety. Specialist Cooper's gallantry was in keeping the highest traditions of the military service and reflects great credit upon himself, his unit, and the United States Army.

Back on the battalion defensive perimeter, the NVA continued to lay small arms and automatic weapons fire on the 1-61 troopers. They were no match for the 50-caliber machine guns and were silenced on several occasions. Sp4 Richard Zelinski repelled one of the larger indirect and small arms assaults on the perimeter with effective machine-gun fire.

**Sp4 Richard Zelinski—Citation—Arcom/V**

Specialist Richard Zelinski distinguished himself by valorous actions on 12 November 1969, while serving as a machine-gunner in Company C, 1st Battalion (Mechanized), 61st Infantry during a sweep and clear operation in the northernmost portion of South Vietnam. That day a well-equipped and deeply entrenched company-size element of NVA Regulars initiated a fierce attack on Company C as they passed below a thickly wooded ridge. The element to which Specialist Zelinski was attached received the brunt of the mortar rounds. Disregarding his personal safety, Specialist Zelinski exposed himself to the hostile mortar fire and was able to locate the enemy positions. Specialist Zelinski put out heavy suppressive fire with his .50 caliber machine gun, silencing the enemy mortar positions. Specialist Zelinski's gallantry was in keeping with the highest traditions of the military service and reflects great credit upon himself, his unit, and the United States Army.

Sergeant Mike McGraw, a member of Charlie Company's first platoon, was spared being in the same predicament as some of his first platoon buddies by the simple luck of his position in the back of the patrol. His view of the cut-off Charlie Company men was from a different angle. Early that morning, when the platoon sweeps were initiated down into those three draws, his squad was third in line in the dismounted patrol. From his location, he could see the draws rise back up and converge on a piece of ground that would prove to be an enemy bunker complex. The first two squads dropped down into the ravine—with the lead squad headed by Sergeant Larry Mosher. Lieutenant Matteffs was somewhere near the front of the column. Sgt. McGraw's squad, led by Sergeant Roger Schaufel, waited for the column to space out as they worked down the incline. While they were waiting to move, a hail of automatic gunfire erupted below. Immediately, McGraw sighted dozens of NVA frantically running across the high ground on the other side of the ravine—no more than a hundred yards away. Some of McGraw's squad began firing at the NVA but others held fire, as they were unable to see the location of the rest of the first platoon, obviously pinned down below. The enemy automatic fire was intense and McGraw estimated the force directly to his front at about one hundred. Eventually Schaufel and his squad found cover and returned fire. It was evident though that those two squads were cut off in the ravine. The memory of those first few moments by McGraw and others reflected that most of the enemy personnel fleeing from their exposed position across the ravine were very tall—much taller in stature than Vietnamese men. It was obvious that there was an element of Chinese infused into the NVA forces—involved both as fighters and advisors. Some of McGraw's memories of that day, together with the days leading up to and after that day, are as follows.

## Sgt. Michael McGraw:

Just before the initial point of contact, we had come up from a draw where we were totally tangled up in this real heavy underbrush but we were in there because that's where they were finding most of the tunnels and bunkers. Leading up to that day we had been finding weapons, ammunition—everything. Every day we were finding more and more of that. Larry Mosher—as I heard it from Ray Melarczik—walked down the hill with his squad and that's when they were ambushed. We really surprised them and there were NVA running everywhere when my squad got there across a little finger of land. Some of us fired but others weren't sure where the rest of the platoon was, but there were mostly NVA without helmets on. Some guys said they saw pretty tall guys—like they were Chinese. The NVA that I saw—quite a few were pretty tall. I think we either caught them just ready to move out or trying to set up for a bigger ambush than what occurred. I wasn't down in the draw but there must have been fifty to one hundred guys [NVA] from all the fire that was going off. Even after the first one or two runs of the Cobras, the fire remained very heavy. It was a well-defended bunker complex. They were still running commo wire. It looked like it was just laid out on the ground to that bunker complex along the fingers of land. Ray Melarczik had told us that Mosher's body had not been recovered. [Recovered by Sgt. Paradis of the 1/502/101st Abn on November 14th.]

I remember Stan Samulak and I believe he might have been a radio operator. He was in Ray Melarczik's and Ken Hahn's squad—who I came with from Grand Rapids—and Jerry Cobb, who was from Tennessee. There was also a black guy but I can't remember his name. They were all down in the draw.

Elmer, the Kit Carson scout, jumped right into a hole—as I heard it—with a bunch of NVA one time—totally fearless. The one thing I can remember about him was when we were out there in that area in August he would find water for us and would know right where the springs were mainly because he was an NVA originally—but was a good scout.

Bill Pierpont was in the same cycle as Lieutenant Ayers—they were very close. Bill was from a little town—White Pines—up in the U.P. of Michigan. They were both out of college and just finished their officer's training that they went through together. Pierpont went through some additional training—ranger or something—and showed up a little later. His platoon—I think it was the second platoon, because of the order of march—but they ended up on our southern flank. There were three assaults down into the valley—and I don't know if he got killed during one of those.

It was pretty chaotic the first half hour from the top of the hill down into the draw. We took out a machine gun nest at the top of the hill. They were throwing grenades at us and Starr threw one of those back and that's how he lost his arm. He and everybody hit the dirt and one of his guys—maybe the RTO or somebody—pulled him down the hill. I remember three helicopters going down before nighttime—or maybe even four. So, it was pretty hot. They had a 51-caliber emplacement somewhere down there and a lot of RPG and RPD fire, so when they medevacked Starr out it was a pretty hot LZ. I remember them landing down the hill and using the hill for protection.

I remember Osteen [1/5th brigade commander] came in on his helicopter and sometime before dark Warne [Starr's replacement] came in to take over the company. We were assigned the east side of the perimeter and we didn't have anything to dig in with. I think third platoon was to our left and then second platoon—I am presuming I was to the north side of the perimeter. As I remember, there were quite a few draws—at least three—and they converged on each other, and that's where this major bunker complex was.

I know we did a listening point at some time before that day down that hill—on 162—and the position we sat in was an old 51-caliber hole with a pedestal in it but then it was quiet. That was kind of funny because leading up to that day, the 1-11th and our unit were finding so much stuff along those ridge lines and in bunkers after artillery and airstrikes and we knew there were a lot of [NVA] personnel in the area. When we went anywhere west of Cam Lo in those hills and valleys—we knew they were there all the time.

[McGraw talking on Captain Blunt:] There were two occasions that day where he [Blunt] took out a machine gun nest and then [the day before] there was another ambush that he broke up with his squads around the backside and on that hill. He knew the area well enough to get the NVA from behind at least two or three times while we were being harassed by mortars. His experience was definitely there.

Late in the afternoon, the entrapped platoon was still stranded and Lt. Colonel Swaren called on Captain Blunt to attempt a rescue just after dark. Captain Stanley Blunt, the D/ 1-11 commanding officer—who also had an NVA price on his head—formed an all-volunteer mission comprised of the 2nd platoon members. But he refused to start until midnight, knowing that if the NVA were given a little time they would pull out after dark. It was obvious that most of the enemy bunkers had been located—albeit the hard way—and it was obvious at least to him that the NVA's only remaining tactic was organized retreat.

In the late afternoon, Lt. Gregory Saxton and five other volunteers dropped off a ridgeline searching for enemy positions on the side hill that would aid in getting information that would help Blunt establish a clear route for his rescue patrol. They immediately came under fire and Saxton, along with Sp4 David Williams, PFC David Goertz, PFC Larry Shores, and PFC Willy Stillwell, distinguished themselves valorously, by assaulting enemy bunkers, running to the aid of fellow wounded soldiers and then carrying them to safety. In the spirit of "no man left behind," Goertz and others went back for the fatally wounded. The names of the Delta men who died were PFC Ronald Lauderdale, Sp4 Gumesindo De La Rosa, and PFC Bruce Walters.

**Citation—Bronze Star/V**

Lieutenant Gregory Saxton distinguished himself by valorous actions on 12 November 1969 as a platoon leader with Company D, 1st Battalion, 11th Infantry during a search and clear operation near Con Thien. While maneuvering toward a well-entrenched NVA position, Lieutenant Saxton's platoon came under intense hostile fire and received several casualties. One of the casualties was helplessly exposed to the enemy fire. With complete disregard for his own safety, Lieutenant Saxton braved the enemy fire and maneuvered toward the exposed man, picked him up, and carried him forty meters back through the hail of enemy bullets to his platoon's defensive perimeter. As a result of the action, a critically wounded man's life was saved. Lieutenant Saxton's bravery and devotion to duty were in keeping with the highest traditions of the military service and reflect great credit upon himself, his unit, and the United States Army.

**Citation—Bronze Star/V**

Specialist Four David Williams distinguished himself by valorous actions on 12 November 1969 as a rifleman with Company D, 1st Battalion, 11th Infantry on a search and clear operation near Con Thien. Specialist Williams' platoon was moving down a ridgeline searching for suspected enemy positions when it came under heavy hostile fire, sustained several casualties, and was ordered to withdraw from its exposed position back to the relative security of the ridgeline. Specialist Williams and his squad leader remained behind when they noticed a seriously wounded comrade fall directly in the line of the enemy fire. Realizing the need for help in rescuing the wounded man, Specialist Williams' squad leader crawled back up the ridgeline while Specialist Williams remained behind to protect his wounded comrade. When his squad leader returned with help, Specialist Williams began carrying his wounded comrade up the ridgeline while the other three men provided protective fire against the enemy. Moving up the ridge, he came under intense enemy fire but relentlessly continued forward until he reached the secured area. As a result of his actions, the life of a seriously wounded soldier was saved. Specialist Williams' personal bravery and devotion to duty were in keeping with the highest traditions of the military service and reflect great credit upon himself, his unit, and the United States Army.

**Citation—Arcom/V**

Private First Class David Goertz distinguished himself by valorous actions while serving as a rifleman with Company D, 1st Battalion, 11th Infantry during a search and clear operation on 12 November 1969 in the Republic of Vietnam. The platoon was moving down a ridgeline searching for suspected enemy positions when they came under heavy enemy fire and sustained several casualties. The platoon leader ordered the platoon to withdraw from their exposed position to a small hill. Upon reaching the hill, PFC Goertz noticed his squad leader attempting to carry the body of a fatally wounded comrade up a hill. With complete disregard for his own safety, PFC Goertz braved the intense hostile fire and moved down the hill toward his squad leader. Upon reaching him, he assisted in carrying the stricken comrade up the hill through the enemy fire. Although the enemy intensified their fire, PFC Goertz and his squad leader continued up the hill until they reached a secure area at the top. As a result of his selfless efforts the fatally wounded soldier was recovered. PFC Goertz' courageous actions were in keeping with the highest traditions of the military service and reflect great credit upon himself, his unit, and the United States Army.

**Citation—Bronze Star/V**

Private First Class Larry Shores distinguished himself by valorous actions on 12 November 1969 while serving as a rifleman for Company D, 1st Battalion, 11th Infantry during a search and clear operation near Con Thien, Republic of Vietnam. PFC Shores' platoon was moving down a ridgeline searching for suspected enemy positions when they came under intense enemy small arms fire that inflicted numerous casualties on the unit. PFC Shores noticed a wounded comrade lying hopelessly exposed to the intense hostile fire at the bottom of a ravine. With complete disregard for his own personal safety, PFC Shores went to the aid of the stricken soldier. Ignoring the enemy rounds that were striking near him, PFC Shores picked up the wounded man and carried him on his shoulders for seventy-five meters through the hostile fire to a secured area. As a result of PFC Shores' courageous actions under intense hostile fire, a critically wounded soldier's life was saved. PFC Shores' personal bravery and devotion to duty were in keeping with the highest traditions of the military service and reflect great credit upon himself, his unit, and the United States Army.

Captain Robert Arrington of the 220th RAC. He was the aerial observer on 12 Nov 1969. Awarded the DFC (courtesy catkillers.org).

**Citation—Bronze Star/V**

Private Willie Stillwell distinguished himself by valorous actions on 12 November 1969 while serving as a rifleman for Company D, 1st Battalion, 11th Infantry on a search and clear mission near Con Thien. When his company became engaged in a fierce battle with a well-entrenched NVA force, Private Stillwell's platoon received several casualties. Ignoring the deadly hostile fire, Private Stillwell moved forward to aid his wounded comrades. Upon reaching the first wounded man, he pulled him through the enemy fire to a position of safety. Private Stillwell then maneuvered back through the hostile fire to aid the remaining wounded men. Through his untiring efforts three additional lives were saved. Private Stillwell's personal bravery and devotion to duty were in keeping with the highest traditions of the military service and reflect great credit upon himself, his unit, and the United States Army.

**Citation—Bronze Star/V**

Sergeant Dan Bozek distinguished himself by valorous actions on 12 November 1969 as a squad leader with Company D, 1st Battalion, 11th Infantry on a search and clear operation near Con Thien. Sergeant Bozek's platoon was moving down a ridgeline searching for suspected enemy positions when they came under heavy fire, and sustained several casualties. The platoon was ordered to withdraw from its exposed position back to the relative security of the ridgeline. Sergeant Bozek and one of his squad members remained behind when they saw a wounded comrade fall directly in the line of enemy fire. Sergeant Bozek attempted to crawl to the aid of the wounded man but was forced back by the intense hostile fire. He returned with two volunteers and, under heavy fire, reached the wounded man. As the wounded man was being extracted from the area, Sergeant Bozek and a comrade remained behind to provide covering fire. An intense barrage of hostile fire fatally wounded Sergeant Bozek's comrade. Refusing to leave without his companion's body, Sergeant Bozek again braved the hostile fire and secured his comrade's body and dragged him up the ridgeline to the secured area. As the result of the action, the life of a seriously wounded man was saved and the body of a soldier was recovered. Sergeant Bozek's extraordinary heroism in close combat against a numerically superior enemy force was in keeping with the highest traditions of the military service and reflects great credit upon himself, his unit, and the United States Army.

During the day, multiple unsuccessful attempts were made to extract Charlie Company's first platoon from the tangle of elephant grass on the valley floor where they were huddled. Two choppers, only smoldering piles of wreckage now, and a third at a short distance lay on the floor of "Helicopter Valley" next to that deep elephant grass where the first platoon formed a perimeter and waited. A fourth Slick was also shot down and made it several clicks away before coming down. Two other gunships were also hit and damaged. The culprit for all these losses was an NVA 51-caliber antiaircraft gun that was entrenched on one of the side ridges on the approach to the ravine and the LZ.

Late in the afternoon, Lancer 28 arrived on the scene. The air commander was Chief Warrant Officer Third Class David "Doc" Smith. His crew was composed of crew chief Sp5 Bruce Nesmith, door gunner PFC Robert Duesenberry, and "Peter Pilot" Warrant Officer Powers. They saw the three helicopters that had been shot down, two of which—the charred remains of a Slick and a Loach—lay at the bottom of the draw where Charlie Company's first platoon was still surrounded. Sergeant Larry Mosher's body was still lying facedown near the still smoldering chopper wreckage. The chopper crews and the rest of the platoon—numbering 22 now—were still huddled in a stand of elephant grass waiting for what they perceived was the inevitable—a final sapper assault. Many were unarmed, those who had weapons were nearly out of ammunition, and everyone was wounded to some extent. Among the worst were Stan Samulak, whose foot was severely damaged, and the Loach pilot First Lieutenant Phillip Miller, whose back was injured and his leg severely lacerated. As Doc Smith circled at altitude with two Cobra gunships and several other Slicks, he assessed the terrain and the location of the 51-caliber NVA antiaircraft gun that had already taken out four helicopters and shot up several Cobra gunships. The 51 had a clear and level angle of fire with perfect natural cover on the side of the ravine, and could not be hit by return fire at that angle. All the previous extraction

**1Lt Carl Drechsel, aerial reconnaissance pilot, at the 220th RAC. Drechsel relieved Captain Robert Arrington on 12 Nov 1969 while he refueled his Cessna observation plane (courtesy catkillers.org).**

attempts the choppers made had been low and fast, and all paid the price dished out by the 51, as they passed directly in front of the gun position.

After consultation with his crew, Doc decided to drop into the LZ from directly above, thus avoiding the deadly low approach. Because they were now in defilade cover from the 51 and were approaching at a new and different angle, the NVA gunner had initial trouble drawing a bead on the fast-dropping Huey, and the tracers missed harmlessly but could still be seen passing close in front of the nose of the Huey. On the other hand, Nesmith had a clear angle over the 51's gun-shield and took out the crew with several bursts of fire. This action would be written up in his DFC citation. Soon, they began receiving automatic small-arms fire from a half-dozen other positions, making it evident it was too hot to attempt the extraction. It was now well past dusk and Lancer 28 was relieved of their mission for the day and returned to Charlie-Two for the night. For their actions, Nesmith, Smith and Powers received the Distinguished Flying Cross and Bob Duesenberry received the Air Medal with Valor. Nesmith recalls the action:

> I served one and a half tours over there. I got there on the 18th of February 1969 and returned on the 25th of April 1970. I spent the entire tour with the same unit—the 158th Aviation Battalion. Our call-sign was Lancers and we were attached to the 101st Airborne. We were based out of Camp Evans and we had a remote location in Quang Tri where we operated out of when we were up that way. There was a platoon always up there and we rotated duty through the battalion. We started out up there supporting the Marines and then the 5th Mech after the Marines pulled out. We had a four-man crew. The Air Commander was Warrant Officer David "Doc" Smith and we were together back in the States before we ever got over to Vietnam. The Peter Pilot was a guy named Powers, and I don't remember his first name. The door gunner was Bob Duesenberry—a

> Sp4 that moved over out of an infantry unit to be a door gunner. He was a cook before he became a door gunner. He volunteered to be a door gunner to get away from being a cook. Doc Smith, I heard—pretty much through the grapevine—in 1994 he got himself a motorcycle and [was] killed in an accident, running into a bridge abutment. He was a real good guy. I was together with him the whole time in Colorado and overseas.
>
> As far as I know, we were not involved on the 11th. We got involved on the afternoon of the 12th. We were with the Special Forces folks that morning. We were returning that afternoon and we heard over the radio on the way back that some helicopters had been shot down to the west—just south of the DMZ—going more for curiosity sake than anything else. We hung around the area a while and there was a whole swarm of aircraft flying around there. We heard there was a hunter/killer team or something that was engaged in an action in the foothills and a Loach got shot down. And there was a Cobra that got shot down as well. Then there were a couple of Slicks that tried to put an infantry team in to pull them out of there and they both got shot down too. And we heard that there were 22 aviation personnel and infantry personnel all balled up there in one area. I guess we surged around out there for a half hour or so and it was getting really dusky dark and the CFC aircraft put out a call asking for volunteers to go in there and attempt a medevac. Doc asked all of us if we wanted to volunteer and we decided we would go ahead in. Everybody else that had gone in low and fast just trying to get in right at the hilltop area, and we decided to make a different approach and come in high and slow, and really I guess that kept us alive. It turned out that the NVA had an antiaircraft gun in there and they had a helicopter trap set up. If you came in low you highlighted against the setting sun so they had perfect visibility and pretty much a level shot. We came high and slow and messed up their aim and he missed us when he opened fire. The 51-caliber antiaircraft gun was less than a hundred yards from us when he opened up and we messed up his aim. I returned fire and got on him and was bouncing rounds off his shield that kept him busy and it confused him just enough that he never did pull back into us before we got away. The tracers went over and under our aircraft. We were so close that the supporting gunships couldn't provide support fire because their fire would have gotten us too. We made it out of there without taking a single hit. We were under fire from the antiaircraft gun and from AKs. That whole hillside kind of lit up on us. I wound up getting the Distinguished Flying Cross for my shooting. We never did get close enough to do anything, though, and had to break off and leave. We went back to Quang Tri and pretty much settled in for the night.

A portion of Nesmith's citation reads:

> Specialist Nesmith distinguished himself by serving as a crew-chief of a UH-1H of Co B (assault helicopter) 158th Aviation Battalion (Airmobile) in Northern I Corp, Republic of Vietnam. The crew volunteered to assist in a medical evacuation of the crew of another helicopter shot down earlier in the day. While the pilots were landing, they came under small arms fire and heavy automatic weapons fire. Although terrain features and the proximity of friendly troops prevented gunships from placing accurate suppressive fire on the North Vietnamese Army machine-gun position, the crew continued to approach. Specialist Nesmith sighted and took under fire with his M-60 machine gun, an enemy 51-caliber gunner who was beginning to fire upon his helicopter. His suppressive fire gave the pilots time to abort the approach and at the same time, silenced the enemy gun position.

Throughout the day, the aerial assets were controlled by Captain Robert Arrington from his single engine O-1 Cessna aircraft. The pilots of the 220 RAC flew low-level reconnaissance missions as aerial observers and marked targets for jet fighters and bombers as well as Spooky mini-gunships and Cobra attack helicopters. They flew with their windows open so that they could readily hear the sounds of battle below and fired 2½-inch white phosphorus rockets to mark enemy positions. Their sights were nothing but a grease pencil cross drawn on the Plexiglas windshield in front of them. They flew at altitudes of 50 to 100 feet, which Arrington and his counterparts felt was much safer than flying at the mandatory minimum of one thousand feet, simply because the enemy antiaircraft gunners had only a second or two to fire on him as he whisked over their positions at treetop level rather than being able to track him and zero in with machine-gun fire for twenty seconds or more. Arrington, along with his "back seat" passenger, Sp4 Phillip Tarr, orchestrated medevacs and resupply helicopters, Cobra gunships, and F-4 or A-4 interceptors and dive bombers, as well as artillery and illumination when dusk had arrived. The latter was the job of the "back seat." For his action, Arrington received the Distinguished Flying Cross. His citations, his own memories, and two witness statements, one by Sp4 Tarr and the other by First Lieutenant Carl Drechsel, his relief while he refueled his Cessna, tell the story with detail and suspense:

Captain Robert Arrington:

We flew in a different plane every day and I was stationed in Phu Bai. I went over unassigned and I reported to a replacement center over there. I looked at the bulletin board every day and one day it said I was assigned to fly out of Da Nang. When I got to Da Nang I was told there were two groups—the headquarters group in Da Nang and another group further north, and they said, "You're going north to Phu Bai." I was assigned to one of three platoons, and the first three to four months I flew mostly in the Ashau Valley. The new guys always got the mortar watch at night. Then they moved me further north, up to Dong Ha, which—unless you are in the field—is as far north as you can go if you're a pilot. Our group was trained by air force people to become forward air controllers. As an army pilot, you didn't have that expertise. We were the only unit that flew the DMZ every day. We were trained to work with the Dong Ha Direct Air Support Center and they would give us all the radio frequencies for a particular mission. They would have contact with F-4s and if we couldn't get them we would get A-4s from the carriers—not coming from the carriers but ones that were returning to the carrier and had not expended all of their munitions. They were Marine or Navy pilots and would be coming back from somewhere—maybe Laos. These guys were high-altitude dive bombers.

The normal routine was to take off from Phu Bai, fly up to Dong Ha and land. This would be early in the morning. We would refuel, pick up a back seat and fly a 2½-hour mission. When the mission was completed, we would spend the night there and go back to Phu Bai in the morning.

When we got to the area of contact that morning there was nothing around. By that I mean aircraft, and there was only one helicopter trying to get in and out of there. We had multiple radios on different channels and I had an Army officer in the back seat with me for artillery. That day, I was talking to an officer on the ground and also his radio man. At that point the back seat [actually Sp4 Phillip Tarr] didn't have much to do except maybe to help me not miss any content of the multiple conversations. I would try to go in very low to assess the situation. Our orders were to never fly below one thousand feet, but we always flew between fifty and one hundred feet because we were harder to hit when the NVA gunners only got a second or two to see us. I did not know that day that there was an antiaircraft gun that was shooting down all those helicopters; otherwise I would have been much more scared. We got shot at that day but mostly by small arms fire. If he shot at us, he didn't come close. We could always tell when we were being shot at because we flew with the windows open and could hear the gunfire and take evasive action. When I got there, I had been flying for a half hour and was on station there for two more hours—eventually running low on fuel. The other guy flying that day [1Lt Carl Drechsel] came and took over while I flew back to Dong Ha to refuel. I then got right back up there and was there for quite a while longer [until dark]. There was one helicopter that crashed while I was there—the Loach. At some point one of the medevac helicopters threw a stretcher and medical supplies down to the unit that was under fire. They were saying, "They are all over us." That's when I contacted Dong Ha DASC [for assets].

Sp4 Phillip Tarr's witness statement: From approximately 1310 hours to 1830 hours on 12 November 1969, Captain Arrington, the pilot for the 1st Brigade, 5th Infantry Division's S-2 Air (Aerial Observer), displayed outstanding skill and coordination in taking responsibility of the complete control and coordination of all aircraft supporting the 1st Battalion, 61st Infantry (M) and the 1st Battalion, 11th Infantry of the 1/5. The above units were pinned down under heavy enemy automatic weapons fire, small arms fire, grenades and RPG fire from almost every direction. Captain Arrington directed the fires of Cobra gunships on station, to where we spotted the enemy fire. After almost running out of fuel, we refueled and he took command from another Catkiller who had relieved us temporarily. By faultlessly directing the suppressing fires of the gunships, he enabled the ground troops to withdraw to a more solid position where they could reorganize. He played a major role in the evacuating of the dead and wounded by helping direct the medevacs into the troop's positions.

I believe that Captain Arrington did a superb job that not only brought great credit upon himself and his abilities, but also on his training and instruction as an aviator. I feel privileged to have worked with a man of his qualities and experience, and I don't know of anyone who could have performed more efficiently or who was more capable of performing as Captain Arrington had.

Sp4 Phillip Tarr
S-2 Air, 517 M I Det
1st Bde, 5th Inf Div.

## 1st LT Carl Drechsel's witness statement:

On November 12, 1969, I was on a visual reconnaissance mission inside the DMZ when I received a call from Captain Arrington to fly cover ship and relieve him if necessary near grid YD 0663, which is due west of fire base Charlie-Two. Captain Arrington was in support of ground troops that were in contact with the enemy. One platoon was stranded about three hundred meters from the main body of the company, with a substantial enemy force between them. The platoon had one KIA plus two or three WIA personnel which had been rescued from a Huey that had been shot down earlier that day. Captain Arrington, realizing the grave situation was becoming increasingly worse, took control of numerous support aircraft—medevac, aerial rocket artillery and Huey gunships—about ten in all and also established ground contact with the ground commander to advise him of enemy positions and movements.

The first priority was the evacuation of the wounded platoon. Captain Arrington guided Roadrunner 16 into the pickup area. On the third pickup, the LOH—Roadrunner 16—took an RPG in the tail rotor and crashed back into the pickup area, [where] enemy fire was now extremely intense. Captain Arrington, with coordination of the ground troops, ran two flights of Aerial Rocket artillery on the enemy positions. With total disregard for his personal safety, he flew dangerously low to ensure proper target coverage as there were friendly troops 50–100 meters away from the enemy positions. Through his courage, the enemy suffered heavy losses and the friendlies were unharmed by the ARA.

At this time Captain Arrington asked me to relieve him as he was dangerously low on fuel. After returning on station, he again attempted to guide a medevac Huey—Dustoff 708—into the area to drop medical supplies to the stranded platoon, but again it was apparent that the enemy ground fire was too intense.

Again Captain Arrington, flying dangerously low to ensure proper target coverage and no friendly casualties, ran eight more flights of ARA, bringing heavy casualties to the enemy. Since it was getting dark, Captain Arrington requested a flare in support of the ground troops, as it was now clear that a rescue before dark would be impossible. However, Captain Arrington did guide a Huey over the friendly troops to drop badly needed supplies and ammunition.

Throughout the more than six-hour ordeal, Captain Arrington was receiving heavy automatic weapons fire—to include small arms as well as [51] caliber. It was later learned that Captain Arrington did silence the [51] caliber through use of ARA gunships. Also, throughout the day, jamming of the FM frequencies by the enemy was plainly evident, which made Captain Arrington's control and coordination efforts more difficult. Despite the deteriorating situation, intense enemy groundfire and frequency jamming, Captain Arrington managed to take control, coordinate and advise all those involved that day, which was a determining factor in the success of the destruction of the enemy and the saving of many American lives. Through his perseverance and dedication to duty, a turning point in the battle was realized and effective offensive attack begun.

Carl L. Drechsel

1LT Signal Corps
220th RAC

## Today, 1Lt Carl Drechsel remembers his military career and that day:

I went to Norwich University in Vermont, which is the nation's only private military college. It was formed in 1819, and it's coming up on its 200-year university, which makes it only 20 years younger than West Point. The school goes back quite a bit. I was very interested in the military back then and graduated there with a plan to be a career officer. I spent four years on active duty and then I spent 24 years in the United States Army National Guard, retiring a full Colonel. I was with the 220th Reconnaissance Airplane Company from April of 1969 until March of 1970. There were 4 platoons in the company and they flew in different AOs. The 1st Platoon, Bob's [Arrington] platoon, flew the DMZ. I was in the 3rd platoon and flew the western A Shau Valley but I filled in on 1st platoon missions when needed. Typically we would check my plane out after our briefing on the particular mission at operations. Then we'd fly up to the DMZ or what was called "the tri-border area" which was pretty remote and mountainous up there. Every once in a while something like this particular event would be happening up there. There was a call and I was up around tri-border when I heard it. Bob radioed out if there was anyone up in his area and that he had to go and refuel. So, I came down there and could see [that] there was a lot of "back and forth" firing near some crashed helicopters. It was getting dark. The situation was not very good and from my standpoint—I thought: "What can we do?" We talked about bringing in flares but once the sun went down there wouldn't be much we could do. So, we were running out of time. While I was there, I wouldn't exactly call it high ship but I was looking for the enemy, but on one of the frequencies, we could hear that one of the platoons was stranded and things were getting worse by the minute. There were casualties and no medevacs were going in there because they had already shot down three helicopters and they were low on ammunition. In my mind they had to bring in some guys to help out or get the other guys on the ground working towards them. Things just weren't working out. They had set up a makeshift position but the radio transmissions indicated they needed ammunition and medical attention really bad. While I was on station I went down low a few times in an attempt to find the enemy—not thinking I was bulletproof or whether they could shoot me out of the air but because the enemy was always pretty smart. They didn't normally shoot at Birddogs unless they definitely could take you down. Because once they shot at me, then I knew where they were and once I knew where they were, I could start calling in fire, whatever it might be that day—gunships, naval gunfire, TAC air or whatever. We were qualified as S4 forward air controllers. But that opportunity did not develop after several low passes—they did not choose to shoot at me anyway. So I held station until Bob came back and I was running out of fuel too so I headed back to Dong Ha to refuel before returning to Phu Bai. Besides, it was getting dark and we were really only equipped for daytime operations.

**Distinguished Flying Cross**

For heroism while participating in aerial flight evidenced by voluntary actions above and beyond the call of duty: Captain Robert Arrington distinguished himself by exceptionally valorous actions while serving as a pilot of a light observation aircraft supporting a ground unit in heavy enemy contact near Con Thien. The lead platoon had been cut off from the main body and was surrounded by an enemy force of unknown size. The platoon had sustained several wounded personnel. Realizing the seriousness of the situation, he immediately scrambled missile-carrying helicopters, medevac helicopters, and helicopter gunships. Upon their arrival on station, Captain Arrington made repeated dangerously low passes in the face of intense enemy automatic weapons fire to mark both enemy and friendly positions accurately. He then proceeded to adjust the missile-carrying and gunship fire close to friendly personnel. After a brief absence for refueling, he returned to the area of operations, and despite heavy enemy fire, directed the medevac helicopters to extract the wounded. By his exceptional flying ability and courage under fire, he was instrumental in the success of the mission. His actions were in keeping with the highest traditions of the military service and reflect great credit upon himself, his unit and the United States Army.

That night, while the bulk of Delta Company reformed to a defensive perimeter, Capt. Blunt led a 7-man volunteer patrol for which he would be awarded a DSC. The team was comprised of his "Hillbillies" that included Lt. Michael Jordan, SSgt. Phil (Iron Man) Phillips, Sgt. Bobby Preece, Sgt. William (Big Daddy) Hammond, Sgt. Ron Gibson, Sp4 Richard Cox, and PFC Dan Switzer. As the patrol left battalion perimeter, they crawled 1200 meters to their destination. Lieutenant Colonel Swaren wanted the patrol to start their trek as dark fell, but Captain Blunt insisted that the NVA would be pulling out and wanted to give them a little time. He figured that the longer he waited, the easier the infiltration would be. It was just after midnight when they started out.

Upon the suggestion of Blunt, Lt. Colonel Jack Swaren called in a set of artillery coordinates to the S3 duty officer, Lt. Jelinek at the TOC, with instructions to fire one round of "Willie Pete" every minute throughout the night. It served a twofold purpose. First, it was a diversionary tactic to keep the NVA bunker line occupied since the Blunt patrol would have to pass extremely close to—and actually through—the enemy bunker complex. It would turn out that they would not retreat north but in fact would move east and stage for a major assault on that aforementioned mortar position of only thirty men that was stranded on Hill 100. Second, Captain Blunt—who was the point man—requested every round to be white phosphorous so that the reflected glare off the Plexiglas bubble windshields of the crashed choppers would help guide them to the predetermined route that the trapped platoon was expecting. That way any other approach from personnel from another direction would initiate the firing upon and expending of what little ammunition the first platoon had left. An odd occurrence happened as Sergeant Ron Gibson—second to last in the file—looked back at one point and noticed that a small section of the lush green growth that all eight men had trod on was glowing with eerie phosphorescence. He thought nothing of it at the time.

As Blunt and his crew neared the trapped platoon, he indicated on the net that he was close at hand. They then made plenty of noise letting the skittish group of wounded GIs know that they were friendly and coming in. Still, pilot 1Lt Miller trained his .38 pistol out into the black night, ready to fire on any unfriendlies. He remained in that posture until he was sure he had friendlies in front of him. He saw Captain Blunt first, who approached with a wry smile on his face. Next, Blunt neared Sp4 Stan Samulak—who was ready to sell his life dearly to the inevitable final NVA assault he was expecting. He was holding a grenade in each hand as Blunt crawled up to Samulak and said, "Put them down, son, we're here now." Samulak was badly wounded in the foot and leg. He would eventually unite with Captain Starr on the hospital ship *Repose* and again stateside at Valley Forge Hospital. Miller, though wounded in the leg, would have to walk out under his own power, as there were others wounded more seriously. Twenty-two men were rescued by "Blunt's Grunts," including two helicopter crews and the first platoon of Charlie Company. Sergeant Mosher, who was killed in the initial ambush about fifteen hours earlier, lay dead near the crashed helicopters. Blunt was not made aware of this until they were well under way. Ken Barkley and Kit Carson Scout Elmer were carried back to the battalion defensive position by members of the first platoon. The names of the survivors are as follows: Sp4 Ezekiel Campbell, PFC Jerry Cobb, Sp4 Sam Cornwell, Sp4 Kenneth Hann, 1LT Charles Matteffs, Sp4 James McAndrew, Sp4 Ray Melarczik, PFC Stanley Samulak, Sgt. Leon Sweeney, PFC Kenneth Vickery, 1LT Phillip Miller, PFC James Oetzel, and eight others—some of them from the air-crew personnel from the downed ships. The remainder of Captain Blunt's DSC Citation reads as follows:

**Staging area outside Con Thien where Captain Gallagher and Alpha Company waited in platoon groups during the late afternoon of 12 Nov 1969 waiting to board the Ghostrider helicopters for insertion into Hill 100.**

In the early morning hours of 13 November, in a continuation of the same operation, Captain Blunt infiltrated a seven-man patrol through some twelve hundred meters of closely defended enemy terrain under cover of darkness in order to reinforce and extract besieged friendly elements. He conducted this perilous mission without incident and undoubtedly saved the lives of the twenty-two trapped American soldiers. Captain Blunt's extraordinary heroism and devotion to duty were in keeping with the highest traditions of the military service and reflect great credit upon himself, his unit, and the United States Army.

## Captain Stanley Blunt remembers:

I figured they might be pulling out if we waited long enough. On the trip down in they [NVA] were there, they were in the same bunkers. They were ... at least a company or more right there. We waited to go back up the hill. We had a couple of kills to carry; many wounded—most of them were wounded but walked. I spoke to the colonel before we left. I didn't want to start until midnight. He wanted us to be back by midnight, but we went down after midnight and it gave the NVA time to pull out because we had to go through them on the way down; they were right below. Eventually, you go through elephant grass at the bottom there. It worked out OK. We got the guys that could walk, [and] they walked. They had no ammo left. I was afraid they were going to open up on us on the way back up—our boys on the perimeter—so we made plenty of noise coming back.

In the cover of the elephant grass, Blunt and his men made litters for the wounded who were unable to walk. The litter cases were loaded on them and the ambulatory were given ammunition and were spaced out for the return trip. The thirty men got under way for the return trip to the night defensive perimeter with Sp4 Ron Gibson on point for the return trip this time. As he moved out, the first leg of the return trip was relatively easy as they moved along an established trail. But as they approached the turn up out of the ravine to the 1-61 perimeter, Ron lost his way momentarily, but then he saw a patch of the same efflorescence he had witnessed on the downhill trip.

It was extremely important to return to the perimeter at the exact preplanned position, because the troopers in that position were forewarned to be aware of the return of the friendlies and not fire on them by mistake. But as fate would have it, for some inexplicable reason, the man in that position had been changed, and it was now operated by a new replacement from Charlie Company. As he had been taught by the 75th Support Battalion, this new recruit had attached clickers to several claymore wires that led out to the concertina to his position. No one had forewarned him of the return of the patrol to his position.

As Gibson panned the hillside of the steep ravine, the pitch-black night was waning in the eastern sky behind him, but the western hillside back to the perimeter was black as night—except for a clear bright trail of green efflorescence that marked the way to safety. Finally feeling relieved from the intense stress of the mission—mainly because the position he was heading to was his old position—he stood a little more erect as he waved the men behind him to move forward. As he began move up the hill, he quickened his pace. He also took comfort in the fact that he had disconnected the claymore wire before the patrol had moved out, not only at the clicker but also at the claymore mine itself. Then all that comfort disappeared as he looked up to his old position and saw two hands raised up from the foxhole. The two hands were frantically squeezing on the clickers and Gibson hit the ground as he screamed a string of epithets up to the perimeter. Nothing happened and the claymores stood just in front of him, silent in the grassy brush. Gibson continued screaming at the unnamed soldier.

Sp4 Ron Gibson:

> I thought I'd remember where the spot was where the trail turned and looked and there was this neon lighting with the fluorescent moss that was leading back up to our position. So we started back up again moving to our left and worked our way back up the hill. I guess somebody was in my foxhole when I got up near the perimeter. Luckily, before we left, we disconnected our Claymores at our positions. When I got back up, I hollered three times, "We're coming in!" Somebody was in my foxhole [and] started cranking on the Claymores. I remember looking through the glow of the Willie Pete, and looking at them cranking and I didn't say anything at first. I just walked by them. We got up to the top and I believe all the wounded were medevacked out from that position. It was just like one of these long, long days that a lot of things happened with all the Birds and Cobras shot down. I think there were five helicopters shot down. We got to the top there and we got out of there later that morning.

The seven men in the recue patrol will be forever known as "The Night Patrol." As for Captain Blunt, he took his company to Fire Base Fuller on the top of Dong Ha Mountain for base security. Dong Ha Mountain is a steep-cliffed stronghold with a close resemblance to Devil's Tower in South Dakota. While there, the company endured a 40-day rocket attack followed by a human wave attack that Delta Company successfully repulsed. Sgt. Joe Prince was wounded with shrapnel in the chest in one of the aerial attacks and still carries that shrapnel today. Blunt served another tour as advisor to the ARVNs and was also back in Quang Tri when the NVA overran Quang Tri and then took it back again. After Vietnam, he bought a sailboat and navigated the coast of Africa, landing on the Somali coast with the idea of forming a mercenary force to fight in that country's civil war. Today he lives in Washington. He often gets phone calls and visits from his "grunts," who love him still.

Back in the warm glow of their friends at the jump CP, some of the men—those not medevacked—began to tell the story of their 20-hour ordeal. Portions of the citations of nine of the beleaguered soldiers of the first platoon of Charlie Company who were cited earlier in this chapter relate just a small slice of the valor exhibited through their ordeal. Few men in war have experienced such a nightmare and lived to talk about it. It is not only a tribute to their courage, but also an acknowledgment of the courage of the men who tried and tried again to save them, and finally did, as well as the officers who led them with such professionalism and exceptional soldiering leadership. They would not give up on the lives of these men.

As night approached on the 12th in another sector of the battlefield, the three rifle platoons of Bravo Company formed in their night defensive perimeter atop Hill 162—they were busy fortifying their position. Foxhole positions were dug deeper, claymores and trip flares were put out, and pre-planned artillery had to be registered. This task fell to Lt. Mike Cowart, Sgt. Jon DeBoer and PFC Fred Dannenfelture. As Cowart worked with 6 batteries of artillery, he progressed his way around the perimeter registering several of the ravines and also several approaches to the Bravo Company mortar position still back on Hill 100 (Gallagher Ridge). Charlie Company mortars had linked up with them earlier in the day. One of Cowart's responsibilities was their perimeter, and he had a clear view of them some fifteen hundred meters below.

While he was registering some of the ravines of Hill 162, suddenly on the radio came the shouted words "Check fire! Check fire! Check fire!" Cowart had come very close to one portion of the perimeter and the rounds were dropping only a few yards away from several positions. To the relief of all, not the least of which was Cowart himself, no one was hit or injured. He tells it in his own words:

> Later that evening I was doing a reconnaissance by fire and establishing defensive ... defcons so we could react if we got hit and could use that as an adjustment point. While doing this, I was walking artillery down a ridgeline and almost killed a squad or something. Some of our people, anyway. It was absolutely sickening—I almost threw up and my knees got weak as I could hear them screaming on the phone—"Check fire. Check fire. Check fire." I thought I had killed my own people and that's the most afraid I have ever been in my life. Even when I was wounded or when I was under fire from as close as thirty feet away I was as calm as I am talking to you right now, but when that happened I just about threw my guts up because I thought I had killed some of our own people. And I just said a prayer right there. All I could say was ... [taking a moment to compose] Please God? [long silence] That's all I could say. Thank God they were OK. My rounds hit so close it set off their trip flares in front of their positions. You know—the fog of war and all. They were scattered here, there and everywhere and nobody knew where everybody was because that's just the way it was. Anybody that doesn't understand, that just hasn't been there. That happened about a little after dark—about 9 o'clock or something like that.

Earlier in the day, as previously stated, Charlie Company's mortar platoon united with the Bravo Company mortar platoon, two or three clicks northeast of Star Valley on Hill 100. They were a small force of thirty and they were vulnerable. The defensive perimeter was already a fully fortified company-size NDP with a circle of APCs and fully dug positions, but what they lacked was numbers. The uniting of the two mortar platoons would double their strength. Still, there were not enough men to man a company-sized perimeter and many positions were unoccupied. Accordingly, they dug in deeper, bracketed some targets and were resupplied by helicopter. The resupply and reinforcement were orchestrated by 1Lt Jelinek at the TOC. They were OK for the time being, but before early evening, they would need to airlift troop assistance to Hill 100. Bravo Company's rifle platoons would be out of the question as they were indispensable as a blocking force for the battalion CP. Another company would be needed and the choices were B/1–11, a company of the 101st Airborne, or most probably, A/1-61. Captain Gallagher had volunteered his Alpha Company troopers and that was the scenario that Colonel Swaren was most in favor of. Otherwise, he might end up relinquishing command of that piece of the battlefield.

# 11

# 12 Nov 1969, Mission "Bald Eagle"

Specialist 4th Class Louis Pepi:

> On November 12, 1969, I was boarding a UH1 Huey with my squad. The bird was call sign Ghostrider. We had been on a knoll outside the southern sally-port of Con Thien. On the chopper with me were Skip Hager, Gary Kent, Archie Donley, Bobby Vandergriff, Steve Smith, David Nicholson, Lt. William Miller, Don Marksberry, and Don Sarsfield. We were told by the door gunner to pack in tight. We were bound for who-knows-where to support who-knows-who for who-knows-what. All we knew was that our sister companies were in trouble. Once we were loaded on the chopper, the pilot throttled the rotor blades. It lifted off the ground, the nose then tilted down, and it pitched forward into flight. We all sat mutely on our steel pots—rifle butts on the deck of the Huey—muzzles all pointing to the heavens. Shouting small talk over the roar of the chopper engine was attempted, but no one bought into it, so we occupied ourselves with staring silently out into the blackness. The western horizon—the direction we were heading—was dark with no sign of dusk. Below us, it was already black night. The lights of the Huey's instrument panel offered the only illumination.

The lead-up to this moment started back during the preceding night. Alpha Company had spent the previous night in a north-south line of platoon perimeters south of Con Thien and several hundred meters west of the service road that led south back to highway 1. At daybreak, the LPs were called in to the service road where hot meals were brought out on a deuce-and-a-half by Master Sergeant Hoyt Sparrow. Whenever we were close to our base of operation—which was Con Thien at that time—the timeworn sergeant saw that we got hot meals. Sparrow was one of those revered and rare Eleven-Bravos who wore a CIB with two stars, having also served as a combat infantryman in World War II and Korea as well. He possessed a genuine love for his enlisted men and he seized every opportunity to make our lives more bearable. He was truly one of the Old Breed.

Sp4 Lou Pepi:

> Let me speak of Sergeant Sparrow. There's a guy named Kenny Love who was in the Fifth Infantry in the 1980s. He spent some time in Germany. And I've been back and forth with him by email and on the phone in 2014, when I learned that he collects soldier scrapbooks. He buys these books online. He sent me an email and he said, "Do you know a guy named Sergeant Sparrow?" And I said, "Geez," and I got right back to him. He started telling me this story about how close he had come while trying to buy his scrapbook. And I said, "What a find that would have been!" Then I thought, "Why would any family give up something like that?"

Charged with base security of Con Thien, Captain Gallagher was given the mission of sweeping the area a little further to the west in synchronized cloverleaf maneuvers. After eating our hot meal in haste, the company split up into platoons again and covered several miles by mid-morning. No sooner did we return to the service road than we were immediately sent back out to sweep again. The rumor was that they were going to airlift us into that firefight in the western hills. Evidently, there were logistical issues that had not yet been worked out and we kept occupied by running continual sweeps. Returning again after another long hump, we were told to square our equipment and be ready to move out again. The rifle platoons were kept busy with more sweeps, and the CP unit remained on the service road.

PFC Sterling Eugene Kelly:

> I was in a rather unique situation because I was driving for the medics. A guy came around at Con Thien and said, "We're going out—we're going out on foot," and one of the drivers popped up and said, "Does that mean drivers?" And he said, "That means everybody." And so we gathered up all our packs and got our steel pots and got pretty much our light marching orders. We went outside of the sally-port at the south entrance of Con Thien and it seems to me we didn't go a very long way and we got into this little depression and we could see that fight going on out there [in the western hills]. We saw aircrafts going in and out and heard the artillery.

At about mid-afternoon, Captain Gallagher formed us up on a small knoll and was standing up on a Jeep. He gave us a pep talk telling us we might get into some heavy stuff. He said we would soon find out what we were made of because we were about to see plenty of action. His voice drifted away as I became consumed with doubt. We were scared. I'll speak for myself—I was scared. Would I be brave? Or would I discredit myself? Then my attention drifted back to the captain's voice. He was reprimanding someone. I don't remember who this soldier was nor did I know the reason for the admonishment. He stood him up and told us that this man was what an REMF looked like. We used that acronym regularly—which stood for Rear Echelon Mother Fucker. It was an inappropriate acronym, and it was certainly unbecoming language by an officer to an enlisted man. All morning we had done sweeps around A-4—the more generic name for Con Thien. Alpha Company was charged with the security of that firebase. It was still a very bad place. It was less than two miles from the DMZ, and on a clear day you could see a huge NVA flag fluttering in North Vietnam. On any given day there were 20 to 40 thousand NVA troops bivouacked no more than three miles north from this rat-infested home of ours—and since bombing the north had been suspended, they were safe from harm.

Sgt. Ken Leach:

> On November 11, I knew something was going on—I didn't know what kind of a big deal it really was, though. They said it was like a couple of battalions of NVA that were out there. I remember early the next morning a track came through there outside A-4 and there was a kid that was driving and Gallagher made him get up on top of the track and he said in front of the company, "Take a good look. This is what an REMF looks like," and he got everyone's attention and humiliated him for about ten minutes. Well, after that we went out on a platoon patrol and I don't remember the LT's name [Lt. Mike Maiorca], but we humped for miles and miles and in the afternoon we came back in and Gallagher yelled at us that we came in too soon and sent us back out for about thirty minutes. I remember we were all pretty worn out when we finally came back in. I had got to 1-61 on October 20—about three weeks before this thing happened—and I got my wish about wanting to get into combat. And it was enough to last me for a while. And as for Gallagher—he ran a tight ship. I remember I hadn't shaved for two or three days one time and Gal-

**Sgt. Clyde "Bud" Wagner, first platoon A/1-61. M-79 grenadier.**

lagher came up to me and said, "Leach, you didn't shave this morning." He was a real stickler—even out in the field.

After Gallagher's words, the company congregated in squads. Some wrote letters and gave them to Lieutenant Miller to mail—just in case. I wrote one but could not bring myself to give it up. I put it in my pocket. I took it out several times and read it. It was surreal to read the line: "If you are reading this, it means that I have been killed." Call it an out-of-body experience if you like, but the fact was that I still had a body and for the time being, it was intact. I remember shrugging and saying to myself, "This is stupid." As I put the letter back in my pocket, my hand came in contact with something else. It was a set of rosary beads that my grandmother Josephine had given me the day I left my hometown for Vietnam. A friend of hers from the Daughters of Italy had been to Rome in 1955 and had attended a group audience with Pope Pius XII—where the rosary was blessed by the pontiff. The crucifix had a compartment in the rear that held a small pebble roughly the diameter of a pencil. Supposedly, it was a piece of rock from Calvary Mount—where Christ was crucified. Oddly enough, it bore a resemblance in size and shape to a 55-grain 5.56 mm full metal jacket bullet—the projectile seated and crimped in an M-16 cartridge. The beads had been in my pocket for the four months to the day since my tour began. I took them out, stared at them for a moment, then—after making sure that the screw that secured the compartment was tightly seated—I put them around my neck and tucked them inside my shirt. What a time for religion. "Just in the nick of time," I thought. Of course, God could see right through that, but it was worth a try. It didn't make me feel much better at the time.

There was a trooper named Kenny Barrett in the First Platoon who was a "born-again" Christian. He circulated amongst the groups and preached that we should put our trust in Jesus and He would pull us through. The troopers in Dave Cowan's squad tried to lighten the mood by playing song trivia. There was a lot of tension.

Ken Leach recalls:

> I remember the guy we called the preacher. He was going up and down to all the groups telling us that we needed to get right with God and everything and that really has stuck in my mind. As I said, he was going up and down to each of us telling us to get ready to meet our maker while we were waiting for our choppers to come in. Then we got the word that the mortars were pinned down and they were under siege and we were going to get choppered in because they were about to be overrun. I was a squad leader at that time and I had gone to noncommissioned officer school. We were divided into eight-man groups to get ready to be choppered out.

As Gene Kelly remembers, the CP group was also isolated in a private group as Captain Gallagher and his RTO were busy monitoring the battalion net and the medics and several other radiomen were squaring their gear. Because Bandaid 6, the senior aid-man, had left on R&R the previous day, Captain Gallagher announced to Kelly that he should stock an aid-bag so that he could fill the shortage and act as a medic that night. Kelly had been driving the medic track for a couple weeks and Gallagher felt that enough knowledge had rubbed off to make him an adequate substitute.

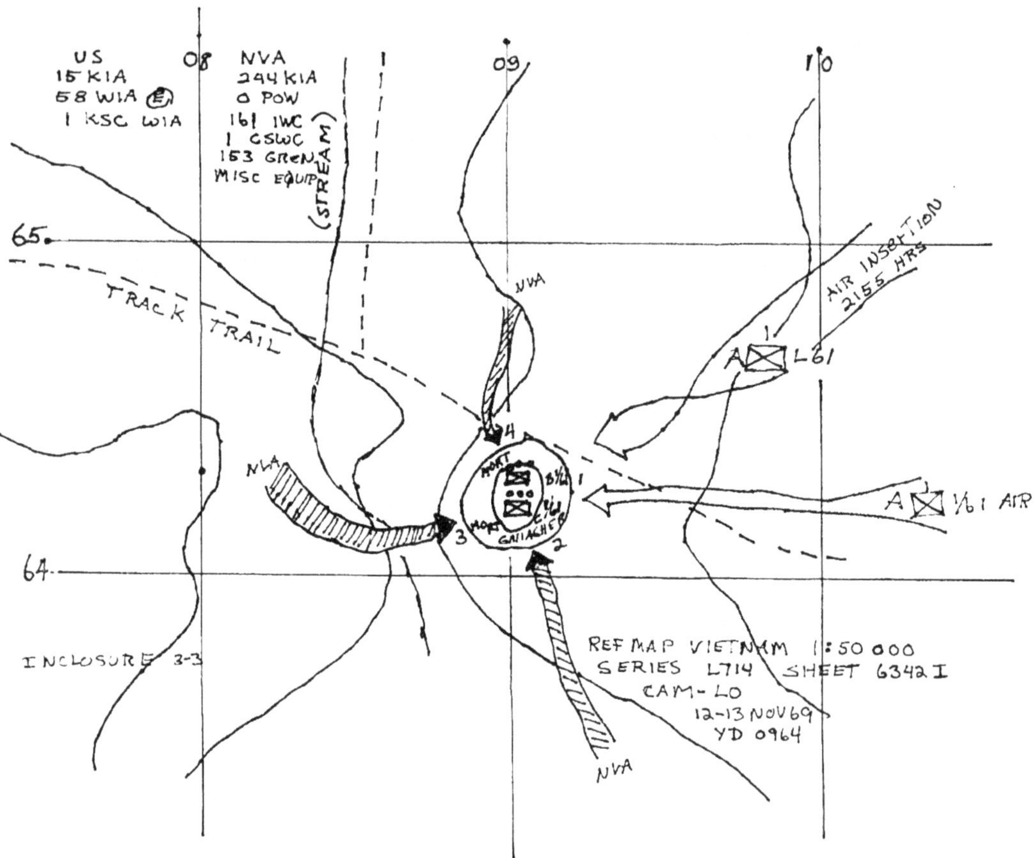


**Map #3: 12–13 Nov 1969 showing Hill 100 and the night defensive perimeter of 4/C/1-61, 4B/1-61 and A/1-61 airlifted from Con Thien as a Bald Eagle Force to support the perimeter at 2255 on 12 Nov 1969.**

**Bravo Company, 1-61, mortar platoon a few weeks after the November Battle. From left to right: Larry Tucker, Charles Loomis, Phillip Frost, Chris Saigh, Archuleta, James Howell, Robert Dietrich, Tim Hurley, J.W. Wagner, Gary Bonzon, Keith Neel, Eric Backer, Charles Jones, Robert Pinkston, John Mastrantoni. Picture taken by Platoon Sergeant William Howard (courtesy Bill Howard).**

PFC Gene Kelly:

> I do remember the first sergeant or maybe it was Sgt. Sparrow. He went around and he said "OK, there's a real good chance we're going to be in this. I want to tell you that I'm going to put this steel pot down here on the ground." And he says, "If there is anything on you, that you don't want to be found on you if you get killed or hit," he says, "I'm going to take a little walk—put it in this steel pot." And he said, "Nothing will be said." And he walked off and then he came back. I don't remember anybody putting anything in there, but it was almost dark when that was going on.

At length, we heard a shout from our platoon leader to gather around him. Now it was our platoon leader's turn to get us in a group and speak to us. It was a day for speeches. Lieutenant William Miller began to speak about "doing your job." He was a recent college graduate with four years of ROTC, 16 weeks of basic and Advanced Infantry Training—and a crash course in leadership training. Again, the speaker's voice drifted away as my inner thoughts kicked in. Then, a few minutes earlier, the voice came back in volume as the LT—similar to Sparrow—placed his steel helmet on the ground: "Anyone that has any contraband, now's the time to get rid of it with no repercussions." We all stood silent and still for a moment or two, and finally several guys from third platoon ambled over to the steel pot and dropped their small stashes in. Unconsciously, I stuck my hands in my empty pockets. I froze abruptly, wondering what I did with my rosary beads. Then I remembered they were around my neck. I fondled them nervously and looked around to see if anyone had noticed my new bling. I tucked them into my fatigue shirt and buttoned the top button in spite of the humidity. Then the song "Plastic Jesus" came into my head—and hard as I tried, I could not get it out. No matter how hard I tried, I couldn't shake the song. It just kept going nonstop—around in a circle and back to the beginning again. That's how it was until dusk when the choppers started rotating to and from our destination. There were only three choppers. I was told at some point that we were going to Hill 89 to support a sister company. It meant nothing to me. We were also told sometimes it was called Hill 100 and it was near Hill 162. Still—it meant nothing.

As it would turn out, that crucifix and necklace of beads would be instrumental in saving my life, much as the plastic Jesus and magnetic Mary on the driver's dashboard provided protection in the song.

Lt. Jelinek at Tactical Operations Center, Lt. Col Swaren out at the Jump CP, and Captain Gallagher waiting outside A-4, labored to find a way to get reinforcements to the weapons platoons. There were several alternatives. The first plan was to bring in several companies, or even a full battalion of the 101st Airborne Division. The 1st Battalion of the 502 Regiment /101st Airborne was at that moment preparing for the airlift and was available. Lt. Col Swaren was not hot on this idea because he would lose control of his mortars and maybe the whole battlefield. Secondly, B/1–11, under Captain Tom Combs, was at C-2 as a ready reaction force if needed, but there was a control issue here as well. His best alternative was to get A/1-61 airlifted out, but they were charged with the security of Con Thien. The plan could not be enacted unless another unit was moved up to A-4 to relieve Alpha/1-61 of their security obligation.

There was a rotary wing element of the 101st flying in the area that could have shuttled Alpha Company to the mortar tracks, but when they were briefed, the unit commander refused the mission, saying they did not want to risk their helicopters. They had been monitoring their radios and knew of the four or five downed birds and several more that were shot up. A short while later, a different flight of 101st helicopters, call sign "Ghostrider," agreed to make the dangerous airlift to the mortar APCs, and at 1700 hours the insertion was initiated. Lieutenant Colonel Swaren, with Charlie and Delta Company in the field, and Lt. Jelinek, from the S3 "shop" manning the TOC that night, both recall the airlift.

Lt. Colonel John Swaren, Battalion CO:

> That evening, we're all farting around, helicopters are getting shot down and Blunt's getting ready to go down over the hill. And we got the mortar tracks over there all by themselves. Jesus Christ, that's where we put them over there, deliberately, figuring this was going to be an easy day and we'd wake up and come out later. The terrain wasn't correct to bring them down where we were. And it's getting dark, and they are over there by themselves. I've got nobody who I could control except A Company and they're back sitting on their butts at A-4, theoretically. So, I relay them a message, I said, "Hey, I don't know how you're going to do it, but you're going to do it. Get some helicopters and bring out Alpha Company out here right now. If I turn around and see a helicopter landing, I'll be happy. If I don't, then you're slow. Get your ass on it. I'm working." Now, I'm talking to the S-3 back in TOC and doing that radio relay through COM at A-4. And I'm doing this through a relay. And I've got an assistant S3 LNO with me and he gets hold of TOC and they do

it! How they did it, I will never know. His name was Marshall. A good man, if there ever was one. Jack Marshal was his name—I'd like to run him down today.

## 1Lt Frederick Jelinek, Battalion S-3 in the TOC

**Sergeant Russ Widener was awarded the Silver Star on Gallagher Ridge. He shipped out shortly after and was promoted to E-6 in Germany. He then left the regular Army and joined the Reserve/Guard, where he received a direct commission in Armor while a full-time student at University of Tennessee in 1976. He graduated in 1980 as a first lieutenant with an RN degree. He then went back on active duty in the Army Nurse Corps and retired as a major in 1994, having served 27 years in the military (courtesy Russ Widener).**

When it became clear that this would be a prolonged engagement, the B company commander radioed me about the APC situation and asked for some help for them. At the time, Alpha Company was responsible for the defense of Con Thien and the artillery there that was firing for the troops in contact. It was midafternoon, too dangerous to move soldiers by foot to the vulnerable APCs, and Con Thien needed a defense force. There was an element of the 101st flying in the area that could have shuttled Alpha Company to the APCs. Pulling the APCs out would have removed combat power that might be needed in the morning. I called Capt. Gallagher and talked over the situation. I proposed that I get the brigade reserve company, fly it up to his location with helicopters and while at the same time flying his company to the APCs using the 101st unit that was there in support of us. Since his company was familiar with equipment on the APCs and the reserve company was not, that seemed better than moving the reserve company directly to the APCs. He agreed to the plan, but when I briefed the 101st unit they refused the mission, saying they did not want to risk their helicopters and would only do it if LTC Swaren directly tasked them to. LTC Swaren was busy working out the rescue of a whole platoon and not available. A few minutes later the unit lead called me and asked to be released as he had no tasks to do. I refused his request and told him to continue to loiter in the area. He made the mistake of asking me why, if he had no tasks to do, he could not be released. I replied I was hoping some NVA gunner would get lucky, shoot his ass down and somebody with some balls would take over the flight. Later he called and said they had to go refuel and flew off. I was not happy. I told A Company the lift was off. A major pile of equipment and firepower was exposed, as well as a number of men, and it was now dark. Then, a bit later, over the air came a call from a different flight of 101st helicopters, call sign "Ghostrider." They had my reserves for Con Thien and were inbound. In a few minutes they landed the reserves. The lead pilot reported mission complete and then said words that still give me goose bumps: "Anything else we can do for you folks?" I quickly asked if he would do a very dangerous and technically demanding night insertion of A Company in rough country with NVA in the area. He agreed immediately. I called Captain Gallagher, told him about the new plan, and he also agreed, knowing the need and risks. Now making this night helicopter move in a very uncertain tactical situation called for cool operators, both flying the helicopters and commanding the rifle company. Both units did a great job and the lift went flawlessly. As it turned out, A Company was desperately needed as the position was attacked a few hours after it got into the position and was successfully defended. Had Captain Gallagher and the Ghostriders not taken that mission, the men in that position would have certainly been killed and the APCs destroyed.

As the 1st squad of the third platoon sat on the cargo deck of our Huey, the dusk glow had all but died out along the western skyline. It was now well after 2200 hours as our Ghostrider quickly dropped altitude. We were the final insertion. We were told by one of the door gunners to prepare to offload as the bird would not actually touch down but would hover just off the ground. As the word was given, we hopped off in twos with fixed bayonets. We landed in a tangle of arms and legs, and somehow, no one was impaled by the bayonets. We were immediately split up and given position assignments to reinforce weak points in the eastern, western and northwestern portions of the perimeter. Kenny Leach, who was a squad leader in the first platoon, and medic's track-driver Gene Kelly remember the airlift:

Sgt. Ken Leach:

So we finally got on our chopper and we went in very fast and low and the crew told us to be ready to unload real quick because they weren't going to linger there very long at all. And when we got there we jumped off and dispersed real quick. And I jumped into a hole with three other guys. It was a shallow bomb crater. There were four of us including Charles Smith, who sometime in the night got a big old piece of shrapnel in his arm—in his elbow, from the first RPG that went off, and he didn't realize he was hurt until it began to swell. He had a long thin piece of shrapnel lodged in his arm.

PFC Gene Kelly:

I think our bird was one of the first ones to take off. I remember seeing them come in and they touched down. I was kind of unattached, I was floating because I was driving for the medics. I was officially part of the headquarters group and I had my shotgun, my forty-five, my Bowie knife, and my light ruck. I was kind of a puppy for the medics. We got on the bird and lifted off and I remember the ride in! That was pretty surreal. When we got to the hill, we all dismounted and I went over by the CP Group where the command track was. I asked the senior aid man, "Well, what do you want me to do?" He said, "Well, kind of stand by, find yourself a hole," you know, not a perimeter position. So, I made myself a spot—I put my poncho liner down next to a little hole—an old [interior] fighting hole. I took out my sleeping bag and aired up my air mattress but it always went flat after about two hours.

PFC Dan Cowan, Sp4 Bud Wagner, and Sp4 Jerry Oliver ran for a large foxhole, but were soon moved to another position on a different section of the perimeter, as Jerry Oliver remembers. This would prove to be fortuitous for them, but not for the three soldiers who took over that position.

Sp4 Louis Pepi:

I was assigned a position with another trooper—Smitty [Steven Smith], I recollect. I have a clear memory of his face and I'm sure it was him. I do remember that he had an M-60 machine gun and we had about five hundred rounds of ammunition. There was already a foxhole there that might have been a month old that was partially collapsed by recent rain. We dug in shifts squaring it off, taking about a foot of mud from the bottom and excavated grenade sumps. Then we filled about 20 sandbags and arched them across our front so that the barrel of our "60" rested on them. As we refortified our position, Lieutenant Miller and Don Sarsfield dropped by with a case of grenades for us. They would visit us often during the night. We pried open the wooden box and began pulling off the additional wire shipping safeties from all thirty grenades. Combat ready, we returned them to the box except for a half dozen that we placed close at hand. After filling a few more sandbags to secure the box, Capt. Gallagher came by our position as he circled the NDP and personally inspected ours and every position's field of fire. He put the whole perimeter at 50 percent alert. It was now about midnight and since I was to pull second guard, I spread my poncho and liner on a piece of flat ground about five feet behind our position. All the digging and preparation of our position had tired me considerably and it took some of the edge off the adrenaline rush that I felt all day. But I could not sleep. Instead, I drifted into a surreal stupor. I remained like this for about an hour.

# 12

# 13 Nov 1969 (DAY 3)

At 0100, the northwestern and southwest sides of the perimeter reported heavy movement near the wire. The NVA were probing the perimeter—most likely looking for claymores and booby traps as well as identifying weak points in our defense. The response was with hand grenades and M-79 fire—both Flechettes and HEs. This woke me out of my restless half-sleep. From our foxhole, we threw about a half-dozen M-26 grenades in unison with pop-flares, but we saw no actual movement in our sector. We could hear frags and thump-guns around the perimeter—but no return fire.

The NVA seemed to have the superior plan that night—don't give away your position by firing and producing muzzle flash inadvertently. What they did do, though, was to put the whole perimeter on alert. Alpha Company was ready and it was obvious to everyone that this was the real thing. The platoon leaders, platoon sergeants and squad leaders moved from position to position to make sure that their men were ready. Lieutenant Miller came by to check fields of fire and to make sure everyone had enough ammunition—M-16, M-60 and grenades. Sarsfield came by to make sure everyone had cigarettes and water. The perimeter was ready to meet the unknown. There was enough fear to go around. I lit a cigarette under the cover of my poncho to cut the tension.

### NVA Tactics

Contrary to public belief back in the U.S. and even among most allied combatants in Vietnam, the NVA unlike the Viet Cong were not just a ragtag force that had no plan other than to ambush and snipe at American forces to inflict a daily number of casualties aimed at demoralizing the American people and eventually swaying public opinion and to deteriorate the will of the United States to continue the war. Yes, they did hit and run and the NVA did not fight to win and hold territory, even less did they seek large-scale battles, in which the U.S. could concentrate their firepower or use their mobility to reinforce at speed. Instead, they had a name for their tactics. They called it the "War Of The Flea," or thousands of hit and run attacks aimed at exploiting to the maximum those vital weapons of stealth and darkness. In a phrase, they owned the night.

On the other hand, all major attacks were characterized by close attention to planning and detail. Planning was usually very long term, anything up to six months from conception to execution, and cancellation was a constant possibility at any stage in the process. Each phase of the operation was broken down into its constituent parts and rigorously rehearsed. Only when and if all parts of the plan appeared practical and achievable was the operation put into effect. These larger attacks were invariably characterized by adherence to the principle of "One Slow, Four Quick"—a doctrine that prevailed in both attack and defense. In offensive operations the "Quick Attack" was further broken down to incorporate the three strong segments—"Strong Fight," "Strong Assault," and "Strong Pursuit." Presented in sequence, the doctrine can be summarized as follows:

SLOW PLAN–This involved a steady but low-key logistical buildup in forward supply areas, being positioned ahead of the fighting forces to make a solid base for the operation. The degree of planning and preparation necessary to undertake a large operation could take as long as 6 months and often included numerous rehearsals.

QUICK ADVANCE–This was a rapid movement forward, up to 40kms in as little as six hours, generally in small and inconspicuous groups, to a forward staging area from where the attack would be launched.

QUICK ATTACK–Here the attacking forces would be concentrated at the weakest point of the target as identified by prior reconnaissance. The duration of an attack could often be measured in minutes and involved:

STRONG FIGHT—an attempt to achieve and exploit the element of surprise.

STRONG ASSAULT—against a pre-arranged position using concentration of force, effort and mass to overwhelm the defense.

STRONG PURSUIT—the attacking force's reserves would be committed to exploit the breaches in the target's defenses so as to deliver a decisive blow.

QUICK CLEARANCE–The attacking force would rapidly reorganize and police the battlefield so as to remove weapons and casualties and was pre-planned to prevent confusion on the objective.

QUICK WITHDRAWAL–Involved a quick egress from the battle area to a pre-arranged rendezvous point where the attackers would again break down into smaller groups to continue their dispersal. A successful withdrawal of this kind was calculated to create an aura of doubt over the enemy because of speed of execution and lack of evidence of ever having been in the area.[1]

Eventually, the probing movement died down and the perimeter became quiet again, but the NVA forces had compiled some valuable information identifying the weak points in Alpha Company's night defensive position. According to the battalion communication logs, the perimeter was hit with an intense barrage of enemy RPGs, mortars and artillery at 0247 hours, and according to SSgt Russ Widener, the first incoming round was an RPG that hit a fuel container strapped to the side of Bravo Company's FDC track. It was the same RPG that wounded Charles Smith in the elbow. Staff Sergeant Russ Widener of Bravo Company's mortar platoon remembers:

Staff Sergeant Russ Widener:

I remember the helicopters coming in with reinforcements and Alpha Company getting off. Initially when the fight started they fired an RPG at our FDC track. It hit the side of the track, but there was a fifty-gallon drum of oil in one of those red oil cans. The viscosity of that oil turned that RPG and I never before or after that saw an RPG turn like that. The viscosity of the oil turned it and there was a big scalloped area out of the side of the track where the aluminum melted out and it looked like a giant tablespoon into the side of the track. That was the first round. Right then we took cover. I was in a foxhole with a guy and it wasn't very long at all until this other guy came by and said that they were breaking through the perimeter on the other side and they needed help. I remember jumping out of the foxhole and running across the perimeter and got in a foxhole on the line and he said that I needed to be farther out. That was between basketball flares and it was dark. So, I crawled out further and got behind this small bush. Then one of the basketball flares went off and I found myself behind a bush the size of a Bonsai plant about six inches tall. I said to myself, "I don't think I'm going to stay out here all by myself." Since that was the only green thing that was out there, I immediately crawled back to the bomb crater. I was firing at one point and turned on my back as I slid down into the crater. When I slid down, a grenade went off just on the edge of the bomb crater. At that point, I could see tracers flying over but I couldn't hear a thing for about five minutes. I had to be one of the luckiest guys that night because that would have taken my head off.

I was one of the guys at one point that was throwing flares out to alert Spooky to the location of our perimeter so that his gunship wouldn't fire inside those markers. I distinctly remember

> one of the guys behind me saying that whatever you do, don't drop any of those trip flares inside the perimeter. I remember seeing the Basketball ship dropping those large phosphorus flares that illuminated 1½ grid squares—or kilometers. When Spooky finally did come in, I was—I believe—on the north side of the perimeter and I had no idea what was happening everywhere else. I was in a big 500-pound bomb crater that had been there previously.

The initiation of the mortar and rocket attack occurred almost simultaneously with the ground sapper assault. Mortars were hitting inside the NDP and outside between the fighting positions and the concertina wire. Enemy and friendly mortars lobbed past each other on their way to their respective targets.

Sp4 Louis Pepi:

> Years later, it is clear to me that another NVA tactic was used that night. It developed as follows. As the mortar attack got underway, the sappers were already charging the perimeter. The probers had already marked the weaker portions of the perimeter and had set command-detonated explosives to blow holes in the wire at those weak points. The sappers charged those weak points and the reinforcing second wave was most likely already in position too. As the first assault wave advanced, each sapper carried one or two blocks of high explosives that they threw to their front in an advancing rhythm, giving the appearance of a walking mortar attack just forward of the assault line. The natural tendency of soldiers in a defensive position is to duck into their holes to shield themselves from the advancing blasts. The majority of the fatal casualties that night—maybe as many as six of them—occurred at several adjoining positions that were overrun on that first or second wave, and this tactic more than likely caused the temporary breech in the defensive line.
>
> I wakened to my foxhole buddy dragging me by the foot into our foxhole—probably saving my life. The scene as I looked skyward was dreamlike. I could see mortars lobbing in and out of our perimeter—that looked like perfect spiraling footballs framed by strings of green and red tracers. Clods of dirt were falling on us and our weapons from explosions in front of our position. Somehow my mind's eye refused to believe this was real and it took a shove from my foxhole buddy to bring me out of that "dream" and back to reality. This was probably the second time that he had saved my life. Illumination rounds burned brightly above and they gently floated under their white parachutes, causing a strobe-like scene of shimmering shadows that added to the surrealism. In the next moment, a new-found reality manifested itself in the shimmering backlight of the basketball rounds in the form of an NVA sapper about 40 feet away. I remember his expression vividly even today—a smooth-faced boy glancing sidelong at me with his head turned slightly to his rear, as if he were looking for the rest of his unit who were just coming through. It looked like he was preparing to retreat. His expression was that of a confused boy with a longing to be somewhere else. I raised my rifle while jacking in a cartridge. I pulled the trigger and the rifle misfired—like shooting in a nightmare. I cycled a new round and it misfired again. The action was sluggish because it was fouled by dirt. Recycling a third round, I jammed it hard into the chamber with my palm. Three was a charm as a short burst discharged from my weapon. As my rifle finally began cycling rounds at the frozen soldier, he collapsed in a heap. Other sappers were advancing to our front at the wire. My foxhole buddy was just starting to fire his M-60, which he also had been clearing. I took this opportunity to clear the dirty receiver of my M-16 by blowing in it. My partner began spraying with the M-60 and other sappers fell from sight. I set my weapon down to reach for another belt of machine gun ammo. I linked on the second belt and then assisted by feeding for him. In a twist of fate—possibly divine fate—the rosary beads that were tucked inside my shirt had evidently fallen out in the intensity of the moment. They now looped over the 7.62 belt and were sucked into the gun action, jamming the M-60. The ammo belt broke and fell to the bottom of our foxhole. At the same moment we both instinctively ducked down to retrieve the ammo belt as a satchel charge detonated at the edge of the foxhole, blowing up our machine gun. Except for a piece of shrapnel that grazed my left hand—the only part of my body not below ground—we were both unscathed. My hearing became muffled like being under water. This was now three times in about ten or fifteen seconds that I had been spared from death. In the morning,

> I reclaimed the rosary beads at the bottom of our foxhole and put them back into their original home in my pocket. Then later, I repaired them, although two beads were missing, but I was still alive, which I consider a fair trade. I have asked myself since then: "Was this an earthly coincidence or God's divine intervention into my life?" I am not a over-religious man, but I guess the answer is obvious—to me anyway—that He holds our lives in His hands.

**Platoon Sgt. William Howard, mortar platoon B/1-61 (courtesy Bill Howard).**

The incoming mortar attack remained heavy and lasted for a full 30 minutes until reverse radar plotted the origin of the mortars from a small hill to the northwest. Away from our position, several waves of sappers from companies of the 27th NVA Regiment staged on the western side of the perimeter. Sappers initiated the attack, and before the western positions could react, the sappers were on them and a portion of the perimeter was overrun. The survivors fought back hand to hand at their foxholes and the assault was eventually reversed. A second attack of grenades and satchel charges ensued, followed by assaulting hostile forces. This one was also repelled, but not without more close-in fighting.

From the summit of Hill 162, Lt. Mike Cowart, the Bravo Company forward observer, and his tech sergeant, Jon DeBoer, adjusted artillery against the sapper assault that they watched develop against the forces on Hill 100 about fifteen hundred meters to the west. They had a bird's-eye view there as they saw wave after wave of NVA sappers charge Captain Gallagher's western perimeter, only to be halted and turned back by their fire missions from five different batteries of 155mm and 175mm. They fired mostly high explosive rounds but a sixth provided air-burst phosphorus illumination canisters.

Cowart relates that the whole hillside was perfectly illuminated by the basketball canisters while burning their bright phosphorus fuel. This assortment of ordnance came from four different fire bases—Con Thien, C-2, Camp Carroll and Vandergrift. Both Marine and Army batteries were among the support that saved the grunts on the ground that night. Cowart and DeBoer observed the hits and adjusted artillery throughout the night.

2Lt Michael Cowart, FO for Bravo Company:

> Alpha Company got airlifted in but we did not see the helicopters coming in. It was my practice—and people made fun of me a little bit—that I loaded up like a pack mule when I went into the bush, which is where I spent most of my time until I got wounded. I carried an extra PRC battery or two most of the time, because commo is everything. On that night, just about everybody else's battery was dead and I had a clear view of the night position, so when that crap hit the fan we heard all this chatter on the radio but of course we were all up and awake anyway. I was totally

disgusted with myself, because I had almost killed those guys earlier in the night and if it happened again, how could I live with myself? I don't know if I could have lived with that or not. About two in the morning, we hear all this stuff and those guys down there just about had their world come to an end. From my position—and of course I'm on the net too—I'm seeing tracers everywhere, I'm seeing outgoing, I'm seeing incoming, I'm hearing it and you could see that everyone was literally fighting for their lives. Had Alpha Company not been flown out there [to reinforce the mortars], all those other people would have been killed. They'd have been slaughtered. There would not have been a man left—at all. The NVA would have overrun them—easily. There's no question that Alpha Company being there saved every one of those people from being killed. God bless Captain Gallagher for volunteering. I had met him casually but I really did not know him, but he was obviously a good soldier. And anyone that would volunteer to go into those circumstances is obviously a brave man. I have nothing but the utmost respect for him and the rest of his men because every one of those people would have been killed if he did not show up with his men. I knew Kevin McGrath, who took over after Gallagher was killed. Kevin was my counterpart for Alpha Company. We talked. He was a first lieutenant—I was a second lieutenant. He was about my height—heavyset with a moustache, I believe. I had met Kevin and he retired as a lieutenant colonel, if I remember right. We were contemporaries.

So this thing kicks off and from my bird's-eye view—you've got Spooky on station, you've got F-4 Phantoms on station and the artillery that I am controlling. I believe there were five batteries of HE and one battery of illumination and it's like the Fourth of July—squared—several times. I could hear Spooky—ah, Puff—you know, C-130s with mini-guns—whatever you want to call it—talking. And he was saying that he was going to have to go back to base for ammunition because he was down to 50,000 rounds. And I don't know how many rounds went out that night, but it was like a solid screen of red going out when he was firing. And I don't know how many rounds from those five HE batteries of 175s went out that night, but it was a lot. It was nonstop explosions for several hours. It went on from about one o'clock until about five o'clock. From my perspective I could see the NVA coming off that hill—going back and forth—it was like ants. It was nonstop. There were lots of them. And my artillery was dropping in all over the place—amongst them. What I was worried about all these years—what made me terrified under those stressful conditions was: one battery is enough, but two, three, four, five or six batteries? I was terrified that I would make an adjustment that wasn't right and kill those guys. That is something that I would never get over. It was tight and all serious business—life and death stuff. Luckily, our perimeter was quiet and luckily, all of our focus could be directed to the attack below. My recollection is that I was a click away—maybe 1200 to 1500 meters away, but it was close enough that I could see. Of course, in those days I had pretty good eyes and I could see. My eyes back then—when they checked them—were 20/10 and they quit checking them after that. Something that was twenty feet away, I could see it like it was ten feet away. I could clearly see the enemy soldiers going on and off that hill. It appeared to me that the enemy assets that had us and Charley Company occupied during the day had shifted to that hill below us because our night was relatively quiet.

Early on, at the rim of Gallagher's perimeter, PFC Sterling "Bo" Kelly was an assistant gunner to PFC Skip Hager on a 50-caliber machine gun. While also periodically going for more ammunition, doubling as an assistant medic and treating wounded, he encountered an enemy sapper and was thrown to the ground and stunned by several grenades thrown towards him. Though he was shaken, Kelly rose to his feet and killed the sapper with his shotgun. A portion of his Bronze Star citation tells the story best.

**Citation**

For heroism in connection with ground operations against a hostile force in the Republic of Vietnam: Private First Class Kelly distinguished himself by valorous actions on 13 November as a machine gunner with Company A, 1st Battalion (Mechanized), 61st Infantry during the defense of a night perimeter in the northernmost portion of South Vietnam. At approximately 0230 hours, a force of NVA soldiers initiated a series of ground assaults on Company A's night defensive perimeter after a barrage of mortar and rocket-propelled grenade fire. During the assault, PFC

> Kelly delivered suppressive fire to all elements of the enemy force with his machine gun. When another platoon began taking heavy casualties, PFC Kelly fearlessly maneuvered about the perimeter, treating the injured and offering encouragement. While resupplying the perimeter with desperately needed ammunition, he was thrown to the ground and stunned by the impacts of several grenades. Although shaken, he struggled to his feet and killed the nearby foe with his rifle. PFC Kelly's courage inspired his fellow soldiers and contributed immeasurably to the successful defense of the perimeter. His gallantry was in keeping with the highest traditions of the military service and reflects great credit upon himself, his unit, and the United States Army.

It was at 0317 that the previously mentioned counter-mortar radar was plotted and Captain Gallagher—through the FO—relayed the plot to 5th/ 4th Arty. The enemy mortar position to the northwest was fired on from one of Cowart's HE batteries and was silenced at 0322. Several calls for medevac were made, but sniper fire and RPGs prevented their landing. Basketball illumination continued to fall and lit the perimeter. At 0340, the command post radio operator, was ordered by Captain Gallagher to pass out heat tabs to all positions to clearly mark the perimeter for Spooky 12 and a flight of four Gunfighter F-4 Fast Movers along with a second Spooky that was en route. Gunfighter was the call sign for the McDonnell Douglas F-4 Phantom jet interceptor. As the heat tabs were passed out, the machine-gun positions were instructed to fire out simultaneously to further mark the limits of the perimeter.

## *Spooky*

Spooky was the call sign for the Airforce Lockheed AC-47 gunship. The AC-47 was a United States Air Force C-47, the military version of the DC-3, that had been modified by mounting three 7.62 mm General Electric mini-guns to fire through two rear window openings and the side cargo door, all on the left (pilot's) side of the aircraft, and the modified craft's primary function was close air support for ground troops at night. Other armament configurations could also be found on similar C-47–based aircraft to include 20-millmeter cannons. The guns were actuated by a control on the pilot's yoke whereby he could control the guns either individually or together, although gunners were also among the crew to assist with gun failures and similar issues. The ship could orbit the target for hours, providing suppressing fire over an elliptical area approximately 47.5 meters in diameter, placing a round every 2.2 millimeters during a three-second burst. The aircraft also carried huge flares it could drop to illuminate the battleground.[2]

One of the crew members of Spooky12—the gun commander—was Bob Schilling. Schilling, a guest speaker at the 2015 Society of the Fifth Infantry Reunion in Columbus, Georgia, presented a slide show concerning the DC-3 and AC-47 crews in Vietnam. During the slide show, he talked of his missions assisting units in the field at night:

> When we had to reload and were in this area [Northern I Corps], we went to Nha Trang, but sometimes we went back to Ben Hoa to reload. You always want a gun on the line. You start out by firing the first two. When the first two are out, you fire the third gun while they are reloading the first two. You always have one gun on line. There was another Spooky hanging about two or three miles back while the first one was on line. Then we would call him and say, "C'mon in, we're out." He usually comes right up if it's a hot target and we head back to home base. If they still need us, then we scramble and get reloaded and come back again. Immediately, when we hit the ground, we are met at the reloading team and they put flares on and reload the ammo magazines. They ask us how the guns are. If they are OK, we are set to go again. We can land, load, refuel

> and take off in fifteen minutes. Under normal conditions we would have two planes that take off at dusk and stay in a sector so that they are already in the air. They are called CAPS. Those two are up until midnight. Two more take off at midnight and fly until dawn in the morning. Then they went back in the morning since we never did any day missions after 1965. Back then, when we flew a lot of day missions, they were shooting us down like flies because we were big slow birds.[3]

## *Gunfighter*

Gunfighter was the call sign for the F-4 Phantom Interceptor Jet. The McDonnell Douglas F-4 Phantom II is a tandem two-seat, twin-engine, all-weather, long-range supersonic jet interceptor aircraft/fighter-bomber originally developed for the United States Navy by McDonnell Aircraft. It first entered service in 1960 with the U.S. Navy. Proving highly adaptable, it was also adopted by the U.S. Marine Corps and the U.S. Air Force, and by the mid–1960s had become a major part of their respective air wings. The Phantom is a large fighter with a top speed of over Mach 2.2. It can carry more than 18,000 pounds (8,400 kg) of weapons on nine external hard points, including air-to-air missiles, air-to-ground missiles, and various bombs.[4]

Again, Lt. Mike Cowart, the Bravo Company forward observer, watched the devastation during breaks in the artillery fire that rained down on the charging sappers from the Spooky mini-guns. As the radio operator left the command post on his mission to distribute heat tabs to mark the company perimeter, Capt. Gallagher was left climbing on top of the command track searching out other enemy positions to relay to the Alpha Company forward observer, 1Lt Kevin McGrath, standing on the ramp of the command track. When the radio operator returned, Spooky 12 was on site and firing. As the operator approached the command post, he saw Captain Gallagher, who had been mortally wounded, lying across the ramp of the APC. The other RTO, Sp4 Tom Landrum, lay mortally wounded near him. One report states that he verbally turned over command to Lt. Kevin McGrath just before he expired. The time was 0354. A radio man recalls:

> We were flown into their perimeter. Once we were all in the perimeter, Captain Gallagher told me to set up the radio watch for the night. I took first watch and Billy Evans from 1st platoon, who was helping out since we were an RTO short, took the second watch. Shortly after I got settled in and fell to sleep, all hell broke loose. I ran to the track where the CP was set up. At some point, Captain Gallagher told me to take a box of heat tabs and hand them out on the perimeter and to tell the men to light them so the Air Force pilots would be able to see our perimeter before they made any bombing runs. Captain Gallagher was climbing onto the top of the track for better vision. I took off as I was told and handed out the tabs. When I returned to the track the captain was dead. That is when Keven McGrath FO took charge. The battalion was notified of the captain's death. The next morning after it was over with, I helped load his body on a chopper.

Ammo resupply was an ongoing issue—especially 81-millmeter mortars. All of 1-61's mortar platoons had an inadequate allotment that was considered too small under the conditions in the field in order to support the patrols, ambushes and listening posts. Mortar sergeants had to beg for resupply, yet there was no shortage. The problem was that even though there was a surplus of ammo, it was allotted to the ARVNs—and they simply sat on it and never used it. An incident related by Sergeant Bill Howard explains the army SNAFU concerning this resupply issue:

> We were in the field in early November and we had run out of ammunition. I needed 81mm ammo. So when my requisition went in they told me that they didn't have any. So I told Captain Perica—it might have been Captain Spencer by then, I'm not sure—that I was going back to Quang Tri to get ammo. I got on a bird and flew back to Quang Tri, then grabbed an APC and went over to the ammo dump. When I got there I was confronted by an E-5 who said, "If you're here to get ammo, where's your requisition?" I said that I didn't have one and he said that I couldn't have ammo. I said, "Yes I can, because I need it." He told me that without a requisition, I couldn't have it. So I challenged him on his date of rank—I was an E-5 also—and I outranked him by two days. I then said, "Because I am taking charge, I'm taking the ammo." I took the APC in—dropped the back—and started throwing ammo in. He had called somebody because the MPs showed up. There was a major, or a colonel maybe, who came up and asked who was in charge and to that, I said that I was. He asked me what I thought I was doing. My comment to him was, "Look. You've got me out there as a platoon sergeant of a mortar platoon to support 136 men and I don't have any ammunition. I need ammo for my eighty-ones. You tell me I have to support those men and because I don't have a requisition, the ARVNs are just sitting on it and they're not even using it"—blank blank blank blank blank. He said, "You can't take it without a requisition." I said, "Sir—I am taking it because I have to support those guys out there that are dying for this country." He looked at me and he said, "Sergeant—don't you EVER come in here and do THAT again. Get over to that track—get it loaded and get out of here." So, I loaded the track and off we went. The whole idea of the political aspect of that fact that the ARVNs can have that ammo and we can't and because the ARVNs never use it—it got me mad. We got the ammo and went back to the field and had our resupply.

The constant issue of having to fight for every round of ammo led to the fourth platoon's never having the number of mortar rounds they would have liked, and the ammo dwindled as the night went on. Platoon Leader Lieutenant Dietrich, FDC Staff Sergeant Russ Widener, and Platoon Sergeant Bill Howard, remembers the beginning of the attack on Hill 100:

> When the shit started, the fire mission was "charge zero or maybe charge one"—they were so close and on us. With that—you shoot it and it goes maybe fifty yards out. It just barely goes up and then comes down—it depends on your elevation. They were so close that we had to cover the wire. We were shooting short rounds—not actually short but you know what I mean. It was like three or four in the morning and we had run out of ammo and we were very selective on our hits. It was not barrages any more; we had to be more selective and it was up to me to decide what we did. Should I hit far out to catch them or bring it in close because they were all around us? That was kind of like the dilemma. When you've got five rounds, what do you do with them? What the hell was I doing? Well, I was doing a job of making sure that the guns fired accurately. I communicated with the FDC and made sure the guns were in. I had no idea of what else was going on around me. I wished I would have, because maybe I could have done more, but I was so involved with the guns.

As the time approached 0400, ammunition supplies were drying up and emergency resupply was needed. Fortunately, Spooky 11 arrived on scene to pick up the slack and foiled another massive assault that was being staged to the southwest of the perimeter. Again, Cowart watched the scene develop from Hill 162. At 0430, a pair of Fast Movers strafed from the southwest and dropped bombs just outside the wire.

At 0500 a flight of four more F-4 Phantoms arrived on station and made multiple passes with napalm and 250-pound bombs—known to the pilots and FACs as "nape and snake." This was a military slang term coined during the Vietnam War by American infantry radiomen, referring to the dropping of 250-lb. MK-81 Snake-eye bombs ("snake") and 500-lb. M-47 napalm canisters ("nape") on a position. Again, Mike Cowart and Jon DeBoer on Hill 162 watched the enemy scatter and run in front of the Gunslingers. Some

**PFC Randall "Tony" Robinson, RTO for Lt. Chelsea Korte, WIA from a grenade blast on 13 Nov 1969 (courtesy Tony Robinson).**

of the bombs struck just outside the perimeter wire and there were dozens of punishing concussions. Many infantrymen on the ground shook their fists and cursed the pilots for dropping their bomb-load too close, but the memories of those pilots and the visual sighting of Cowart and DeBoer attest that swarms of NVA were very close to the wire strung around the NDP. One of those was an NCO for 4/B/1-61—SSgt Russ Widener—who shouted into his radio for the TAC Air pilots to back off. Today he realizes how close the enemy really were, as well as the huge role those pilots played in saving the lives of every man on that perimeter. Widener remembers:

> I just have flashes of things like this that I remember. Somehow, I ended up talking to the FAC that night on the radio when they brought the jets in. When the first bomb was dropped, it felt like it went off just outside the edge of the perimeter and it knocked me off my feet. I can distinctly remember—and I don't know how I knew that the radio handset that was hanging down from the door of the track was the one that this guy was using to talk to the FAC—getting on the handset and saying, "Get them the hell out of here. That was too close." Then I hear this calm voice on the other end of the mike. It was the FAC and he was talking like he was sitting in a lounge chair and quietly watching TV. He said something like, "Roger, I understand that was a little close. I'll move it out." To this day I can remember holding the handset at arm's length away and shouting, "A LITTLE CLOSE!!! A LITTLE CLOSE!!!" I would give anything to find out who that FAC officer was to thank him and maybe kiss the soles of his feet.

Russ spent a good portion of the night when he wasn't carrying ammo to positions.

A portion of Russ Widener's Silver Star citation reads as follows:

> Sergeant Widener distinguished himself by valorous action on 13 November 1969 as a mortar section leader of Company B, 1st Battalion (Mechanized), 61st Infantry Regiment, 5th Infantry Division (Mechanized) during defense of a night perimeter. A numerically superior force of North Vietnamese Army regulars engaged the company's perimeter with a devastating barrage of mortar, rocket-propelled grenades and small arms fire. Sergeant Widener, with complete disregard for his own safety, fearlessly moved from position to position, providing encouragement and leadership, administered first aid to more than fifteen injured comrades, and personally eliminated an aggressor about to throw a grenade into the position where he was treating a casualty. His knowledge of first aid saved many lives and was largely responsible for conserving the unit's fighting strength. Sergeant Widener's gallantry and selflessness were in keeping with the highest traditions of the military service and reflect great credit upon himself, his unit and the United States Army.

Back at C-2 Firebase at 0500—after only a few hours of sleep—Doc Smith was awakened and asked if he and the Lancer 28 crew would volunteer for another dangerous mission. Alpha Company's perimeter on Hill 100 was completely out of 81-millimeter mortar rounds and was also nearly out of small arms munitions. After consulting his tired crew, they unanimously accepted the dangerous mission. They were to replace another chopper that was grounded because of mechanical problems. At 0515 Lancer 28 was loaded with eighty-one millimeter mortar rounds, small arms M-16 cartridges, machine gun belted ammunition, and grenades. At 0530 the heavily laden chopper lifted off and turned southwest to make the seven-mile trip to Hill 100. Reaching the ammo-depleted perimeter, they were waved off temporally by the Forward Air Controller while TAC-Air finished their bombing runs. After that, Spooky 12 began its circular reign of terror, sending hundreds of thousands of rounds in a red rotating curtain. At 0545 all fire missions were complete and Lancer 28 was okayed to enter the airspace to resupply Alpha Company. The plan was also to medevac two serious stretcher cases and several other wounded men. It would turn out that the perimeter was still too hot and the medevacs would have to be postponed.

As Lancer 28 started its approach in total blackout mode, Doc Smith spotted the two flashlight beams that were to guide them in. They were held by Sgt. Bill Howard—the Bravo Company mortar platoon sergeant—who stood sixty feet outside the positions on the edge of the perimeter. As Doc dropped altitude, he now saw that the whole perimeter was covered in a thick blanket of NVA bodies. There was no clear spot to land and as he approached the flashlight beams, he was forced to set his skids on several NVA corpses. By now Howard was receiving sniper fire as he rushed to the side door of the Slick and started pulling the several dozen ammo crates to the ground. At the same time, several men rushed from the perimeter to carry the ammo back inside the NDP. Among them were Gary Higgins, Bud Wagner, Tim Hurley, Russ Widener and others. As Howard was pulling the crates out, two large crates of mortars were still on the far side of the chopper deck. Knowing the desperate need for those mortars, Howard began running around the front of the chopper in a low crouch. Howard pulled the last two boxes off just as a rocket-propelled grenade exploded directly over him. It peppered the side of the Huey, and Bruce Nesmith—the crew chief—was sprayed by a swarm of small particles, which would later prove to be bits of dirt and stone. Nesmith believed Bill Howard was hit more substantially when he watched him fall to the ground. Nesmith reached for him in an attempt to pull him aboard. As Nesmith pulled with all his strength, the Slick began to lift and turn. The force of the lift and Howard's two-hundred-pound mass was too much for even the six-foot-eight Nesmith to lift and he lost his grip. Howard fell away to the ground and the chopper crew member could only watch Howard's form fade into the darkness of the night. For forty-six years Nesmith carried a deep survivor's guilt about not being able to save Howard and blamed himself for his probable death because he had not done enough or tried hard enough to save him. It was not until this author told him that Bill Howard got himself back to the perimeter, that he realized that he had survived the battle. In the morning, Howard nursed a few small scratches on his legs from the RPG blast, but aside from that was OK. Bruce Nesmith recalls the mission:

> They called us back out and said there was a 5th Mech unit loggered up in the same area as the day before and in danger of being overrun. They were out of ammo and an emergency ammo resupply was needed. It was kind of an all-hands-on evolution and whoever could get up and get out fastest, just got up and went out. We were the first crew out on the pad by I guess quite a while. We loaded up with ammo—basically overloaded, really—and we just barely got off the ground and headed off to that area. When we got in visual range, of course we could see all the fire where the battle was taking place and Spooky was just finishing up circling overhead putting down his fire. It was pitch dark—you couldn't see anything except the tracers everywhere. We bypassed the area and went off to the east while Spooky finished his rounds. Then we were called in. We were taking ground fire most of the time—mostly AK fire. We didn't return fire or anything because they couldn't see us—they were just shooting at the sound. We had all of our running lights and everything turned off and there was no illumination. When we finally made our approach and came in, I think there was a guy with a flashlight out there outside the perimeter wire. We didn't expect to see a flashlight and couldn't believe it when Doc turned on the landing lights for the final approach. You literally couldn't see the ground, it was so completely littered with bodies. You couldn't even see the grass, either. We actually landed on a carpet of bodies—no grass to be seen anywhere. We started chucking ammo out and two or three guys—I know one guy on my side and one or two on Bob's side—just jumped out there and we just started chucking ammo. About the time we finished chucking ammo out, there was a blast—it was a mortar, or satchel charge or RPG—went off right under the tail rotor. We were still on the ground when it hit and Doc put it in full pitch to head out. The man standing next to my side where we were kicking ammo off looked hit, and I made a grab for him and he fell backwards and fell away from me. That whole side of the aircraft was peppered with shrapnel. I always wondered if he was all right or not.
>
> We did not come back to take any medevacs out after that. We were not in any shape to after that. I don't remember where the nearest fire base was—maybe A-4—but we landed on a firebase right near the DMZ to see what kind of shape we were really in. The whole tail boom was shot up. We had holes in the tail rotor drive shafts. The nose cap from the RPG—or whatever it was—went through the engine compartment and just missed the engine. The nose cone was still on the deck in the engine compartment. I had it for years but finally lost it. That was our last engagement and we flew the aircraft back to Quang Tri the next day and got a chewing out because we did. They then craned it back to Evans. It was in the hangar for about six weeks. It got a new tail boom and the engine compartment was messed up. There was a lot of sheet metal work to do. It was pretty much a mess. Doc got a DFC. Peter pilot got the DFC. Door gunner got the Air Medal with valor. I did not get a Purple Heart, but I had a few nicks and dings at times, but we never did apply for Hearts. When you're hauling out people that have lost arms and legs you didn't worry about Hearts.

As the saying goes, there are two sides to every story, and surprisingly, both sides of this story coincide perfectly. Bill Howard describes the resupply from his point of view on the ground and what a perfect target he must have been to the attacking NVA. Again, these are his words as told to this author:

> About the resupply helicopter and Bruce Nesmith [laughs heartily]—love him dearly. When I… It was kind of a surreal issue—I was talking to Lancer 28 and my call sign was Four Five. He said, "I'm coming into a hot LZ and I need light." He wanted two white lights to land by. So, I grabbed two flashlights and—for the mortars—we had the L-shaped flashlights. I took the red lens off them and I went out and stood probably fifty yards outside the perimeter and stood there and held the lights up for him to see. They came in and started to land and were about twenty to thirty yards off the ground when they flipped on the landing lights. I felt like I was a naked man standing in the middle of Hollywood and Vine. I was the only man that that whole part of Vietnam could see [laughs]. We've got green tracers coming this way and red tracers going that way and here I am standing up with two white flashlights and this guy turns his lights on. And I thought, "Oh shit. I'm dead." So, he landed and we started unloading. I don't know how many cases of eighty-one were on that deck, and that's when that RPG came in and just blew the side out of the chopper. When it did, Doc—the pilot—looked at me and said, "I'm out of here." Doc—I've been looking for him for forty-five years because I wanted to thank him. But Doc's no longer with us and I never got a chance to meet him. I jumped up on the skid after the RPG hit to grab two more boxes of ammo, and at the same time, Bruce [Crew Chief of Lancer 28] reached down to grab my arm. He thought I was hit from all that shrapnel and I'm thinking I've got to hold on to those last boxes of ammo. I'm keeping them. I grabbed them and pulled back while the chopper was three or four feet off the ground. He was on his way out. When I pulled on them, I fell backwards and landed on the ground with the two boxes of ammo. So, Bruce has always wondered what happened to me. On the other hand, I've got my two boxes of ammo and here I lay outside the perimeter with green tracers going one way and red tracers going the other. I laid there for maybe two minutes and I was scared shitless because I'm in the middle of a whole mound of eighty-one millimeter rounds with tracers going both ways. "What do I do now?" So, I low-crawled back to the perimeter with the two boxes of ammo. When things lulled down later, we had Tim and some of the other guys in the fourth platoon go out and retrieve the rest of them. That whole incident is just embedded in my head until this day because that's what I remember of the night. I was hit by the shrapnel but it was just scrapes and cuts—nothing deep—no Purple Heart. I got some on my legs because they were exposed when the RPG hit the chopper. And when they turned on the landing lights you could see all these NVA lying dead everywhere—I had no idea up to that point. If I'd have known that, I'd have been even more scared.

Staff Sergeant Widener also remembers the flashlight incident:

> When the flashlights came on, the helicopter was just coming in to hover and I followed one of our guys out there pulling ammo boxes off the helicopter. About the same time a mortar round or maybe an RPG round went off and exploded pretty close to the helicopter. He did an emergency take-off right from there and went up. The guy with the flashlight—that was Bill Howard.

At this point, a dozen or so positions on the eastern perimeter were thinned from two-man to one-man positions to reinforce the hard-hit western perimeter and replace the wounded and dead. These relocated troopers carried the recently resupplied ammo with them to their new positions.

Sp4 Louis Pepi:

> My position was no exception. Lt. William Miller and Sp4 Don Sarsfield—our track driver but acting squad leader that night—showed up a few minutes after we watched the Slick rise off behind us following a bright ball of fire. Lt. Miller, seeing my bloody hand, suggested I be medevacked after the more seriously wounded were soon to be lifted out. I heartily refused, stating that I wasn't going to get into an RPG magnet. For that he rewarded me with the task of pulling a 50-caliber gun off the track behind us and bringing it to a foxhole several positions down. Reluctantly, and as scared as I have ever been in my life, I jumped up on the PC, detached the 86-pound gun, and jumped to the ground with it all in one motion. How I didn't break both ankles, I'll never know. But today my good ankle is severely deformed and the other has been fused. Sarsfield (with a tripod and a box of ammunition) and the lieutenant (with two more boxes of fifty) led me to

> the vacant position. Sarsfield and I set up the gun and he assisted for a few bursts to establish sectors of fire. He left briefly, but then returned with a new partner—a spare barrel, a sandbag full of grenades, cigarettes and a canteen of water. He returned several times in the course of the night to assist and pass on information. By now it was an hour or so until daylight and, except for sporadic sniper fire and an occasional mortar round, it appeared that the enemy was withdrawing. Still, every few minutes the intensity of fire would escalate as someone spotted movement—maybe sappers trying to retrieve their dead and wounded, policing the battlefield. There were no other positions visible from my foxhole, and that was a very long hour until first light.

It was now evident that the enemy was starting its withdrawal—or in their tactical jargon, that of Quick Clearance and eventually Quick Withdrawal. Still, sniper fire and the occasion mortar caused the perimeter to keep their collective heads low. But you could almost breathe again and savor the thought that you might have actually survived the night.

At other positions around the perimeter the situation was worse and many other stories developed. Lieutenant Chelsea Korte's story was one of those. Korte, a young newly commissioned officer who hailed from the state of Washington, was the weapons platoon leader, but this night he and his mortar-men were airlifted into Gallagher Ridge as riflemen. When the attack started, the NVA below his position began hurling grenades from several rows of old foxholes oriented in concentric rings. This hill had been used many times by both Marines and Army soldiers over the years and the ring of foxholes used on any given night depended on the size of the unit in the field. Evidently, Hill 100 had been used as a larger battalion-sized NDP many times. The NVA occupied those outer foxholes situated 50 meters beyond and below the positions that Alpha Company was using that night. As the firefight started, the NVA below began firing and hurling Chicom grenades. As Korte's RTO, PFC Randall (Tony) Robinson tells it, a grenade fell in front of a large foxhole where he lay wounded with PFC Robert Parker from his platoon. Immediately, Korte fell on it, whether on purpose or not, shielding his men from the blast. Korte states today that he slipped and accidently fell on it, but his men saw it much differently. He was wounded with a large piece of shrapnel in the side of his thorax, but managed to rally himself—and then his men—and directed fire on the positions below. Robinson describes the first minutes of the firefight on the southwestern side of the perimeter:

> I was hit when we were first attacked. I was inside the perimeter and not on bunker guard. I can't say exactly where I was, but I was on the corner where the six guys got killed. They broke through the perimeter right there. They were inside the perimeter and they threw grenades and they hit me before I even realized what was going on. The only one [of the dead] I remember was the guy that had just been transferred from Germany. He was killed right in front of me. This guy was a Sp4 [Sp4 Norman Benedik]. He had got to the company that day when we were set up there between C-2 and A-4. He had volunteered to come to Nam. Yeah—he got killed that night. The whole perimeter got hit hard—I know that, but when they initially broke through, it was on our side. I had carried Korte's radio. After I got hit, Fox found out I was hit and he tried to get me on a chopper but I didn't make it in time. So, I went back and got in a foxhole with a guy named [PFC Robert] Parker. I got hit in the back—all up my back. It blew my boot off—I got hit in the foot too. Just shrapnel. I wasn't hit as bad as I thought it was at the time. Korte was coming around checking on the perimeter and he saw that I was wounded. While he was checking on me, they threw another grenade in. It hit right in front of the foxhole. When it landed in front of the foxhole, Korte laid down on it and it blew him up. From that point, he took off and I never saw him until the next morning when we took off on the same chopper. On the medevac chopper, I saw he had a big hole blown in his chest and I believe he had been hit somewhere else before that too. I know he had a big hole because on the medevac, it was daylight and he was in a lot of pain.

They gave him morphine and I could see the big hole and I didn't know whether he was going to make it or not. I never did hear from him, not until he sent us a care package back from the States. (I was told) ... that he got the Distinguished Service Cross. I should have put him in for something. He should have gotten the Medal of Honor. After the medevac, I was out for three or four weeks, and when I came back, I started carrying the radio for [Capt.] Neely. Korte was originally an enlisted man—he had been drafted and they sent him to Nam. He wanted out of there so he re-upped for three years to go back to OCS—officers school. Well, he went through officer's school and they sent him right back there.

Though in pain and losing blood, Korte kept his elbow tightly pressed to his side to slow his bleeding. He continued to expose himself and point out positions to his men. In the murderous enemy fire, his men began to fall wounded. He pulled and carried them back up the hill to the military crest where they could be tended to by the medics who had gathered all the WIAs in one place near the CP. He then would rally replacements back to his section of the perimeter. Through his pain and loss of blood, he did this many more times. He passed out at one time from the fatigue and severity of his wound, but eventually got himself back to his men to direct fire. In the morning, many men remember seeing a young lieutenant lying on a stretcher waiting for the first medevac. It was Chelsea Korte. He was nominated for the Medal of Honor but was awarded the Distinguished Service Cross. It reads as follows:

**Citation**

The President of the United States takes pleasure in presenting the Distinguished Service Cross to Chelsea C. Korte, Second Lieutenant (Infantry), U.S. Army, for extraordinary heroism in connection with military operations involving conflict with armed hostile force in the Republic of Vietnam, while serving with Company A, 1st Battalion, 61st Infantry, 1st Infantry Brigade, 5th Infantry Division (Mechanized). Second Lieutenant Korte distinguished himself while serving as platoon leader of a weapons platoon during the defense of a night perimeter just south of the Demilitarized Zone. Early that morning, waves of North Vietnamese regulars assaulted Lieutenant Korte's position under cover of rocket-propelled grenade, mortar, and automatic weapons fire. Although hit in the abdomen by an enemy round early in the fighting, Lieutenant Korte refused medical aid and continued to direct the return fire of his men. When the blast of a rocket-propelled grenade threw one of his men outside the perimeter, Lieutenant Korte, though weakened by his own wound, moved through a hail of enemy fire to his fallen comrade and pulled him back within the perimeter. Lieutenant Korte attempted to administer first aid to the wounded soldier, but he lapsed into unconsciousness from exhaustion and loss of blood. When he regained consciousness, Lieutenant Korte ordered the medical aid-man treating his wound to attend to the soldier he had just retrieved. He then staggered off to the perimeter and resumed command of his defenses. Sighting two enemy soldiers firing from behind a clump of bushes, Lieutenant Korte summoned a rifleman to his side and gave the soldier two hand grenades. He then stood up in the open to attract the attention of the enemy soldiers. As the two enemy rose to open fire, Lieutenant Korte's companion hurled his grenades and killed both enemy soldiers. Noticing then that machine gunners on the perimeter were low on ammunition, Lieutenant Korte three times crawled over thirty meters under fire to the gun emplacements with re-supplies of ammunition. Despite Lieutenant Korte's determined efforts to hold back the enemy onrush, one side of the perimeter was about to be overrun. Lieutenant Korte then crawled to the other side of the perimeter and ordered reinforcements to the endangered side. While deploying these troops to defensive positions, Lieutenant Korte collapsed unconscious on the battlefield. Emboldened by Lieutenant Korte's indomitable fighting spirit, his men, though overwhelmingly outnumbered, emerged from their foxholes and charged the enemy attackers. So stunned were the enemy that they broke contact and fled, leaving over a hundred dead and wounded on the battlefield. Second Lieutenant Korte's extraordinary heroism and devotion to duty were in keeping with the highest traditions of the military service and reflect great credit upon himself, his unit, and the United States Army.

PFC Edwin Martin was a member of Lieutenant Korte's platoon. In his words he remembers the previous day and that night:

> It was late in the afternoon and the battalion commander and the chaplain came out in the field. Lieutenant Korte told us that Captain Gallagher was going to lighten up on us because we were sure to see some combat [that] night. Some guys said that the real change of attitude was that he wanted body count or something, but that was hearsay. So in the afternoon, Gallagher got orders that he was to be airlifted to Hill 100 to support mortar elements of B and C Company that were there, and there were about thirty men as I remember. The choppers picked us up and we headed towards the DMZ while darkness was setting in. We were flying at about 1000 feet. From above, you could see thousands of bomb craters and there was no vegetation. It was a desolate area. And finally—one by one—the choppers landed on the ridge there. And this always bothered me. We landed on the hill on the southern part of the hilltop where they had an area cleared for the choppers to land there. My squad exited to the right of the chopper and moved about thirty feet or so and filled a couple large foxholes, which I believe, were on the southeastern side of the hill. And these foxholes formed the outer perimeter ring of positions that encircled the hill. My squad and another squad filled these large holes. We had five men in each hole. They were about 3 feet deep. In my hole the first guy to my left was named Denny [Collie]. That's all I knew him by. A lot of the guys wanted to go by their first names only. He was a close friend to me there. And then there was me. The next guy was a black guy, Sp4 [Kenny] Brown with his M-79 grenade launcher, then Staff Sgt. Hearn, who had recently joined us, and the fifth guy in that hole was Sergeant Bob O'Day—the squad leader. To the right of the hole were some of the other guys in our squad, I believe. Then over to the left were some of the guys from B and C Company. It was pitch dark when we got there and I was a little disoriented. The defense emplacements there consisted of three concentric circles. There was the outer circle that we were in where 50 machine guns were set up, and at the peak of the hill was a circle of APCs. Between our positions and the APCs was another ring of staggered positions with M-60s. I've got to hand it to the guys of B and C Company because they dug nice deep foxholes where you could kneel down and be completely protected. They handed out to each of us 4 or 5 frag grenades. I didn't know this at the time, but General Giap, the commander of all NVA forces, had this thing about timing an attack at exactly 2 o'clock [in the morning] when most would be asleep or tired. So, exactly at 2 in the morning they hit us. Denny and I were on guard and O'Day and Hearn were sleeping on the ground. O'Day and Hearn piled into the foxhole when the mortars started hitting and they let up a little bit when the NVA started charging up the hill. We opened up with the fifty caliber and the small arms fire started increasing. Then I noticed artillery started shooting illumination flares over us. After about 20 minutes or so, I started worrying about running out of ammunition, so I slowed down the rate of fire a little bit. Then the enemy started advancing and advancing until they got closer and closer to our position and finally close enough to start throwing concussion grenades at us, and we responded by throwing some of our frag grenades at them. One of their concussion grenades exploded behind us and to the left [followed] by a second grenade that exploded [immediately] behind us. Then what happened next was the scariest thing that ever happened to me when an NVA threw another grenade into our foxhole to the left of Denny and it ended up right next to Denny's side. Of course, it exploded and took a chunk out of his leg and side. The best that we could do was to lay him on his back in the bottom of the hole while we yelled for the company medic to come for assistance. It turned out that he was also one of the first casualties in the opening barrage. He had been peppered with fragments of a white phosphorous shell. Another guy was lying there on the ground on top of the hill. He was a black guy. Now here's one of the weirdest things—it was like a miracle I guess. Sergeant O'Day decided to get up and walk out of the foxhole. He stood up straight and was moving to the next hole when a guy in a [staggered] position behind us thought O'Day was an enemy soldier and opened up with his M-60, firing about a dozen rounds before we started screaming at him to cease fire. I was surprised to see Bob still standing there cursing the guy that fired at him who was not 20 feet away and missed completely. Bob came out of that with only a hole in his fatigue shirt. Then I looked forward and there was a little fireball headed toward us and an RPG passed about three feet over us and blew up in

the dirt behind us about twenty feet to the rear. They were obviously aiming for those tracks behind us. Then our artillery—and I think that this was 155 artillery—started shelling around the base of the hill and [later] I saw a Cobra gunship moving over the hill just to the right and above us and started firing a mini-gun and the tracers were streaming down into the valley. I'll never forget that loud buzz—you couldn't hear the individual rounds firing—just an incredible buzz going on—an incredible sound. Then the word from Lieutenant Korte was for all of us on the outer perimeter to open up with the 50-calibers simultaneously. This was to enable the jet aircraft overhead to spot the perimeter so they could see the perimeter more accurately and to start bombing. Shortly after, the jets started rolling in. One of the bombs hit just below us and the ground shook. I remember dirt clods raining down on us. It was a really close one and I think that's why Lt. Korte called off the airstrike because we were being endangered. So I'm still working with the 50-caliber while Sgt. Hearn directed Brown to start firing his M-79 at clusters of NVA muzzle flashes down below us with his grenade launcher. After a couple hours of fighting, Lt. Korte came down to me and ordered me up the hill to drag some more ammunition down and that's when I noticed he was wounded. He was hit in the leg [and side] and was dragging himself up and down the hill bringing ammunition to the positions. I grabbed my M-16 and ran to the top of the hill and grabbed some ammo cans and started dragging them back, proceeding toward my foxhole, where I encountered a shocking sight there. One of the guys—and I believe he was from B or C Company—had jumped into my foxhole in the exact same place where I was just a few minutes before—and he was laying there dead. And, and, uh, uh … [emotionally] [after a pause]. He was kind of a heavyset guy—kind of a good-looking kid—and he was laying there in the foxhole with a little hole in his chest. He had been shot through the heart. That was tough. He was in the bottom of the foxhole. I couldn't get back in the foxhole so I did the low crawl back up the hill. I found an old tree stump and I used it as cover as best I could and kind of got flat down behind it. It was kind of a risky place to be, but I could see a little bit better what was going on down there. I actually saw enemy soldiers for the first time. It was kind of a dark shadow out in front of the foxhole I was [just] in. It was an NVA in the brush about 10 feet out in front the foxhole where O'Day and all of the rest were. I yelled out to O'Day: "There's a dude out there in front of you, frag him." I ran into a guy on the medevac chopper who was in one of the mortar platoons on top of the hill. They had been sitting around and convinced some of his superiors to let him fire some zero charge 81-millimeter mortars from the mortar track that was behind us. So they supported us the rest of the night. It was about 5 a.m. when things were starting to let up some, and at the foot of the hill I saw a flash of an RPG round. I immediately opened fire on him with my M-16 and I believe I got him. It was too dark to tell for sure. Then at six o'clock the light of day began coming on and the enemy was gone—they were retreating. In the morning, Sgt. O'Day took a look me and ordered me to get on the last medevac chopper. I was wounded when the frag fell in the foxhole next to Denny and some of the fragments hit me in the face. I had a steel pot on which protected my head and I had a flak jacket, which protected the rest of me. My face was all bloody. I was hit in the face—shrapnel in the nose and my left eardrum was burst. I had this ringing sound and I couldn't hear much. We lifted off that hill and it was just like—ah—one moment you're fighting for your life and then all of a sudden this chopper comes and you lift off and it's all just a memory then. Such a drastic switch, you know. You switch from terror and then you're up in the sky taking a nice little ride and landing on the hospital ship. At the ship, this guy comes up to me and takes my rifle and they bring me down and start picking shrapnel out of me. Then they sent me to a hospital in Japan. I had some metal fragments in my eye they had to get out—in my cornea, so they operated and I spent about two months there. Then they sent me to Fort Hood, Texas, where I finished out my time.

Sp4 (Squad Leader) Donald Sarsfield relates his memories of November 13:

I was always in the 3-1 squad. Everybody else was getting hit out to the west. We were actually the reserve [for A-4] and I don't know if Gallagher volunteered us or if we were called in. The thing I remember about that is when we got out there fortunately our squad was put in an open area where there were a few bomb craters, but with some of the other guys on the perimeter, the jungle came right up to their positions and they were the ones that were getting their asses kicked all night. It's funny what sticks in your mind, but we had two guys from California and it really looked like we were going to get overrun there, so they put their rifles down in front of their foxhole and started smoking weed [since] they were sure we were going to die. I went over and kicked one's ass and told the other if he didn't get into shape he was going to get it too. So they picked up some after that. At one point I didn't want to see any of the guys exposed so I began bringing ammunition to them and I was really glad when dawn arrived. Of course, looking over that hill, the 3-1 guys had an open area, but the other guys weren't so lucky, and I really broke down and cried. I was just thankful that dawn arrived, and of course, looking over that hill we had an open area and you could see all those dead [NVA]. That's when I broke out and cried. On the other side, the cover for the NVA was right up to the perimeter and that's why all our dead were over there. It's amazing how luck plays a factor in so many things, but being over on the open side really helped us guys. I remember doing a sweep the next morning and I also remember I had a piece of shrapnel in my neck, which they took out right there on the spot. I also remember I got into it with the colonel who was flown over from the next hill and he said he wanted me to walk a sweep. I said, "Like hell I am. My guys have been up all night and you guys have been sitting on your ass." Fortunately his top sergeant got me aside and said to wait, mostly because I had this shrapnel in my neck when a satchel charge went off which actually blew my glasses off and all the buttons on my shirt. I was wearing a St. Christopher medal and that got blown off too. The tanks and bulldozers came out in the morning. There was fog and they couldn't find their way for a while.

PFC Alton "Skip" Hager remembers November 13:

I arrived in July of 1969, maybe the 12th. I remember I talked to Gallagher that day and had a conversation with him before we choppered out. I just shot the shit with him a little bit. I mean our company was really only about the size of a platoon and they choppered us in to these other guys before they got hit. We all knew we were going to get hit that night. As far as what happened at my position, I really don't want to talk about that because it brings bad thoughts back to me. I got shot somewhere between A-4 and C-2 later in January. It was just one of those freak deals is all that I can say. Nobody was paying attention and they just jumped out of the bushes and shot. That sapper got me. I stayed out on the hospital ship about a month and in February they shipped me down south to the 1st Cav. I am still messed up by the wound. You never heal over that shit. I stayed with the Cav until July and they shipped me home through Oakland.

As it grew light, it was apparent that the enemy was withdrawing, but several times sniper fire and enemy mortar blasts sounded in the dawn and return fire was restarted on all sides of the perimeter. Every man in every foxhole experienced some level of fighting as the perimeter was attacked on all sides. Many other men who braved the vicious fighting on Gallagher Ridge that night have vivid memories and have offered to share them in this narrative. Below are their memories in their own words.

Dan Cowan:

I remember waiting outside of A-4 all afternoon. We knew we were waiting to go help B and C Company but I don't think we understood how serious things were. I remember playing song trivia with some of the guys and just passing the time until it was getting dark and then the choppers came and got us. I think we landed on Hill 100. As soon as we jumped off we were assigned our positions. We made up a guard list and then bedded down for the night. I was opposite the side that got the brunt of the ground attack. Anyway, I fell fast asleep since my guard slot was not until early morning. Next thing I remember was waking up to a full-blown fire fight and low crawling as fast as I could to a foxhole which seemed so far away, and I was sure I would not make it without getting hit. As I landed in our foxhole, two more guys came seconds after me. One was Bud Wagner and I cannot remember the other guy's name. I know he was a short timer. I was an M-60 gunner and I remember it jamming at first but then I got it going. Adrenaline was crazy and I was firing too high and the short timer patted me on the back and said to keep the line of fire low. An RPG came over our heads and hit one of the mortar tracks. I saw a guy come crawling out of track yelling he had been hit. Another guy in our squad came to our hole and informed us Captain Gallagher had been killed. I remember the supply chopper coming in and Bud ran over to get us more ammo. "Thanks, Bud." I remember how terrifying it was when jets began dropping bombs outside perimeter. When illumination was up, I could see dead NVA to the left of our position but not in front of us. Nobody was wounded in our foxhole. I remember as daylight came and we heard "cease-fire," and it would be quiet for a while, but then firefight would start up again. When it was over, I would be one of the guys who lifted Cpt. Gallagher onto stretcher. I talked to the guy who was sole survivor in a foxhole that took a direct hit. I thought it was a Chicom grenade. He said he was OK but I could tell that emotionally he was not OK. I remember hearing about Lt. Korte, who had a chest wound and yet kept running under fire helping others. I saw him laying on a stretcher waiting for medevac. The guy who kicked the grenade—or whatever happened—and was wounded and sent home, left a lasting impression on me. I wish I remembered his name. He had a conversion with me in boot camp and called himself born again. We thought he was fanatical, but 8 years later I would have a similar conversion and then I understood his passion for God.

Sgt. Tim Hurley, one of the members of the stranded mortar platoon, remembers:

November 12–13, 1969: That morning started the same as any of my three or so weeks in the field—scared shitless. The company went out on a sweep leaving mortar guys. We were on the north side of the perimeter and Charlie's mortars were on the south side. We might have fired a couple of fire missions for them throughout the day. There was a lot of radio chatter throughout the day about buildup of NVA and possible contact. It was starting to get dark and we realized that our company was pinned down and would not be able to return to us. We were starting to get foxhole assignments and Bob Pinkston (Pinky) and I went out and set two trip flares on the north side before they called us back in. The north side was fairly flat and open. The west side of the perimeter dropped off pretty steeply and we had plotted a lot of our preplanned fire. The south side dropped off a little but had high ground beyond it. The east side dropped off but no major problems as I remember. The pucker factor was about 100 percent plus. It was uneventful until Alpha Company was choppered in. At night, when a trip flare went off, we started taking incoming. I remembered diving in a foxhole inside the perimeter and two guys ended up on top of me. We stayed there for a moment and then the top guy said, let's get out. The guy on top of me did not want to get out. I had to get by him because I did not want to die in a foxhole. We started stripping mortar rounds because we were firing charge zero and charge ones. The concentration of firing was intense. The smell of gunpowder was quickly burning your nose.

**2Lt Chelsea Korte, platoon leader of the mortar platoon, A/1-61. He was wounded on 13 Nov 1969, and was nominated for the Medal of Honor. He was eventually awarded the Distinguished Service Cross for his actions on the 13th.**

I remember someone coming to get a barrel or machine gun from the top of our track. We heard fairly quickly that Captain Gallagher had been killed. I remember Russ Widener going around acting as a medic. He was supposed to have caught an earlier chopper to return to base camp as he was leaving for home. At one point, Lt. Dietrich was sort of on top of our APC trying to see where the firing was coming from. The two tracks were trying to beat each other hitting the targets that he was pointing out. When Spooky came in, it was reassuring, but to me it was like, "Those things are bad boys." Watching them firing did improve everyone's spirit a bit. When the resupply helicopter came in, I ran out twice to get mortar ammo. I can remember running past dead NVA. When the F-4s came in, that was scary. I think the first run wasn't bad, but the next one, I can remember lying on my side and the whole sky was lit up in one giant flash with all kinds of weight pressing down on us. I remember Pinky getting on the radio and yelling, "Get those fucking jets out of here." Everybody thought they were too close, but someone said that the pilots could see hundreds of NVA coming over a hill towards us and they dropped the bombs right in the middle of them. I can remember someone screaming all night long. A couple of hours into the battle we took some more incoming and we went back into the holes. Above all the firing we could hear Gary Bonzon yell out, "Who shit in this foxhole?" He had dived in headfirst and his nose stopped a couple of inches from a fresh turd. I remember the sun coming up and the tanks getting there and one tank running over a one-legged NVA. Then people started searching for souvenirs or whatever and a grenade or booby trap went off. We had all the powder bags that we had stripped off from all the mortar rounds in a bomb crater next to one of our tracks and they caught fire. Something went off in the bomb crater from the fire. Pinky was going around trying to act cool eating spaghetti and meatballs while looking at all the bodies. An hour later he curled up in a ball crying like a baby. I can remember them taking the bodies out in the morning and the poncho fell off from one and he had terrible head injuries. I remember the 101st coming in with more helicopters than I thought existed. As far as you could see to the southeast were Chinooks, most of them slinging nets of supplies. I know that night I was with some of the bravest people that I have ever known. I can remember our company coming back later on to that hill and our Kit Carson scout made a stupid statement about NVA kicking the GI's ass. The captain's RTO kicked him in the ass and he flew at least 10 feet and they had to pull the RTO off him. I know all of us who did not have any physical wounds that day, surely left that hill a lot different than when we arrived there. I felt bad for Alpha [Company] because they took all of the losses and injuries. Later the next day when we went back into C-2, we went to the ammo dump and we were told that we had used our allocation of ammo for the month. We went back to Captain Spencer and let him handle it. I can close my eyes and I can see the layout of the APCs.

## Sp4 Darrell Alexander on some of those who were killed:

Dennis Ross was from Parker, Kansas. I know he had a daughter. I called information and asked for the phone number for Dennis Ross but I got his brother instead. I talked to his brother and told him we served together in Vietnam and were in the same firefight. My wife and I went down and visited the family and his daughter couldn't come by because she was at work but she did write me a letter. We would talk on the phone and I did get an invitation from Denny's granddaughter to come to her graduation. We went down to Parker, Kansas, for that. The guys, Ross, Caswell and Rose, got hit with a mortar round or grenade. Their foxholes were all in the same area. Tom Landrum was one of Gallagher's RTOs that night. My foxhole was within sight of the foxhole where Gallagher, Landrum, and the Forward Observer were. All three were standing on the ramp of an APC—I could see all three of them—and the next time I looked over there, it was just the FO [1Lt Kevin McGrath]. Ken Berry was wounded in the leg. His gun had misfired or malfunctioned.

## Sgt. Kenneth Leach:

We were on the southwest side and out in front of us was a ravine that had a lot of woods and we couldn't see them very well when they were coming. There was a ravine off to the right leading down and the guys facing that ravine to the west and northwest got hit the hardest because they came up that ravine. It started out quiet after we got dug in. We had taken on a little light fire but then they hit us hard. Then I remember there was a guy behind us that was screaming real loud. I had never heard anything like that before. He kept screaming that he was hit and probably knew he was going to die. I remember a little piece of shrapnel hit my arm and I pulled it out. We had an M-60 that Smith was firing and we were just putting down a suppressing fire. What I do remember very vividly was concerning one of those big illumination rounds. They have this thin aluminum housing on them and when they're coming down that aluminum cylinder comes off and just falls to the ground. Well, I heard this sound and it didn't sound like that swishing sound of a mortar, but it was kind of wobbly-sounding, and this piece of aluminum about eighteen inches long and two inches thick landed about 6 inches from my head. That was a close one—you know. And then this guy—I think he volunteered because he was a rear guy—he was the supply sergeant at A-4 and his name was Jennings. He was going around to all the foxholes and he told us that Gallagher had been killed. One of the last things Gallagher did was to have us throw these flares out in front of us to mark our position for the jets that came in—the F-4s that were dropping five-hundred-pound bombs coming in low just above the trees and dropping them just outside of our perimeter. The concussion from those things would knock you right down and make your eyeballs feel like they were going to come right out of your head. It's probably the only thing that kept us from being overrun. And that's when Jennings came by right after that and told us that Gallagher had been killed. Then we were running out of ammunition and they had this ammo point near the headquarters with all the ammo piled up. So I got up and ran over there for ammunition and I remember running by Gallagher. They had him covered up, mostly, but his arm was sticking out and I remember seeing that turquoise ring of his on his finger. So, I kind of silently paid my last respects to old Gallagher there, and then I ran on to the ammo point to resupply my little area. It went on like that all night, off and on. Then the next morning when it started to get light it slowed down a bit. And when it got light there was this dead NVA lying there on his stomach only a few feet from us inside the perimeter and the guy that we called the Preacher [Barrett] walked up to him and was standing over him. And then he kind of rolled him over with his foot and there was a grenade under him, and I don't know whether he set it under himself before he died or he was getting ready to throw it when he died, but anyway it went off when the Preacher rolled him over and he was wounded and they had to medevac him. He was there a shorter time than me. I got there in mid-October—about three weeks before this fight—and the Preacher got there after me. I am glad to hear that he made it. I remember a few guys on stretchers and one guy in particular lying in a pool of his own blood just mumbling and gurgling. We loaded him on a chopper but he probably didn't make it. I remember vividly the smell of the battlefield—there is no smell like it, no other feeling like it—to hear people screaming. It's an experience that you can't get from movies. They get as close as you can get—but you can never get that feeling, that ground rush, that smell, the bullets going over you—and the realization that it's real life and people are dead and dying there. The chopper guys the next day when we were loading the wounded told us they could see the enemy retreating while they were flying in for the medevacs and they looked like ants going over the hill—too many to count. But we held them off. I don't know what others say, but on my side we were pretty close to getting overrun. I remember there on that hill in the morning—I shaved with cold water in my steel pot. Gallagher went by the book and I think everyone respected him—I know I did. He had leadership qualities. I don't remember who it was I was talking to—maybe it was one of the medics tending to him—but they said he was up on top of the track directing artillery fire when he got hit. I hope he was killed immediately and didn't suffer.

### PFC Gary Higgins:

I don't remember what platoon I was in with 1-61, maybe first platoon. I was only there for about six weeks. I was in three different units in Vietnam. I was with the 9th Infantry and I was with the 4th of the 5th artillery. So, I got around. I was with SSgt. Orman with 1-61—I became his RTO. I remember Evilisizor. He was killed. He was new. He was to the left of where I was. Maybe one or two foxholes over. It looked as though it could have been a single bullet in the head. I was in a foxhole with three others. Three of us shooting and one of us loading ammo. Then during the night, Sergeant Orman wanted me to go around the perimeter to see if anybody needed any help. I saw a lot of dead NVA over on one side of the perimeter. We had a bunch of dead NVA in front of us, but they never got up to the foxholes, they never breached the line there. The other side did. A Huey helicopter came and they landed right outside the perimeter where we were. There was a few of us running back and forth unloading. Then artillery hit the tree line out in front of us when the chopper took off. In the morning, I helped put Gallagher on the helicopter with some other guys. He was carried in a poncho liner. I remember we got underneath the rotor and we were putting him in the chopper and the wash from the rotor blew the liner off and I could see his face laying there. He was on top of a track calling fire, I heard.

PFC Sterling "Gene" Kelly:

The level of tension started to rise when we got hit by that barrage. I got in my hole until that barrage lightened up. I naturally gravitated back to my old squad after that and I found Hager. I don't know who the assistant gunner was for him, but someone was feeding Hager's gun. Hager needed water and more ammunition. I went back to one of the mortar tracks and the ramp was open. I got a fifty barrel and I tucked that under my arm and I grabbed two fifty cans and I got back to Hager. I then crawled over to the next hole and there was another fifty over there that had quit firing. The two guys behind the gun that were wounded, were nearly out of ammunition. They had minor wounds from shrapnel. I went back and got water and ammunition from the same track and brought it back to them. I continued to work this sector of the perimeter until I came across this other guy that had his leg blown off. It was his right leg and it was blown off right below the knee—just hanging on with some ligaments. He was howling! I had come across an aid-bag with a corner shot out of it and some of the stuff was dumped out but there was still some morphine and some battle dressings and things like that in it. I didn't have a tourniquet. So, I took his belt off and tried to make one for him. While I was doing this, the dog handler came by and I told him to stay with this guy. Before I returned to Hager's foxhole, I gave him some morphine and stuck the empty syringe in his flak jacket at his collar. I bent the needle and I used his blood to put a mark on his forehead. He started to quiet a little. I tied his leg behind him so he couldn't see it and was telling him silly things like, "Yeah, you're fine," before I started back to Hager's hole. I found another guy that was hurt and got him back to the dog handler. We were kind of collecting these guys that were hurt and getting them out of the line of fire, below a little depression. When I got back to Hager, his barrel was burnt out and the rounds were just corkscrewing out of the barrel. The barrel was really hot and ready to melt down. From then on, I was pretty much finding anybody that was down and trying to get them back to the dog handler. Then I remembered going back to the command post for more medical supplies and passed by the commo track. Captain Gallagher was down in a little depression next to the track in the left-hand corner by the ramp. It looks like he had his RTO with him and I think they were directing fire. So, I headed back to see how my wounded people were doing and I saw two guys underneath a track. At first, I didn't know if they were hit or not, so I poked my head under there. One was a medic. I don't know what his name was but he had taken a piece of shrapnel in his head right above his hairline. It wasn't a penetrating wound. I checked it out. It was just one of those flesh wounds that bleeds like hell and he thought he was dying. I got a field dressing on him and he was pretty concussed. There was somebody else with him and he wasn't coming out. He was no good to anyone by then anyway. So, I moved back to where the dog handler was and I just went back to work trying to collect people and carry ammunition and water. Things had settled down. But then it would get hot, then settle down a little bit, and then get hot again. Then, the gunships and jets came in. There was a lot of shit flying through the air. I returned to the dog handler [PFC Michael Wyatt] and his dog was flipping out and he needed more bandages. I traversed back to the command post and coming around the corner of the commo track, Captain Gallagher had just finished rolling to the bottom of the ramp. He was lodged in between a blown-off tree stump and the ramp. I went over to check for vital signs and he was gone. That really shook things up because we didn't have a CO now. I didn't see anyone else around there. No RTO or anything. So, I went back and then the jets came in. I just tried to keep people supplied with ammunition and water and smokes. Then there was the sapper with grenades. He had a couple of damn frags he got off real close to me and my mind goes completely blank after that. I did have my shotgun, and later when we finished on the hill, eighteen or twenty rounds were gone, so I must have fired it. I don't remember firing the shotgun [speaking about his Bronze Star citation]. Most of the time I was trying to help wounded guys—and not having any medical training or anything. There were a couple of guys that I couldn't do anything for. There was a guy that somebody had put on a stretcher close to our area. He was laying belly down with his face to the side and there were big bubbles coming out from blood that was gathering in the stretcher. I tried to turn him over on his side. He was obviously hit really bad. What really pissed me off was that nobody had done anything for him that I could see. I didn't know what the hell to do for him. You know, I wasn't really a medic. I just turned his face so he wouldn't breathe in that stuff and I didn't recognize him. I pretty much kissed him off. I always figured we were all going to get it in the end—that they were going to regroup and overrun us. I really didn't expect to see daylight or the sun come up. But it started to get a little light and I was sitting at that hole with Hager and pretty soon, people were getting up and walking around. A helicopter dropped a pallet of ammunition. Later, I remember the tanks coming up and I remember these guys coming down in a Huey and they were clean. They were officers, and they were looking around. They were pointing and they were saying this and that, the way that people in a movie would do. There was this shell crater, and there had been grenades and stuff, which didn't go off—Chicom grenades—and they were rolling down in this hole all night. It was full of all that shit from ammunition cases, and stripped off mortar charges and God only knows what. One of the officers comes up and says the most stupid thing I could ever remember anyone saying. "Let's police up the battlefield." I just looked at him and so did Hager. He said, "Put it all in there with all that packing material and burn it." I kind of piped up and said something to the effect of, "There's live ammunition in there and if you set it on fire, it's not going to be good." But surer than shit, he insisted on burning it. And it got burning pretty good and then grenades start going off. We hit the deck. There were those two guys who walked out looking for souvenirs. Some guys had been throwing grenades that night with those wire retainers still on them that held the spoon down. There was a lot of ordnance out there, but these guys wanted to get some souvenirs and they stepped on something. Finally, the tanks came and brought us back to Con Thien. They gave us two bottles of whiskey and I slugged a few sips and took a nap.

### 2Lt Chelsea Korte:

We knew something was up. We were in reserve. And I remember my boys stole a Prick 25, so we knew what was going on. We were sitting there listening. What you could hear was the communication between the captain and the battalion commander—the battalion net. We knew what was going on. We knew that they [the mortars] were on that hilltop and helicopters had gone down in the valley below. It was a severe firefight. During the day, we had been operating dismounted because too many of the tracks were screwed up or in for repair. We were operating as straight leg and I'm pretty sure it was early in the day that they put us into this great big field where they separated us into individual groups to be picked up by a chopper flight, but the flight didn't come in until nearly dark. They flew us in in support of another unit. I remember coming in to that perimeter and there was confusion. We sat in that field all day and I guess they flew out most of the company. My platoon was mostly absent. I don't remember if it was one squad or two squads but some of our platoon by error were put on the other hilltop with the battalion main troop force. We were all short anyway. That's how it was. They never counted the AWOLS and desertions because of the politics. So we were always way shorter than we were supposed to be. On that hill, I remember setting up nine firing sectors. My platoon had this particular sector. We checked out the foxholes the best we could and we didn't sleep in them in case they were booby-trapped. We set up some claymore mines and trip flares and then hit the rack. Then, of course, all hell broke loose. Then it was just a matter of replacing people, hauling ammo and trying to stay alive. I was waiting for a bullet to go right between my eyes, but of course it never happened. I was told was that … they expected an attack on the other hill and that we were choppered in only to provide support, and they said, "Well, just to be on the safe side, let's put a company in there for the security of that poor mortar platoon." Instead of going after the battalion, they came after us instead. It was very smart on their part. I don't remember much except hauling ammo and hauling bodies and moving people to make sure there was firing going on. Because I was hit early on, I must have been semiconscious a little bit because parts of it I just don't remember. I remember the cold air, the nice cool air. Our guys lighting little fires to keep warm. The Navy came in and the fighter jets … I got on the horn and said, "Jesus Christ, you're killing us! Now, stop that!" I mean they were dropping five-hundred-pound bombs. Large chunks of earth were coming down and landing on us. It was amazing. There were Puff the Magic Dragons. It was amazing. Just like something out of a book. I had no idea that the other side of the perimeter was almost flat, the exact opposite of what I was on. I remember seeing the foxholes below and remember thinking the field of fire was so grand. Early on, I had a hand grenade fragmentation hit the right side on my thorax—just under the arm about six inches below the armpit. The first grenade came in hit the APC behind me and got my radio operator. He was a kid from Kentucky, Tony Robinson! The next one came in and you could hear it clanking and it got me but I was still operative. I just had to close my elbow against the side. I didn't know how serious it was. I could feel the blood running down but I couldn't see it. I was able to function just fine. I was kind of one-handed but that was it. On our side of the perimeter, it was quite steep and you could see them. There was one that I remember in particular that was pretty well exposed. There were concentric rings of positions from a bunch of different battles and big rocks. The lowest foxholes were where they were. I remember just having to replace a lot of guys. Those mortar tracks had dismounted most of the fifty-calibers.. They dismounted those 50-calibers. I know I had.

In the mortar platoon, the guy who does all the computations was a sergeant, and we used to call him "the computer." There were guys all over the middle of the perimeter. I don't know what they were thinking they were going to do from t`here. I grabbed this kid and dragged him back to the perimeter. He couldn't talk and I put him in the foxhole. I had my hand on his collar behind his neck and BAM! He got hit! His whole face was gone and I remember feeling my hand jerk back. And he's up against the back of the foxhole unconscious—a bloody mess. I just assumed he was dead. In Japan, where they took a lot of those wounded, they took me down to this burn unit, and it turns out he was alive and not even seriously wounded. As a child, he had been in a car accident, and they had done extensive reconstructive plastic surgery. So when this grenade hit, it knocked all that dirt with tremendous force up into his face and literally took the plastic surgery off.

I had to replace him, so I walked back into the center of the perimeter and found another one of those guys and dragged him down there. We just needed bodies. We just needed people to shoot. Eventually, the main problem was ammunition for the machine guns. An APC, as any mechanized trooper knows, has 50-caliber ammo cans lining the whole floor. So, I started hauling those cans out to my sergeant. He just sat up in the back of the foxhole, exposed. If anyone deserved a medal, it wasn't me, it was him. I don't know how I got the medal. I really don't. I'm still embarrassed by it today because he was the hero. He just sat there, boom, boom, boom, boom, boom.

In the morning when they put me on the medevac—I'm thinking, "There is no fucking way we are getting out of here." We're going to get shot out of the sky, but they were pulling back at that point. In fact, those pilots were pretty amazing. I remember when the helicopter banked around. I think he was trying to be evasive, and as it banked around and put its nose down to get some speed, you could see the bodies all laying in concentric circles at the edge of the perimeter. As badly hurt as we were, we surely put a big dent in their roster. The medevac took me out to the *Repose* and a lot of the guys were on the hospital ship. In the Navy, they made a big deal about the officers. We had this little round room. It was in the center of the ship. There was this big dining table where they served family-style meals with waiters. There were individual rooms, and that's where the surgeries were performed. And there I stayed until they shipped me to Japan. I married one of those nurses in Japan. About my award, the commander of the hospital said, "Come on in here, lieutenant." I went into his office and he's got his feet up on his desk and he says to his aide, "Bob, get the Pentagon on the phone." The commander gets on the phone and I can tell by the way they are talking they know each other—both were probably career guys, you know—and he says to me finally, "Well, Lieutenant, I got good news and bad news and I'll give the bad news first. Well, you didn't get the Medal of Honor. You got a Distinguished Service Cross." I thought, "You must have the wrong guy."

When Korte and the other seriously wounded were evacuated, it was Captain Tousignant and Dustoff 708 that got the mission. By 0600, medevacs were ferrying wounded directly to the hospital ship, and the Spooky 11 gun commander, Bob Schilling, was still firing on his return mission between the medical evacuations. Sporadic mortar and small arms fire continued for 90 more minutes as dawn approached. Tousignant adds his memories of that morning.

I got Korte out the morning of the 13th. I flew 5½ hours that day. It must have been early in the morning because I have some night flying listed in my log, which would have been before sunrise. So, I must have got him out at first light. His first wife was a bridesmaid in my wedding on December 13, 1969, in Japan. It was a month to the day after I picked him up that I had his soon-to-be wife in my wedding party—Virginia Kam. Since then I've been in touch with my first wife and she has talked to Virginia, and has told Chelsea that I am the one that picked him up that morning, which is really ironic because I never did meet him after that and I only knew of his wounds. I did know that he was awarded the DSC. I stayed in the service and continued to manage medical facilities that treated Vietnam vets in VA hospitals. I did stay with it for quite a while. I continued in the Medical Service Corps but stopped flying in the mid–1970s. I became operational commander of a number of medical units in the reserves. I sent a number of units to Desert Storm and Desert Shield at the end of my career. I retired in 1997 as a colonel. I was more administrative than operational late in my career. I thought it was so true of so many of those that we served and their incredible bravery and just how adrenalin and good training could take over when put into a situation like what you guys were in because the outlook those couple days was not very encouraging at all.

In the morning, Jim Jackson and the Recon Platoon were gathered for a sweep by Lieutenant Hosfield. They slid off the steep hill that had been their night defensive position and worked down into the elephant grass in the narrow valleys below.

PFC Jim Jackson:

In the morning, they told us we were going to move down to a finger on the south side of the hill we were on and it had a little bit of elephant grass on it. It was the only logical way to get down. As we were going down there, we were supposed to meet Charley Company. We went a while and then they stopped us and we waited. Finally, I believe it was Bravo Company that passed by us heading back to their APCs and their mortar platoon. By that time, the 101st was flying in and being dropped on the hilltops, and Colonel Swaren sent us and the other units a warning to be careful of their gunships rolling into that valley and shooting rockets. Well, they didn't have any high rounds and didn't really come that close to us. When we got down in the elephant grass, Lieutenant Hosfield stopped us before we broke out from some bushes, and that's when Bravo Company crossed in front of us. We were one of the last units out of there. We did not suffer any casualties. We were lucky. In hindsight, I can't believe they told us to pack so lightly, knowing where we were going in the middle of everything. I had only brought 7 mags and one frag grenade and I was more heavily armed than most. Some guys had almost nothing, thinking we were just going out there for a minute, you know. It would have been better to have made two trips with those three helicopters so we could bring some M-60s and more ammo than what they did. I'm sure they were overwhelmed with all the things going on, besides the fact that all the corps commanders and field grade officers wanted to get a helicopter and go out there, get on the radio and get a look at what was going on. I still can't believe that they had C Company and D Company so spaced apart.

First Lieutenant Matteffs came to the Recon Platoon as platoon leader after he recovered from his wounds [in Helicopter Valley]. I remember we had set up an ambush and his RTO and FO both were hit, so he had to call in artillery himself. I thought it was coming in about 50 meters from us. We had several wounded. He was a short-timer by then. That was sometime in May. Matteffs was not only very brave but just a good platoon leader for Charley Company—I know he was for us. He was a quiet, soft-spoken guy.

***Top:*** **Sgt. Robert Vandergriff (left), third platoon, A/1-61. He was KIA on 30 Nov 1969 in a mortar accident. He is standing with Sp4 Joseph Vetrano, also of third platoon, A/1-61.** ***Bottom:*** **PFC Gary "Cool-Breeze" Kent, first squad, third platoon, A/1-61. He was WIA in the 30 Nov 1969 mortar accident.**

With the rumbling of approaching tanks in the distance, the enemy withdrew and sounds of battle ceased. The tanks were led by HQ66—commanded by Sgt. Walter Evans. They were headquarters section from A/1–77 Armor. As they approached, Alpha Company began stirring from their foxholes. That ended abruptly as two men were wounded when one kicked an unexploded grenade. This was followed by sporadic sniper fire. Eventually Alpha Company—what able-bodied men were left—would leave a grateful pair of mortar platoons to secure their own perimeter and await the return of their rifle platoons. Alpha rode back to Con Thien on the top of A/1–77's tanks. The word came down that a battalion of the 101st Airborne—the 1st of the 502nd—was being inserted airmobile to mop up and chase the retreating 27th NVA Regiment. Again, it would be the Lancers who would be called to assist for the battalion insertion.

They would disperse on Hills 162 and the Three 100s and search and clear into the adjoining ravines, finding hundreds of abandoned NVA bodies. Tim Hurley, remaining on the hill with Bravo Company's mortar platoon, would comment years later that the sight of so many choppers in the sky at one time was one of the great wonders of his life. The other compelling sight was the burial of all the NVA in a common grave by bulldozers that accompanied the tanks. The Valorous Unit Citation documentation presented by the 5th Infantry cites a count of 288 bodies. On the 14th of November, Larry Mosher's body, still lying next to the burnt skeletons of three choppers, would be recovered by the 101st. The 1st/502 would list him as a chopper pilot, but he was later identified as Mosher.

**PFC David Nicholson (left) with Skip Hager, third platoon, A/1-61. Nicholson was killed on 30 Nov 1969 in a mortar accident.**

For several days, the 101st would chase the withdrawing 27th NVA Regiment north to the DMZ, towards an area northwest of Con Thien where A/1-61 would have one last skirmish on November 17 with the 27th NVA Regiment before that unit was deemed combat ineffective and was assimilated into other NVA units. It occurred at first light and was believed to be a diversionary tactic to enable the main force to escape back into North Vietnam. Bravo Company and Alpha Company were set up about a thousand meters apart when a small NVA force began firing on both companies. Bravo had dusters with them on their perimeter—tracked vehicles armed with twin 40-millimeter cannons. As they fired at the NVA in a hollow between the two companies, they overshot their mark and the rounds landed in Alpha Company's perimeter. Gary Higgins was wounded in the arm and a 50-gunner had a finger shot off. A total of 14 were wounded in Alpha Company. Besides Higgins, the medevacs were PFC Gene Kelly, Sp4 Kenneth Brown, PFC Ron Karr, PFC John Tripp, PFC Jeffrey Brooks, Sgt. Anatoli Puschkin, Sp4 Bruce Sampson, 1Lt Buford Bagby, Sp4 Kevin Lopeman, and Sp4 Lewis Nunez. Coincidentally, another 50-gunner from B Company also had a finger shot off by enemy automatic weapons fire.

In the three days of fighting, there were no fewer than 84 Army Commendation Medals for Valor, 62 Bronze Stars for Valor, 4 Silver Stars for Valor, and 4 Distinguished

Service Crosses for Valor, 4 Distinguished Flying Crosses, 1 Air Medal for Valor, and 1 nomination for the Medal of Honor awarded for valor and gallantry on Gallagher Ridge. Captain Gallagher, who was awarded a Bronze Star posthumously, would have been proud of his men.

The aftermath that morning was a decisive victory. The enemy dead were buried in a common grave on the northwestern side of the perimeter. They lay piled atop each other—their final resting place after succumbing to the full force of the United States Army. Also in evidence were scores of blood-soaked drag-trails as the NVA carried their dead out of the line of fire. During the firefight, the NVA used grappling hooks slung on ropes to pull their dead out of exposed areas in the line of fire. These "probables," along with the several hundred bodies the 101st found, were estimated at well over five hundred. For several months after, the 5th Infantry would find scores of NVA bodies west and north of Gallagher Ridge on their escape trails. Lt. Col. Swaren had this to say:

> Well, Gallagher might have been psychic. I truly was absolutely amazed that that NVA unit was able to spin off several companies—or more—and make that loop around that hill that Recon was on to get to the mortar position, but they did! Gallagher apparently put his men in the right places. He did a good job and his guys did a good job. There was no question that there was some serious shooting going on up there. At night, we could see the tracers through the illumination. We could not see actually on the ground. Now, while all of that was going on, we've got the Scout Platoon and they have gotten around the corner now and we've got that major unit boxed in and we're pouring shit on them like you can't believe—artillery and small arms. They pull out, and it turns out that is a Regimental Headquarters, with at least one and probably two battalions of infantry protecting them as well. They all pull their asses out. And the other guys that are hitting Gallagher do not pull out and it's just starting to get light. Then, they pulled out too and they disappeared. Now, as soon as I could get enough light for them to do it, I told the tank company to get their asses out there too and reinforce Alpha Company. And they did. That pretty much was the end of the fighting there on Gallagher's perimeter. Now, all that's happening, and I'm getting radio calls now from helicopters relaying that the people in charge back at Red Devil want me to get my butt up to the TOC and I said well, that's fine. You give me a helicopter and I'll fly out. And they can do helicopters now because the 51-caliber is gone. So, I go back there and General Zais is there and the brigade commander is there. They have a big plan to bring in a battalion of the 101st and a battalion of ARVN to chase these guys down. I had to point on a map where we were because they didn't really know where we were, and which direction these guys were taking to the high ground back towards the DMZ and where we could get troops in to block them. We went through all of that and then I said, you know, boss, those fellows left about first light and if there is anything they are good at is they can boogie down the trail. Those fellows can pick up their gear and move. And it's mid-morning now and we haven't even alerted the ARVN unit or 101st unit to get their ass up to that hill. It'll be 12:00 before they get here. It'll be futile; they'll be gone. They'll just beat their feet against the mountain out there. Well, they probably agreed with me, but they didn't say so, and so they ended up sending a battalion of ARVN and a battalion of the 101st out.

Lt. Colonel Swaren, along with the other brass, lifted off the TOC landing zone to observe the troop movements. What they observed was that the sky was filled with other rotary wing aircraft for the airlift of two airmobile battalions. On the ground, a platoon of tanks lumbered down the tank trails carrying Alpha Company from Gallagher Ridge back to Con Thien—packed tightly on top of their hulks. Bravo Company was on foot heading back to meet their mortar platoon on Gallagher Ridge and would remain in the field. Charlie Company was also linking with their mortar component and would also set up nearby in the field. The Scout Platoon was preparing to be airlifted back to C-2. Through all this, the advance elements of the 101st were on scene and were scouting the ravines and hills for places to drop troops. They rolled in and out of the many valleys looking for enemy movement and good landing zones. As Charlie Company walked up out of Starr Valley, Bravo Company was moving back toward Gallagher Ridge where their tracks were, and the recon platoon was working through the elephant grass in the thin valley below their NDP. Delta 1–11 was awaiting their airlift from Hill 162 back to C-2. Swaren had a scare as he watched his men sweeping through various draws and ravines from his bird's-eye view in the battalion Loach:

> And the 101st Battalion has got two Cobras that were flying escort for them. Now, our troops are coming out, on foot, down the hill off 162. You could see it from where I'm sitting. I'm watching them come down that trail. And here, these goddam Cobras start to roll in on them—taking them for VCs for Christ sake! "Oh my God," I said! That's all I need, just make my day! I'm obviously talking nastily on the radio. So, somehow they got it through their heads: "Don't shoot, those are Americans." And, they didn't. I was scared to death that that roll-in was going to be made and they were just going to wipe out a whole bunch of our good guys. They didn't, but it just bothered the hell out of me. And everybody came in and everybody made out After Action Reports. Everybody put in for awards and I—I feel very guilty on the award thing. I changed my mind now, but back in those days my theory was that with the infantry guys, it was their job to fight and to kill. So, if you did that, you were just doing your job. What the hell? You're going to get a medal for doing your job? And some people did more than their job … Starr, Blunt. I believe they ought to get some kind of award, but GI Joe over there who shot sixteen magazines out of his foxhole because he was being attacked, that's what he's paid to do. Jesus, don't tell me he needs an award for doing that.

Lt. Frederick Jelinek:

> The morning after the battle, I was alone in the TOC working up air support missions for the units on the ground. Over the radio came a call for me from "Silver Eagle Alpha" requesting landing instructions. I knew that the "Alpha" in a call sign meant the caller was a general's aide and heard it with dread as I had never had personal contact with general officers. What I was very familiar with was stories of high-level officers flying above fights and causing lots of distraction for very busy folks on the ground. LTC Swaren was still in the field. I replied, "Silver Eagle Alpha, I know what you are but not who you are. You are cleared to land on our pad, but I cannot come and meet you as I am the only officer here. I am in the TOC bunker under all the antennas." Over the radio came the response, "This is Silver Eagle, roger out," my first traffic received directly from a general. A few minutes later, I heard the chopper land and a few minutes [after that] the sound of several pairs of boots coming down the stairs of the bunker. Then a voice said, "All of you wait here" and Major General Wright, commanding general of the 101st Division, came in to the operations area alone. There is no doubt in my mind he was aware I was stressed. As I sat him down to brief him from the big "official" briefing map on the wall, he held up his hand and asked, "Is this the map you are controlling the units in the field with?" I said, "No sir," and he said, "Why don't you brief me from that?" So we went around to my well-worn operations map that I always carried and he simply said, "Tell me what happened." I did and he asked some very basic questions. Then he looked at me with smiling eyes and said, "Well, you are doing a fine job." Now, I suspect he said that regardless of what he might have believed, but I never forgot how good that made me feel and how he ensured the lowest stress level possible by having his staff members cool their heels outside while I briefed him. I liked him a lot. LTC Swaren came in from the field later in the day. Major General Wright airlifted some of his troops to try and catch the NVA as they fled west. As part of recovering from the battle the next day, LTC Swaren put a quick after-action briefing together and flew out to our companies to give them an idea of exactly what role they played in the three-day fight. As we were flying from one company to another, we spotted some troops on the ground taking a break. The 101st were the only other troops in the area, so we dropped in on them to see what they were doing. We were wrong. The troops "taking a break" were dead NVA that must have been caught by some artillery or air strike, as they were not in an

area where they would have been in contact with our infantrymen. We hopped back in the chopper and got out of there in a flash once we realized our mistake.

Gallagher Ridge suffered remarkably few friendly losses considering what they had been up against. There were 17 serious litter cases, but as is remembered, almost everyone on that hill was bloodied in some way. Most of the wounded were flown directly to the hospital ship *Repose*. Among them were: PFC Archie Donley, Sp4 Richard Spillman, Lt. Chelsea Korte, PFC Vernon Wayson, PFC Randall Robinson, PFC Michael Stalcup, PFC Edwin Martin, PFC Robert Conley, Sp4 Raymond Elwell, PFC Kenneth Barrett, PFC Dennis Collie, PFC Theodore Sescinski, PFC Kenneth Berry, PFC James Green, Sp4 Charles Smith, PFC Joseph Curtis and PFC James Tanner. Those who paid the ultimate sacrifice in the wee hours of November 13 on Gallagher Ridge were: Sp4 Dennis Ross, PFC Norman Benedik, Sp4 Thomas Landrum, Sp4 Kenneth Caswell, SSgt Ralph Evilsizor, PFC Mark Rose—and Captain Robert Patrick Gallagher, all from Alpha Company. The brave dead will be in our hearts forever.

Those who died on November 11 and 12 on Hill 162 were: Sgt. Ruben Carbajal, Sp4 Michael McQueer, PFC Ronald Lauderdale, Sp4 Gumesindo De La Rosa, Sp4 Kenneth Barkley, PFC Bruce Walters, Lt. William Pierpont, and Sgt. Larry Mosher.

In the morning—out of reverence and respect—our commanding officer was carried to the chopper wrapped in a poncho liner. Among the bearers were Dan Cowan, Jerry Oliver and Gary Higgins. As they approached the bird, Higgins remembers the wind wash from the rotor blowing open the poncho liner and exposing the captain's lifeless body. With the loss of this valiant man and along with the others—wounded and dead—Alpha Company lost its identity for a time. Added to the nearly 30 lost to the company either killed or wounded that night were the fourteen wounded losses of November 6. Subsequently there would be fourteen more wounded losses on November 17, and two friendly fire losses on November 30. In victory, Alpha Company paid its dues in November of 1969. By the end of November, A Company was down to under 50 men.

These losses of the day somewhat dull the overwhelming victory that was accomplished. There are so many questions and some of us have been unable to talk about our experiences for years. However, time both softens grief and stiffens our resolve to remember, and through this documentation, many of us have made our way back to each other. Sometimes, in each other's company, we have even smiled. Tears are OK too, though. They release the burden of the survivor and cleanse the soul. To quote Thoreau: *Man hath no greater joy than that seen through a tearful eye.*[5]

Sp4 Louis Pepi:

Shortly after first light, the tanks arrived and were running over the NVA bodies partly because Ken Barrett had been wounded when a corpse was rolled over and detonated a live unexploded grenade. I climbed out of the second foxhole I had manned during the night. It took only a shallow hop as the position contained about 2 feet of fifty-caliber casings and links. I walked to my first foxhole to find Smitty, who was fine. I moved to the front of that position to look at the first NVA soldier that I killed in the initial assault. I found him forty feet away and he was shot in the neck. The exit wound was in his calf, causing a compound fracture of his tibia. He was also peppered with grenade shrapnel. He was lying on his side in a fetal position. I squatted near him, and noted the look of youth in his face I remembered from the previous night. I recall that he had a musky odor about him that was foreign to me. An SKS lay beyond him and I picked it up to keep as a souvenir. I had no further desire to touch or search him, partly from the thought that he might have booby-trapped himself, but more out of reverence and respect for the dead. One of the tanks was approaching and I was shifting my weight to stand up erect when—to my great shock—his eyes opened. He had a distressed glance on his face as the rumbling tank approached, but he was clearly alive. I tried to yell but the tanker waved me off as he made straight for the body. I back-pedaled several more steps as the near track ran over the NVA soldier. His skull crushed with a loud, sharp report—like a light bulb popping. His face was smashed flat into the ground. The scene of that very moment is the nightmare that I can still see today. Whenever I hear a lightbulb burst I flinch.

Lt. Michael Cowart, FO for Bravo Company:

After Alpha Company left on the tanks, we reformed to our mortars on that perimeter below. Thank goodness they had already gotten out our dead and the wounded, but there were dead gooks all over the place—heads, arms, legs with boots, guts, body parts all over the perimeter—lots of them. The controller that night did a good job, whoever he was. He did a lot to blend all the activity and deserves a lot of credit for keeping some of my rounds from going where they shouldn't go. One of the things I was concerned about was not only not hitting the men but also not hitting the Puff, because all those things were in play. It was one thing to keep the rounds "on" the perimeter and not "in" the perimeter, but it was totally another to make sure you don't shoot down a bird.

Sergeant William Howard:

The morning was surreal. I had had no idea of the magnitude and the thought of what we had been through was unfathomable. But like any other nasty situation we were in over there—you put it aside and moved on. And all of the bodies and our own dead—you can't dwell on it. You just keep going.

The fluid situation of those three days caused most of the original strategy to be thrown out the window. What is commonly said about all battles is: "All strategy goes out the window after the first shot is fired." When asked about the strategy and decisions of the top brass, Lt. Cowart defended his battalion commander with this answer: "There is something called the burden of command, and where you are responsible for the lives of people, you do what you have to do to make sure the mission gets accomplished but also you protect your people. Swaren had my respect back then and he's got my respect even more now."

# 13

# Unfriendly Fire and Survivor's Guilt

November 30, 1969, was the Sunday after Thanksgiving and we were on stand-down at Con Thien. Three days earlier, the Army made us a Thanksgiving dinner that served only to make us more homesick. We had spent Friday and Saturday performing maintenance on our APCs—while restocking supplies and ordnance for each track. The 50-cals and M-60s were field-stripped, oiled and reassembled, as were our personal weapons. The squad was completely squared away and the day appeared to be ours to waste. TF/1-61 had been through a savage month and Alpha Company in particular. A few weeks before, there was a large influx of replacements. There was new meat in every squad. Morale was very low and we needed time to unwind and chill. Even the hellhole that was our rat-infested bunker looked good on this day as we primed to lounge the day away.

Our platoon leader Lt. Miller had other ideas, though. He had been ordered to practice adjusting mortar-fires with another officer. With the platoon RTO Douglas Free, Miller's driver Frank Williams, and the other officer in tow, he pushed through the bunker entryway. He announced that he needed three of our squad to saddle up the 31 APC and come along too—just in case. Of the eight of us packed into our hovel, four were FNGs. This left Dave Nicholson, Gary Kent, Skip Hager and me to "volunteer" for this mission. Hager was sound asleep so he got a pass. Sgt. Bobby Vandergriff, one of the other squad leaders in the platoon, announced that he wanted to come along too—mainly because Cool-Breeze [Gary Kent] had just opened a piece of mail containing the latest issue of *Playboy*. With the proper amount of griping, we grabbed our weapons and hopped on the 31. Since Don Sarsfield was on R&R, I was the only experienced driver present, so I got that job.

The two PCs exited Con Thien and proceeded down the service road a short distance to clear the mine field. Then we turned east. We set up on an elevated berm 3 clicks east of Con Thien, just west of an old destroyed NVA bunker system. This small bench consisted of short grass and dusty-dry red dirt. It was poised about ten feet above a large expanse of tall elephant grass extending in all directions to the artillery-fractured tree lines five or six hundred meters distant. As the RTO and the two officers were talking to the FDC guys, our group huddled around Cool-Breeze and the magazine. The centerfold was a photo layout of Paulette Lindberg.

The first round was called to the location of those enemy bunker ruins situated further east of our position and we heard it chunk out of the tube through the radio squawk.

A few seconds later it swished by overhead and hit 700 meters out. The next round was called to a correction of "drop 200 meters," but it impacted in the same vicinity as the first. About that time, my bowels started rumbling and I went to the back of the track for toilet paper. The third round was called to a correction of "drop 200 meters and left 100 meters" as I found the TP. This round also hit in the same vicinity as the first two. There was definitely a problem, but too far away to concern us. As I watched the black smoke from the blast drift in the wind and the disturbed soil freefall back to earth, I was moved by the long grass undulating near and far in the gentle wind. I marveled at the movement of the grass that seemed to be giving me the feeling of a sea of arms beckoning to me. Sometimes Vietnam was so beautiful. This thought and feeling, I still remember distinctly.

For the fourth round, the platoon leader gave the correction: "Left 200, drop 400." This round never reached our position, and instead, hit 50 meters short of our position, and Miller immediately called check fire. Hindsight is always 20/20, they say, but if you total all the adjustments, the last round hit right where it was supposed to. None of us realized that at the time—instead I thought, "Good time to jump off the edge and relieve myself." I turned away from my squad group. As I walked to the edge of the berm, I heard some inaudible squawk over the radio. What I didn't hear was the mortar platoon's request to try again on an "azimuth of 2200 mils." As I jumped the small berm, the round hit the spot where I had been standing a single moment before. In a flash of fiery red, everything went numb and then turned pure white. I was driven face first into the loose dirt below. At some point, maybe five seconds later, I came to and my senses started to return. I scrambled up the hill—still deaf from the blast and concussion. I was clawing wildly and spitting out dirt. I thought we were under attack and I was trying to get under the track—where I assumed the other guys were already huddled. As I scurried up the berm, my hand grabbed a familiar object—it was an army boot with a sock hanging out of it—which turned out to belong to Dave Nicholson. The dust was drifting off and I saw Nicholson's bare foot. When I got to him he was vibrating and I saw his wound—a golfball-sized hole through his left eye socket. I hugged him in some futile attempt to revive him but he was nearly gone. Then I saw Bobby Vandergriff, thrown against the bogie wheels of our track. He was grasping at a gaping hole in his throat and some of his vocal cords were fluttering out of the wound like white elastic bands. He was making a low, raspy, guttural sound. I pulled his dirty hands away from the wound and shrieked that he was going to be OK. As I held his two wrists down, a few more seconds elapsed and his body relaxed somewhat. I hugged him more out of futility and shook him to try to revive him. It was pointless, and I believed he was dead. I found out later he actually died on the medevac. Then I heard Cool-Breeze screaming, "Where am I hit?" His fatigue pants were blown completely off and what was left was on the ground, smoldering at the tattered edges with a red glow. So intense was the explosion that only his belt and belt loops were completely intact on his waist. He was reaching for his crotch as he asked me again where he was hit. As I looked at his half-missing penis and the gash on his leg, the lieutenant—who was bleeding from the shoulder—had reached him and was pushing him back down, saying: "Don't worry. You are going to be fine," and then looking at me said, "He'll be OK." I was in near shock. As I watched the white exposed tissue of his wounds just beginning to saturate in red, I disagreed with the lieutenant's optimism. I was told later that he did make it—but I knew that he wasn't going to be all right. Meanwhile, the driver and the RTO (Williams and Free) had shrapnel wounds and they were to be medevacked with Cool-Breeze, Vandergriff and Nicholson. I felt some wetness on my neck because I had blood coming out of my left ear. Paulette Lindberg and the *Playboy* magazine must have vaporized because we never found it. Finally, the dust-off arrived and took Cool-Breeze and the others. I drove the 3-1 track back to Con Thien but I don't remember who drove the 36 track.

Back at Con Thien that night, I was devastated and finally was at what I thought was my wit's end. Being in a confused and concussed daze, I went to the aid station and complained of dizziness and headaches. The medics gave me 22 downers—Davrons—and in a morbid knee-jerk reflex, I swallowed all 22 of them and lay on my rack waiting to die. At some point, I must have drifted from consciousness because I awoke at length covered in vomit. In a panicky rush, I struggled to my feet and staggered in the darkness back to the medic's hooch—wishing now to live again. I crashed heavily through the door and disclosed to the doc that I had taken all 22 Davrons. His retort was an instant burst of laughter, and then he added: "You're not going to die. You'll throw up first and it looks like you already have." He was right. After heaving my guts up, I crawled back to my rack, exhausted. Today I consider November 30, 1969, as the worst day of my life.

The sterile comment in the Daily Journal reads like this: While A/1-61 was practicing 81mm, the 3/6 element adjusted fire and there was an accident when the round landed on top of the element resulting in 2 KIA and 5 WIA.

But I believe there is more to the story than this antiseptic explanation. Racked once with survivor's guilt, I could not forget this incident while I have long forgotten many others. That inability to forget drove me to find family and friends of the fallen to explain what happened. I found a girlfriend, Rebecca Byrd; a brother, Rick Vandergriff, and his wife Linda; and two good friends, Dan Powel and Ken Ford. I think I helped them get closure from the deaths of these two men. I certainly have helped myself with closure. I still feel sadness when I think about Dave and Bobby, but the guilt has abated to a manageable level. I have no doubt that some higher force loomed over us that day. I did a stupid thing by jumping outside the perimeter during a fire mission—and was rewarded with my life. I would like to think that there was a purpose to what happened and that those of us who survived have lived lives that will validate that purpose.

This is the first piece about Vietnam that I put to pen and paper in the mid–1980s, and a book has formed around it. I wrote more stories and they are dotted throughout this book. Then I started contacting some of the other men in the Fifth Infantry Division who took part in Operation Fulton Square. Each story was different, but they also were the same. I hope I have done justice to their stories. Some others refused to talk and would just like to forget Vietnam. We cannot forget, though, partly because there should be a record for the future.

Don Sarsfield remembers:

> I was on R&R. I was coming back and I ran into four guys that I knew who were leaving for R&R and they talked me into staying an extra day with them. I came back to the unit and I was pretty toasted. Of course, I was happy to have been on R&R, but when I got back all the guys were super-down, and that's when I found out those guys got hit with that 81 mortar.

# 14

# Going Home

Starting on or about August 1, 1969, I began writing a series of letters that I mailed to Ted Kennedy, one of my home state's U.S. senators. I was applying for a 90-day educational deferment, and at the same time, I applied for admission to the University of Massachusetts' College of Engineering. I wrote Kennedy a letter once a week for the next three months with no response from the Massachusetts senator. In like fashion, my father, who was a big fan of the Kennedys, began mailing similar requests on my behalf to the senator's Washington office. They received the same lack of response. Then in early November, I sent one similar request to Senator Edward Brook, an African American and Massachusetts' other U.S. senator. A few weeks later, and a day or so after the friendly fire incident, we were on stand-down at Firebase C-2. I was called to the company clerk's office and informed that I had received a senatorial deferment to return to my college studies at the University of Massachusetts in Amherst. Having just come through the worst month of my 21-year-old life, I was ecstatic. Evidently, the Kennedys had come through for me. I stated that emphatically to the clerk, who looked at me strangely, as he shook his head in the negative. The deferment had come from someone in the office of a Senator Brook. Had Kennedy simply ignored the nearly two dozen letters his office received, or had he passed them to Brook, the state's junior senator? I don't know. I never saw the actual deferment.

Although the clerk could not give me an exact date, it seemed probable that I would be leaving Vietnam just after the first of the year instead of my actual DEROS date of March 28. After six months in a combat infantry unit, there was a glimmer of hope that I might actually live long enough to return home. I was due for a three-day R&R to China Beach in a few days on December 3 and a full seven-day R&R on December 13—to return on December 23—including travel and stayover in Da Nang. It seemed that it was a cinch that I would not be going back to the field. I was partially correct. Since I was going home, my three-day in-country R&R was canceled, and I would instead return to the field for about ten days.

I would have to endure those ten days one second at a time. They would pass by like an eternity. On the brighter side, I was spared the one-day-at-a-time countdown for the 115 days until my actual DEROS date. Instantly, 88 days were erased from the countdown. Now I needed an exact date, which probably would be sometime between Christmas and New Year's. Back with my platoon, my news was bittersweet as I observed the envy in everyone's eyes. The ten days passed slowly. I still was involved in the platoon mix—patrols, guard duty and ambushes. Luckily, it was quiet and peaceful the whole time.

On December 12, I returned to the rear and pulled my A-bag from storage to get a couple sets of khakis starched, and to pack for Bangkok. Not much to pack—money and my camera. On the flight to Da Nang, I met someone from another company in the battalion and we partnered up for our seven days in Thailand. I don't remember his name, but I do recall that he was from Montana and was formerly a smoke jumper. His description of his Big Sky Country home enthralled me, and I would visit Montana many times and trek and ride through the wilderness on fishing and hunting trips in my later years. I even bought acreage in the North Fork area—Flathead River—which bordered on Glacier National Park in an area that teemed with elk, grizzly and wolves. We got a letter at one time from the Department of the Interior stating that there was a den of wolf pups on our property, and asking would we please avoid that corner of our property until the fall.

The R&R was "just what the doctor ordered," and we would spend the next seven days stoned, drunk and naked in the company of a series of beautiful Thai ladies. On our return, I bade my new friend farewell and have never heard from him since. I wish I could remember his name. On my return to Da Nang, I ran into John Crutchfield, an old friend from the 52nd Ordnance Company. He was now a sergeant in Bravo Company and was heading to Australia on R&R. He had spent the night of November 12–13 on an NDP on Hill 162 with Captain Spencer, Mike Cowart, Jon DeBoer and company. We talked briefly about that major engagement we were just in from our different perspectives, but our emotions and the traumatic shock from those several days mostly muted the conversation. I told him that I was returning to the States in about a week. His DEROS date was still in mid–July. It was a sad departure as we shook hands and departed each other's company. I never have reconnected with John.

I returned to C-2 on December 23 and remained on company-area work detail. I remember nothing about the holidays. About a day or two after Christmas, I had the bright idea that I would ride the meal chopper out to the company, which was set up with base security just outside of Qua Viet Naval Base on the DMZ. It would be a short, easy hop. After talking with the pilot, I told him I would jump off the chopper, say my goodbyes and return in less than a minute.

The chopper landed on the smoke and I jumped out as two men ducked in to pull off the hot chow containers. Then I saw that the chopper was lifting off again and my heart sank. Evidently, Captain Neely had ordered the pilot to take off immediately. Here I was back in the field with just my M-16, Kabar and one clip of ammunition. What was worse, my squad had drawn an ambush that evening, and since they were shorthanded, I was a welcome addition. There would be one more night of putting my frayed nerves through the ringer. My pals gave me a bandoleer of M-16 ammo, along with several grenades, a poncho liner and a canteen. I had no choice. I had to borrow a mess kit so that I could partake in the hot chow, and I readied myself mentally for one more night of horror. There would be several hours for this contemplation since the sun was still high in the sky.

Somehow, the squad learned that I had a pocket full of money, and Don Sarsfield produced a deck of cards and suggested one last farewell poker game. I remember that there were more than seven players because we could not play our favorite game of seven-card stud and had to settle for five-card stud and acey-deucy. The game lasted a little over an hour and I remember winning the first eight or ten hands. When the game ended with loud grumbling, I had almost $3000 in my wallet—enough to buy a new car when I got home.

At dusk, I fell into the spaced march to our ambush point. It was a quiet night and the weather actually cooperated, giving us mild and dry conditions. On the way back to the perimeter, a smile developed as I reached back to pat my full wallet. A grimace abruptly replaced my smile as I fumbled my hand into an empty pocket. The wallet was gone and so was the $3000. Lieutenant Miller refused my insistence on returning to the ambush site when we returned to the perimeter. No, we could not go back! I was broke but I was going home.

I do not remember New Year's Eve, except that I heard that the third platoon withstood a vicious assault that night, while on a defensive perimeter outside Qua Viet Naval Base. I heard this from the supply sergeant while I was processing out at Camp Red Devil. Lieutenant Miller, SSgt Chuck Krabel, Sgt. Todd Orman, Sgt. Archie Donley and Sp4 Steve Smith received Bronze Stars for Valor with most of the group also wounded. It was Lt. Miller's third Purple Heart. The sergeant also said my captured SKS had disappeared and he knew nothing about it.

On January 2, 1970, I processed out of the Fifth Mech through the 75th Replacement Company. The flight down to Da Nang and then to Ben Hua was quite different from that of my arrival six months earlier, and so was my flight across the Pacific on the Freedom Bird on January 3. After two days of medical and psychological exams, I was a civilian again. I boarded an airliner at Seatac Airport and flew via Chicago to Logan Airport in Boston, where my parents and siblings were waiting for me. My mother cried and hugged me while my father shook my hand. My brother and three sisters fidgeted and looked on. My brother John, 13, and my sisters Linda, Lisa and Nancy, 18, 12 and 9, formed the second row in the family reception line. I hugged Linda and mussed the hair of the other three. Years later, my sister Nancy told me, "Back then you seemed like a rock star to us kids." I certainly did not feel like one. My father was an Army Air Corps Veteran of thirty-eight B-29 missions over the Japanese islands as a door gunner. The army awarded him two Distinguished Flying Crosses and an Air Medal with five stars. He never asked me about nor did he want to listen to me talk about any of the actions I was in in Vietnam. He also was emotionally unable to discuss the war, due to his wartime involvement. I came to recognize the post-traumatic stress that he endured, when I became aware of my own PTSD issues. I wish I could have helped solve the issues he wrestled with. I am sure that he never did.

I have tried to put on paper what happened to Alpha Company in mid–November of 1969, but maybe that is impossible. The cold facts are there but the emotion is harder to relate. You just cannot explain in words those feelings of the extreme chaos and the horrendous cacophony of battle. Bullets are crackling. Friendly and enemy mortars are exploding. Grenades, RPGs, and satchel charges are detonating. High performance jet engines at treetop level are careening just above you and dropping napalm and 250-pound bombs on your wire. The concussion is so great that it feels like your body is being compressed to its bone-breaking limits. The Spookys sound like giant high-speed drills. The air is full of steel. There is the random shouting of those taking charge, muffled by the constant screaming of the wounded. Through that entire din, you can hear the unnerving sound of the NVA coming—commanders blowing whistles to initiate sapper attacks and enemy forward observers shouting coordinates in high-pitched Asian dialect. I guess the closest thing to the sound of battle is probably silence in a vacuum—they are so far from each other on opposite sides of the sound spectrum, that they actually meet on the other side.

Some of the events in your life that you witness or take part in are so crushing to the soul that you will never be able to shake them from your subconsciousness. They will stay with you forever. You are haunted by them, but somehow, you deal with them by locking them away—or letting them out. We will never forget the men who sacrificed and died so that others could live. Some died but most of us lived, as I did; and you love all of them all.

That is life!

# 15

# Utah Mesa and Bravo Company, 18 Jun 1969

Although the engagements in this chapter occurred a month before I arrived in Vietnam, I have included his chapter, because it involved two men that I spent the night with on the Gallagher Ridge perimeter on November 13. They were Sgt. William Howard and SSgt Russell Widener. This was their first large engagement in Vietnam and it certainly prepared them for the key roles they would play on the 13th. Briefly, here is a recollection of that night along with the memories of several others.

In June of 1969, Bravo Company, 1-61 was based at LZ Sharon. They had been operating out towards the Khe Sanh Plateau several times with little or no action since the April 28 battle—a significant battle in which Alpha Company fought. This time Bravo Company would be involved in significant action.

This is how Sgt. David Gattis, Sgt. Bill Hambleton, Sgt. Dan Tyrrel and Sgt. William Howard remembered it. There had been some sniper fire and the odd rocket, but it was quiet out there. Under the operational control of the Third Marine Division, they would patrol the area along with platoon elements of the 1st Battalion of the 9th Marine Regiment, a.k.a. "The Walking Dead."

Dave Gattis, Sgt. Tyrrel and Bill Hambleton were part of the original troopers of the 5th Infantry Division's move en masse from Fort Carson. The 1st Brigade of the 5th Infantry Division was dispatched to Vietnam after the Tet Offensive to replace the entire 3rd Marine division. The change of command would not be completed until November 6, 1969—some sixteen months after the Fifth arrived.

Like the 1/9 Marines, Bravo Company, 1-61 got the unlucky draw this time. Sgt. Gattis, Hambleton and Tyrrel were nearing the end of their tours. Gattis was on medical profile with a punctured eardrum. A few weeks earlier, he was out in the field and manning an M-60 machine gun in an M113 armored personnel carrier when it was hit by two successive rocket-propelled grenades (RPG). The RPG was effective for penetrating armored steel because it was armed with a shape charge, enabling it to explode forward and burn through the armor plate. The second RPG burst a hole in one of Gattis's eardrums, so he was on light duty in the rear. Also wounded in the incident was trooper and squad member Mike "Sandyman" Saunders. He sustained a severe laceration of his trigger finger from shrapnel which would keep him out of the field on June 18.

Nevertheless, Lt. Gallagher,[1] Gattis's platoon leader, informed him that he would be needed on this upcoming mission, because they were sure to get into some heavy contact, and because of the recent influx FNGs, he would also need all the battle-tested veterans he could muster as a stabling force for the new men. Because they needed bodies in the field, he told Gattis he would not be driving for his old squad, but he would be on safer duty with the motor-pool track instead. This time he would not be with third platoon men—Sgt. Harry Diehl, Sp4 James Hennessy, Sp4 Charles Emmert, an African American he remembers only as "Foots," and Sp4 Charles Emmert—his replacement driver.

From LZ Sharon, it took the better part of two days to get to an area south of Highway 9 near FB Vandergrift and a lone sheer rock escarpment situated on the flat, surrounding plain 12 miles to the northeast called the Rockpile. When they arrived at the elongated ridgeline where they would set up their night defensive perimeter, two things would be out of the norm. This was the first time they had ever used concertina wire to circle the perimeter, and it was also the first time that they were instructed to dig such elaborate foxholes, furnished with grenade sumps. Appearing as an afterthought by the company commander, multiple rolls of wire were choppered out to the night defensive perimeter. The coordinates of the NDP were 48QXD883383.

About midday, the tracks split into platoon-mounted patrols, ran cloverleaf search, ran clears in several directions, and received minor contact in the way of limited small arms fire. Meanwhile the command track, mortar track and motor-pool track personnel, under the direction of Captain Perica, stretched out the concertina in a large circle and dug deep foxholes. Gattis worked at this too, with his newfound comrades from the motor pool. Theoretically, the concertina wire was supposed to ring the perimeter, but the ends of the wire where it started and finished were concentrically off by almost forty feet. Unable to restring the wire to align it, because it was now dark, Captain Perica chose to fill that gap with the M48 tank belonging to Delta Company 1–77 Armor that was along with them. This would prove to be a fatal mistake that night. The motor-pool track was placed directly behind the tank, and Gattis's deep foxhole was located in front of the motor-pool track.

Bill Hambleton, who was from Pennsylvania, was Captain Perica's RTO and was set up in a foxhole near Perica in the center of the perimeter. Hambleton had heard the orders come over on the battalion net that a large enemy element of unknown size—possibly battalion magnitude—was out near the old Khe Sanh Marine base. Two more companies of 1-61 were also in the general area.

At dusk, the squads returned. Listening posts were not put out, and the perimeter was on 100 percent alert. According to Keith Short's *History of the 5th Infantry Division*, at about 0335, the NVA hit and they hit hard.[2] The mortars fired HE (high explosive) and WP (white phosphorus illumination), but the sapper assault was not stopped. As it turned out, the tank was not enough to plug the gap in the wire, and NVA poured into the perimeter as the tank was hit by two RPGs. Killed instantly by AK-47 fire were Delta/1/77 tank commander Staff Sergeant Michael Hodge from Flint, Michigan, and company medic Sergeant James Dolvin from St. Albans, New York.

Meanwhile, Gattis's field of fire was compromised and he could not return fire on the assaulting NVA. He spotted a silhouette close to the ground crawling toward him and thinking it was a tanker escaping the hit vehicle, he held fire until the approaching man was very close. Seeing now that he was in fact an NVA sapper, Gattis opened fire at point-blank range, killing the enemy soldier. At the same time, the tank driver, seeing that he was now alone and vulnerable, backed the tank out of the gap in the wire, finally giving Gattis and his M-60 machine gun a clear field of fire. The machine gun did what the tank could not do—namely, to spray the entire gap with concise grazing fire—thus stopping the assault through that breach. However, the damage had been done, and there were sappers inside the wire. At some point Spooky arrived on the scene and provided circular fire around the perimeter. Bill Hambleton remembers the firefight:

> I was Perica's RTO. It had come in from battalion that they were expecting a big element of NVA to be in that area. So we had orders to move on this large element—a battalion, I guess. I think three companies went out. I was with B Company. The first day or so there was one of our patrols that made contact but never determined the size of the element and moved back to set the perimeter. It was getting dark when all the platoons got back. This was the first time we used concertina wire that they flew out to us—although we might have had some wire but not on every track. The concertina wire was set up but it did not line up. There was a gap. They were out of wire so they plugged it with a tank. The gooks must have been watching and saw that and when they hit us, that is where they came through. It was about 3:00 or 3:30 in the morning when we first were hit and it lasted until almost daylight. Some of them were inside the wire. There were two dead gooks about ten meters from where I was. I was with the command post in the center of the perimeter. They did capture one gook that was still alive in the morning. [Also in the morning], a platoon of Marines was inserted into our company perimeter. I left the field on the 20th of June a few days later and left Vietnam when my tour was up in July. They sent me back a little bit early. I was part of the initial group sent from Fort Carson. The Puffs were there for us that night—then and two nights later.

Meanwhile, on the opposite side of the perimeter, Sgt. William Howard and Sp4 Roy Curry of the weapons platoon shared a deep foxhole. This is how Bill put it:

> We knew that they were going to hit us because we could smell 'em. That is why we ground-mounted the 50 and went deep into the ground. The first thing we heard was the tank blow and then the yelling that they were inside the wire. That is when the trips went off in front of us and all hell broke loose. I will never forget that night—I remember it like it was last night—and Roy? We were in the foxhole together when the shit started. He would not run the 50; he said it jammed every time he touched it. They were penetrated on the opposite side of the perimeter from us when our lieutenant called for me to come and help him. Roy said he would go—I was to stay and run the 50. I gave him my steel pot and flak jacket (drivers always lost their stuff), and out of the hole he went. We heard incoming and he dove for a hole. The mortar or rocket landed there with him. That is how Roy Curry was killed. I cried like hell that next morning when I was told. We were close.[3]

As stated, the damage had been done. Sergeant Gattis's 2nd Platoon, third squad was nearly wiped out. Gone were Staff Sergeant Harold Diehl, Sergeant Robert Graham, Specialist 4th Class James Hennessy, Specialist 4th Class Charles Hunter, Specialist 4th Class Marc Aurele, Sergeant Paul Nervaez, and the track driver, Specialist Charles Emmert[4]—the man who took Gattis's place. The lone survivor was "Foots." In the middle of the carnage, Foots—himself wounded—had no other option but to play dead and pull the body of one of his departed comrades over him.[5] It saved his life, but he felt abysmal about what he had to do in order to live another day. Two motor pool mechanics—Specialist 5th Class Melvin Mize and Specialist 5th Class Joseph Smith—were also killed.

The final toll of battle was 12 U.S. troops killed and 18 seriously wounded. Enemy casualties were 38 NVA KIA and 1 POW. As Danny Mathers—a rifleman from Bravo—was searching some thickets inside the perimeter, an NVA sapper squirted out, but he had nowhere to run. He was subdued with a small burst of gunfire but was only wounded. Captured were 9 AK-47s, 50 Chicom grenades, and 100 pounds of satchel charges. When this author asked Dave Gattis if he remembered roughly how many were medevacked, he responded, "Well, yeah. I have a list of 'em right here. OK, here's what I've got," and he read off a string of names: "Howell, Stingle, Lambert, Gignac, Osborne, Connelly, Messer, McCarty, Moran, McLaughlin, Washington, Goods, Milton, Green, Grennus, and Givens." Then he explained, "When we got back in the rear—it wasn't but a few days later, we were all settin' around drinkin'—I had an old set of orders in my pocket and I made a list. I continue to carry a copy of that list until today. There were so many dead and wounded and we'd never be able to remember them. So I set down and wrote all the names on those orders and put it in my billfold where I still carry a copy today." Dave keeps the original is his scrapbook protected behind cellophane. In addition to this list, counting the two tankers that were also medevacked, the actual number was eighteen.

At 0530, the NVA element withdrew except for light sniper fire. The 18 wounded were medevacked first, then 1Lt Gallagher ordered Gattis back out of the field since he was still on medical profile. He flew back to LZ Sharon with the dead. At 0700, an insertion of Marines from A & D/1-9 was dropped in the area. They immediately moved out on recon patrols. One group was ambushed by small arms fire and grenades. One Marine was killed and 6 were wounded. Enemy casualties were 6 NVA KIA and one wounded. Two AK-47s and some enemy documents were captured. Another Marine recon element, C/1–9, was ambushed by 51-caliber fire. Three Marines were killed but the machine gun was captured. As the Marines moved in to extract their dead, they were ambushed from three sides. Air strikes and artillery were called in and the outcome was 35 NVA killed, 4 AK-47s and 16 Chicom grenades captured. C/1–9 suffered 9 KIA and 14 wounded. At the end of the day, D/1-9 was airlifted to reinforce Bravo Company on their night perimeter.[6] That ended that day's fighting.

Sgt. Russ Widener was with the mortar platoon with their three eighty-one-millimeter gun emplacements. His point of view from his position was slightly different. Here is how Widener remembers what he calls the Khe Sanh fight:

> I had only been there [Vietnam] three or four weeks and our mortar crews were just on the other side of the hill from where the main battle was taking place. I was the only one running ammunition back and forth from the track to one particular gun. Track to the gun—track to the gun—back and forth. It was a little bit of a transfer and I was a little exposed but I never thought that I was getting any fire at all. It was all happening on the other side of that little hill in the middle of the perimeter. The three guns were set up back there. I remember the next day when we were getting ready to move, I went out to pull out the aiming stakes and there were two bullet holes through one of the aiming stakes approximately about a foot above the ground. From the angle of the entrance and exit holes, I could see that they were shooting at me and I didn't even know it at the time.

**Citation:**

The President of the United States takes pride in presenting the Silver Star Medal (Posthumously) to Walter J.L. Griffin (2450222), Private First Class, U.S. Marine Corps, for conspicuous gallantry and intrepidity in action while serving as a Machine Gunner with Company C, First Battalion, Ninth Marines, Third Marine Division, in connection with combat operations against the enemy in the Republic of Vietnam. On 18 June 1969, Private First Class Griffin's platoon was conducting a patrol in the Khe Sanh Valley, Quang Tri Province, when the Marines came under a heavy volume of automatic weapons and rocket-propelled grenade fire from an estimated company-sized North Vietnamese Army force occupying well-concealed emplacements. Although seriously wounded during the initial moments of the fire fight, Private First Class Griffin commenced delivering devastatingly accurate fire against the enemy unit. Resolutely maintaining his exposed position, he enabled his platoon to reorganize and evacuate the injured to a position of relative safety. Steadfastly refusing medical attention, Private First Class Griffin completely disregarded his own painful wounds and continued to fire at the enemy until he was mortally wounded by a hostile hand grenade, which impacted near him. His bold initiative and timely actions inspired all who observed him and contributed significantly to the defeat of the North Vietnamese Army force. By his courage, aggressive fighting spirit and selfless devotion to duty in the face of extreme personal danger, Private First Class Griffin upheld the highest traditions of the Marine Corps and of the United States Naval Service. He gallantly gave his life for his country.

On the 19th of June, the Marines of C/1–9 found a large bunker complex 2 clicks west of the previous day's fighting. Airstrikes and artillery resulted in 7 more NVA KIA. Meanwhile, Bravo Company and D/1-9 encountered an enemy force. Spooky was again called in and enemy casualty results were unknown.[7] There was one Marine killed. Bravo Company had a relatively quiet night on the 19th but fired M-79 all night as recon by fire. This was a strong indication that the men on the perimeter could hear the NVA probing for weak spots. Hambleton again remembers: "On the 19th we didn't get hit, but the whole night long we were shooting M-79 rounds—H&Is all night long. That may have deterred the NVA that night."

On June 20, B/1-61 and D/1-9 Marines at 48QXD827385, were attacked at 0530. Bravo suffered two killed. They were the XO, 1Lt William Long from El Paso, Texas, and Staff Sergeant James Parker from Blauvelt, New York. Enemy casualties were 26 NVA KIA and 1 POW. Captured were 18 AK-47s and 4 machine guns. On the same day, in a rocket attack at FSB Vandergrift, Lt. Brian Heath, Sp4 Theodore Baltezore and Sgt. Richard Joy (Captain John Langston's track driver) were killed, having been sent to the rear by the CO to be in a place of supposed safety.[8]

RTO Bill Hambleton:

Then on the 20th we got hit again. They came in on the third platoon side of the perimeter with small arms fire and RPGs. Lieutenant Long, who was the XO, and a platoon sergeant, Staff Sergeant Parker, got killed that night. Lieutenant Heath and Richard Joy were in the rear at a base camp and there was a mortar attack and they were in a jeep. Joy was an RTO. Gattis, Terrell and I were the last to leave the company of the originals that came from Fort Carson.

In three days of fighting, total friendly casualties of the combined Army/Marine force were 27 killed, some 51 stretcher wounded, and as many walking casualties. Enemy casualties were 132 NVA KIA and 2 POWS with another 200 probable KIAs.

In an unrelated incident at 1600 hours, an M-48 tank from D/1-77 and attached to Team Bravo ran over a mine, wounding 6 tankers.

***Army Soldiers Killed***

| | | |
|---|---|---|
| Sp4 Roy Curry | age 21 | Gresham, OR |
| PSgt Harry Diehl | age 28 | Oceanside, CA |
| Sp4 Charles W. Emmert | age 23 | Navarre, OH |
| Sgt. Robert L. Graham | age 22 | Eota, MI |
| Sp4 James D. Hennessy | age 22 | Mount Clemens, MI |
| Sp4 Charles L. Hunter | age 23 | Starksville, MS |
| Sp4 Marc Aurele | age 20 | Voluntown, CT |
| Sp5 Melvin L. Mize | age 22 | Lake City, FL |
| Sgt. Paul R. Navaez | age 21 | San Antonio, TX |
| Sp5 Joseph F. Smith | age 21 | Jacksonville, FL |
| SSgt Michael Hodge | age 22 | Flint, MI |
| Sgt. James Dolvin | age 21 | St. Albans, NY |
| Sgt. James Parker | age 29 | Blauvelt, NY |
| Lt William Long | age 24 | El Paso, TX |
| Lt Brian Heath | age 20 | Tampa, FL |
| Sgt. Richard Joy | age 25 | Binghamton, NY |

**Dave Gattis's handwritten list of wounded and killed in Operation Utah Mesa on 18Jun69 (author's photograph, courtesy Dave Gattis).**

| | | |
|---|---|---|
| Sp4 Theodore Baltezore | age 21 | Gettysburg, SD |
| Francis G. Ruppert | age 21 | Cumberland, MD |

***Marines Killed***

| | | |
|---|---|---|
| PFC Michael D. Boyer | age 21 | Portland, OR |
| PFC Robert G. Carr | age 21 | South Holland, IL |
| LCpl Edward W. Charles | age 21 | Gillet, AR |
| LCpl Frank Cruz | age 21 | Yakima, WA |
| PFC Walter J. Griffin | age 21 | Hawkins, TX |
| 2Lt Garry W. Letson | age 21 | San Francisco, CA |
| Cpl Enrique Miramontez | age 21 | Anthony, TX |

***Naval Corpsmen Killed***

| | | |
|---|---|---|
| Hm Thomas D. Naughton | age 21 | Dearborn, MI |
| Hm3 Paul A. Rezendes | age 21 | Plymouth, MA |

# 16

# Chris Martin and the Americal Division

This chapter documents my friend from the 52nd Ordnance Company at Clarksville Base. It is a brief commentary of his gallant tour in Vietnam after we parted ways. After our service, we lived only several miles apart. We met once by accident in 1971, but our war experiences were still painful open wounds then, and we never met again. I regretted that deeply. At his funeral in 2010, I met his brother and his son Chris Jr. I found out in 2014 that several good friends of mine that I grew up with had been friends with Chris for years after his return from Vietnam. Surprisingly, I still never crossed paths with him. Then in 2015, I traveled to Paxton, Massachusetts, a few miles from my home and reunited with Chris Jr. and met Chris's former wife, Katherine. This chapter is for Chris Jr. and Katherine.

Chris Martin was sent to the 3rd Battalion, 21st Infantry Regiment, 196rd Infantry Brigade of the Americal Division. He arrived in mid-July like the rest of the 52nd Ordnance levy. Chris was awarded a Silver Star, two Bronze Stars, an Army Commendation Medal for Valor, and three Purple Hearts. He distinguished himself on many occasions but particularly on September 22, 1969. While a sister company had been ambushed and pinned down by an aggressive NVA force of unknown size, Martin and his squad volunteered to be choppered in hot to see if they could spring their Americal brothers loose. Nine were already dead and more than a dozen wounded. Coming in under heavy fire, his squad scattered and everyone but Chris and one other were instantly pinned down in some sparse cover on an open and exposed hillside. He rallied his men and organized an assault, placing his men in strategic positions. Continuing up the hill now with good cover fire from his men, he took out a machine-gun bunker singlehandedly and redirected the fire of his men onto the remaining NVA bunkers and spider holes. At some point Corporal Martin and James O'Shields were wounded. Corporal Martin—bleeding heavily—zigzagged his way up to O'Shields, first pulling him to cover and then treating his wounds to stop the bleeding and prevent shock until a medic could make his way up the hill through the machine-gun fire. Then he devoted his attention to the remaining positions and returned to the point of contact. He and his men then routed the rest of the enemy force. Nine men from Martin's sister company Bravo, including a helicopter pilot, were killed, and eighteen were wounded. Martin had five other of his men wounded. Martin was instrumental in getting all twenty-three loaded on medevacs before he was extracted from Nui Lam Mountain.

Martin recovered from his wound and was promoted to sergeant. He was also called into the battalion HQ and was told by a colonel that he would be awarded the Distinguished Service Cross and nominated for the Medal of Honor. There was one catch—he had to extend his tour six months. Without hesitating to think it over, Martin replied in the negative, and the DSC offer was withdrawn. The meeting with the battalion commander ended there. Many years later, while Chris was battling cancer, an attempt was made to renominate him for the Medal of Honor by the U.S. Congressman in his district, but due to his failing health, he died before he could receive this honor and the family let the process die with him.

When Chris died a few years ago, I met his brother, son and ex-wife. His citations are below with the witness statements written on his behalf.

**Letter from Robert Amey**

I am writing in regards to Christopher Martin whom I served with in Vietnam. We were in company D, 3rd Battalion, 196th light infantry Brigade. I witnessed a man, who I considered a real American Hero. Chris put his life on the line more than once, with no regard for his own safety to save his fellow Soldier. A soldier, James O'Shields, was wounded seriously in the open on the side of a hill. Chris crawled down the hill to him while under intense enemy fire, completely in the open, and placed his own body over the soldier. He covered him until the dustoff arrived, picked Jimmy O'Shields up and carried him down the hill to the chopper. Again still under fire, and almost by himself, Chris loaded the wounded on the helicopter. After the chopper left, Chris maneuvered up the hill while the remaining few of us shot cover for him. He made it to the enemy fortification, fought with two enemy soldiers in hand-to-hand combat using a bayonet that he took from one of them, and he killed both enemy soldiers. The personal bravery and numerous risks to his own safety, for that matter his own life—to me—were unbelievable. I have seen many heroes during my time in Vietnam, but I never witnessed someone who so distinguished himself above and beyond the call of duty. When you see someone put his own life on the line repeatedly in battle situations, it is beyond belief. We were under intense circumstances where we lost many of those with us, and several others wounded. I would strongly recommend and urge that this man—Chris Martin—is deserved of any medal ... of the highest order—The Medal of Honor be awarded in this case. I can think of no one who would deserve it more. I am proud to have served with such a unique individual, a true hero and never will I forget what he did for all of us that served with him.

Robert Amey

**Letter from James O'Shields**

I, James E. O'Shields, Company D, 3rd Battalion, 21st Infantry, 196th Infantry Brigade, was with Corporal Christopher Martin on September 22nd 1969. Our platoon was dropped off on a hill to reinforce other friendly elements near Vinh Deng, Vietnam.

It was late afternoon. Corporal Martin and I were working our way up the hill. As we approached the top of the hill, I was shot by a sniper. I called for Corporal Martin to help me. We were under enemy fire and Corporal Martin worked his way over to where I was. Corporal Martin called for medical help and stayed with me. I was seriously wounded and Corporal Martin covered me from enemy fire and kept me from going into shock until medical help arrived.

Corporal Martin arranged to have me moved back down the hill and out of hostile fire. I did not know it at the time but seven people were killed and 18 were wounded. Six others and I were airlifted to the rear area. I was in the hospital for over 10 months due to my injury.

I feel that Corporal Martin's personal bravery and the risk of his own life under fire to come to my aid, distinguishes himself above and beyond the call of duty. I know without Corporal Martin's help, I would not be alive today.... James O'Shields.

**Cpl Christopher Martin Silver Star**

For gallantry in action against an armed hostile force in the Republic of Vietnam. Corporal Martin distinguished himself by intrepid actions on 22 September 1969 while serving as a squad leader with company D, 3rd Battalion 21st infantry. On that date the company was combat-assaulted into an area near Vinh Dong to reinforce other friendly elements that were engaged in heavy fighting with a large enemy force. Immediately upon touchdown, Corporal Martin organized his men and led a fierce assault against the enemy fortifications. After successfully deploying his comrades, Corporal Martin quickly succeeded in overrunning a key hostile bunker and then directed effective suppressive fire on the remaining enemy positions. Although seriously wounded during the ensuing battle he continued to move about the area to distribute ammunition until he spotted a wounded fellow soldier fall in an exposed area. With complete disregard for his personal safety, Corporal Martin maneuvered through the hostile fusillade to the side of the casualty and carried him from the battlefield. After skillfully administering first-aid he returned to the point of contact, rallied his squad members and again began advancing against strategic enemy emplacements. Closing with the determined insurgents, Corporal Martin successfully routed them from the area, enabling subsequent airlifts to be completed with minimal delay. His courageous and timely actions were instrumental in saving the life of a fellow soldier, and in defeating the large enemy force, and in the overall success of the mission. Corporal Martin's personal heroism, professional confidence and devotion to duty are in keeping with the highest traditions of the military service and reflect great credit upon himself, the Americal Division and the United States Army.

**Bronze Star with V**

Sargent Christopher Martin of the United States Army who distinguished himself by outstandingly meritorious service in the connection with military operations against a hostile force in the Republic of Vietnam during the period July 1969 to March 1970. He consistently manifested exemplary professionalism and initiative in obtaining outstanding results. His rapid assessment and solution of the numerous problems inherent in a combat environment greatly enhance the allied effectiveness against a determined and aggressive enemy. Despite many adversities, he invariably performed his duties in a resolute and efficient manner. Energetically applying his sound judgment and extensive knowledge, he has contributed materially to the successful accomplishment of the United States' mission in the Republic of Vietnam. His loyalty, diligence and devotion to duty were in keeping with the highest traditions of the military service and reflect great credit upon himself in the United States Army.

**Army Commendation Medal with V**

For heroism in connection with a military operation against a hostile force in the Republic of Vietnam. Corporal Martin distinguished himself by valorous actions on November 10th 1969 while serving with Company D 3rd Battalion 21st Infantry. On that date the company was establishing its night defensive position near Quan Tam Ky when it came under intense hostile grenade fire from a well-concealed enemy force. In the ensuing battle, two friendly soldiers were critically wounded and a medevac aircraft was dispatched to the site. When the helicopter arrived, Corporal Martin gallantly left his relatively secure position and exposed himself to the hostile fusillade to guide the helicopter to the designated landing zone. He then assisted in evacuating his wounded comrades, remaining in an open area until the casualties had been removed from the battle zone. His courageous and timely actions were highly instrumental in the swift extraction of the wounded personnel and served as an inspiration to the remainder of the unit. Corporal Martin's heroism and devotion to duty are in keeping with the highest traditions of the military service, and reflect great credit upon himself, the Americal Division, and the United States Army.

The names of those killed on the Mountain are as follows: Barry Alexander (helicopter pilot), Danny Dupres, Larry Ellis, Fred Gold, James Hall, Clinton Miller, Mark Surber, Johnnie Williams, and Lowry Cuthbert. The last eight are from the sister company, Bravo.[1]

# Epilogue

## *The Air Show*

I remember going to an air show at Pease Air Force Base in New Hampshire sometime in the 1990s with my wife and 2 kids, and watching the Blue Angels put on a show. It was the first time I had been in a military installation since being discharged on January 6, 1970. For some reason, I was shaking like a leaf and my wife and kids could not understand what was wrong with me. Hell, I did not either. Then several fast movers took off. There was an F-4 and I think an F-15. They flew off and disappeared past the horizon. My wife asked me if I wanted to leave and I shook my head, no. Several minutes later, they came back—first appearing as two dots on the horizon and in a moment, they were bearing down on the onlooking crowd. At that moment, the audience seemed collectively to feel the same fear that had been coursing through me the moment before, while the distress drained out of me in a flood, as I remembered the Gunfighters on November 13. It was the same warm sensation that I felt back then—signaling that help was on the way. With a calm smile on my face, I experienced a purging thrill watching them coming in on a shallow dive, then pulling back in a steep, accelerating, nearly vertical climb—spewing first dark brown smoke, then ascending with condensation streams coming off the wing tips. It was a realistic re-enactment of the real thing in every way—except for the fact that there were no "High-Drag Delta-Ones" falling off the wings. Thankfully, you never forget being saved by the cavalry.

# Afterword by Clyde "Bud" Wagner

*A Company, 1/61st,*
*5 Mechanized Division*

Several years ago the phone rang in my office and I found myself talking to Lou Pepi. After he introduced himself, he told me that he and I had fought together on November 12–13, 1969, on Hill 100—later coined Gallagher's Ridge by us. It was one of the fiercest battles in 1969 in all of Vietnam. Gallagher's Ridge was our company's part of the engagement that took place that November against three reinforced battalions of the 27th NVA Regiment. Lou sensed my emotional state as I tried to respond to this subject, and he quickly realized that I was not ready to talk about Gallagher's Ridge. Accordingly, he told me he would call at another time to interview me about that night.

That phone call was the "beginning of the end" of my gradual decline into the throes of PTSD, which had taken place over a period of years. By the end of 2015, I knew I was in serious trouble. I was depressed and suffering from severe insomnia, followed by long bouts of anxiety, and I just did not know why. I had led a year-round Christian youth camp and retreat center for twenty-eight years, but I found myself no longer able to lead. I gave the retreat's board of directors six months' notice that I was resigning effective June 1, 2016.

Shortly after my resignation on June 3, 2016, my wife and I found ourselves heading to a state park in Kentucky where I was about to reunite with some of the men from Alpha Company, 1-61, of the Fifth Mechanized Infantry Division. This was the very company I served with, and several of those men, including Lou Pepi, were going to be there. After our emotional, face-to-face meeting, I learned that he had brought along with him a draft of the manuscript he was writing about the aforementioned battle.

Lou allowed me to read his manuscript and I found I could not put it down. I wept openly many times, but amazingly, I was ultimately able to find deep healing in much of what I was reading. Since that weekend, I have come to realize that this book helped save my life. It also brought great clarity to that tragic and painful November night. More importantly, Lou's writing helped me see the good from that night, that came in the form of the selfless sacrifices many of our brothers displayed.

Lou's journey in writing his book brought much-needed healing to his own life and to the many men he personally interviewed during his research. Lou has allowed many of us to find peace in the tragedy of war, especially the war deep inside our spirits. He tells us that this book is dedicated to all the men who served in Vietnam, especially those who gave their lives defending our freedoms and beliefs.

*Clyde "Bud" Wagner served, alongside the author, with A Company, 1/61, 5th Infantry (Mechanized) in the area of Con Thien on the DMZ. After three years in the Army, he was discharged with the rank of Sergeant (E-5).*

# Appendix A: What They Are Doing Today

- Bill Hambleton lived in New Providence, Pennsylvania, and passed away in 2016.
- Bill Starr, a retired educator, lives in Illinois and attends many reunions. He can be seen at them with his Charlie Company men gathered around him for the whole weekend.
- Bob Arrington resides in Fort Lauderdale, Florida, and still works as a sales manager for a large truck firm.
- Bob Gattis resides in Ringgold, Georgia, where he and his wife Dimple live on a farm. They once had a large commercial chicken concern, but now Dave buys young steers in the spring, grass-feeds them through the summer, and then sends them off to be finished in the fall. His grandsons Trevor and Garrett are accomplished bluegrass musicians.
- Bob Schilling is a certified tour guide at the South Dakota Air and Space Museum. He travels around the country talking about Puff gunships and his time as a Spooky gun commander.
- Bob Ziessler and his wife Hai Minh live in New Jersey. Bob is active in many veteran organizations and he and Minh love gardening. He and his wife visit Vietnam every year.
- Bruce Horn is retired and resides in Wisconsin.
- Bruce Nesmith resides in Cookeville, Tennessee.
- Bud Wagner and his wife Malinda reside in Pennsylvania. He is a retired director of a youth Christian retreat center.
- Chelsea Korte married one of the nurses who attended him in Japan and practices law in Ellensburg, Washington.
- Dan Cowan is retired and resides in California.
- Dan Tyrell lives in Arizona. He rejoined the Army and is retired from the armed services.
- Darrell Alexander and his wife Jeannette reside in Missouri. He has been retired for eleven years. He has contacted several families of the fallen on Gallagher Ridge.

- Dave Tousignant married one of his nurses and—as he says—has had a blessed life, residing in Massachusetts, New Hampshire and now Pennsylvania. He provided me with valuable information about various helicopter units as well as providing a narrative of his role as a medevac pilot on November 12 and 13, 1969.
- Don Marksberry worked in the horse-racing business and lives in Berry, Kentucky. We speak often on the phone.
- Don Sarsfield resides in Rochester, New York, and is retired. He traveled throughout the Americas working in commercial construction.
- Fred Jelinek resides in Stella, North Carolina.
- Gary Higgins resides in San Mateo County, California, and is deeply involved with the Purple Heart Society, the American Legion, and other veteran organizations. I see him every year at the Society reunion.
- Gary Kent, from Georgia, passed away in 2008.
- Gene Franck, a helicopter pilot with the 101st, helped immensely in finding other pilots and other information through the VHPA. He resides in Oklahoma.
- Gene Kelly and his family reside in Magalia, California. Gene loves playing his guitar, writing songs and singing. He performs at many benefits and loves to entertain.
- Jack Swaren passed away in 2016. Jack received an appointment to the United States Military Academy at West Point in 1950. He graduated in 1954 and was commissioned a 2nd lieutenant. In 1955, he started his first assignment with the 2nd Battalion of the 3rd Infantry Regiment and was promoted to 1st Lieutenant when his duties were expanded to XO, then CO. He married Noreen McGann in 1957. Jack was then assigned to the 2nd Battalion of the 85th Infantry Regiment in Germany, and then to the 1st Battalion of the 48th Infantry Regiment as their CO, also in Germany. Promoted to captain, Jack returned to the States in 1960, where he was assigned as an instructor at the Infantry School. Captain Swaren's first combat assignment was as a battalion advisor to the 25th ARVN Division in 1963. He was promoted to major prior to his return to the US. His next assignment was as a professor of military science at the University of San Francisco. In 1967 he was promoted to lieutenant colonel and returned to Vietnam in mid–1969 to the 1-61/1-5 (Mech) as the commanding officer of Task Force 1-61. Lt. Col. Swaren distinguished himself in the November Battle, November 11–13, 1969. He remained in Vietnam patrolling the Northern I Corp and the DMZ till mid–1970 and commanded his battalion to other victories in January, March, April and June of 1970. In 1970, Jack returned to the 48th Infantry in Germany for two more years before returning to the States as staff chairman of the Armed Forces Staff College for next three years. Following this, he was deployed to the I Corp of the Korean theater for a year. He then returned to the States, where he directed the Army Training Support Center of the U.S. Army Training and Doctrine Command prior to his retirement. His decorations include the Silver Star, Legion of Merit, Bronze Star with V with 3 OLC, Meritorious Service Medal with 2 OLC, Air Medal with 6 OLC, Joint Commendation Medal with 2 OLC, Army Commendation Medal with 2 OLC, Purple Heart, Vietnamese Honor Medal with 2 OLC,

Vietnamese Gallantry Cross with 3 OLC, Korean Order of National Merit, Combat Infantry Badge, Expert Infantry Badge and Jump Wings.

- Jerry Oliver has passed away. His wife resides in Eddyville, Kentucky.
- Joe Prince and his wife Linda live in Pickerington, Ohio. Joe is a retired lieutenant from the Columbus (Ohio) Fire Department. He spends part of his time taking his red GTO to car shows. He is involved with karate and has earned high degree belts.
- John Ginty lives with his wife Fran in the New Paltz area of New York and still works as an electronics specialist. John's tour in Vietnam was in 1971 and he served with 1st Squad, 3rd Platoon, A/1-61.
- Keith Short—once the Society of the Fifth Infantry Division's historian—has devoted a significant portion of his life to military archival work, specifically with the history of the 5th Infantry spanning every war from World War I to the Invasion of Panama. His book on Vietnam[1] is one of the more informative pieces on the 5th Mech. Without his help at the start in providing me with volumes of information as well as the knowledge of how and where to find more military documentation, this book would never have been possible.
- Ken Leach is a semi-retired veterinarian from Missouri.
- Lyle Kohmetsher resides in Arkansas and attends all the 5th ID reunions.
- Michael Stalcup resides in California.
- Mike Cowart resides in Florida and enjoys his large family. His children and grandchildren number 19.
- Mike Maiorca was a school principal in the Midwest.
- Mike McGraw spent his professional life in the field of education in the Michigan education system.
- Phil Bienvenue—formerly from western Massachusetts—now resides in North Carolina and has a vast collection of 5th Infantry military documents. He helped me with research.
- Phil Marshall was a dustoff pilot and author of several books who helped with finding helicopter personnel.
- Phil Miller retired a lieutenant colonel and spends his summers in Minnesota and winters in Panama.
- Phil Phillips and his wife Judy hail from Palestine, Texas. He is a retired steel fabricator.
- Ron Gibson resides in Arkansas.
- Ron Van Beek is presently the chaplain of the Society of the 5th Infantry.
- Russ Widener reenlisted and retired a major in the Hospital Corp. He resides in Pagosa Springs, Colorado.
- Sam Cornwell resides in Virginia near Westminster.
- Stan Samulak and his wife Cindy reside in Lansing, Michigan. He is an avid deer hunter, turkey hunter and fisherman. He was a past president of his local VFW post and is active in the Purple Heart Society.

- Skip Hager resides in Arkansas.
- Stan Blunt is alive and well living with his granddaughter Sonya in Washington State. He served four tours in Vietnam.
- Tony Robinson resides in Verona, Kentucky.
- Vern Sondgeroth lives in Iowa and is active in the Society of the Fifth Inf. Div.

# Appendix B: Awards Index

### *Valor Citations Awarded in the November Battle*

| *Name* | *Rank* | *Date/Action* | *Award* | *Unit* |
|---|---|---|---|---|
| Blunt, S. | CAPT | 11–12-Nov-69 | DSC | CoD1stBn11thInf |
| Starr, W. | CAPT | 12-Nov-69 | DSC | CoC1stBn61thInf |
| Korte, C. | 2LT | 13-Nov-69 | DSC | CoA1stBn61stInf |
| Miller, P. | 1LT | 12-Nov-69 | DSC | 163ACo101AGp101AD |
| Arrington, R. | CAPT | 12-Nov-69 | DFC | 220TH RAC |
| Nesmith, B. | SP5 | 12-Nov-69 | DFC | 158TH AvGrpAmbl |
| Smith, D. | CAPT | 12-Nov-69 | DFC | 158TH AvGrpAmbl |
| Powers | WO | 12-Nov-69 | DFC | 158TH AvGrpAmbl |
| Duesenberry, J. | PFC | 12-Nov-69 | Amdl V | 158TH AvGrpAmbl |
| Widener, R. | Sgt | 13-Nov-69 | SSM V | CoB1stBn61stInf |
| Danenfelture, F. | PFC | 12-Nov-69 | SSM V | CoB1stBn61stInf |
| Cunningham, L. | SP4 | 12-Nov-69 | SSM V | CoC1stBn61thInf |
| Matteffs, C. | 2LT | 12-Nov-69 | SSM V | CoC1stBn61thInf |
| Preese, B. | PFC | 11-Nov-69 | BSM V | CoD1stBn11thInf |
| Phillips, H. | Sgt | 11-Nov-69 | BSM V | CoD1stBn11thInf |
| Willingham, W. | SP4 | 11-Nov-69 | BSM V | CoD1stBn11thInf |
| Vanbeek, R. | SP4 | 11-Nov-69 | ACM V | CoD1stBn11thInf |
| Gibson, R. | SP4 | 11-Nov-69 | BSM V | CoD1stBn11thInf |
| Jordan, M. | 1LT | 11-Nov-69 | BSM V | CoD1stBn11thInf |
| Libertowski, S. | PFC | 11-Nov-69 | ACM V | CoD1stBn11thInf |
| Kowalski, K. | PFC | 11-Nov-69 | ACM V | CoD1stBn11thInf |
| Horn, B. | 2LT | 11-Nov-69 | ACM V | CoD1stBn11thInf |
| Sondgeroth, V. | PFC | 11-Nov-69 | ACM V | CoD1stBn11thInf |
| Adkins, C. | SFC | 11-Nov-69 | ACM V | CoD1stBn11thInf |
| Roberts, D. | Sgt | 11-Nov-69 | BSM V | CoD1stBn11thInf |
| Washington, J. | PFC | 11-Nov-69 | ACM V | CoD1stBn11thInf |
| Myers, R. | SSG | 11-Nov-69 | BSM V | HHQ1stBn61stInf |
| Williamson, D. | SP4 | 11-Nov-69 | ACM V | CoB1stBn6stInf |
| Quiroga, E. | CSM | 11-Nov-69 | BSM V | HHQ1stBn61stInf |
| Stillwell, W. | PFC | 11-Nov-69 | BSM V | CoD1stBn11thInf |
| Green, E. | SSG | 11-Nov-69 | BSM V | CoB1stBn6stInf |
| Saxton, G. | 1LT | 12-Nov-69 | BSM V | CoD1stBn11thInf |
| Samulak, S. | PFC | 12-Nov-69 | ACM V | CoC1stBn61stInf |
| Oetzel, J. | PFC | 12-Nov-69 | ACM V | CoC1stBn61stInf |
| Cobb, J. | PFC | 12-Nov-69 | ACM V | CoC1stBn61stInf |
| Thorton, T. | SSG | 12-Nov-69 | BSM V | CoC1stBn61stInf |
| Williams, D. | SP4 | 12-Nov-69 | BSM V | CoC1stBn61stInf |
| Shores, L. | PFC | 12-Nov-69 | BSM V | CoC1stBn61stInf |
| Goertz | PFC | 12-Nov-69 | ACM V | CoC1stBn61stInf |
| Wyatt, M. | PFC | 12-Nov-69 | ACM V | 43rdInfPlt(Scout Dog) |
| Coplin, M. | SP4 | 12-Nov-69 | ACM V | 43rdInfPlt(Scout Dog) |

| *Name* | *Rank* | *Date/Action* | *Award* | *Unit* |
|---|---|---|---|---|
| Cooper, J. | SP4 | 12-Nov-69 | BSM V | CoC1stBn61stInf |
| Bishop, J. | SP4 | 12-Nov-69 | ACM V | CoC1stBn61stInf |
| Bozek, D. | Sgt | 12-Nov-69 | BSM V | CoD1stBn11thInf |
| Melarczik, R. | SP4 | 12-Nov-69 | BSM V | CoC1stBn61stInf |
| Tucker, T. | SP4 | 12-Nov-69 | BSM V | CoC1stBn61stInf |
| Otto, D. | SP5 | 12-Nov-69 | ACM V | CoC1stBn61stInf |
| Reiner, T. | PFC | 12-Nov-69 | BSM V | CoC1stBn61stInf |
| Lawson, L. | Sgt | 12-Nov-69 | BSM V | CoC1stBn61stInf |
| Hann, K. | SP4 | 12-Nov-69 | BSM V | CoC1stBn61stInf |
| Zelinski, R. | SP4 | 12-Nov-69 | ACM V | CoC1stBn61stInf |
| Campbell, E. | SP4 | 12-Nov-69 | BSM V | CoC1stBn61stInf |
| Towery, R. | SP4 | 12-Nov-69 | ACM V | CoC1stBn61stInf |
| Dell, R. | Sgt | 12-Nov-69 | BSM V | CoC1stBn61stInf |
| Morgan, J. | Sgt | 12-Nov-69 | BSM V | CoC1stBn61stInf |
| Myllymaki, R. | PFC | 12-Nov-69 | BSM V | CoC1stBn61stInf |
| Villicana, M. | SP4 | 12-Nov-69 | ACM V | CoC1stBn61stInf |
| Bienvenue, P. | SP4 | 12-Nov-69 | ACM V | CoD1stBn11thInf |
| Hubbard, S. | SP4 | 12-Nov-69 | ACM V | CoD1stBn11thInf |
| Tate, D. | SP4 | 12-Nov-69 | ACM V | CoD1stBn11thInf |
| Juliar, S. | PFC | 12-Nov-69 | ACM V | CoD1stBn11thInf |
| Smith, R. | Sgt | 12-Nov-69 | BSM V | CoC1stBn61stInf |
| Cornwall, S. | SP4 | 12-Nov-69 | BSM V | CoC1stBn61stInf |
| Kelly, M. | SP4 | 12-Nov-69 | BSM V | CoC1stBn61stInf |
| Sweeney, L. | Sgt | 12-Nov-69 | BSM V | CoC1stBn61stInf |
| Striker, G. | SP4 | 13-Nov-69 | ACM V | CoA1stBn61stInf |
| Kelly, S. | PFC | 13-Nov-69 | BSM V | CoA1stBn61stInf |
| Murray, J. | Sgt | 13-Nov-69 | BSM V | CoA1stBn61stInf |
| Lynch, J. | PFC | 13-Nov-69 | BSM V | CoC1stBn61stInf |
| Vandergriff, R. | SP4 | 13-Nov-69 | ACM V | CoA1stBn61stInf |
| Golden, B. | SP4 | 13-Nov-69 | BSM V | CoC1stBn61stInf |
| Perreton, W. | SP4 | 13-Nov-69 | ACM V | CoC1stBn61stInf |
| Weeks, J. | SP4 | 13-Nov-69 | ACM V | CoC1stBn61stInf |
| Anderson, K. | Sgt | 13-Nov-69 | BSM V | CoB1stBn61stInf |
| Kent, G. | PFC | 13-Nov-69 | ACM V | CoA1stBn61stInf |
| Tucker, L. | SP4 | 13-Nov-69 | BSM V | CoB1stBn61stInf |
| Hubenschmidt, J. | SP4 | 13-Nov-69 | BSM V | CoC1stBn61stInf |
| Barrett, O. | PFC | 13-Nov-69 | ACM V | CoB1stBn61stInf |
| Pepi, L. | SP4 | 13-Nov-69 | ACM V | CoA1stBn61stInf |
| Spillman, R. | 2LT | 13-Nov-69 | ACM V | CoA1stBn61stInf |
| Zahzinger, T. | PFC | 13-Nov-69 | ACM V | CoA1stBn61stInf |
| Green, J. | SP4 | 13-Nov-69 | ACM V | CoA1stBn61stInf |
| Smith, S. | PFC | 13-Nov-69 | ACM V | CoA1stBn61stInf |
| Higgins, G. | PV2 | 13-Nov-69 | ACM V | CoA1stBn61stInf |
| Wood, J. | PFC | 13-Nov-69 | ACM V | CoA1stBn61stInf |
| Benton, W. | PFC | 13-Nov-69 | ACM V | CoA1stBn61stInf |
| Leonard, M. | PFC | 13-Nov-69 | ACM V | CoA1stBn61stInf |
| Whitt, B. | PFC | 13-Nov-69 | ACM V | CoA1stBn61stInf |
| Lamotte, N.. | SSG | 13-Nov-69 | BSM V | CoA1stBn61stInf |
| Phillips, F. | PFC | 13-Nov-69 | ACM V | CoA1stBn61stInf |
| Hulanick, M. | Sgt | 13-Nov-69 | ACM V | CoA1stBn61stInf |
| Glass, G. | SP4 | 13-Nov-69 | ACM V | CoC1stBn61stInf |
| Jones, D. | PFC | 13-Nov-69 | ACM V | CoC1stBn61stInf |
| Ames, C. | PFC | 13-Nov-69 | ACM V | CoA1stBn61stInf |
| Sampson, B. | SP4 | 13-Nov-69 | ACM V | CoA1stBn61stInf |
| Villalon, R. | PFC | 13-Nov-69 | ACM V | CoA1stBn61stInf |
| Shipley, J. | PFC | 13-Nov-69 | ACM V | CoA1stBn61stInf |
| Pfetzing, E. | PFC | 13-Nov-69 | ACM V | CoA1stBn61stInf |
| Karr, R. | PFC | 13-Nov-69 | ACM V | CoA1stBn61stInf |
| Zeiba, S. | SP4 | 13-Nov-69 | ACM V | CoA1stBn61stInf |
| Ulasinski, S. | PFC | 13-Nov-69 | ACM V | CoA1stBn61stInf |

| *Name* | *Rank* | *Date/Action* | *Award* | *Unit* |
|---|---|---|---|---|
| Vega-Garcia, J. | PFC | 13-Nov-69 | ACM V | CoA1stBn61stInf |
| Tard, A. | SP4 | 13-Nov-69 | ACM V | CoA1stBn61stInf |
| Porraz, J. | SP4 | 13-Nov-69 | ACM V | CoA1stBn61stInf |
| Vetrano, J. | PFC | 13-Nov-69 | ACM V | CoA1stBn61stInf |
| Obney, K. | SP4 | 13-Nov-69 | ACM V | CoA1stBn61stInf |
| Berry, M. | PFC | 13-Nov-69 | BSM V | CoA1stBn61stInf |
| Wagner, C. | SP4 | 13-Nov-69 | ACM V | CoA1stBn61stInf |
| Wayson, V. | PFC | 13-Nov-69 | BSM V | CoA1stBn61stInf |
| Donley, A. | SP4 | 13-Nov-69 | ACM V | CoA1stBn61stInf |
| Wood, N. | PFC | 13-Nov-69 | ACM V | CoA1stBn61stInf |
| Sweeney, W. | PFC | 13-Nov-69 | ACM V | CoA1stBn61stInf |
| Cheek, R. | PFC | 13-Nov-69 | ACM V | CoA1stBn61stInf |
| Alexander, D. | PFC | 13-Nov-69 | BSM V | CoA1stBn61stInf |
| Humes, K. | SP4 | 13-Nov-69 | ACM V | CoA1stBn61stInf |
| Southard, R. | PV2 | 13-Nov-69 | ACM V | CoA1stBn61stInf |
| Gawron, R. | SP4 | 13-Nov-69 | ACM V | CoA1stBn61stInf |
| Milton, J. | SP4 | 13-Nov-69 | ACM V | CoA1stBn61stInf |
| Sarsfield, D. | PFC | 13-Nov-69 | ACM V | CoA1stBn61stInf |
| Miller, W. | 2LT | 13-Nov-69 | ACM V | CoA1stBn61stInf |
| Williams, F. | PFC | 13-Nov-69 | ACM V | CoA1stBn61stInf |
| Orman, T. | SSG | 13-Nov-69 | ACM V | CoA1stBn61stInf |
| Gentry, C. | PFC | 13-Nov-69 | ACM V | CoA1stBn61stInf |
| Black, D. | PFC | 13-Nov-69 | ACM V | CoA1stBn61stInf |
| Hager, A. | PFC | 13-Nov-69 | ACM V | CoA1stBn61stInf |
| Graves, N. | PFC | 13-Nov-69 | ACM V | CoA1stBn61stInf |
| Cowan, D. | PFC | 13-Nov-69 | ACM V | CoA1stBn61stInf |
| Morano, G. | Sgt | 13-Nov-69 | ACM V | CoA1stBn61stInf |
| Mcgrath, K. | 1LT | 13-Nov-69 | ACM V | BtryC5thBn4thArty |
| Oliver, J. | SP4 | 13-Nov-69 | ACM V | CoA1stBn61stInf |
| Leach, K. | Sgt | 13-Nov-69 | ACM V | CoA1stBn61stInf |
| Smith, C. | PFC | 13-Nov-69 | BSM V | CoA1stBn61stInf |
| Brown, E. | PFC | 13-Nov-69 | ACM V | CoA1stBn61stInf |
| Evans, T. | PFC | 13-Nov-69 | ACM V | CoA1stBn61stInf |
| Swann, R. | SP4 | 13-Nov-69 | ACM V | CoA1stBn61stInf |
| Brown, K. | SP4 | 13-Nov-69 | BSM V | CoA1stBn61stInf |
| Carlson, H. | PFC | 13-Nov-69 | ACM V | CoA1stBn61stInf |
| Fox, G. | PFC | 13-Nov-69 | BSM V | CoA1stBn61stInf |
| Seay, C. | SP4 | 13-Nov-69 | BSM V | CoC1stBn61stInf |
| Karnes, R. | 1LT | 13-Nov-69 | BSM V | CoC1stBn61stInf |
| Hoffman, L. | SP4 | 13-Nov-69 | ACM V | CoA1stBn61stInf |
| Robeson, F. | SP4 | 13-Nov-69 | BSM V | CoA1stBn61stInf |
| Kuhaulua, J. | PFC | 13-Nov-69 | BSM V | CoC1stBn61stInf |
| Addeo, W. | PFC | 13-Nov-69 | BSM V | CoB1stBn61stInf |
| Dennis, R. | SP4 | 13-Nov-69 | BSM V | CoA1stBn61stInf |
| David, R. | PFC | 12-Nov-69 | BSM V | CoB1stBn61stInf |
| Mosher, L. | Sgt | 13-Nov-69 | BSM V | CoC1stBn61stInf |
| Benedik, N. | Sgt | 13-Nov-69 | BSM V | CoA1stBn61stInf |
| Gallagher, R. | CPT | 13-Nov-69 | BSM V | CoA1stBn61stInf |

# Appendix C: Valorous Unit Citation

DEPARTMENT OF THE ARMY
Headquarters, United States Army Vietnam
APO San Francisco 96375

GENERAL ORDERS
NUMBER 2045

14 June 1971

AWARD OF THE VALOROUS UNIT AWARD

TC 439. The following AWARD is announced.

By direction of the Secretary of the Army, under the provisions of paragraph 202, 1g,(2), AR 672-5-1, the Valorous Unit Award is awarded to the following named units of the United States Army for extraordinary heroism while engaged in military operations during the period indicated:

1ST BATTALION (MECHANIZED), 61ST INFANTRY, 1ST INFANTRY BRIGADE, 5TH INFANTRY DIVISION (MECHANIZED) and its assigned and attached units:

Headquarters and Headquarters Company, 1st Battalion (Mechanized), 61st Infantry
Company A, 1st Battalion (Mechanized), 61st Infantry
Company B, 1st Battalion (Mechanized), 61st Infantry
Company C, 1st Battalion (Mechanized), 61st Infantry
Company D, 1st Battalion (Mechanized), 61st Infantry
Company A, 1st Battalion, 77th Armor
Company D, 1st Battalion, 11th Infantry
2d Platoon, Company A, 7th Engineer Battalion
Demolition Team 4, 3d Platoon, Company A, 7th Engineer Battalion
Demolition Team 11, 3d Platoon, Company A, 7th Engineer Battalion
Team 1-61, Interogation of Prisioners of War Section, 517th Military Intelligence Detachment
Teams 1, 2, 3, 4, and 5, Section A, 43 Infantry Platoon (Scout Dog)

The citation reads as follows:

1ST BATTALION (MECHANIZED), 61ST INFANTRY, 1ST INFANTRY BRIGADE, 5TH INFANTRY DIVISION (MECHANIZED) and its assigned and attached units distinguished themselves through extraordinary heroism while engaged in military operations from 11 November to 15 November 1969 in Military Region 1, Republic of Vietnam. After establishing contact with two reinforced battalions of the 27th NVA Regiment occupying a strongly defended bunker complex in rough, hilly terrain, the officers and men of the battalion demonstrated aggressive determination and uncommon valor in pursuing the enemy and directing supporting fire from tactical air support, Cobra gunships and artillery on enemy positions. Facing a highly motivated and well equiped enemy force, the members of the 1ST BATTALION (MECHANIZED), 61ST INFANTRY, 1ST INFANTRY BIRGADE, 5TH INFANTRY DIVISION (MECHANIZED) enlisted all available resources and, without regard for their personal safety, maintained an offensive which succeeded in rendering the 27th NVA Regiment combat ineffective. Through unfailing tenacity, professional competence and gallantry, battalion personnel significantly advanced the Free World military effort in the Republic of Vietnam. The

General Orders Number 2045, dated 14 June 1971, DA, Headquarters, United States Army Vietnam, APO San Francisco 96375 (Cont)

extraordinary heroism and devotion to duty displayed by the members of the 1ST BATTALION (MECHANIZED), 61ST INFANTRY, 1ST INFANTRY BRIGADE, 5TH INFANTRY DIVISION (MECHANIZED) are in keeping with the highest traditions of the military service and reflect distinct credit upon themselves, their unit and the Armed Forces of the United States.

FOR THE COMMANDER:

CHARLES M. GETTYS
Major General, USA
Chief of Staff

C. A. STANFIEL
Colonel, AGC
Adjutant General

DISTRIBUTION:
5-Each unit concerned
2-AVHGA
1-AVHIO
1-AVHAG
1-AVHAG-A
1-AVHAG-AR
50-AVHAG-PD
6-CINCUSARPAC
1-COMUSMACV, ATTN: MACAG-PD
2-TAGO, DA, ATTN: AGPB-AB
2-TAGO, DA, ATTN: AGPB-AC
2-ATGO, DA, ATTN: AGSD
2-Chief of Military History
DA, ATTN: HSD-OHB

# Appendix D: Glossary

**1/502/101** 1st Bn, 502nd Inf Regiment, 101st Airborne Division

**11B** MOS of an infantryman

**11C** MOS of a mortar man

**20th TASS** 20th Tactical Air Support Squadron BARKY

**21st TASS** 21th Tactical Air Support Squadron BARKY

**220th RAC** 220th Reconnaissance Airplane Company based out of Da Nang, Phu Bai and Dong Ha

**2nd/501st/101st** 2nd Battalion, 501st Infantry Regiment, 101st Airborne Division

**4/5 Arty** 4th Battery, 5th Artillery

**5th Mech** 5th Infantry Division (Mechanized)

**A/1-61** Alpha Company, 1st Battalion, 61st Infantry Regiment

**A/1-77** Alpha Co/1stBn,77th Armor

**A-4** Also Called Con Thien. A Fire support base near the DMZ. Hill 158

**ABCCC** Airborne Battlefield Command and Control Center

**Actual** Example: 6 is the call sign of the commander or radio man. Actual is the CO himself

**Agent Orange** A toxic chemical herbicide used on a wide scale and designed to defoliate vegetation

**AH-1** Bell Cobra Helicopter Gunship

**AIT** Advanced Infantry Training

**AK-47** Also called an AK. It was the standard infantry weapon used by VC/NVA soldiers

**Ambush** A squad size unit set up on a known trail

**AO** Area of Operations

**AO Orange** The hot spot in Northern I Corps in 1969

**APC** Armored personnel carrier

**Arc-light** Saturation or blanket bombing by B-52s (carrying up to 58,000 lbs. of conventional bombs)

**Arty** Artillery

**ARVN** Army of the Republic of Vietnam; the South Vietnamese army

**Automatic** A device such as a claymore mine rigged with a tripwire and battery to detonate

**Bald Eagle** Ready Reaction Force, company size

**BARKY** Call sign for forward air controllers of the 20th and 21st TASS

**Basketball** Call sign for flare shipped—dropped illumination

**Batman** Call sign helicopter unit attached to the 5th Infantry

**Ben Hai River** Boundary between North and South Vietnam

**Bird** A helicopter

**Bird Dog** Aerial observer in light single engine plane from the 220th FAC

**BMNT** Beginning of Morning Nautical Twilight

**Bracket** Artillery term of establishing coordinates for all 4 sides of a position

**C-2** Fire support base south of Con Thien YD132644 16.8532443°, 107.0010536°

**C-4** Plastic explosive, although intended for detonating purposes

**Camp Eagle** Home of the 101st Airborne Division

**Camp J.J. Carroll** Artillery Fire Base 4/8 Arty

**Camp Red Devil** 5th Infantry Division HQ YD240597 16.8097732°, 107.1019033°

**CAR-16** Later version of the M-16

**Catkiller** Call sign for 220 RAC observers

**CH-47** Boeing Larch transport helicopter

**Charlie** The nickname for the VC, or Vietcong—a Vietnamese Communist and enemy soldier

**Chicom** Grenade originating in Communist China

**Claymore** Small antipersonnel mine used on defensive perimeters (C-4 explosive)

**Click** Slang for kilometer, which is approximately .62 miles

**CO** Commanding Officer

**Cobra** A heavily armed attack helicopter

**Com Check** Communication check

**Con Thien** Also called A-4. A fire support base near the DMZ. Hill 158

**Concertina wire** Barbed wire rolled out and stretched along a perimeter

**CSW** Crew Served Weapon

**D/1-11** Delta Company, 1st Battalion, 11th Infantry Regiment

**Daily Journal** Communication Log of the Company Duty

**Daisy Chain** Mechanical ambush

**DEROS** Date of expected return from overseas service

**DMZ** Demilitarized Zone

**DOA** Department of the Army

**DoD** Department of Defense

**Dong Ha Base** Fire support base

**Dong Ha DASC** Direction Air Support Control Center

**Dust off** Medical evacuation of wounded by helicopter

**Duster** Tracked vehicle with twin 40mm cannons

**EENT** End of Evening Nautical Twilight

**FAC** Forward Air Controller

**Fast Mover** Fixed Wing Jet fighter/bomber

**FDC** Fire Direction Control Center

**Flechette** Antipersonnel rounds containing darts and usually fired from a M-79 grenade launcher

**FNG** Fuckin' new guy

**FO** Forward Observer

**Frag** A fragmentation hand grenade

**Frag Order** Fragmentary or partial Op Order

**Free Fire Zones** Areas with no restrictions on firing

**FSB** Fire Support Base

**Gook** A Korean word for "person," but a derogatory word for NVA soldiers

**Grunt** An infantryman

**HE** High explosive

**Hill 162** Prominent landmark west of Con Thien and just south of the DMZ

**Huey** Popular name for the UH-1 helicopter

**I Corps** I Corps (Eye Corps) started at the DMZ and IV Corps was in the Delta

**Indirect Fire** Artillery fire

**IPDF** Individual Personnel Deceased File

**KCS** Kit Carson Scout

**Khe Sahn** Abandoned Marine air strip near Laos and the DMZ

**KIA** Killed in action

**Kit Carson Scout** A VC/NVA soldier who surrendered under the Chieu Hoi program

**Lancer** Call sign for helicopter unit attached to the 5th Infantry

**LNO** Liaison Officer

**LOH** Light observation helicopter OH-6 (pronounced "loach")

**LP** Listening post set up to detect enemy movement outside a unit perimeter

**L-T** Lieutenant (2nd or 1st) (pronounced "L Tee")

**LZ** Landing zone; a helicopter pick-up or drop-off spot in the field

**LZ Angel** Fire support base YD211490 16.7133878°, 107.0736563°

**LZ Pedro** Fire support base

**LZ Sharon** Fire support base YD437397 16.6271501°, 107.2845034°

**LZ Stud** Fire support base

**LZ Tombstone** Fire support base

**M-1125 A1** Mortar APC

**M-113 A1** Armored Personnel Carrier

**M-2** 50-caliber machine gun—Browning

**M-26** Grenade

**M-48** Tank

**M-60** Machine gun

**M-67** Baseball grenade

**M-79** Grenade launcher

**M-88** Tank Recovery Vehicle

**Ma Deuce** 50-caliber browning machine gun

**MACV** Military Assistance Command Vietnam

**McNamara Line** Series of firebases and listening devices on the DMZ between Laos and the South China Sea

**Mechanical** A device such as a claymore mine rigged with a tripwire and battery to detonate

**Mechanized unit** An infantry unit using APCs as primary transportation

**MIA** Missing in action

**M-l6** Standard semiautomatic rifle made by Colt Firearms and which fired 5.56 mm bullets

**MOS** Military Occupation Specialty

**Napalm** Jellied gasoline dropped from aircraft, which ignited with devastating effect

**NDP** Night defensive perimeter

**NVA** North Vietnamese Army

**OH-6** Hughes Cayuse, later version of a Loach
**Onrush** Call sign for the battleship USS *New Jersey*
**Op Order** Operational Order
**Phase Line** A line on a map used to transmit a unit position without alerting enemy listeners
**Pig16** Call sign for Charlie Company 1st platoon leader
**Pig26** Call sign for Charlie Company 2nd platoon leader
**Pig36** Call sign for Charlie Company 3rd platoon leader
**Pig46** Call sign for Charlie Company 4th platoon leader
**Pig6** Call sign for Charlie Company CO
**POW** prisoner of war
**Puff** As in "Puff, the Magic Dragon." A C-130 fitted with 7.62 mm mini guns and 20mm cannons
**Qua Viet** Naval base on the DMZ
**QuangTri Combat Base** Fire support base in the Northern I Corp YD304518 16.7377879°, 107.1611202°
**Recon** Reconnaissance
**REMF** Rear Echelon Mother Fucker
***Repose*** Hospital ship anchored off the coast of the Northern I Corp
**RFPF** Regional Force Public Force
**RPG** Rocket-propelled grenade, a favorite of the VC
**RRF** Ready Reaction Force
**RTO** Radio telephone operator fire coordination center (FCC).
**S1** Administration/ Headquarters
**S2** Intelligence Officer
**S3** Operations and Transportation Officer
**S4** Supply Officer
**Sapper** VC/NVA soldier trained in explosives/demolition and infiltration
**Satchel charge** Enemy TNT charge
**Search and Clear** Patrol to secure an area
**Search and Destroy** Patrol to destroy enemy forces in an area
**Shake 'n' Bake** Noncommissioned officer who won graduation from NCO
**Sit Rep** Situation report
**SKS** Semiautomatic Russian rifle
**Slow Mover** Helicopter or propeller aircraft
**SOP** Standard operating procedure
**Sparrow Hawk** Ready Reaction Force, platoon size
**Spooky** Call sign for C-47 gunships (Puff)
**Starr Team** Elite ambush team
**Straight Leg Unit** Light infantry (on foot), sometimes airmobile
**TDY** Temporary Duty
**The Old Man** Unit Commander
**The Pig** M-60 Machine Gun
**Thump Gun** M-79 grenade launcher
**TOC** Tactical operations center
**Trace** Area 1000 yds. wide and 4000 yards long just below the DMZ, defoliated and bulldozed
**Track** Any vehicle with treads, e.g., tank, artillery, etc.
**Trip Flares** Defensive flares attached to trip wires, set off by intruders or sappers
**UH-1** Bell Iroquois 204/205Medium sized helicopter used for medevac, transport and as a gunship
**WIA** Wounded in action
**Willie Pete** Name given to white phosphorus or incendiary rounds
**XXIV Corp** 24 Corps, northern sector of Vietnam

# Appendix E: Communication Logs, 11–13 Nov 1969

CONFIDENTIAL Memo 20 Copies

| DAILY STAFF JOURNAL OR DUTY OFFICER'S LOG For use of this form, see AR 220-15; the proponent agency is Office of Deputy Chief of Staff for Military Operations. | PAGE NO 1 | NO OF PAGES 6 |
|---|---|---|

| ORGANIZATION OR INSTALLATION | LOCATION | PERIOD COVERED FROM HOUR | FROM DATE | TO HOUR | TO DATE |
|---|---|---|---|---|---|
| S2, S3 Section 1st Bn (M), 61st Inf | C2 YD 134645 | 0001 | 11 Nov 69 | 2400 | 11 Nov 69 |

| ITEM NO. | TIME IN | TIME OUT | INCIDENTS, MESSAGES, ORDERS, ETC. | ACTION TAKEN | INITIALS |
|---|---|---|---|---|---|
| 1. | 0001 | | (U) Journal opened, cipher check with Bde loud and clear. | Staff | WJT |
| 2. | 0030 | 0400 | (U) Sit Reps no change. | Staff, Bde | WJT |
| 3. | 0430 | | (C) Spot Report. A: D/1-11, B: 110429 Nov 69, C: YD 077638, D: D/1-11, while in NDP, took unknown group of individuals under fire. Individuals were moving in a South-Easterly direction, E: Continuing to observe area. F-N: Negative. | Staff, Bde | WDT |
| 4. | 0630 | | (C) Weather Report. From 110600 to 120600. Visibility is 5 miles. Wind is from the West at 8 knots. 24 hour outlook is for scattered showers with a high of 82 and a low of 70 with the humidity at 80%. BMNT is at 0628 and EENT is at 1838. Sunrise is at 0650 and sunset is at 1816. Moonrise is at 0802 and moonset is at 1921. Illumination is 2% in a new phase. | Staff, Units | WDT |
| 5. | 0635 | | (C) D/1-11 moves company to track trail left by elements which were reconning their NDP. | Staff, Bde | WDT |
| 6. | 0650 | | (C) Mine sweep from C2 to QL9 is starting at this time. | Staff | WJT |
| 7. | 0700 | | (C) Mine sweep from A4 to C2 is now starting. | Staff | JRG |
| 8. | 0710 | | (C) D/1-11 hit by a grenade ambush (YD 066635) with results being 2 US KIA, 2 US WIA (E), NVA unknown. | Staff, Bde | JRG |
| 9. | 0715 | | (C) D/1-11 requested medivac for 3 litter patients WIA. | Staff, Bde | JRG |
| | | | DOWNGRADED AT 3 YEAR INTERVALS; DECLASSIFIED AFTER 12 YEARS. DOD DIRECTIVE 5200.10 GROUP FOUR | | |

CONFIDENTIAL

| DAILY STAFF JOURNAL OR DUTY OFFICER'S LOG<br>For use of this form, see AR 220-15; the proponent agency is Office of Deputy Chief of Staff for Military Operations. | | | PAGE NO<br>2 | NO OF PAGES<br>6 |
|---|---|---|---|---|

| ORGANIZATION OR INSTALLATION | LOCATION | PERIOD COVERED FROM HOUR | FROM DATE | TO HOUR | TO DATE |
|---|---|---|---|---|---|
| S2, S3 Section<br>1st Bn (M), 61st Inf | C2 | 0001 | 11 Nov 69 | 2400 | 11 Nov 69 |

| ITEM NO. | TIME IN | TIME OUT | INCIDENTS, MESSAGES, ORDERS, ETC | ACTION TAKEN | INITIALS |
|---|---|---|---|---|---|
| 10. | 0720 | | (C) CO of 1-61 directs B/1-61 element to move, dismounted, to ridge vicinity of YD 066643 and to sweep South-West along the ridge. | Staff, Bde | JRG |
| 11. | 0725 | | (C) CO of 1-61 directs C/1-61 to move to position of D/1-11 to reinforce that element. | Staff, Bde | JRG |
| 12. | 0725 | | (C) Medivac on station, instructed to orbit East of C2. | Staff, Bde | JRG. |
| 13. | 0730 | | (C) CO of 1-61 is on the ground and joins D/1-11. | Staff, Bde | JRG |
| 14. | 0810 | | (C) C/1-61 completes link-up with D/1-11, maneuvers to North side of ridge and establishes fire. B/1-61, vicinity of YD 062641 provides enfilade fire on NVA positions. Cobras on station and firing. NVA on three high spots with automatic weapons in bunkers, vicinity YD 064635. | Staff, Bde | JRG |
| 16. | 0845 | | (C) Team Tank reaction force is in position at bridge between A4 and C2. | Staff | JRG |
| 17. | 0856 | | (C) Spot Report. A: D/1-11 (initial), B: 110745 Nov 69, C: YD 059634, D: Illumination fired till first light. Barky came on station at 0630H. D/1-11 proceeded to follow withdrawal of enemy on tank trail towards hill 162. On the way they found 2 NVA KIA. Contact was again made near crest of ridge. D/1-11 now in contact. C/1-61 and D/1-11's 1/6 element have united. B/1-61 is moving to back side of ridge. D/1-11 has 3 personnel WIA. LZ is not secure and cannot medivac wounded. Gunships received small arms fire and was unable to strike because of close proximity of contact. E: Continuing contact and trying to conduct medivac. F-H: Negative. | Staff, Bde | JRG |
| 18. | 0935 | | (C) Medivac for D/1-11, which was controlled by C/1-61, is now complete. | Staff, Bde | JRG |

CONFIDENTIAL

DAILY STAFF JOURNAL OR DUTY OFFICER'S LOG
For use of this form, see AR 220-15; the proponent agency is Office of Deputy Chief of Staff for Military Operations.

| PAGE NO | NO OF PAGES |
|---|---|
| 3 | 6 |

| ORGANIZATION OR INSTALLATION | LOCATION | PERIOD COVERED FROM HOUR | DATE | TO HOUR | DATE |
|---|---|---|---|---|---|
| S2, S3 Section<br>1st Bn (M), 61st Inf | C2 | 0001 | 11 Nov 69 | 2400 | 11 Nov 69 |

| ITEM NO. | TIME IN | TIME OUT | INCIDENTS, MESSAGES, ORDERS, ETC. | ACTION TAKEN | INITIALS |
|---|---|---|---|---|---|
| 19. | 1010 | | (C) D/1-11 maneuvers against second strong point under cover of C/1-61, B/1-61 and Cobra fire. Artillery continues to fire blocking fires. C/1-61 has 2 US WIA (E). | Staff, Bde | JRG |
| 20. | 1105 | | (C) B/1-61 is receiving small arms fire from ridge to front and draw to the South. Possibly 82mm fire. | Staff, Bde | JRG |
| 21. | 1110 | | (C) Elements remain in contact. B/1-61 is on rear ofridge. D/1-11 is still on front side of ridge. | Staff, Bde | JRG |
| 22. | 1140 | | (C) D/1-11 and C/1-61 on line to assault final strong point. | Staff, Bde | JRG |
| 23. | 1155 | | (C) (To Bde from Major Golvach): D/1-11 engaged unknown size enemy force vicinity of NDP at YD 070635. Engaged with claymores, grenades, M-79's and small arms fire. Pursued enemy to West vicinity of YD 059634. Blocking fire placed to West and South and also to the South-West. C/1-61, reinforced, is moving from NDP, YD 075623, to YD 057633. B/1-61 is committed and moves to YD 056637. Continues to move behind enemy. | Staff, Bde | JRG |
| 24. | 1225 | | (C) C/1-61 and D/1-11 are at YD 058645 and B/1-61 is at YD 046655. | Staff, Bde | JRG |
| 25. | 1230 | | (C) D/1-11 and C/1-61 is on final strong point and sweeping hill. | Staff, Bde | JRG |
| 26. | 1245 | | (C) Spot Report. A: B/1-61, C/1-61 and D/1-11. B: 111230 Nov 69, C: C/1-61 and D/1-11 are at YD 059646. B/1-61 is at YD 052634. D: Elements at above coordinates have broken main contact and are taking sporadic sniper fire. At present there are 7 NVA KIA and 2 NVA WIA in the area. There are numerous weapons and equipment in the area. Further details will follow. F-H: Negative, | | |

GROUP FOUR

CONFIDENTIAL

CONFIDENTIAL

DAILY STAFF JOURNAL OR DUTY OFFICER'S LOG
For use of this form, see AR 220-15, the proponent agency is Office of Deputy Chief of Staff for Military Operations.

| PAGE NO | NO OF PAGES |
|---|---|
| 4 | 6 |

| ORGANIZATION OR INSTALLATION | LOCATION | PERIOD COVERED FROM HOUR | FROM DATE | TO HOUR | TO DATE |
|---|---|---|---|---|---|
| S2, S3 Section 1st Bn (M), 61st Inf | C2 | 0001 | 11 Nov 69 | 2400 | 11 Nov 69 |

| ITEM NO | TIME IN | TIME OUT | INCIDENTS, MESSAGES, ORDERS, ETC. | ACTION TAKEN | INITIALS |
|---|---|---|---|---|---|
| 26. | 1245 | contd | I: 7 NVA KIA, K: 2 WIA, M-N: Negative. | Staff, Bde | WDT |
| 27. | 1300 | | (C) Pos Reps. A/1-61 is at A4, B/1-61 is at YD 052634, C/1-61 is at YD 059646, D/1-11 is at YD 059646. | Staff, Bde | WDT |
| 28. | 1310 | | (C) 2A/1-77 closed A4 coming from bridge between A4 and C2. | Staff, Bde | WDT |
| 29. | 1315 | | (C) A/1-61 is leaving A4 to assigned AO South of A4. | Staff, Bde | WDT |
| 30. | 1350 | | (C) D/1-11 has one platoon in light contact vicinity of YD 066632. | Staff, Bde | WDT |
| 31. | 1350 | | (C) C/1-61 and B/1-61 link-up vicinity of YD 061639. | Staff, Bde | WDT |
| 32. | 1355 | | (C) Bde CO and Bde S2 on ground by LOH joins D/1-11 and then C/1-61. | Staff, Bde | WDT |
| 33. | 1414 | | (C) 1A/1-77 and 2 tanks have left C2 for A4. | Staff, Bde | WDT |
| 34. | 1430 | | (C) All units move toward their NDP. | Staff | WDT |
| 35. | 1430 | | (C) Following information is submitted and corresponds to journal number 26. 9NVA KIA, 2 NVA WIA POW, 2 RPG's with 5 rounds, 1 RPD, 8 AK-47, 1SKS, 27 chi-com grenades. | Staff, Bde | WDT |
| 36. | 1440 | | (C) A/1-61 CP, 1/6 and 4/6 are at YD 123698. 2/6 is at YD 105675, 3/6 is at YD 120663. | Staff, Bde | WDT |
| 37. | 1520 | | (C) Message to HHC 1-61 from CO of 1-61: Wants showers, hot chow, clean clothes etc. for D/1-11 when that element comes in today. Maximum effort is expected. Pass to 1st Sergeant, A/1-11 and HHC CO | Staff | WDT |

GROUP FOUR

CONFIDENTIAL

CONFIDENTIAL

DAILY STAFF JOURNAL OR DUTY OFFICER'S LOG
For use of this form, see AR 220-15; the proponent agency is Office of Deputy Chief of Staff for Military Operations.

PAGE NO 5 | NO OF PAGES 6

| ORGANIZATION OR INSTALLATION | LOCATION | PERIOD COVERED FROM HOUR | DATE | TO HOUR | DATE |
|---|---|---|---|---|---|
| S2, S3 Section<br>1st Bn (M), 61st Inf | C2 | 0001 | 11 Nov 69 | 2400 | 11 Nov 69 |

| ITEM NO. | TIME IN | TIME OUT | INCIDENTS, MESSAGES, ORDERS, ETC. | ACTION TAKEN | INITIALS |
|---|---|---|---|---|---|
| 38. | 1540 | | (C) D/1-11 links-up with B/1-61 tracks. | Staff. | WDT |
| 39. | 1620 | | (C) B/1-61 off-loads equipment and moves to NDP. | Staff | WDT |
| 40. | 1630 | | (C) B/1-61 and C/1-61 are in NDP. D/1-11 is enroute to C2. Cobra 6 in LOH in area. Visits all units. | Staff | WDT |
| 41. | 1640 | | (C) (From S3 Air 1061): Reports that the airlift of C/1-61's 2nd platoon to his 1st platoons area is completed at 1630H. | Staff | WDT |
| 42. | 1705 | | (U) B/1-61 and C/1-61 resupply complete. | Staff | WDT |
| 43. | 1720 | | (C) Night Acts. A/1-61 has NDP at YD 123679, platoon size ambushes at YD 128674 and YD 113688. LP's are at YD 121678, YD 122682, YD 125681. B/1-61 has NDP at YD 085645 with 6 LP's within 100 meters of C/1-61 NDP YD 061641. Team tank is at A4 and Team scout is at C2, D/1-11 is at C2. | Staff, Bde | WDT |
| | | | BUSHMASTER REPORT<br>11P, 1GG, 1BB, 5Z, 12AA, 3CC | | |
| 44. | 1830 | | (C) Total body count for todays contact: 12 NVA KIA, 2 NVA POW, 1 POW from C/1-61 and one from D/1-11. 2 KIA by B/1-61, 3 from C/1-61, 3 from D/1-11 and 2 by gunships and 2 by artillery. | Staff, Bde | WDT |
| 45. | 1833 | | (C) D/1-11 closed C2. | Staff, Bde | WDT |
| 46. | 2000 | 2100 | (U) Sit reps no change. | Staff, Bde | WDT |
| 47. | 2101 | | (C) C/1-61 reports movement 50-75 meters from his NDP. Fired M-79, grenades and called for more H and I fires. | Staff, Bde | WDT |
| 48. | 2130 | 2330 | (U) Sit reps no change. | Staff, Bde | WDT |

CONFIDENTIAL
GROUP FOUR

CONFIDENTIAL

**DAILY STAFF JOURNAL OR DUTY OFFICER'S LOG**
For use of this form, see AR 220-15; the proponent agency is Office of Deputy Chief of Staff for Military Operations.

PAGE NO: 6 | NO OF PAGES: 6

| ORGANIZATION OR INSTALLATION | LOCATION | PERIOD COVERED FROM: HOUR | DATE | TO: HOUR | DATE |
|---|---|---|---|---|---|
| S2, S3 Section<br>1st Bn (M), 61st Inf | C2 | 0001 | 11 Nov 69 | 2400 | 11 Nov 69 |

| ITEM NO | TIME IN | TIME OUT | INCIDENTS, MESSAGES, ORDERS, ETC | ACTION TAKEN | INITIALS |
|---|---|---|---|---|---|
| 49. | 2400 | | (C) 24 hour summary. A/1-61 left NDP at A4 and moved to their assigned AO. At 0430H D/1-11 detected movement around perimeter and fired organic weapons. At first light they conducted a sweep and made heavy contact with an unknown size NVA force. B/1-61 and C/1-61 were called to reinforce D/1-11 and with these forces along with Artillery, TAC air and gunships the enemy withdrew leaving behind: 12 NVA KIA, 2 POW WIA NVA and numerous items of material including 2 RPG 2's with 5 rounds, 1 RPD, 8 AK-47's, 1 SKS and 27 chi com grenades. US casualties were 2 KIA and 2 WIA. D/1-11 returned to C2 for stand down at night and Bravo and Charlie companies 1-61 manned NDP's in the general vicinity of contact area to resume sweep at first light. A/1-77 escorted mine sweep from A4 to C2 and manned day and night NDP's at A4. Scouts 1-61 escorted mine sweep to QL 1. Manned day and NDP's at C2. | Staff, Bde | [illegible] |
| 50. | 2400 | | (U) Journal closed. | Staff | [illegible] |

CONFIDENTIAL

TYPED NAME AND GRADE OF OFFICER OR OFFICIAL ON DUTY: FREDERICK M. JELINEK CPT Infantry S3 Air

SIGNATURE:

DA FORM 1 NOV 62 1594 — PREVIOUS EDITION OF THIS FORM IS OBSOLETE.

CONFIDENTIAL

Memo 20 Copies

DAILY STAFF JOURNAL OR DUTY OFFICER'S LOG
For use of this form, see AR 220-15; the proponent agency is Office of Deputy Chief of Staff for Military Operations.

| ORGANIZATION OR INSTALLATION | LOCATION | PAGE NO | NO OF PAGES |
|---|---|---|---|
| S2, S3 Section<br>1st Bn (M), 61st Inf | C2<br>YD 134685 | 1 | 5 |

| PERIOD COVERED | | | |
|---|---|---|---|
| FROM | | TO | |
| HOUR | DATE | HOUR | DATE |
| 0001 | 12 Nov 69 | 2400 | 12 Nov 69 |

| ITEM NO. | TIME IN | TIME OUT | INCIDENTS, MESSAGES, ORDERS, ETC. | ACTION TAKEN | INITIALS |
|---|---|---|---|---|---|
| 1. | 0001 | | (U) Journal ~~closed~~ open, cipher check with Bde and B/1-61 is loud and clear. | Staff, Bde | WDT |
| 2. | 0030 | 0630 | (U) Sit Reps no change. | Staff, Bde | WDT |
| 3. | 0635 | | (U) Weather Report. From 120600 to 130600. Visibility is 6 miles and winds are out of the North-East at 8 knots. 24 hour outlook is for scattered showers. High of 78 and low of 70 is expected with the humidity at 81%. BMNT is at 0628 and EENT is at 1838. Sunrise is at 0651 and sunset is at 1816. Moonrise is at 0908 and moonset is at 2083. Illumination is 6% in a new phase. | Staff, Units | JRG |
| 4. | 0700 | | (U) Sit Reps no change. | Staff, Bde | JRG |
| 5. | 0715 | | (C) Mine sweep from A4 to C2 is starting at this time. | Staff | JRG |
| 6. | 0735 | | (C) Mine sweep from C2 to QL 9 has started. | Staff | JRG |
| 7. | 0743 | | (C) From Battalion Commander to B/1-61 and C/1-61's CO's: B/1-61 to make thorough search of fingers, valley's and hills vicinity of hill 162. Check area for bunkers, bodies and equipment. C/1-61 to sweep West to South to East retracing route they followed yesterday. Searching all valleys, hills, draws etc. Using 2 days time if necessary. Making sure to check area for bodies, weapons, bunkers and equipment. Making sure to try to make unit identification for Bde S2. Also made C/1-61 and B/1-61 aware of possibility of enemy mortar attacks and whenever unit stops to dig in. | Staff, Bde | JRG |

CONFIDENTIAL

DOWNGRADED AT 3 YEAR INTERVALS
DECLASSIFIED AFTER 12 YEARS
DOD DIRECTIVE 5200.10
GROUP FOUR

CONFIDENTIAL

| DAILY STAFF JOURNAL OR DUTY OFFICER'S LOG<br>For use of this form, see AR 220-15; the proponent agency is Office of Deputy Chief of Staff for Military Operations. | | | PAGE NO 2 | NO OF PAGES 5 |
|---|---|---|---|---|
| ORGANIZATION OR INSTALLATION<br>S2, S3 Section<br>1st Bn (M), 61st Inf | LOCATION<br>C2 | PERIOD COVERED | FROM: HOUR 0001 DATE 12 Nov 69 | TO: HOUR 2400 DATE 12 Nov 69 |

| ITEM NO | TIME IN | TIME OUT | INCIDENTS, MESSAGES, ORDERS, ETC. | ACTION TAKEN | INITIALS |
|---|---|---|---|---|---|
| 8. | 0755 | | (C) Minesweep from A4 to C2 is at YD 126672. | Staff | JRG |
| 9. | 0815 | | (C) Minesweep is at Cam Lo bridge at this time. | Staff | JRG |
| 10. | 0820 | | (U) Bde notified 1-61 that helicopter for defolation mission is on way to C2 pad. | Staff | JRG |
| 11. | 0824 | | (C) Minesweep from A4 to C2 is complete. | Staff, Bde | JRG |
| 12. | 0830 | | (C) Notified Bde change in plans for today. B/1-61 and C/1-61 will work area of yesterdays contact. All other units no change. | Staff, Bde | JRG |
| 13. | 0900 | | (C) Pos Rep. A/1-61 CP and 4/6 element reports no change. 1/6 is at YD 110670, 2/6 is at YD 110660, 3/6 is at YD 110680. B/1-61 is departing CP at this time. D/1-11 is at C2. | Staff, Bde | JRG |
| 14. | 0905 | | (C) Minesweeps complete. | Staff, Bde | JRG |
| 15. | 0925 | | (C) Pos Reps. B/1-61; 1/6, 2/6, 3/6 and CP are at YD 076637, 4/6 is at NDP. | Staff, Bde | JRG |
| 16. | 0945 | | (C) B/1-61 requested a medivac for a man with facial burns. Being medivaced by chopper flying defolation mission. | Staff, Bde | JRG |
| 17. | 0954 | | (U) Medivac complete at 0954. | Staff | JRG |
| 18. | 1007 | | (C) Pos Rep. A/1-61 reports no change, B/1-61 is at YD 076637, C/1-61 is at YD 061640. | Staff, Bde | JRG |
| 19. | 1021 | | (C) Spot Report. A: B/1-61, B: 12 Nov 69 1015H, C: YD 076637, D: B/1-61 on sweep of yesterdays contact found 3 NVA KIA in wood line, 2 AK-47's and 5 to 6 chi com grenades. E: Continuing sweep of area will evacuate weapons. F-H: Negative. I: 3 NVA KIA, K-L: Negative, M: 2 AK-47's, 5 to 6 chi com grenades, N: Negative. | Staff, Bde | JRG |

CONFIDENTIAL

GROUP FOUR

CONFIDENTIAL

| DAILY STAFF JOURNAL OR DUTY OFFICER'S LOG<br>For use of this form, see AR 220-15; the proponent agency is Office of Deputy Chief of Staff for Military Operations. | | | | PAGE NO 3 | NO OF PAGES 5 |
|---|---|---|---|---|---|
| ORGANIZATION OR INSTALLATION: S2, S3 Section, 1st Bn (M), 61st Inf | | LOCATION: C2 | PERIOD COVERED — FROM: HOUR 0001, DATE 12 Nov 69 | TO: HOUR 2400, DATE 12 Nov 69 | |

| ITEM NO. | TIME IN | TIME OUT | INCIDENTS, MESSAGES, ORDERS, ETC. | ACTION TAKEN | INITIALS |
|---|---|---|---|---|---|
| 20. | 1050 | | (C) Spot Report. A: C/1-61, B: 121040 Nov 69, C: YD 061634, D: C/1-61 found 2 bodies vicinity of above coordinates in hammocks with poles through them. Looked like they were trying to be evacuated and were stopped by artillery fire. Also finding various items and bunkers. Report on bunkers and equipment to follow. E: Continuing search of area. F-H: Negative, I: 2 NVA KIA, L-H: Negative. | Staff, Bde | JRG |
| 21. | 1107 | | (C) Spot Report. A: B/1-61, B: 121050H Nov 69, C: YD 064634, D: B/1-61 at above coordinates found 3 AK-47's, 1 RPG launcher, 13 chi com grenades and 10 dehydrated food packets and assorted web gear. E: Continuing sweep of area and will evacuate weapons. F-L: Negative, M: 3 AK-47's, 1 RPG 7 launcher. N: 13 chi com grenades, 10 dehydrated food packets. | Staff, Bde | JRG |
| 22. | 1121 | | (C) Pos Rep. A/1-61 no change, B/1-61 is at YD 064634, C/1-61 has CP and 3/6 element at YD 069634, 2/6 is at YD 057636, 1/6 element is at YD 064633. | Staff, Bde | JRG |
| 23. | 1144 | | (C) Spot Report. A: B/1-61, B: 121105H Nov 69, C: YD 062632, D: B/1-61 took 1 NVA in the open under fire with small arms fire, resulting in one NVA KIA and 1 AK-47. E: Consolidating elements and sweeping area. F-H: Negative, I: 1 NVA KIA, K-L: Negative, M: 1 AK-47, N: Negative. | Staff, Bde | JRG |
| 24. | 1235 | | (C) CO of C/1-61 reported his 1/6 element was in contact with unknown size force at YD 057633. | Staff, Bde | JRG |
| 25. | 1240 | | (C) Pos Reps. C/1-61 has CP at YD 062635, 1/6 is at YD 057633, 2/6 is at YD 062637, 3/6 is at YD 060630, SS sweep YD 060635, STB YD 061641, B/1-61 has CP and 4/6 element at NDP 1/6, 2/6, 3/6 YD 064634. | | |
| 26. | 1105 | | (C) (late log) At YD 062632 B/1-61 engaged one NVA in open with results being 1 NVA KIA and one AK-47. | Staff, Bde | JRG |

CONFIDENTIAL

GROUP FOUR

CONFIDENTIAL

**DAILY STAFF JOURNAL OR DUTY OFFICER'S LOG**
For use of this form, see AR 220-15; the proponent agency is Office of Deputy Chief of Staff for Military Operations.

PAGE NO 4 | NO OF PAGES 5

| ORGANIZATION OR INSTALLATION | LOCATION | PERIOD COVERED FROM HOUR | DATE | TO HOUR | DATE |
|---|---|---|---|---|---|
| S2, S3 Sectio[illegible] 1st Bn (M), 61st Inf | C2 | 0001 | 12 Nov 69 | 2400 | 12 Nov 69 |

| ITEM NO. | TIME IN | TIME OUT | INCIDENTS, MESSAGES, ORDERS, ETC. | ACTION TAKEN | INITIALS |
|---|---|---|---|---|---|
| 27. | 1212 | | (C) (Late log) At YD 061634 a UHS reports unidentified unit North-West of above coordinates and unit is transporting the wounded to an unknown area. | Staff, Bde | JRG |
| 28. | 1700 | | (C) Chronological summary of days events: While on search and clear following contact of 11 November, 1/C/1-61 made contact with an unknown sized enemy force. Received small arms fire, grenades and automatic weapons fire. Returned small arms fire, grenades, automatic weapons fire and M 79's. Medivac requested that B/1-61 be committed into the contact area at coordinates YD 057632. 3/C/1-61 was committed to assist 1/C/1-61 to secure UH1H which was shot down and to extract crew at YD 055628 (D/1-11 also went on this mission). 1/C/1-61 and D/1-11 made contact with unknown size enemy force. Received small arms fire, automatic weapons fire, and grenades. Returned fire with small arms fire, automatic weapons and M 79's. Gunships were also supporting. Scouts/1-61 were airlifted into LZ at YD 054637 to reinforce D/1-11 and 1/C/1-61. At 1545H an OH6A was shot down vicinity of YD 054630 while assisting with a medivac. At 1625 hours, Captain Warne, LNO, was airlifted to jump CP location at YD 054628 and assumed command of C/1-61. B/1-61 ordered to move to YD 052642 to block enemy threat from North-West as a result of radar sightings. 10 element (Communications Section) C/1-61 reported taking mortar fire, 82mm type mortar vicinity of YD 061641 at 17[illegible]. 2/A/1-61 was airlifted to YD 061641 to reinforce C/1-61's 10 element at 1820. | Staff, Bde | JRG |
| 29. | 2000 | | (C) A4 is receiving incoming from an unknown position Type of incoming was 60mm mortar. 6 rounds impacted near helipad. | Staff, Bde | JRG |
| 30. | 2155 | | (C) A/1-61 airlifted into YD 085645 to reinforce 4/B/1-61 and 4/C/1-61. Lift complete at 2155. | Staff, Bde | JRG |
| 31. | 2245 | | (C) Add. to night acts: 3D/1-11 at YD 070636. | Staff, Bde | JRG |
| 32. | 2300 | 2400 | (C) Sit Reps no change. | Staff, Bde | JRG |

CONFIDENTIAL
GROUP FOUR

CONFIDENTIAL

| DAILY STAFF JOURNAL OR DUTY OFFICER'S LOG<br>For use of this form, see AR 220-15; the proponent agency is Office of Deputy Chief of Staff for Military Operations. | | | | PAGE NO | NO OF PAGES |
|---|---|---|---|---|---|
| | | | | 5 | 5 |

| ORGANIZATION OR INSTALLATION | LOCATION | PERIOD COVERED FROM HOUR | DATE | TO HOUR | DATE |
|---|---|---|---|---|---|
| S2, S3 Section<br>1st Bn (M), 61st Inf | C2 | 0001 | 12 Nov 69 | 2400 | 12 Nov 69 |

| ITEM NO | TIME IN | TIME OUT | INCIDENTS, MESSAGES, ORDERS, ETC | ACTION TAKEN | INITIALS |
|---|---|---|---|---|---|
| 33. | 2400 | | (C) 24 Hour Summary. On morning of 12 Nov 69 B/1-61 and C/1-61 while making a search and clear of yesterdays contact made contact with an unknown size enemy element at coordinates YD 057632. C/1-61 made initial contact and B/1-61 was committed to contact area. UHLH was shot down. D/1-11 was airlifted into contact area along with Scouts/1-61 and A/1-61. Efforts to retrieve downed chopper and crew were met by heavy fire. Cpt. Warne replaced CO of C/1-61. Contact continued till nightfall when units moved to NDP's. Spooky, Flare ship and Barky remained on station into the night. | Staff, Bde | JRG |
| 34 | 2400 | | (U) Journal closed. | Staff | JRG |

CONFIDENTIAL
GROUP-FOUR

| TYPED NAME AND GRADE OF OFFICER OR OFFICIAL ON DUTY | SIGNATURE |
|---|---|
| FREDERICK M. JELINEK CPT Infantry S3 Air | Frederick m Jelinek |

DA FORM 1 NOV 62 1594 PREVIOUS EDITION OF THIS FORM IS OBSOLETE.

GPO: 1969 O—343-783 (343)

CONFIDENTIAL

| DAILY STAFF JOURNAL OR DUTY OFFICER'S LOG<br>For use of this form, see AR 220-15; the proponent agency is Office of Deputy Chief of Staff for Military Operations. | | | | PAGE NO | NO OF PAGES |
|---|---|---|---|---|---|
| | | | | 1 | 9 |
| ORGANIZATION OR INSTALLATION | LOCATION | PERIOD COVERED | | | |
| | | FROM | | TO | |
| | | HOUR | DATE | HOUR | DATE |
| S2, S3 Section<br>1st Bn (M), 61st Inf | C2 | 0001 | 13 Nov 69 | 2400 | 13 Nov 69 |

| ITEM NO. | TIME IN | TIME OUT | INCIDENTS, MESSAGES, ORDERS, ETC. | ACTION TAKEN | INITIALS |
|---|---|---|---|---|---|
| 1. | 0001 | | (U) Journal opened, cipher check with Bde loud and clear. | Staff | WDT |
| 2. | 0015 | | (C) Message to CO of 1-61 from CO of 1/5: 1st Bn ARVN (-) will conduct a heliborne assault at 1200H 13 Nov 69 on LZ Hawk YD 052648 with one company assaulting at YD 066653. There will be a meeting of 101st to work out details. It is not anticipated assault will be conducted prior to 1200H. ARVN objective is hill 208, they will sweep South-West to cut off enemy rear. They will be prepared to change direction if we have not taken it at that time. Overlay and details will be sent in morning. CO of 1/5 recommends we make maximum use of supporting fires. He also recommends CO 1-61 return to C2 to work out plans and details of operation: He feels CO of 1-61 can do more for unit in the rear initially and then move back into the field. He also wants maximum blocking fires placed to North-West. | Staff | WDT |
| 3. | 0100 | | (C) 1/6 element, C/1-61, reports heavy movement near their NDP vicinity of YD 085646. | Staff, Bde | WDT |
| 4. | 0200 | | (U) Sit Reps no change. | Staff, Bde | WDT |
| 5. | 0247 | | (C) 4B/1-61, 4C/1-61 and A/1-61 reports taking heavy incoming. | Staff, Bde | JRG |
| 6. | 0300 | | (C) A/1-61 reports heavy mortar fire. (Incoming) | Staff, Bde | JRG |
| 7. | 0301 | | (C) Spooky 1/2 requested to assist A/1-61 in contact at YD 085645. | Staff, Bde | JRG |
| 8. | 0302 | | (C) Artillery is being employed as a blocking force. | Staff, Bde | JRG |
| | | | CONFIDENTIAL<br>DOWNGRADED AT 3 YEAR INTERVALS<br>DECLASSIFIED AFTER 12 YEARS<br>DOD DIRECTIVE 5200.10<br>GROUP FOUR | | |

DAILY STAFF JOURNAL OR DUTY OFFICER'S LOG
For use of this form, see AR 220-15; the proponent agency is Office of Deputy Chief of Staff for Military Operations.

PAGE NO 2 | NO OF PAGES 9

| ORGANIZATION OR INSTALLATION | LOCATION | FROM HOUR | FROM DATE | TO HOUR | TO DATE |
|---|---|---|---|---|---|
| S2, S3 Section 1st Bn (M), 61st Inf | C2 | 0001 | 13 Nov 69 | 2400 | 13 Nov 69 |

| ITEM NO. | TIME IN | TIME OUT | INCIDENTS, MESSAGES, ORDERS, ETC. | ACTION TAKEN | INITIALS |
|---|---|---|---|---|---|
| 9. | 0305 | | (C) Spot Report. A: A/1-61 along with the mortar platoons of B/1-61 and C/1-61, B: 130247H Nov 69, C: YD 085645, D: Under heavy indirect and direct attack at their NDP. Receiving large amount of incoming, satchel charges and grenades. E: Called for spooky and are firing artillery into area. F-N: Negative. | Staff, Bde | JRG |
| 10. | 0307 | | (C) Counter mortar radar plotted, 60mm originating from YD 077647. | Staff, Bde | JRG |
| 11. | 0307 | | (C) C/1-61's 4th platoon is requesting through A/1-61 CO to fire 81mm fire to the West. | Staff | JRG |
| 12. | 0310 | | (C) A/1-61 is receiving hand grenades and a sporadic ground attack. | Staff, Bde | JRG |
| 13. | 0311 | | (C) C/1-61's 4th platoon had their FDC track hit by an RPG round. As of yet one WIA. | Staff, Bde | JRG |
| 14. | 0314 | | (C) 4/6's mortar section requests a medivac. | Staff, Bde | JRG |
| 15. | 0315 | | (C) A/1-61's CO reports illumination is good. They are receiving satchel charges from sappers. | Staff, Bde | JRG |
| 16. | 0316 | | (C) Artillery was fired to the South of A/1-61's position. | Staff, Bde | JRG |
| 17. | 0317 | | (C) A/1-61's CO to all his sections; prepare to mark positions again, Spooky is on the way. | Staff | JRG |
| 18. | 0321 | | (C) Spooky 1/2 relayed by B company will be at position in 20 minutes, A/1-61 had radio transmitter trouble. | Staff | JRG |
| 19. | 0322 | | (C) Incoming mortars have stopped, artillery hit the suspected mortar position YD 077647. | Staff, Bde | JRG |

CONFIDENTIAL

| DAILY STAFF JOURNAL OR DUTY OFFICER'S LOG<br>For use of this form, see AR 220-15; the proponent agency is Office of Deputy Chief of Staff for Military Operations. | | | | PAGE NO<br>3 | NO OF PAGES<br>9 |
|---|---|---|---|---|---|

| ORGANIZATION OR INSTALLATION | LOCATION | PERIOD COVERED FROM HOUR | DATE | TO HOUR | DATE |
|---|---|---|---|---|---|
| S2, S3 Section<br>1st Bn (M), 61st Inf | C2 | 0001 | 13 Nov 69 | 2400 | 13 Nov 69 |

| ITEM NO. | TIME IN | TIME OUT | INCIDENTS, MESSAGES, ORDERS, ETC | ACTION TAKEN | INITIALS |
|---|---|---|---|---|---|
| 20. | 0335 | | (C) A/1-61's CO to Barky control; Barky and Spooky should be in position in 10 minutes. | Staff, Bde | JRG |
| 21. | 0340 | | (C) B/1-61's CO relayed to A/1-61; CO is to have trip flares and heat tabs ready to mark perimeter for Spooky. | Staff | JRG |
| 22. | 0342 | | (C) Spooky will start run North to West to South 300 meters out to 100 meters in a 360 degree perimeter. | Staff | JRG |
| 23. | 0344 | | (C) Trip flares and heat tabs are lit. | Staff | JRG |
| 24. | 0347 | | (C) Spooky is at A/1-61's position and ready to fire. | Staff, Bde | JRG |
| 25. | 0350 | | (C) A/1-61 and elements are receiving fire from the West. | Staff, Bde | JRG |
| 26. | 0351 | | (C) A/1-61 is remarking perimeter with trip flares. | Staff | JRG |
| 27. | 0354 | | (C) A/1-61's CO has been KIA. | Staff, Bde | JRG |
| 28. | 0355 | | (C) Alpha company's FO is in charge of the company. | Staff, Bde | JRG |
| 29. | 0356 | | (C) FO is requesting 360 degree fire from Spooky. | Staff, | JRG |
| 30. | 0359 | | (C) Second Spooky requested. | Staff, Bde | JRG |
| 31. | 0400 | | (C) Request ammo ASAP! No ammo. | Staff, Bde | JRG |
| 32. | 0402 | | (C) B/1-61's CO to all elements; use ammo disicipline. S4 1-61 alerted, Bde notified lift ship and gunships needed for emergency resupply. | Staff, Bde | JRG |
| 33. | 0406 | | (C) Alpha company needs medivac. | Staff, Bde | JRG |

GROUP FOUR

CONFIDENTIAL

CONFIDENTIAL

DAILY STAFF JOURNAL OR DUTY OFFICER'S LOG
For use of this form, see AR 220-15; the proponent agency is Office of Deputy Chief of Staff for Military Operations.

PAGE NO 4 | NO OF PAGES 9

| ORGANIZATION OR INSTALLATION | LOCATION | PERIOD COVERED: FROM HOUR | FROM DATE | TO HOUR | TO DATE |
|---|---|---|---|---|---|
| S2, S3 Section<br>1st Bn (M), 61st Inf | C2 | 0001 | 13 Nov 69 | 2400 | 13 Nov 69 |

| ITEM NO. | TIME IN | TIME OUT | INCIDENTS, MESSAGES, ORDERS, ETC. | ACTION TAKEN | INITIALS |
|---|---|---|---|---|---|
| 34. | 0407 | | (C) B/1-61 has detetected movement by perimeter. | Staff, Bde | JRG |
| 35. | 0411 | | (C) Barky, Basketball and Shadow are all on their way to the contact. A/1-61 says illumination fired in center of perimeter drifting over perimeter. | Staff, | JRG |
| 36. | 0413 | | (C) FO asks Spooky; how much ammo and flares left. Answer was 8 flares. | Staff | JRG |
| 37. | 0415 | | (C) Barky, Huey and Gunships are on the way. | Staff | JRG |
| 38. | 0420 | | (C) A/1-61 is receiving heavy fire. | Staff, Bde | JRG |
| 39. | 0422 | | (C) Spooky 1/1 is on the way to replace Spooky 1/2. | Staff | JRG |
| 40. | 0425 | | (C) A/1-61 needs illumination. Spooky has 5500 rounds of ammo left. | Staff, Bde | JRG |
| 41. | 0426 | | (C) Artillery illumination is on the way. | Staff | JRG |
| 42. | 0427 | | (C) 1/6 element of A/1-61 is being hit by shrapnel. | Staff, Bde | JRG |
| 43. | 0430 | | (C) Basketball ship is 15 minutes away. | Staff | JRG |
| 44. | 0430 | | (C) Spooky 1/2 is firing to the South-West. | Staff | JRG |
| 45. | 0430 | | (C) TAC air is going in on red flare dropped by Spooky. | Staff | JRG |
| 46. | 0430 | | (C) CO notified A/1-77 to move with all elements to assist A/1-61. | Staff, Bde | JRG |
| 47. | 0431 | | (C) A/1-77 (+) are on their way to contact. | Staff, Bde | JRG |
| 48. | 0453 | | (C) Spooky has expended ordnance and flares. | Staff | JRG |
| 49. | 0455 | | (C) Spooky 1/[illegible] is 10 miles away. Basketball is at 6000 feet. | Staff | JRG |

CONFIDENTIAL

GROUP FOUR

DAILY STAFF JOURNAL OR DUTY OFFICER'S LOG
For use of this form, see AR 220-15; the proponent agency is Office of Deputy Chief of Staff for Military Operations.

PAGE NO 5 | NO OF PAGES 9

| ORGANIZATION OR INSTALLATION | LOCATION | FROM HOUR | FROM DATE | TO HOUR | TO DATE |
|---|---|---|---|---|---|
| S2, S3 Section 1st Bn (M), 61st Inf | C2 | 0001 | 13 Nov 69 | 2400 | 13 Nov 69 |

| ITEM NO. | TIME IN | TIME OUT | INCIDENTS, MESSAGES, ORDERS, ETC | ACTION TAKEN | INITIALS |
|---|---|---|---|---|---|
| 50. | 0446 | | (C) D/1-11 has recovered the C/1-61, 1/6 element. Requesting 2 stretchers and one medivac. | Staff, Bde | JRG |
| 51. | 0450 | | (C) Report of 12 WIA and 2 KIA at A/1-61's position. | Staff, Bde | JRG |
| 52. | 0453 | | (C) A/1-61 is receiving AK-47 fire from an unknown number of snipers. | Staff | JRG |
| 53. | 0455 | | (C) Spooky 1/1 is 10 miles away, Basketball is at 6000 feet. | Staff | JRG |
| 54. | 0505 | | (C) Medics requested from C2 aid station to get to pad ASAP. | Staff | JRG |
| 55. | 0508 | | (C) Shadow on station. | Staff | JRG |
| 56. | 0510 | | (C) 3 resupply birds are on the ground. | Staff | JRG |
| 57. | 0512 | | (C) Air strikes on the way. | Staff | JRG |
| 58. | 0520 | | (C) Requested medivac and gunships at first light for personnel at D/1-11 CP. Requested 2 litters be on board. | Staff, Bde | JRG |
| 59. | 0525 | | (C) Bunker was reported to have been firing on elements of A/1-77. | Staff | JRG |
| 60. | 0526 | | (C) C/1-61's position thought they received an RPG round. | Staff | JRG |
| 61. | 0530 | | (C) Choppers are on way to make medivac, bringing medics from C2 on same mission. | Staff, Bde | JRG |
| 62. | 0536 | | (C) TAC air has one run left but will try to make two out of his remaining ordanance. | Staff | JRG |



TYPED NAME AND GRADE OF OFFICER OR OFFICIAL ON DUTY | SIGNATURE

DAILY STAFF JOURNAL OR DUTY OFFICER'S LOG
For use of this form, see AR 220-15; the proponent agency is Office of Deputy Chief of Staff for Military Operations.

PAGE NO 6 | NO OF PAGES 9

ORGANIZATION OR INSTALLATION: S2, S3 Section, 1st Bn (M), 61st Inf

LOCATION: C2

PERIOD COVERED: FROM Hour 0001 Date 13 Nov 69; TO Hour 2400 Date 13 Nov 69

| ITEM NO | TIME IN | TIME OUT | INCIDENTS, MESSAGES, ORDERS, ETC | ACTION TAKEN | INITIALS |
|---|---|---|---|---|---|
| 63. | 0545 | | (C) TAC air has completed mission. | Staff, Bde | JRG |
| 64. | 0550 | | (C) A/1-61 reports it has 6 KIA. | Staff, Bde | JRG |
| 65. | 0550 | | (C) Choppers will drop off supplies and will take out medivacs. | Staff | JRG |
| 66. | 0551 | | (C) Chopper to be guided in with flashlights and incendiary grenades. | Staff | JRG |
| 67. | 0553 | | (C) Incendiary grenades out, guiding chopper in and need more illumination to come in. 2 litters on first bird and 3 ambulatory. | Staff | JRG |
| 68. | 0600 | | (C) Many people to be evacuated. No fire in the last 30 minutes. | Staff, Bde | JRG |
| 69. | 0600 | | (C) Incoming reported by A/1-61. | Staff, Bde | JRG |
| 70. | 0603 | | (C) Spooky 1/1 is to fire 100 meter 360 degrees entire perimeter. | Staff | JRG |
| 71. | 0604 | | (C) Tank spotted at YD 1065. | Staff, Bde | JRG |
| 72. | 0605 | | (C) Medivacs to be taken out to hospital ship immediately. Spooky is requesting more pinpoint position. Barky is to mark in with white phosphorous. A/1-61 has nothing to mark with but will fire in all directions to mark positions. | Staff, Bde | JRG |
| 73. | 0614 | | (C) A/1-61 received one incoming round. Barky is looking for position of mortar tube. Believed South of friendly position. | Staff, Bde | JRG |
| 74. | 0623 | | (C) Mortar flashes are coming from the North-East. | Staff | JRG |
| 75. | 0627 | | (C) Barky has four sets coming in at this time 0645, 0715, 0730 | Staff | JRG |





TYPED NAME AND GRADE OF OFFICER OR OFFICIAL ON DUTY | SIGNATURE

CONFIDENTIAL

DAILY STAFF JOURNAL OR DUTY OFFICER'S LOG
For use of this form, see AR 220-15; the proponent agency is Office of Deputy Chief of Staff for Military Operations.

PAGE NO 7 | NO OF PAGES 9

ORGANIZATION OR INSTALLATION: S2, S3 Section, 1st Bn (M), 61st Inf
LOCATION: C2
PERIOD COVERED: FROM HOUR 0001 DATE 13 Nov 69 — TO HOUR 2400 DATE 13 Nov 69

| ITEM NO. | TIME IN | TIME OUT | INCIDENTS, MESSAGES, ORDERS, ETC. | ACTION TAKEN | INITIALS |
|---|---|---|---|---|---|
| 76. | 0628 | | (C) 16 WIA still to be medivaced. A/1-61 has 15 litter patients. | Staff, Bde | JRG |
| 77. | 0630 | | (C) A/1-77 has linked up with A/1-61. | Staff, Bde | JRG |
| 78. | 0630 | | (C) 1 Chopper is unflyable on C2 pad. | Staff | JRG |
| 79. | 0641 | | (C) A/1-61 needs medivac and resupplies. | Staff, Bde | JRG |
| 80. | 0643 | | (C) B/1-61 is calling for Defcons. Section 3. | Staff | JRG |
| 81. | 0645 | | (C) Barky 1/7 is now on station and taking over. | Staff, Bde | JRG |
| 82. | 0646 | | (C) Chopper is on way to pick up individuals needing medivac. | Staff, Bde | JRG |
| 83. | 0648 | | (C)Gun is ready for Defcon firing. 5 rounds. | Staff | JRG |
| 84. | 0648 | | (C) Medivac has left C2 pad. | Staff, Bde | JRG |
| 85. | 0648 | | (C) Barky has TAC air on station over contact area. | Staff, Bde | JRG |
| 86. | 0650 | | (C) Resupply chopper to B/1-61 will take out medivac personnel. Chopper 1/4 is on station to go toward rocket ridge to observe possible movement North. | Staff, Bde | JRG |
| 87. | 0737 | | (C) Fighter on station for second and third st. | Staff, Bde | JRG |
| 88. | 0745 | | (C) B/1-61's 4th platoon has one WIA by booby trap. | Staff | JRG |
| 89. | 0820 | | (C) Minesweep from A4 to C2 is at YD 126684. | Staff | JRG |
| 90. | 0830 | | (C) Minesweep from Cam Lo to C2 is complete at this time. | Staff, Bde | JRG |

CONFIDENTIAL
GROUP FOUR

TYPED NAME AND GRADE OF OFFICER OR OFFICIAL ON DUTY | SIGNATURE

CONFIDENTIAL

**DAILY STAFF JOURNAL OR DUTY OFFICER'S LOG**
For use of this form, see AR 220-15; the proponent agency is Office of Deputy Chief of Staff for Military Operations.

PAGE NO 8 | NO OF PAGES 9

| ORGANIZATION OR INSTALLATION | LOCATION | PERIOD COVERED FROM: HOUR | DATE | TO: HOUR | DATE |
|---|---|---|---|---|---|
| S2, S3 Section 1st Bn (M), 61st Inf | C2 | 0001 | 13 Nov 69 | 2400 | 13 Nov 69 |

| ITEM NO | TIME IN | TIME OUT | INCIDENTS, MESSAGES, ORDERS, ETC | ACTION TAKEN | INITIALS |
|---|---|---|---|---|---|
| 91. | 0915 | | (C) All minesweeps are complete. | Staff, Bde | JRG |
| 92. | 0925 | | (C) B/1-11 and B/1-61 are at YD 075642, C/1-61 is at YD 076645, A/1-61, A/1-77 and B/1-61 are at YD 084645. 10 element C/1-61 and 2A/1-61 are at YD 062641. | Staff, Bde | JRG |
| 93. | 1140 | | (C) Pos Rep. Scouts 1-61, B/1-11 and C/1-61 are at YD 076645, A/1-61, A/1-77 and B/1-61 are at YD 084645. 10 element C/1-61 and 2A/1-61 are at YD 062641. | Staff, Bde | JRG |
| 94. | 1240 | | (C) C 10 reports mortar fire. | Staff | JRG |
| 95. | 1230 | 2000 | (C) 0100 A/1-61 reported a heavy movement near their NDP. At 0245H they reported taking heavy unknown type of mortar fire. Thie incoming was recieved by the 4C/1-61, 4B/1-61 and A/1-61 elements. Counter mortar fire was plotted as 60mm originating from YD 077647. The A/1-61 element is receiving hand grenades, satchel charges, RPGs, and AK-47 fire. At the same time the 4th platoons FDC track of C/1-61 took a direct hit by RPG fire. Spooky 1/2 is airborne and called in at 0301H that it would be on station at 0351H. Main force of NVA is hitting the Western side of the perimeter. At 0354H A/1-61's CO and wound proved to be fatal. Artillery is being fired to South and Westo of A/1-61's position. At 0322H mortar attack stopped, suspected mortar position was hit by artillery. A/1-61's element stil is receiving hand grenades, RPG's and small arms fire from the West. At 0407H the B/1-61 elements began to pick up movement at their NDP. FO of A/1-61 is now in charge of the company and is requesting ammo ASAP, to include M-79, M-60, M-16 and 81mm ammo. The second Spooky ship is now enroute to the area of contact. At 0422H the A/1-77 element along with one platoon at C2 was committed and is enroute to the contact area as a reinforcement element. At 0440H the 1/6 element from C/1-61 and the downed huey and [illegible] crew have been linked up and recovered by the B/1-11 element. At approximately [illegible] A/1-61 is reporting incoming along with SAF from all sides of the NDP. At 0510H the resupply and medivac birds are on the ground at the LZ and are taking | | |

GROUP FOUR

CONFIDENTIAL

TYPED NAME AND GRADE OF OFFICER OR OFFICIAL ON DUTY | SIGNATURE

CONFIDENTIAL

DAILY STAFF JOURNAL OR DUTY OFFICER'S LOG
For use of this form, see AR 220-15; the proponent agency is Office of Deputy Chief of Staff for Military Operations.

PAGE NO 9 | NO OF PAGES 9

ORGANIZATION OR INSTALLATION: S2, S3 Section, 1st Bn (M), 61st Inf
LOCATION: C2
PERIOD COVERED: FROM HOUR 0001 DATE 13 Nov 69; TO HOUR 2400 DATE 13 Nov 69

| ITEM NO. | TIME IN | TIME OUT | INCIDENTS, MESSAGES, ORDERS, ETC. | ACTION TAKEN | INITIALS |
|---|---|---|---|---|---|
| 95. | 1230 | 2000 | out serious medivacs. They then proceded to the Hospital ship. At 0600H the A/1-61 element is again receiving incoming from the North-East and also taking sporadic SAF from the North. This occasional fire took place till 0745 when contact was broken. The 4th platoon of B/1-61 had two individuals WIA when they disturbed a booby trapped NVA body. Medivacs are now at scene of contact and fighters are presently on station. | Staff, Bde | JRG |
| 96. | 2000 | 2130 | (C) Sit Reps no change. | Staff, Bde | JRG |
| 97. | 2131 | | (C) Cpt Luce is now with the 3/5 Cav. Will RON. | Staff | JRG |
| 98. | 2135 | | (C) Admin bird from 0800 to 1200H, log bird from 0730 till completion, log bird from 1300 till completion. | Staff | JRG |
| 99. | 2200 | 2400 | (C) Sit Reps no change. | Staff, Bde | JRG |
| 100. | 2400 | | (C) 24 hour summary. While in their NDP's D/1-11, C/1-61, B/1-61 and A/1-61 received incoming, small arms fire, and sapper attacks throughout the night. At approximately 0100 A/1-61 reported heavy movement and soon after came under heavy indirect and direct fire attack. FTC track of 4/C/1-61 took a direct hit from an RPG. Spooky gunships and barky were on station through the night. Emergency resupplies were flown in to A/1-61 as they were nearly out of ammunition. Captain Gallagher, CO of A/1-61, was KIA and Captain Neckey was choppered out to take his place. Heavy contact continued until 0745 when the enemy withdrew and contact was broken. Results are forthcoming as to WIA's and KIA's both friendly and NVA. | Staff, Bde | JRG |
| 101. | 2400 | | (U) Journal closed. | Staff, Bde | JRG |

CONFIDENTIAL

GROUP FOUR

TYPED NAME AND GRADE OF OFFICER OR OFFICIAL ON DUTY: FREDERICK M. JELINEK CPT Infantry S3 Air
SIGNATURE: Frederick M. Jelinek

DA FORM 1 NOV 62 1594 — PREVIOUS EDITION OF THIS FORM IS OBSOLETE. GPO 1969 O—343-753 365

# Appendix F: The "Rules" of Engagement

As I think back on my days in Vietnam and how the powers that be chose to make us fight that war, I am totally astounded that supposedly intelligent men came up with such suspect strategies and tactics. We would take a hill and then give it up and end up fighting for it again several months later. The After-action reports used lopsided "body count" to spin their victories. After November 15, the 27th NVA Regiment was deemed "combat ineffective," but the several thousand survivors were just assimilated into another unit. When we did set up a perimeter on one of those hills, the forward observer would have a standing order to register the position, which involved calling for artillery from a nearby firebase and "walking" rounds up to our wire on each side of the perimeter. The idea was that a pre-planned fire mission might be needed during the night, but little attention was paid to the fact that our position was being broadcast to any NVA within several miles. It was a pointless, wasteful and counterproductive exercise—but that's how it was supposed to be done, so that's what we did.

And then there was President Johnson's bombing halt of North Vietnam. Being so close to the DMZ, we knew that there were regiments and divisions comprised tens of thousands of NVA only a few miles away, staging in complete safety for their missions against us. The rules of engagement were such in Vietnam that we were sometimes completely hamstrung as a fighting unit when cease-fires and bombing halts were instituted, forcing American fighting men to bide their time and hold their fire while the NVA and VC would openly ignore the truces. Captain Bob Arrington—a Birddog pilot—related the following story to me, about a reconnaissance mission he flew across the DMZ while serving with the 220th RAC. Light-hearted yet grim, this anecdote drives home the absurdity of some of what we experienced, and how it shaped us, during the war.

Bob's routine for missions in Quang Tri Province and across the DMZ was to fly into Dong Ha to pick up his Backseat—a position filled by a Third Marine officer prior to November of 1969. That changed when the Third Marines pulled out on November 6, 1969, and left Northern I Corps to the charge of the Fifth Infantry. After that 5/4th artillery or S-2 Air from the 517 M I Detachment fulfilled those duties. The duty of the Backseat was to communicate with ground artillery on an FM frequency if needed, and to relay coordinates if that weaponry was needed or otherwise help the aerial observer.

Bob recalled meeting this particular Marine for the first time. He was an NCO who was given a commission in trade for committing to a second tour. On that day, Arrington touched down at the Dong Ha strip and immediately saw an individual on the edge to the tarmac—putting golf ball-sized rocks into an empty sandbag. As Bob taxied up, the Marine jumped into the back seat—with his M-16, a bandolier of mags and the bag of rocks. After topping off his fuel and exchanging quick introductions with his new partner, Bob got clearance from the tower and they took off. Between them, they were patched into three or so radio nets as well as the intercom. This way they could call a range of assets through Dong Ha DASC—or even ABCCC out of Laos. If needed, they could call on the Gunslingers (F-4 Phantoms), carrier-based Marine Hellbornes (A-4 Sky-hawks), various ground-based artillery batteries or even ONRUSH (USS *New Jersey*)—if she was available with her 16-inch guns. This was not one of those days.

During this period, President Johnson's bombing halt of North Vietnam was still in force and there was a standing order not to fire unless fired upon when going Tally Ho—the code name for crossing into North Vietnam. The suspense was killing Bob, so he finally spoke into the intercom, "By the way—what're the rocks for?" The Marine replied, "You'll see. Maybe..."

As they crossed the middle of the Demilitarized Zone and entered the No-Fire Zone, Bob swung northwest—paralleling the border. In a short time, they spotted a uniformed NVA soldier standing out in the open—looking up at them. The Marine tapped Bob's shoulder, saying, "Drop a wing and circle that guy for me sir."

Bob—flying at much less than the mandatory minimum of 1,000 feet—complied, and put the Type 4 Cessna 01 into a slow, tight 360-degree turn. The Marine officer, after inserting a clip into his weapon, began chucking rocks at the NVA soldier who had to jump aside several times, but never raised his AK-47. The Marine—disappointed—ceased his rock throwing and the rest of the day was uneventful, but they flew many missions together after that.

# Chapter Notes

## *Chapter 2*

1. Actually, we traveled to Maguire Air Force Base and boarded three olive-drab military buses for the short trip to Dix.

## *Chapter 4*

1. *Worcester Telegram and Gazette*, taken from Chris Martin's obituary guestbook.

## *Chapter 5*

1. History Place, http://www.historyplace.com/unitedstates/vietnam/index-1969.html, accessed 1999.
2. This Day In History, http://www.history.com/this-day-in-history/the-nixon-doctrine-is-announced, accessed 2015.
3. Department of State, Office of the Historian, letter from Richardson to Kissinger, https://history.state.gov/historicaldocuments/frus1969-76v01/d42, accessed 1969.
4. Department of State, Office of the Historian, letter from Moynahan to Nixon, Document 45, https://history.state.gov/historicaldocuments/frus1969-76v01/d42, accessed 1969.
5. *The Economist*, article on Hess's book *Culture*, http://www.economist.com/sections/culture, accessed 2014.
6. The opinion of this author, which would eventually be backed up by North Vietnamese intelligence reports captured near Saigon.
7. History Place, http://www.historyplace.com/unitedstates/vietnam/index-1969.html, accessed 1999.
8. The History Place, Nixon's Silent Majority Speech, http://www.historyplace.com/unitedstates/vietnam/nixon-silent.htm, accessed 1969.

## *Chapter 9*

1. The McNamara Line, http://www.u-s-history.com/pages/h1887.html.

## *Chapter 12*

1. Vietnam War Resource, http://web.archive.org/web/20030521033516/www.gruntonline.com/NVAandVC/nva_vc_offense.htm.
2. Wikipedia, https://en.wikipedia.org/wiki/Douglas_AC-47_Spooky, accessed 5 October 2015.
3. From Bob Schilling's slide show and presentation in September 2015 at the Society Reunion.
4. Wikipedia, https://en.wikipedia.org/wiki/McDonnell_Douglas_F-4_Phantom_II, accessed 1 February 2016.
5. *The Maine Woods*, by Henry David Thoreau.

## *Chapter 15*

1. This is not the same Gallagher who was the commander of A/1-61 and was killed on November 13, 1969.
2. Keith Short, *A Reference Source for Military Documentation*, Units of the Fifth Infantry Division, Quang Tri Province from July 1968 to August 1971.
3. Sgt. William Howard.
4. Virtual Wall.
5. Sgt. David Gattis.
6. Keith Short, *ibid.*
7. Keith Short, *ibid.*
8. Joint Task Group Guadalcanal After Action Report—Operation UTAH MESA, 12 June 1969–9 July 1969.

## *Chapter 16*

1. The information in this whole chapter was given to me by the family of Chris Martin. The letters were from eyewitnesses in Chris's unit in a petition to upgrade his Valor award to the Medal of Honor.

## *Appendix A*

1. Keith Short, *ibid.*

# Index


Alexander, SP4 Darrell 32, 174, 180, 185
Arrington, Capt. Robert 92, 107, 109–13, 179, 183, 213; *see also* Catkiller "18"

Basketball 66, 129–33, 189
Blunt, Capt. Stanley 45–9, 51–4, 57, 67–77, 79–82, 183
Burke, General 52, 68

Catkiller "18" 92, 107, 109, 112, 189; *see also* Arrington, Capt. Robert
Cornwell, SP4 Samuel 85, 87–8, 94, 114, 181, 184
Cowart, Lt. Michael 61, 88, 91, 98, 117, 131, 133–6, 157, 162, 181
Cowen, PFC Daniel 122, 126, 144, 156, 179, 185

Drechsel, Capt. Carl 109, 111–3
Dustoff "708" 99–100, 112, 151; *see also* Tousignant, Capt. David

Gallagher, Capt. Robert 1, 3–11, 35–40, 46, 58, 77, 115, 118, 120–6, 131–4, 140–9, 154–6, 185
Gattis, Sgt. William David 165–70, 179, 215
Gibson, PFC Ron Gibson 48–9, 71, 78–81, 101, 114, 116, 181, 183

Hager, PFC Alton 27–36, 119, 132, 144, 148–9, 153, 158, 182, 185
Hambleton, Sgt. William 165–7, 169, 179
Higgins, Pvt2 Gary 137, 147, 153, 156, 184
Horn, Lt. Bruce 72–6, 179, 183
Howard, Sgt. William 123, 131, 134–5, 137–9, 157, 165, 167, 216
Hurley, SP4 Timothy 4–6, 123, 137, 145, 152

Jackson, SP4 James 89, 95, 151
Jelinek, 1Lt. Frederick 72, 83–4, 114, 118, 124–5, 155, 180

Kelly, PFC Sterling Eugene 1, 28, 35–6, 40, 57, 59, 120–6, 132–3, 148, 153, 180, 184
Korte, Lt. Chelsea 59, 78, 97, 136, 140–6, 149, 151, 156, 179, 183
Kowalski, PFC Kenneth 72–4, 183

Lancer "28" 108–9, 137, 139; *see also* Nesmith, SP5 Bruce
Landry, PFC James 80–1
Leach, Sgt. Kenneth 34, 57, 59, 120–2, 126, 146, 181, 185
LZ Sharon 27, 34–6, 40–4, 68, 165–6, 168, 190

Martin, Sgt. Christopher 16–20, 172–4, 215
Martin, PFC Edwin 59, 142, 156
Matteffs, Lt. Charles 85–92, 94–6, 104, 114, 151, 183
McGraw, Sgt. Michael 104–6, 181
Miller, 1Lt. Phillip 90–5, 108, 114, 181, 183
Miller, Lt. William 30, 35, 77, 115, 121–3, 126–8, 139, 158–9, 163, 185

Nesmith, SP5 Bruce 108–10, 137–9, 179, 183; *see also* Lancer "28"
Nicholson, PFC David 35, 59, 119, 153, 158–60
Nixon, Pres. Richard 20–3, 69, 215; Silent Majority Speech 24

Oliver, SP4 Jerry 126, 156, 181, 185

Pepi, SP4 Louis 119, 126, 130, 139, 156, 184
Phillips, Sgt. Harold 46, 48–9, 70–2, 78–9, 114, 181, 183
Priest, Sgt. Kevin 28, 33–5, 38
Prince, Sgt. Joseph 46, 49, 70–3, 80–5, 118, 181

Roadrunner "16" 112; *see also* Miller, 1Lt. Phillip
Robinson, PFC Randall 59, 136, 140, 150, 156, 182
Ross, SP4 Dennis 146, 153, 156

Sondgeroth, PFC Vernon 73–5, 183
Spooky 78, 110, 129, 132–35, 137–8, 146, 151, 163, 167, 169, 179, 191, 215
Starr, Capt. William 67–8, 79, 83–5, 89, 91, 97–105, 114, 155, 179, 183
Swaren, Lt. Col. John 4, 35, 54, 60, 67–8, 72, 82–4, 91, 95, 106, 114, 118, 124, 151, 154–7, 180

*Time* magazine 68–9
Tousignant, Capt. David 97–100, 151, 180; *see also* Dustoff "708"
Tyrrel, Sgt. Dan 165, 179

Vandergriff, Sgt. Robert 35, 119, 152, 158–60, 185
Vetrano, PFC Joseph 35, 37, 152

Wagner, Sgt. Clyde "Bud" 121, 123, 126, 137, 144, 177, 179, 185
Widener, SSgt. Russell 125, 129, 135–9, 146, 165, 168, 181, 183
Wright, Maj. Gen. 155

Zais, Gen. Melvin 60, 68
Zeissler, Sgt. Robert 5, 38–9, 179

www.ingramcontent.com/pod-product-compliance
Ingram Content Group UK Ltd.
Pitfield, Milton Keynes, MK11 3LW, UK
UKHW060611180726
13836UKWH00012B/2509